T0211202

Lecture Notes of the Institute
for Computer Sciences, Social Informatics
and Telecommunications Engineering   480

The LNICST series publishes ICST's conferences, symposia and workshops.

LNICST reports state-of-the-art results in areas related to the scope of the Institute.

The type of material published includes

- Proceedings (published in time for the respective event)
- Other edited monographs (such as project reports or invited volumes)

LNICST topics span the following areas:

- General Computer Science
- E-Economy
- E-Medicine
- Knowledge Management
- Multimedia
- Operations, Management and Policy
- Social Informatics
- Systems

Rui Hou · Huan Huang · Deze Zeng ·
Guisong Xia · Kareem Kamal A. Ghany ·
Hossam M. Zawbaa
Editors

Big Data Technologies and Applications

11th and 12th EAI International Conference, BDTA 2021
and BDTA 2022, Virtual Event, December 2021 and 2022
Proceedings

Springer

Editors
Rui Hou (ID)
South-Central Minzu University
Wuhan, China

Huan Huang
South-Central Minzu University
Wuhan, China

Deze Zeng
China University of Geosciences
Wuhan, China

Guisong Xia
Wuhan University
Wuhan, China

Kareem Kamal A. Ghany (ID)
Sadat Academy for Management Sciences
Cairo, Egypt

Hossam M. Zawbaa (ID)
University College Dublin
Dublin, Ireland

ISSN 1867-8211   ISSN 1867-822X (electronic)
Lecture Notes of the Institute for Computer Sciences, Social Informatics
and Telecommunications Engineering
ISBN 978-3-031-33613-3   ISBN 978-3-031-33614-0 (eBook)
https://doi.org/10.1007/978-3-031-33614-0

This Springer imprint is published by the registered company Springer Nature Switzerland AG
The registered company address is: Gewerbestrasse 11, 6330 Cham, Switzerland

Preface

It is our great pleasure to introduce the proceedings of the 11th and 12th European Alliance for Innovation (EAI) International Conferences on Big Data Technologies and Applications (BDTA 2021 & BDTA 2022). Although the two conferences took place in an online-only form due to COVID-19, they also attracted many researchers, scholars and practitioners around the world who are involved in developing and researching big data technology theories and applications.

The technical programs of BDTA 2021 and BDTA 2022 consisted of 23 full papers. The main scope of the two conferences included all the big data technologies, such as big data collection and storage, big data management and retrieval, big data mining approaches, big data visualization, and new domains and novel applications related to these technologies. BDTA 2022 also featured 3 tracks, which were Track 1 - Software Engineering and Blockchain Technologies; Track 2 - Machine Learning and Big Data Applications; and Track 3 - Deep Learning Applications and Bio-inspired Optimization. Beside high-quality technical paper presentations, the conference technical programs also featured two keynote speeches by Lin Li, who is from Wuhan University of Technology, China, and Ayman Taha, who is from the Technological University Dublin, Ireland, respectively.

We deeply appreciate the guidance from and coordination with the steering committee, Imrich Chlamtac, Honghao Gao and Jason J. Jung, who were essential for the success of the conferences. The same appreciation is also given to the excellent organizing committee team for their efforts in organizing and supporting the conferences, and especially for the construction of a fully-fledged online platform. In particular, we thank the Technical Program Committee, Dongliang Duan, Xiaobin Tan, Xiaoping Wu, Bing Li, Pan Chen, Junqiang Han, Hao Li, Tao Lin, Huan Zhou, Wenbin Hu, and Hesham Hefny, who helped to arrange the peer-review process and scheduled a high-quality technical program. We also greatly appreciate the Conference Managers, Jacqueline Sirotová and Veronika Kissova, who devoted themselves to the preparation and organization of the conferences. Finally, we are grateful to all the authors who gave strong support to BDTA 2021 and BDTA 2022. We strongly believe that the BDTA conference provides a wonderful platform for all researchers, scholars and practitioners to extensively discuss all scientific and technological aspects relevant to big data. We confidently hope that future BDTA conferences will be even more strongly attended, more attractive and more successful.

Rui Hou
Huan Huang
Deze Zeng
Guisong Xia
Kareem Kamal A. Ghany
Hossam M. Zawbaa

Conference Organization - BDTA 2021

Steering Committee

Imrich Chlamtac	University of Trento, Italy
Honghao Gao	Shanghai University, China
Jason J. Jung	Chung-Ang University, South Korea

Organizing Committee

General Chairs

Deze Zeng	China University of Geosciences, China
Guisong Xia	Wuhan University, China

TPC Chair

Rui Hou	South-Central Minzu University, China

Sponsorship and Exhibit Chair

Jing Zhao	South-Central Minzu University, China

Local Chair

Yang Wu	South-Central Minzu University, China

Workshops Chair

Linjing Wu	Central China Normal University, China

Publicity and Social Media Chairs

Tanupriya Choudhury	University of Petroleum & Energy Studies, India
Min Hu	Hubei University of Chinese Medicine, China

Publications Chair

Huan Zhou   China Three Gorges University, China

Web Chair

Huan Huang   South-Central Minzu University, China

Posters and PhD Track Chair

Shuai Yuan   South-Central Minzu University, China

Technical Program Committee

Dongliang Duan	University of Wyoming, USA
Xiaobin Tan	University of Science and Technology of China, China
Xiaoping Wu	Wuhan University, China
Bing Li	Shenzhen University, China
Pan Chen	China University of Geosciences, China
Junqiang Han	South-Central Minzu University, China
Hao Li	Central China Normal University, China
Tao Lin	Amazon, USA
Huan Zhou	China Three Gorges University, China
Wenbin Hu	Wuhan University, China

Conference Organization - BDTA 2022

Steering Committee

Imrich Chlamtac	University of Trento, Italy
Honghao Gao	Shanghai University, China
Jason J. Jung	Chung-Ang University, South Korea

Organizing Committee

General Chair

Kareem Kamal A. Ghany	Sadat Academy, Egypt

General Co-chair

Ibrahim A. Hameed	Norwegian University of Science and Technology, Norway

TPC Chairs and Co-chairs

Kareem Kamal A. Ghany	Sadat Academy, Egypt
Hossam M. Zawbaa	Technological University Dublin, Ireland
Hesham A. Hefny (Co-Chair)	Cairo University, Egypt

Sponsorship and Exhibit Chair

Waleed Ead	Beni-Suef University, Egypt

Local Chair

Cristina Albert	Sadat Academy, Egypt

Workshops Chair

Tarek Gaber	University of Salford, UK

Publicity and Social Media Chair

Heba M. Sabri   Sadat Academy, Egypt

Publications Chair

Eid Emary   Arab Open University, Egypt

Web Chair

Amr Abdulaziz   Beni-Suef University, Egypt

Posters and PhD Track Chair

Ali Wagdy   American University in Cairo, Egypt

Honorary Chair

Mohamed Hassan Abdel-Azim   President of Sadat Academy, Egypt

Technical Program Committee

Makram Soui	Saudi Electronic University, Saudi Arabia
Fahad Kamal	Beni-Suef University, Egypt
Pezhman Kazemi	Manchester University, UK
Sahar Elkazzaz	Saudi Electronic University, Saudi Arabia
Aliaa Abdella	Sadat Academy, Egypt
Abdulwahab Qureshi	Saudi Electronic University, Saudi Arabia
Adrian Byrne	University College Dublin, Ireland
Taha Mansouri	University of Salford, UK
Abdulhamid Ardo	University of Salford, UK

Contents

Deep Learning Applications and Bio-inspired Optimization

Artificial Intelligence and Data Mining in Education

Hardware and Software Solutions for Big Data Storing and Management

New Domains and Novel Applications Related to Big Data Technologies

Software Engineering and Blockchain Technologies

Using Requirements Clustering to Discover Dependent Requirements for Hidden Impact Analysis

Ahmed Safwat[✉] and Mostafa Mohamed Yacoub

Sadat Academy for Management Sciences, Faculty of Computers and Information, Cairo, Egypt
asafwat@sadatacademy.edu.eg

Abstract. Since one of the most important practices in any software development lifecycle is Requirements Engineering. Weakly applied RE is one of the main causes for the development breakdown. Main practices of RE processes are specification and elicitation, verification, cooperation, and implementation management. Since ULS systems are increasing in complexity and difficulty, it has observed a growing call for smart modules, methods, and applications that would support improving RE practices. In this paper, we focus on how various kinds of recommendation technologies can be applied to support ULS participants in the completion of the RE tasks; first, we provide an overview of the research related to the application of recommendation tools in RE that was already described in a high level. Second, we show in detail how clustering method as one of Model-based filtering technique can be applied to proactively strengthen "Measuring Change Ripple Effect", Third, new ideas need to be discussed and future research explored. We have used Natural Language Processing (NLP) and Similarity Models to support the model.

Keywords: ULS · ULS Challenges · Software Engineering · Requirements Engineering · NLP · Similarity Model · Change Management

1 Introduction

Change is inevitable in all large-scale projects. Changes are pushing the system to respond to external and internal requirements changes as long as the demands change. In previous work we were able to measure the impact of single or group of changes on ULS requirements repository using NLP similarity model. However, the existing requirements could be deleted or changed themselves without exposing to external change requests.

Therefore, in this paper, we propose a module to automatically cluster the existing requirements based on similarity measures. An empirical evaluation is managed using the same ecosystem ERP [1] dataset to evaluate our model. The experimental results showed that the proposed model specified semantic clustering according to k-means unsupervised clustering method.

R. Hou et al. (Eds.): BDTA 2021/2022, LNICST 480, pp. 3–23, 2023.
https://doi.org/10.1007/978-3-031-33614-0_1

Since one of the most important practices in any software development lifecycle is Requirements Engineering. Weakly applied RE is one of the main causes for the breakdown of the development. Main practices of RE processes are specification and elicitation, verification, cooperation, and implementation management. Since ULS systems are increasing in complexity and difficulty, it's observed a growing call for smart modules, methods, and applications that would support improving RE practices.

In this paper, we focus on how various kinds of recommendation technologies can be applied to support ULS participants in the completion of the RE tasks [2].

A recommender system can be defined as any system that guides a user in a personalized way according to his/her interest in useful objects in a large space, recommendation systems are useful for suggesting products or services such as books, movies, goods, and financial assistances. Such systems help the end customers in the selection of related items in circumstances where the volume of varieties exceed their ability to review it and to get a choice [3].

Low-movement items like movies and products are also suggested by observing customer's preferences for an equally scoring behavior. The related form of suggestion is called Collaborative Filtering [4], Which is a clear applichation of word-of-mouth ads where buying decisions are prejudiced by relationships and colleagues' views: In the event that two consumers viewed related objects in a similar manner in the long-ago, a mutual filtering-based recommendation framework will propose to one consumer new things that the other has already rated with confidence. For example, Netflix online movies platform recommends movies already viewed by customers with a similar ranking. [5].

A substitution tool for endorsing low-movement products is content-based filtering [6]. It is a filtering technique in which characters of items are used by a user ranked in the history to identify new suggestions for the same customer. For instance, where a customer of amazon.com has purchased Linux OS-related products, books (related to Linux) will be recommended for potential recommendation transactions. Fast-movement or related objects such as mobiles are endorsed based on knowledge-based recommendation methods, Where the Recommendation System uses predefined parameters for the identification of a selection of candidates [7]. Usually, ranking-built recommendation methods are not appropriate for slow-moving items since these items are not purchased routinely and thus no recent ranking data are provided.

Collaborative recommenders are one of the recommendation methods, which provides good proposals and recommendations. Collaborative filtering (CF) methods pay attention to the likeness and relationship among users' favorites. Therefore, associations among users are key instruments during the recommendation methods [8]. Recommender system methods and organization are given in Fig. 1.

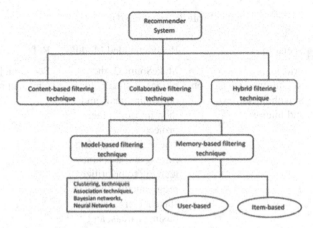

Fig. 1. A Summary of Methods of Recommender Systems Methods and Categorization

The major contributions of this paper are the following. First, we provide an overview of the research related to the application of recommendation tools in RE that was already described in a high level in Sect. 2.6. Second, we show in detail how clustering method as one of Model-based filtering technique can be applied to proactively strengthen "Measuring Change Ripple Effect" described paper 3 to support ULS technical participants in RE change management. Third, new ideas need to be discussed and future research explored (Table 1).

Table 1. Overview of Recommendation Methods in Supporting RE

RE Activity	Scenario	Recommended Module	Ref
Stakeholders Analysis	Recommending Stakeholders	Stake Source Using Social Networks and Crowdsourcing	Soo et al. [9]
Requirements Elicitation	Recommending Requirements	Data Mining and Recommendation Systems and k-Nearest Neighbor Algorithm: kNN detects like-minded users with similar rating history Content-based filtering Social network analysis Collaborative filtering	Niolofar et al. [10] Dumitru et al. [11] Soo et al. [12] Mobsher et al. [13]

(*continued*)

Table 1. *(continued)*

RE Activity	Scenario	Recommended Module	Ref
Requirements Prioritization	Prioritizing Requirements based on Stakeholders position and interests	StakeSource2, the ratings of stakeholders on requirements and their impact in the project The method uses data mining and machine learning to prioritize requirements fitting to stakeholders' interests, business areas, and concerns	Soo et al. [14] Chuan et al. [15]
Requirements Prediction	Predicting based on similar stakeholders' interest	Collaborative filtering to predict other requirements [12]	Soo et al. [14]
Quality Assurance	Finding Requirements Conflict Consistency Management Dependency detection Managing Feature requests	StakeSource2.0 which highlights stakeholders with conflicting preferences for requirements [14] Knowledge-based recommendation Clustering Clustering	Soo et al. [14] Felfernig [16] Cleland-Huang et al. [17]
Managing Requirements uncertainty	Specifying uncertainty within requirements model	Using MAVO to convey reduction of uncertainty in RE models	Rick et al. [18]

In the following section, we discuss existing research for requirements clustering in support of requirements planning and change management based on the collections of textual functional and non-functional requirements.

The basic concept is to evaluate the needs that are present in the requirements repositories and to apply clustering methods for the smart classes of these user requirements that can be evaluated in the future to identify hidden change impacts within similar clusters and for completeness control. The module proposed is to use k-means to detect the similarity between textual requirements. The module proposed is to use k-means to detect the similarity between textual requirements.

2 Requirements Management

The elicitation and interpretation of requirements emphasizes the collection of requirements to from different stakeholders. The elicitation and interpretation of requirements emphasizes the collection of requirements from different stakeholders. For example, textual requirements specifications, business processes, use cases and prototypes and user interfaces are representative resulting artifacts [2].

Particularly in large-scale and spread software developments, it is unmanageable to establish individual conferences on a steady base. In cases like those, users Requirements are also outlined in online-based discussions that respond to the difficulties of information overwork, duplication, information imperfection and diverse participants' deviating thoughts. C-Huang et al. [13] and C-Herrera et al. [19], in their strategies to boost subsistence for participants in the production of ULS Systems, they illustrate the way of using clustering methods to categorize customer requirements and further on to allocate (recommended) participants to groups based on content-based filtering [6]. A major driver for such an allocation of stakeholders to requirement clusters is to achieve a succinct coverage, that is, an appropriate number of participants will evaluate and prove each requirement.

In contrast to their tactics of recommending (assigning) stakeholders to requirement clusters (topics), the tactics addressed in Cleland-Huang et al. [13] and Castro-Herrera et al. [19] often pay attention to supporting participants' requirements, focused, for example, on the ideas of collective filtering, based on the concepts of collaborative filtering for example, A big reason for implementing collaborative filtering in this scenario was the awareness of correlation effects that help to increase quality requirements (participants getting proposals concerning requirements they are concerned in have a high degree of similarity of evaluating their needs). Another reason for collaborative filtering presentation is to enhance the understanding of the requirement model when creating adapted navigation ways for participants.

Because requirements are expressed informally on a regular basis, usually relationships between requirements are illustrated in terms of conjunctions (e.g., requirement A requires requirement B or requirement A is incompatible with requirement B) defined by participants. Recommendation systems allow for the provision of extra information that proactively assists participants in defining requirement relationships.

The discovery of dependence between requirements can be based, for example, on clustering methods which are gathered into clusters of similar subjects (see, e.g., C-Huang et al. [17]). The basic idea is that needs which are assigned to the similar group depend on both sides. Though useful, this tactic isn't ended up to a broad description of the nature of reliance but then helps as a foundation for an additional investigation by stakeholders. Fantechi and Spinicci list some initial effort related to requirements and discovery of inconsistencies in "Open-Source Software Creation (OSSD)" based on the "Natural Language Processing (NLP)" techniques [20].

3   Requirements Clustering

There are different methods when there is a need to generate clusters from textual requirements collected by ULS stakeholders. Machine learning solutions those are expended most founded in for this resolution can be either "supervised" or "unsupervised". In supervised systems, classes are essentially to be predefined [21].

In supervised learning, the human experts who are involved to tag some amount of data with predefined classification, in that case the amount of data or requirements are controlled by the knowledge workers. While Unsupervised learning algorithms permit the automatic specification of clusters without any earlier guidance supported by professionals [21].

Clustering in overall is a significant and valuable method that automatically classifies a group with a considerable number of data substances into a much lesser number of similar sets. In the specific situation of textual documents, clustering has verified to be an operational method and an exciting investigation issue as well. It is rising even more motivating and challenging with the growth of the internet and the development of Web 2.0. For example, outcomes resulted from search engines are clustered to aid end users rapidly classify and emphasis on the applicable set of outcomes. Client notes are grouped in numerous online stores, such as netflix.com, to deliver cooperative advice. In collaborative bookmarking or tagging, clusters of customers those have common specific characters are recognized by their behaviors [22].

Precise clustering needs an accurate description of the nearness between a couple of items, by either the likeness or distance. A diversity of likeness or distance methods have been offered and broadly affected, such as the Jaccard correlation coefficient and cosine similarity [23].

In the clustering method, we'll also have to distinguish the dissimilarity/similarity between two clusters or between a cluster and an entity.

3.1 Hierarchical Clustering

"Hierarchical clustering" algorithms recognized their term since they shape a set of clusters that may be represented as a hierarchy of clusters. The hierarchy would be built-in top to bottom (called divisive) or bottom to top (called agglomerative) style. Hierarchical clustering methods are one of the Distance based clustering processes, i.e., using a similarity method to calculate the intimacy among text documents.

In the top to bottom method, it starts with single cluster that contains all the text documents. it repetitively divides this cluster into sub-sets or sub-classes. In the agglomerative method, each document is originally reflected as a single cluster. Then sequentially the utmost alike clusters are combined till all documents are contained in one cluster.

Three diverse merger modules for agglomerative algorithms:

1) Single Linkage Clustering: In this method, the likeness among two groups of documents is the uppermost similarity among any couple of documents of these clusters.
2) Group-Average Linkage Clustering: In that type of clustering, the likeness between two clusters is the average likeness among couples of documents in these clusters.
3) Complete Linkage Clustering: within this technique, the likeness between two clusters is the poorest situation similarity between any couple of documents in those clusters [24].

Numerous algorithms are been projected for automatically clustering words founded on a huge corpus. They are divided into two categories., One category is built on rearranging words from group to group initially from some early set of classes. The second type repeats assembling classes beginning from a set of singleton classes (which contain only one word).

Both categories are share the same end function, in most conditions by confusion or average joint information. The value of the other category for the sake of building hierarchical clustering is that it could easily change the past of the merging method to a tree-structured forming of the vocabulary.

The other way around, the second category is disposed to be stuck by a local minimum.

The first category is stronger to the local minimum problem, but then the excellence of clusters importantly relies on the primary group of classes and discovery of an opening set of good quality is itself an identical problematic. Additionally, the first method only offers tools of dividing the vocabulary and it doesn't deliver a method of building a hierarchical clustering of words bags [25].

3.2 Clustering Using K-Means

K-means clustering [26] is an important technique for identifying clusters, where k states the number of clusters obtained. K requirements may be chosen as cluster cores in the preliminary repetition, and the other requirements are assigned to the closet cluster most.

Table 2. Example of System Requirements

Requirement	Category	Description
R1	Database	Indexed Configuration in DB
R2	User Interface	UI with internet help available
R3	Database	Isolated layer for DB
R4	User Interface	User Interface with enterprise identity

Table 3. Tokens extracted from System Requirements

Requirement	Extracted Tokens
R1	Indexed Configuration DB
R2	UI internet help
R3	Isolated layer DB
R4	User Interface enterprise identity

The likeness of the pull-out tokens – Eq. 1 reveals a basic clear resemblance metric for example, sim (r1, r3). 0.17, if we undertake tokens (r1). {indexed, configuration, DB} and tokens(r3). {isolated, layer, DB}:

$$Sim(s, r) = \frac{|tokens(s) \cap tokens(r)|}{|tokens(s) \cup tokens(r)|} \tag{1}$$

Different matching scoring could be implemented – For the sake of this case, we ask that the tokens be similar (see Table 3) mined from the written statements of our sample requirements ({r1; r2; r3; r4} in Table 2). The centroid (mean) per cluster is then defined for each cluster and requirement specifications are allocated to clusters. For that case, both clusters c1:{r1; r3} and c2:{r2; r4} are expected to be recognized after one step where sim(r1; r3) is 0.17 and sim (r2; r4) is0.5. The algorithm ends if a significant reiteration depth is reached or all clusters remain steady [2].

So, the centroid's value in individual dimension is the calculated mean of that dimension above all the entities in the cluster. Let C be a set of documents. Its centroid is defined as

$$\vec{tc.} = \frac{1}{|C|} \sum_{\vec{td} \in C} \vec{td} \tag{2}$$

where it is the mean value of all vectors' terms in the group [27].

4 Determining the Good Number of Clusters

The clustering of requirements, though, is considerably harder than the clustering of normal documents in several behaviors. The cluster granularity, i.e., the exact value of clusters count is one of main issues that needs to be specified automatically in requirements clustering at a very acceptable level of granularity. While document clustering originates from the need to sort or filter huge groups of textual materials, such as journals, books, feeds, or internet pages, the resolution, that is frequently the main driver, of data clustering, is to classify the documents into a controlled number of classes to simplify some basic activities such as surfing and searching. The amount of the classes is naturally minor and is typically recognized beforehand. Instead, the objectives for clustering of requirements are very dynamic and are reliant on the activities for which the produced clusters will be use [28].

One of the basic problems in k-means methods is determining the good value of clusters. The right choice of k is often unclear; various experts used different methods to solve this problem, Elbow method is one of them to get the good number of K for K-mean algorithms.

Cross-validation would be extra method for inspecting the good value of clusters planned by Smyth [29], depending on cluster solidity to find out the correct k.

Another technique based on the average silhouette of the data is useful and reliable to identify the number of clusters accepted. The silhouette of a data instance is a degree of how narrowly it is ties to data point inside its own cluster and how roughly it is alike to data of the near cluster [30].

Intra and Inter Cluster Distances, the main objective after implementation of the clustering algorithm is to get a shortened and well-separated subsequent clustering. As a result, the intra-cluster distance (within cluster scatter distance) has to be minimized and the inter-cluster distance has to be maximized (between cluster separations) [31].

Hence, cluster density in K-means can be estimated using the intra-cluster distance dimension average. Inter-cluster distance is the distance between centers that shows separation of clusters, which must be amplified. The combination of these two measures (Elbow and Silhouette) can help calculate the fineness of the clustering as described by Siddheswar et al. [32]. Validity = intra/inter.

Given the fact that there is no adequate solution to the difficulties of measuring true K value estimation, which is accurate in each dimension, but some heuristic rules are used to calculate K value, (Intra and Inter-cluster distances) with k-mean++ allow a sensible choice of the preliminary centroid and it is significantly quicker and can be used in many ways to achieve the end result. [30].

4.1 Suggested Model for Calculating Good Number of K Clusters

It's not easy to divide a set of documents D into separate partitions or clusters and solid procedure since it requires to shadow a methodical process to cluster text data. The phases are utilized to highly conclude the clustering outcomes in the entire document clustering methods are examined in below:

Preprocessing
Preprocessing is the main obligatory step to clear up the data for text mining processes. It is useful for reducing data noise and for cleaning the data. As far as preprocessing is concerned, the actual purpose is to transform the originated data into a logical machine type. Preprocessing process requires tokenization, filtering, stemming or the elimination of stop-words.

Filtering Words
The terms that give low value below vector methods must be removed before the actual calculation; filtering is the way to achieve this mission. In addition to several documents, each document includes numerous words such as punctuations, special characters, stop words and redundant words. It provides imperfect information to distinguish between several documents, although it also contains infrequent words which offer no meaning and requests to get out [30].

Stemming
The fundamental goal of the stemming method is to adapt the words to their source (root/stem) words, which are extremely activity-based language. The method respects immensely the stemming method in English. It is a procedure that serving to increase the effectiveness and decline duplications [33].

Stop-Word Removal
"Stop words are the continuous words that occur, such as prepositions, articles, conjunctions: is, an, a, when, but etc., or terms that are not important and some terms of high frequency. While Stop-word elimination is the method used to dismiss these words from the vocabulary as a vector space perspective they do not confer any value and measure less important. Stop-word elimination procedure assists in implementation and significantly impacts the entire clustering process [34].

Processing
Like the K-Means and K-Medoids, the centroid-based cluster operators make a centroid model and a categorized set of clusters. The model of the centroid cluster has details about the clustering achieved. It states which cases are part of which cluster. It also contains

details on the centroids of each cluster. The Cluster Distance Performance operator returns this centroid cluster model and clustered collection as input and evaluates model output by cluster centroids. There are two output algorithms provided: Cluster distance average and Davies-Bouldin index [35].

Average Within Cluster Distance:
The average distance within a cluster is calculated by measuring the mean distance between the centroid and all points in a cluster [36].

Davies-Bouldin Index:
It is good to know that index (DB) is based on the fact that the inter-cluster separation and intra-cluster similarity and solidity should be high for a good partition. Then, the dispersion measure and the measure of cluster similarity must be defined to determine the DB index.

Since the goal is to achieve the lowest scattering within the cluster and the highest segregation between the clusters, the number of clusters c that minimizes VDB is considered the best value of c [37].

Representation
The important requirement is to transform our corpus into machine-detectable form vectors, described as VSM (Vector Space Model) before clustering the documents into sets $z = \{x_1, x_2, x_3, \ldots, x_n\}$. The term x_1 in Z represents the item vector d for each text document while $d = \{w_1, w_2, w_3, \ldots, w_n\}$. The w_i is a term weight demonstration of term t_i in a document that results in the impact of each word in a text. It is highly reliable and easier to make logical use of the TFIDF methodology for SVM corpus vectorization (Term Frequency Inverse Document Frequency) which is extremely utilized one, that calculates a position within the corpus for each term of a text. That calculates a position within the corpus for each term of a text. The TFIDF can be computed as follows:

$$w_{ji} = tf_{ji} * idf_{ji} = tf * log_2(\frac{n}{df_{ji}}) \tag{3}$$

The tf_{ji} is the occurrence of object i in a text j. Though df_{ji} specify the docs count that term i has checked, and n is the total number of documents present in a corpus. The statistical measurement of the word weight under this method tests the frequency of presence in a text for one word in addition to the entire corpus. Whether a phrase exists, it is most frequently mentioned as a stop-word in various documents, TFIDF eliminates those words when the TFIDF score changes to zero or near zero for stop-words [38, 39].'

Experiment and Results for Good Number of k Determination
The data used for our experiment is retrieved from the whole requirements dataset from
Functional requirements document for ERP ecosystem [40], and the researchers tried
both Average within cluster distance and Davies-Bouldin index to determine the most
suitable number of K Clusters according to the below model design in Fig. 2 and 3.

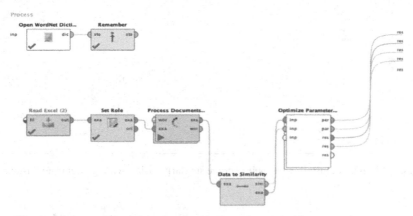

Fig. 2. High Level Model Design for Finding Most Suitable "K Cluster Value"

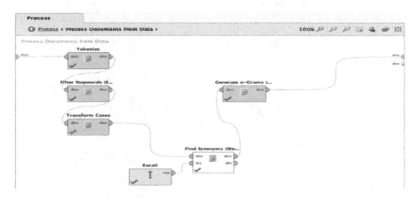

Fig. 3. Detailed Tasks View for Finding the Most Suitable 'K Cluster Value'

We have tested the proposed two methods, the first method – Average Centroid
Distance as Silhouette Index – is the one shown in Figs. 1, 2, 3, and 4 showing the
optimum number of k is 70 Clusters with average requirements similarity 0.586 and 250
attributes, and the average similarity is described in detail for each cluster in Fig. 5 after
many iterations in order find the good number of k extracted from model output through
RapidMiner [41].

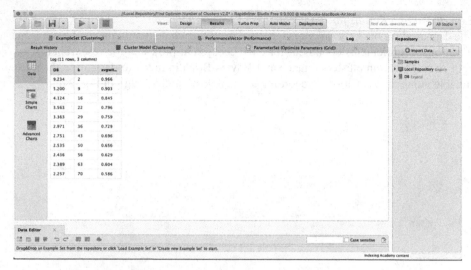

Fig. 4. Different k clusters with their average similarity using Average Centroid Distance

```
Parameter set:                                              -----Avg. within centroid distance_cluster_34: 0.470
                                                            -----Avg. within centroid distance_cluster_35: 0.000
Performance:                                                -----Avg. within centroid distance_cluster_36: 0.584
PerformanceVector {                                         -----Avg. within centroid distance_cluster_37: 0.742
*****Avg. within centroid distance: -0.586                 -----Avg. within centroid distance_cluster_38: 0.468
-----Avg. within centroid distance_cluster_0: 0.712        -----Avg. within centroid distance_cluster_39: 0.501
-----Avg. within centroid distance_cluster_1: 0.668        -----Avg. within centroid distance_cluster_40: 0.753
-----Avg. within centroid distance_cluster_2: 0.547        -----Avg. within centroid distance_cluster_41: 0.556
-----Avg. within centroid distance_cluster_3: 0.635        -----Avg. within centroid distance_cluster_42: 0.294
-----Avg. within centroid distance_cluster_4: 0.712        -----Avg. within centroid distance_cluster_43: 0.399
-----Avg. within centroid distance_cluster_5: 0.372        -----Avg. within centroid distance_cluster_44: 0.249
-----Avg. within centroid distance_cluster_6: 0.749        -----Avg. within centroid distance_cluster_45: 0.520
-----Avg. within centroid distance_cluster_7: 0.765        -----Avg. within centroid distance_cluster_46: 0.686
-----Avg. within centroid distance_cluster_8: 0.626        -----Avg. within centroid distance_cluster_47: 0.660
-----Avg. within centroid distance_cluster_9: 0.613        -----Avg. within centroid distance_cluster_48: 0.130
-----Avg. within centroid distance_cluster_10: 0.764       -----Avg. within centroid distance_cluster_49: 0.531
-----Avg. within centroid distance_cluster_11: 0.672       -----Avg. within centroid distance_cluster_50: 0.645
-----Avg. within centroid distance_cluster_12: 0.664       -----Avg. within centroid distance_cluster_51: 0.350
-----Avg. within centroid distance_cluster_13: 0.840       -----Avg. within centroid distance_cluster_52: 0.656
-----Avg. within centroid distance_cluster_14: 0.627       -----Avg. within centroid distance_cluster_53: 0.636
-----Avg. within centroid distance_cluster_15: 0.749       -----Avg. within centroid distance_cluster_54: 0.725
-----Avg. within centroid distance_cluster_16: 0.677       -----Avg. within centroid distance_cluster_55: 0.701
-----Avg. within centroid distance_cluster_17: 0.228       -----Avg. within centroid distance_cluster_56: 0.638
-----Avg. within centroid distance_cluster_18: 0.765       -----Avg. within centroid distance_cluster_57: 0.434
-----Avg. within centroid distance_cluster_19: 0.395       -----Avg. within centroid distance_cluster_58: 0.477
-----Avg. within centroid distance_cluster_20: 0.656       -----Avg. within centroid distance_cluster_59: 0.488
-----Avg. within centroid distance_cluster_21: 0.627       -----Avg. within centroid distance_cluster_60: 0.666
-----Avg. within centroid distance_cluster_22: 0.725       -----Avg. within centroid distance_cluster_61: 0.255
-----Avg. within centroid distance_cluster_23: 0.411       -----Avg. within centroid distance_cluster_62: 0.286
-----Avg. within centroid distance_cluster_24: 0.767       -----Avg. within centroid distance_cluster_63: 0.447
-----Avg. within centroid distance_cluster_25: 0.308       -----Avg. within centroid distance_cluster_64: 0.697
-----Avg. within centroid distance_cluster_26: 0.355       -----Avg. within centroid distance_cluster_65: 0.689
-----Avg. within centroid distance_cluster_27: 0.422       -----Avg. within centroid distance_cluster_66: 0.324
-----Avg. within centroid distance_cluster_28: 0.660       -----Avg. within centroid distance_cluster_67: 0.421
-----Avg. within centroid distance_cluster_29: 0.000       -----Avg. within centroid distance_cluster_68: 0.296
-----Avg. within centroid distance_cluster_30: 0.268       -----Avg. within centroid distance_cluster_69: 0.584
-----Avg. within centroid distance_cluster_31: 0.463       }
-----Avg. within centroid distance_cluster_32: 0.359       Clustering.k      = 70
-----Avg. within centroid distance_cluster_33: 0.555
```

Fig. 5. Average Similarity Centroid per each Cluster

The second method – Davies-Bouldin Index evaluates intra-cluster similarity and inter-cluster differences – is the one shown in Figs. 1, 2, 3, 4 and 5 showing the optimum number of k is 70 Clusters with average requirements similarity 0.586, and the average similarity is described in detail for each cluster in Fig. 7.

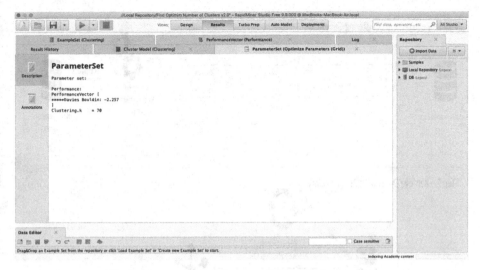

Fig. 6. Recommended Number of K by Davies Bouldin

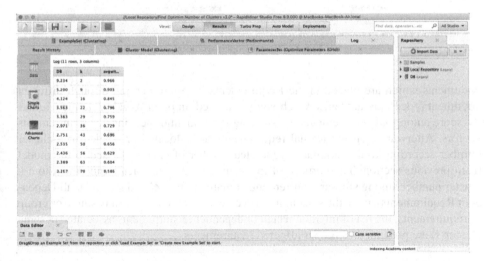

Fig. 7. Different k clusters with their average similarity using Davies Bouldin

5   K Clustering Model Implementation

The following chart illustrates a High-level functional model for how to create the requirements clusters using the calculated similarity score among Systems Requirement R after passing through different activities, then retrieve all the dependent set of requirements those could be affected by any in-place requirements amendment or deletion.

In the model, finding the interconnected set of requirements as end results are passed through two main steps, first step (Requirements Clustering Generation) all requirement

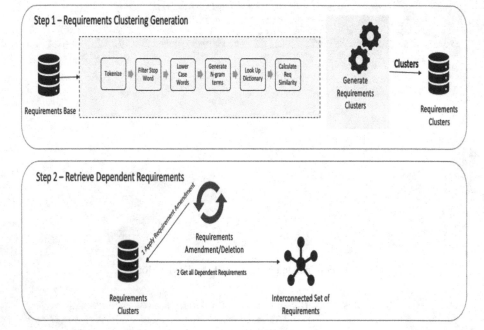

Fig. 8. Model Implementation

documents which are placed in the Requirements base, are passing through different document processing activates which were described, in order to calculate the similarity score among all requirements considering the semantic meaning for requirements vectors. Afterwards, all the textual requirements are allocated or labeled to a cluster number according to the automatic generated number of clusters passed to the model from previous section. The purpose of this step is to allocate each requirement to a k cluster number among similar requirements. Finally, in the second step (Get all Dependent Requirements), once the stakeholders decide to amend or delete any single or group of requirements, the list of interconnected or dependent requirements associated in same cluster(s) are presented as proper affected requirements.

5.1 Detailed Model Data Examination

Aiming to investigate the potential benefits of the clustering model, we have applied the k clustering on the real industrial requirements for around 4000 Requirements Statements.

The following section describes each process in detail among the flow of activities applied in RapidMiner [41] for the requirements repository in order to allocate them to different clusters.

Remember Wordnet Dictionary
This operator utilized to save the wordnet dictionary into the object store of the activity in order to minimize the I/O process for each vector during the model run. The saved

object would be restored in the future using Recall function mentioning the same name and class.

Read Data

This function used to read data from Microsoft Excel sheets, where the whole requirements are stored in spreadsheets. The table must be arranged in such a way that each row is an example, and each column is an attribute. For attribute titles which could be specified as parameters, see the first row of the Excel sheet.

Tokenize

Mainly, that operator separates the document's text to sequence of tokens. There are numerous choices just how to determine the segregation themes. Whichever it can be used all non-letter character. The mode that was used is to separate the text into English linguistic tokens.

Filters Stop Words (English)

This function filters out English stop words from a document by eliminating every token that matches a stop word from the embedded stop word list. Every token should represent a single English word only.

Transform Case

This operator transforms all characters in a document to either lower case or upper case, correspondingly.

Recall Dictionary

This operator recalls the itemized wordnet dictionary from the object recall of the procedure. The objects can be held in the object store by using the Remember Operator.

Find Synonyms

This operator uses wordnet dictionary file, as it received the text vector and find all the synonym or different meaning for each word or vector.

Generate n-gram

This function produces tokens in a document with term n-Grams. It defines a word n-Gram as a series of repeated tokens of length n. The term n-Grams generated by this operator includes all the following series of n-length tokens, the default length being 2.

Data to Similarity

The "Data to Similarity Data" operator measures the similarity of an Example Set among all requirements. Even requirements are comparable to those of themselves. So, if the Example Set includes n examples of specifications, this operator returns similarity comparisons to n^2. The Data to Similarity Data Operator returns an Example Set called a view, so that there will be no memory errors here.

K-means Clustering

This Operator performs the clustering using k-means algorithm. Clustering groups Examples together which are similar to each other, Clustering can be used on un-labelled data and is an algorithm of unsupervised machine learning.

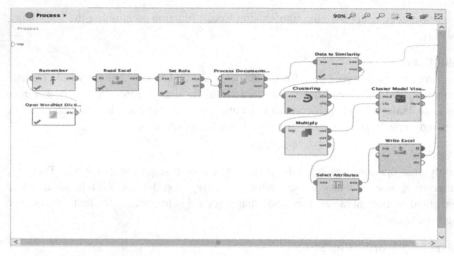

Fig. 9. Clustering Model Technical Description

6 Clustering Model Results

As explained, k-means clustering is used to see how the model can correctly detect if a certain requirement itself has changed or deleted during ULS system run and get the auto discovered or dependent set of requirements those could be impacted.

So, the following Figs. 11, 12 and 13 show the allocation of requirements into several clusters, each cluster contains at least one to n requirements.

Cluster Model

Cluster 0: 78 items	Cluster 24: 32 items	Cluster 48: 41 items
Cluster 1: 50 items	Cluster 25: 35 items	Cluster 49: 37 items
Cluster 2: 29 items	Cluster 26: 28 items	Cluster 50: 16 items
Cluster 3: 26 items	Cluster 27: 19 items	Cluster 51: 53 items
Cluster 4: 30 items	Cluster 28: 26 items	Cluster 52: 28 items
Cluster 5: 36 items	Cluster 29: 48 items	Cluster 53: 25 items
Cluster 6: 28 items	Cluster 30: 37 items	Cluster 54: 25 items
Cluster 7: 96 items	Cluster 31: 27 items	Cluster 55: 42 items
Cluster 8: 52 items	Cluster 32: 31 items	Cluster 56: 27 items
Cluster 9: 30 items	Cluster 33: 34 items	Cluster 57: 89 items
Cluster 10: 82 items	Cluster 34: 53 items	Cluster 58: 42 items
Cluster 11: 29 items	Cluster 35: 26 items	Cluster 59: 14 items
Cluster 12: 22 items	Cluster 36: 32 items	Cluster 60: 34 items
Cluster 13: 23 items	Cluster 37: 47 items	Cluster 61: 50 items
Cluster 14: 25 items	Cluster 38: 35 items	Cluster 62: 1 items
Cluster 15: 57 items	Cluster 39: 137 items	Cluster 63: 41 items
Cluster 16: 29 items	Cluster 40: 39 items	Cluster 64: 53 items
Cluster 17: 35 items	Cluster 41: 46 items	Cluster 65: 69 items
Cluster 18: 77 items	Cluster 42: 39 items	Cluster 66: 25 items
Cluster 19: 40 items	Cluster 43: 16 items	Cluster 67: 62 items
Cluster 20: 47 items	Cluster 44: 68 items	Cluster 68: 66 items
Cluster 21: 44 items	Cluster 45: 20 items	Cluster 69: 48 items
Cluster 22: 37 items	Cluster 46: 45 items	Total number of items: 2898
Cluster 23: 42 items	Cluster 47: 47 items	

Fig. 10. Requirements allocation to Clusters

The below Fig. 13 shows if there is any change on a specific requirement, all the cluster related requirements have the same probability of propagation since they belong to same cluster.

Requirements Cluster

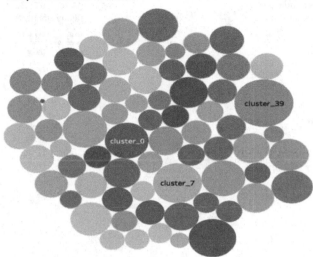

Fig. 11. Clusters Size

Cluster Details

Req Seq	Label	Req Text
R0001	cluster_48	All systems should be integrated with other subsyste
R0002	cluster_48	Provides interaction with other related systems to pa
R0003	cluster_58	All systems must be able to produce an electronic file
R0004	cluster_37	Security is required for each application with the abili
R0005	cluster_49	Limit based on role and allow exceptions using role-ba
R0006	cluster_7	Provides application and system performance measur
R0007	cluster_67	Ability to generate report files in delimited, ASCII, PD
R0008	cluster_46	Provides field level edits to ensure validity of the data
R0009	cluster_37	Help is searchable, editable and County specific.
R0010	cluster_33	Ability to request reports on-line for immediate or del
R0011	cluster_48	On-line training and demo module included with appli
R0012	cluster_67	Ad-hoc report writer packaged with application softw
R0013	cluster_67	Provide GUI-based end-user report viewing and query
R0014	cluster_7	System supports electronic workflow throughout all s
R0015	cluster_48	Integrated systems pass transactions, data and infor
R0016	cluster_32	Ability to view audit trail via screens and reports. Use
R0017	cluster_32	Ability to archive audit trail data
R0018	cluster_32	Ability to record audit trail for all data updates and sp
R0019	cluster_45	Ability to link to files located in a document managem
R0020	cluster_58	Supports electronic signatures
R0021	cluster_45	Document and diagrammatically represent workflows
R0022	cluster_39	Permits easy modification of work flows by end user o
R0023	cluster_49	Supports role-based workflow levels (different user, s
R0024	cluster_39	Changes to the work flow approval path do not affect
R0025	cluster_38	Workflow items that are in-process are able to be inqu
R0026	cluster_39	End users have an individual workflow-driven work qu
R0027	cluster_37	Automated e-mail notification for specific events and,
R0028	cluster_38	Inquire on open approval items in a workflow approva
R0029	cluster_55	Supports single sign-on
R0030	cluster_3	Supports different security structure for internal cou
R0031	cluster_63	Limit enforcement of transaction execution via a com
R0032	cluster_56	Limit enforcement of transaction execution via a com
R0033	cluster_7	System Administrator can view list of logged-in users
R0034	cluster_49	Supports group level permissions
R0035	cluster_3	Produces user security profile report Limit access by s

Fig. 12. Example of Cluster 0 and its allocated requirements IDs

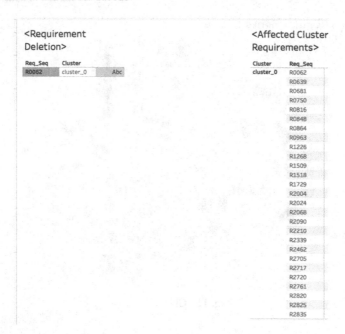

Fig. 13. Change in one single requirement and its impact on the whole cluster's requirements

7 Conclusions

In this work, we proposed a model to measure the impact of change request submitted in a free natural language against a large set of requirements. The key characteristics of the approach are that it exploits the synonyms of text in which the user is representing the change against the list of requirements through NLP similarity models.

Automated similarity analysis is used widely in many different business areas started by search engines, recommender systems and sentiment analysis and become a promising technique for supporting requirements engineers to manage requirements evolution since it has been managed in a decentralized way by crowdsourcing stakeholders and development team in ecosystems.

The model showed noticed results since there are no control over neither the structure of written textual requirement, the change requests, the formal semantics of requirements relation types or even the domain knowledge of the system. In addition, it can run over bulk of changes simultaneously with no barrier statements volume.

Since, it's an unsupervised prediction model, consequently, there is no predefined training data set to feed the model, so it's scaling up wherever needed.

We have implemented our model on RapidMiner, it's a data science application for machine learning, data mining, text mining, predictive analytics, and business analytics [41]. Each function in the suggested model is represented in one more task in the tool. Figures illustrate the tasks flow starting from reading each of requirements and changes repositories, applying the similarity model till providing the results at the end through a table showing the distance value between each change and requirement.

Finally, in this paper, we described a feasible model that utilizes unsupervised cluster technique and similarity models to scale-up the change impact analysis model of ULS requirements change management. We believe if combined both models change impact analysis problems can be solved in a noticeable way, we would be in a much stronger situation to challenge some of the higher-level difficulties identified in the ULS Systems report [42], like those related to unbalanced requirements, immediate requirements, and continues changes that happen alongside different interconnected system.

References

1. Functional Requirements for Enterprise Managment Systems. https://mulco.us/file/47449/download
2. Felfernig, A., Ninaus, G., Reinfrank, F., Weninger, L., Pagano, D., Maalej, W.: An Overview of Recommender Systems in Requirements Engineering, in Managing Requirements Knowledge, pp. 316–318. Springer, Munich (2013)
3. Burke, R.: Hybrid recommender systems: survey and experiments. UMUAI 12(4), 331–370 (2002)
4. Terveen, L., Herlocker, J., Konstan, J., Riedl, H.: Evaluating collaborative filtering recommender systems. ACM Trans. Inf. Syst. 22(1), 5–53 (2004)
5. Linden, G., Smith, B., York, J.: Amazon.com recommendations: item-to-item collaborative filtering. IEEE Inter. Comput. 7(1), 76–80 (2004)
6. Pazzani, M., Billsus, D.: Learning and revising user profiles: the identification of interesting web sites. Mach. Learn. 27, 313–331 (1997)
7. Felfernig, A., Burke, R.: Constraint-based recommender systems: technologies and research issues. In: Proceedings of IEEE ICEC'08, Innsbruck (2008)
8. Zayed, R.A., Ibrahim, L.F., Hefny, H.A., Salman, H.A.: Shilling attacks detection in collaborative recommender system: challenges and promise. In: Barolli, L., Amato, F., Moscato, F., Enokido, T., Takizawa, M. (eds.) WAINA 2020. AISC, vol. 1150, pp. 429–439. Springer, Cham (2020). https://doi.org/10.1007/978-3-030-44038-1_39
9. Soo, L., Cornelius, N.: Social networks and crowdsourcing for stakeholder analysis in system of systems projects. In: 8th International Conference on System of Systems Engineering, Hawaii (2013)
10. Mulla, N.: A new approach to requirement elicitation based on stakeholder recommendation and collaborative filtering. Int. J. Softw. Eng. Appl. 3(3), 51–60 (2012). https://doi.org/10.5121/ijsea.2012.3305
11. Dumitru, H., Gibiec, M., Hariri, N., Cleland-Hunang, J. Castro-Herrera, C.: On-demand feature recommendations derived from mining public product descriptions. In: Proceedings of ACM/IEEE, Waikiki/Honolulu (2011)
12. Lim, S.L., Finkelstein, A.: StakeRare: using social networks and collaborative filtering for large-scale requirements elicitation. IEEE Trans. Softw. Eng. 38(3), 707–735 (2012). https://doi.org/10.1109/TSE.2011.36
13. Mobasher, B., Cleland-Huang, J.: Recommender systems in requirements engineering. AI Mag. 32(3), 81–89 (2011). https://doi.org/10.1609/aimag.v32i3.2366
14. Soo, L., Daniela, D., Anthony, F.: StakeSource2.0: using social networks of stakeholders to identify and prioritise requirements. In: ICSE'11 Proceedings of the 33rd International Conference on Software Engineering, pp. 1022–1024 (2011)
15. Chuan, D., Paula, L., Cleland-Huang, J., Kwiatkowski, C.: Towards automated requirements prioritization and triage. Requirements Eng. 14(07), 73–89 (2009)

16. Felfernig, A., Schubert, M., Mand, M., Ghirardini, P.: Diagnosing inconsistent requirements preferences in distributed software projects. In: Proceedings of 3rd International Workshop on Social Software Engineering, Paderborn (2009)
17. Cleland-Huang, J., Dumitru, H., Duan, C., Castro-Herrera, C.: Automated support for managing feature requests in open forums. Commun. ACM **52**(10), 68–74 (2009)
18. Rick, S., Marsha, C., Jennifer, H., Alessio, D.S.: Managing requirements uncertainty with partial models. Requirements Eng. **18**(2), 105–106 (2013)
19. Castro-Herrera, C., Duan, C., Cleland-Huang, J., Mobasher, B.: Using data mining and recommender systems to facilitate large-scale, open, and inclusive requirements elicitation processes. In: Proceeding of the 16th IEEE international conference on requirements engineering (RE'08), Barcelona (2008)
20. Fantechi, A., Spinicci, E.: A content analysis technique for inconsistency detection in software requirements documents. In: WER05 – workshop em Engenharia de Requisitos, Porto (2005)
21. Belsis, P., Koutoumanos, A., Sgouropoulou, C.: PBURC: A patterns-based, unsupervised requirements clustering framework for distributed agile software development. Requirements Eng. **19**(2), 213–225 (2013). https://doi.org/10.1007/s00766-013-0172-9
22. Anna, H.: Similarity Measures for Text Document Clustering (2008)
23. Salton, G.: Automatic Text Processing. Addison-Wesley (1989)
24. Allahyari, M., et al.: A brief survey of text mining: classification, clustering and extraction techniques. In: KDD Bigdas, Halifax, Canada, August 2017
25. Ushioda, A.: Hierarchical clustering of words and application to NLP Tasks. In: Fourth Workshop on Very Large Corpora, Association for Computational Linguistics, pp. 28–41 (1996)
26. Can, F., Ozkarahan, A.: Concepts and effectiveness of the clustering methodology for text databases. ACM Trans. Database Syst. **15**(4), 483–517 (1990)
27. Jain, A.K., Murty, M.N., Flynn, P.J.: Data clustering: a review. ACM Comput. Surv. **31**(3), 264–323 (1999). https://doi.org/10.1145/331499.331504
28. Duan, C.: Clustering and its Application in Requirements Engineering. College of Computing and Digital Media, Via Sapientiae (2008)
29. Smyth, P.: Clustering using monte carlo cross validation. In: 2nd International Conference Knowledge Discovery and Data Mining (KDD-96), Portland (1996)
30. Naeem, S., Wumaier, A.: Study and implementing K-mean clustering algorithm on english text and techniques to find the optimal value of K. Int. J. Comput. Appl. **182**(31), 7–14 (2018)
31. Davies, D.L., Bouldin, D.W.: A cluster separation measure. IEEE Trans. Pattern Anal. Mach. Intell. **PAMI-1**(2), 224–227 (1979). https://doi.org/10.1109/TPAMI.1979.4766909
32. Siddheswar, R., Rose, H.: Determination of Number of Clusters in K-Means Clustering and Application in Color Image Segmentation (1998)
33. Julie, B.: Development of a stemming algorithm. MIT Information Processing Group, Electronic Systems Laboratory (1968)
34. Christopher, D., Prabhakar, R., Hinrich, S.: An Introduction to Information Retreival, p. 26. England, Cambridge University Press, Cambridge (2007)
35. Core, R.: Cluster Distance Performance (2018). https://docs.rapidminer.com/8.0/studio/ope rators/validation/performance/segmentation/cluster_distance_performance.html. Accessed 11 2019
36. Rapidminer: Cluster Distance Performance. Rapidminer, Jan 2020
37. Li, S., Liu, C., Wang, Y. (eds.): CCPR 2014. CCIS, vol. 484. Springer, Heidelberg (2014). https://doi.org/10.1007/978-3-662-45643-9
38. Mehdi, A.: A Brief Survey of Text Mining: Classification Clustering and Extraction Techniques in KDD Bigdas. Halifax, Canada (2017)
39. Shah, N., Mahajan, S.: Document clustering: a detailed review. Int. J. Appl. Inform. Syst. **4**(5), 30–38 (2012)

40. Functional Requirements for ERP Ecosystem (Cuyahoga County Government Functional Requirements). http://it.cuyahogacountry.us. Accessed Oct 2019
41. R. Miner. www.rapidminer.com
42. Feier, P., et al.: Ultra Large Scale Systems: The Software Challenge of the futhure. Technical Report, Software Engineering Institue (2006)

A Proposed Keyword-Based Feature Extraction Approach for Labeling and Classifying Egyptian Mobile Apps Arabic Slang User Requirements Reviews

Rabab Emad Saudy[1,2](), Alaa El Din El-Ghazaly[2], Eman S. Nasr[3], and Mervat H. Gheith[1]

[1] Faculty of Graduated Studies for Statistical Research, Cairo University, Giza, Egypt
`[email protected]`
[2] Sadat Academy for Management Sciences, Cairo, Egypt
[3] Cairo, Egypt

Abstract. Mobile applications (apps) review feature is supplied by most mobile apps platforms, which authorize users to evaluate, comment, and rate apps after utilizing it. User reviews are identified as an oriental source to enhance mobile applications (apps) and raise the importance for users. With the acute rise in the quantity of reviews, how to functionally and efficiently analyze and mining the user reviews and recognize serious user requirements from them to enhance the mobile apps. In this paper, we suggest an automatic approach for identifying and classifying requirements into Functional Requirements (FR), Non-Functional Requirements (NFR) and Sentimental Requirements (SR) from Egyptian Mobile Apps Arabic Slang Reviews (MASR), utilizing a group of techniques Term Frequency – Inverse Document Frequency (TF-IDF), Bag of Words (BOW) and Natural Language Processing (NLP) techniques with keywords selection. We suggest applying Classifier Chains (CC) approach to convert classifying multi-labeled data problem into one or more problems of single labeling, and utilizing the hybrid stack classification model, which combines Machine Learning (ML) and Deep Learning (DL) approaches consist of Logistic Regression (LR), Random Forest (RF), and Multi-Layer Perceptron Neural Network (MLP-NN). The hybrid stack classification model accomplishes high accuracy results for classifying Egyptian MASR user requirements as follow: (99.7%) for classifying Performance, (99.5%) for classifying Dissatisfied Users, (98.8%) for classifying Others, and (98.1%) for classifying Security, (97.9%) for classifying Usability, and (97.4%) for classifying Feature Requests.

Keywords: Mobile Applications · Mobile Applications Arabic Slang Reviews · User Requirements · Functional Requirements · Non-Functional Requirements · Sentimental Requirements · Term Frequency – Inverse Document Frequency · Bag of Words · Natural Language Processing · Classifier Chains · Machine Learning · Deep Learning · Logistic Regression · Random Forest · Neural Network

E. S. Nasr—Independent Researcher.

1 Introduction

With the rising ubiquity and income of mobile applications (apps) market, and app stores have turned into the essential hotspot for the division and possession of mobile apps [1]. Mobile applications (apps) review feature is supplied by most mobile apps platforms like (Google, Apple) app store that authorize users to evaluate, comment, and rate apps after utilizing them, which supplies a feedback technique from users to mobile apps developers. Mobile apps reviews are identified as an oriental source to enhance mobile apps and raise the importance for users [2, 3], as the reviews assist mobile apps developers to recognize better user requirements [4] for meet requirement maintenance, development, and evolution tasks [5, 6]. However, present mobile apps platforms support limited assistance for mobile apps developers to systematically assemble, clarify, and classify feedbacks to recognize user requirements [3]. User review and rating information have been explored for business and technical objectives such as mobile app price prediction [7]. Scientists have therefore fostered various approaches to automatically summarize user reviews contents to elicit the most helpful information they convey [8–10]. For instance, few methodologies plan to classify user reviews into various groups (e.g., feature request, bug report, aspect evaluation, etc.) [11, 12], while some studies focus on cluster and prioritize user reviews to distinguish the most significant topics [13]. Chandy et al. [14] suggested an automatic approach to identify spam reviews in iOS App Store. However, there is few works on automatically and systematically recognizing and classifying requirements from mobile apps user reviews, which will seriously enhance requirements elicitation and analysis in mobile app development.

To this end, the contribution for this research can be summarized as follow: we suggest an automatic approach to recognize requirements information from Egyptian Mobile App Arabic Slang Reviews (MASR) and classify them into Functional Requirements (FR), Non-Functional Requirements (NFR), Sentimental Requirements (SR), and Others requirements, which cannot be classified as FR or NFR or SR. This approach focuses on applying recommended Egyptian keywords selection for identifying, and classifying subcategories for main requirements such as: FR contains [feature requests, bugs, and update], NFR contains [security, performance, usability, frequency, and response time], and SR contains [satisfied users, and dissatisfied users].

In the rest of this paper: Sect. 2 discusses related work and compare some of them with our proposed approach. Section 3 suggests our proposed approach and the process of choosing keywords for automatically identify and classify various requirements for Egyptian Mobile Apps Arabic Slang Reviews. Section 4 displays the evaluation results for classifying Egyptian MASR user requirements. Section 5 summarizes this research with proposed future works.

2 Literature Review

This section debates and abbreviates relevant researches containing user reviews mining, filtering, and classification and their relation to our research in this section. Mobile apps store analysis has become a common subject in Software Engineering (SE) especially for requirements evolution. It allocates users suggest their sentiments, and opinions about the mobile apps they utilized in various app platforms.

Various researches [7, 15, 16] that mining mobile app stores concentrates on analyzing the feature information during user reviews, and recognition their inter-relations with different factors, e.g., code, rating, price, and downloads. Our research approach purposes to integrate mining of mobile app store reviews and identifying Requirements Engineering (RE) to assist developers enhance mobile apps to meet requirements evolution process. Many researchers [17–23] have concentrated on mining and analyzing user reviews in order to derive NFR that can assist developers maintaining and enhancing software systems according to requirement evolution. Our research approach aims to identify and classify various requirements categories: FR, NFR, SR, and other.

Finkelstein et al. [7] presented a technique to extract feature which results are also utilized as the input to estimate the prices of mobile apps, while our research concentrates on user requirements extraction from mobile app reviews. Villarroel et al. [24] classified reviews into proposal for new features, bug reports, and other types, in addition clustered together similar user reviews together and advised developers to address the user review cluster in the following release. Guzman et al. [25] utilized a feature and sentiment approach to elicit various opinions regarding utilizing mobile apps user reviews. Al-Subaihin et al. [26] elicited features from textual specification of mobile apps to cluster the mobile apps utilizing hierarchical clustering and generated mobile apps categorization. Panichella et al. [27] proposed merged technique automatically classify reviews into: information giving, information seeking, feature request, and problem discovery. Chen et al. [13] suggested an automatically framework to mine informative user reviews for mobile app developers, and moreover rank informative reviews. Our research purposes to recognize and classify users' reviews to FR, NFR, SR and others. Rastkar et al. [28] created bug report summaries in order to assist developers to find duplicate bug reports more quickly. Oh et al. [29] devised an automatically algorithm that recognizes informative reviews mirroring user interference to decrease developers' information overload. Chandy et al. [14] suggested an automatic approach to recognize spam reviews in mobile app store utilizing a latent class model with an understandable structure and minimal complexity. Lu et al. [18] attempt to apply supervised Machine Learning (ML) techniques to filter out non-informative reviews in addition to classify reviews into different categories (FRs, NFRs, and Others). Sorbo et al. [9] compiled reviews to suggest future software modifications based on user reviews summarization. Yang et al. [30] integrated regular expression and TF-IDF in addition human participation to classify reviews into NFRs and FRs. Hoon et al. [31] developed combined three emotion, quality, and functional ontologies to classify reviews into three groups. Gao et al. [32] created AR-Tracker tool, which automatically gathers user reviews of mobile apps and rates them in order to improve the reviews set exemplification. Tian et al. [33] analyzed the specifications of mobile apps reviews and recognized the factors of high-rated mobile apps. This research presents that analytics tools will assist developers in managing the vast volume of reviews via filtering, classifying them, to determine what requirements to add, change, or remove [34]. Galvis Carreño et al. [35] concentrated on altering requirements and developing new requirements utilizing the topics recognized from reviews, while our research try to recognize and classify various requirements from Arabic Slang mobile apps reviews. Our proposed approach results can consider to be as inputs to be recognized and classified as new requirements topics in requirements evolution. Wei et al. [36] proposed a multi-label classification dataset of mobile apps user reviews. Results show that it's possible to identify automatically new features requests. Our research concentrated on multi-label identification and classification for Arabic Slang Mobile apps reviews dataset which is requirements are categorized into FR, NFR, SR, and others and each main category include many multi-labels topics. Yang et al. [37] develop TOUR tool for detecting app reviews, identifying sentiments, and prioritizing important reviews for facilitating developers' examination. It applies topic modeling approach. It evaluates by a survey that includes various developers, and All of them attest to the features TOUR suggests changing's practical utility. Sany et al. [38] suggest model for predicting covid-19 reviews into depressed or not. The prediction accuracy is 91% for applied ML algorithms, and 79% for DL algorithms.

3   A Proposed Keyword-Based Feature Extraction Approach for Identifying and Classifying of User Requirements from Egyptian Mobile Apps Arabic Slang Reviews (MASR)

We suggest an automated approach with for identifying and classifying requirements into FR, NFR, and SR from mobile apps Arabic slang reviews especially Egyptian reviews. There are four phases in this approach: MASR collecting, preprocessing, keyword extractor, identifying and classifying requirements, categorize requirements.

Figure 1 specifies the sequence workflow of proposed approach, which involves the following many phases will be discuss in details:

3.1   Phase One: Egyptian Mobile Apps Arabic Slang Reviews (MASR) Collection

In this phase, MASR [39] was elicited according to three main steps including: Scraping, Mobile App Categorizing, and Filtering, as shown in Table 1.

Table 1. MASR Collection phases.

Scraping	Scraper Tool	Applying Appbot Scraper Tool
	App Store	Choose specific Play Store (Google Play Store)
Categorizing	App category	Select various 9 categories of mobile apps (Social, Lifetyle, Travel & Locals, Shopping, Tools, Medical, Productivity, Education, Maps & Navigation)
	App Rating	Determine mobile applications were selected based on their rating of more than 4 scores on google play store in order to ensure the quality of the comments that guarantee the needs of the users,

(continued)

Table 1. (*continued*)

Filtering	Reviews Filtering	Choose Country/Language, and Date for crawled reviews. In this research we concern on mixing reviews of Egyptian mobile apps, and another Egyptian reviews for non-Egyptian mobile apps such as: Instagram
	MASR Dataset	Save extracted reviews in CSV file which are contained the following columns: app name, store, app id, review id, country, a star rating from 1 to 5, date, the reviewer's username (author), a review data (body), a translated review body, a review polarity (positive, negative, neutral)), language, reply URL, and app category
	Attributes Filtering	select specific attributes for analyze and classify reviews like: app category, app name, review, rating, and review polarity

3.2 Phase Two: Keyword-Based Feature Requirement Identification and Classification Approach (KBRIC) for Egyptian (MASR)

In this research, we focus on extracting three user requirements categories: FR, NFR, and SR. FR specifies "a task that a system must be capable to execute", NFR is limited to a few distinct characteristics other than functionality, and SR is relating to or involving feelings. In this phase, we suggest to perform three steps: Keyword-based Search for Extracting Annotated Reviews, MASR Preprocessing, Keyword Feature Extraction.

Keyword-Based Search for Extracting Annotated Reviews. This paper utilizes a keyword-based search technique to automatically categorize requirements with FR, NFR, and SR. Some reviews include multi-label classifier. We select a limited set of keywords as shown in Table 2. We focus on the sentences including keywords relevant to keyword search requirements types mentioned in Table 2, for example: ((regex = عطل/معطل/تعطيل/تعطيل*), (regex = تامين/امان/امن)). If sentences include any of the keywords: ((تحسين ، تعديل ، اصدار ، تحديث)), we assume the review is relevant to the Update issue category), ((اضافة ، مكالمة ، فيديو ، صوت ، خاصية ، ميزة ، بلوك، حذف،)), we assume the review is relevant to the Feature Requests issue category), ((مستاء ، اخفاء), we assume the review is relevant to the Dissatisfied users issue category)). Such a limited set of keywords assist to decrease false positives.

MASR Preprocessing. The primary step is to perform pre-processing so as to develop the performance of classifiers by converting the text into a form as suitable as possible. This approach applies many stages (normalization, tokenization, stop-word removal and stemming) as shown in Table 3.

Keyword Feature Extraction. To estimate classifiers performance, we utilized various variety of features. Those features can be Bag-of-Words (BOW) with Term Frequency Inverse Document Frequency (TF-IDF) as mentioned in Table 4.

Table 2. Keywords for various Requirements Types.

Requirement Category	Requirements Type	Keywords
FR	Feature Requests	اضافة ، مكالمة ، فيديو ، صوت ، خاصية ، ميزة ، بلوك ، حذف ، اخفاء
	Bugs	خطأ، عطل ، متوقف ، معطل
	Update	تحسين ، تعديل ، اصدار، تحديث
NFR	Frequency	وقت ، مستمر ، مرة ، مرات ، ثانية، دقيقة، ساعة ، معدل ، متوسط ، باستمرار
	Security & Accounts	مستخدم ، سر ، حساب ، شخصى ، معلومة ، خاص ، احتيال ، فيرس ، الكاميرا ،استماع ، مراقبة ، تصنت ، تجسس ، سرقة، صلاحية، خصوصية
	Performance	تهيئة ، كفاءة ، فعالية ، جدارة، حالة ، وضع
	Response Time	سرعة ، سريع ، بطيئة ، بطىء، استجابة ، انتظار ، تاخير ، تحميل ، متجمد ، متوقف ، معطل ، مختصر ، طويل ، دائم ، متقطع
	Usability	سهل ، صعب ، استهلاك ،مرنة ، استخدام ، شاشة، اجتماعى، التعلم ، تشغيل ، تصفح ، صفحة
SR	Satisfied users	راضى ، سعيد ، ممتاز ، جيد ، متحمس

3.3   Phase Three: Automated Supervised Single/Multi-label Classification

This paper utilizes the automatically annotated mobile apps reviews from the preceding phase as training reviews for supervised learning of multi-label classification as mentioned in Table 5. Then utilizes different manually annotated dataset as our validation set for evaluating the of multi-label classifier performance. We first tokenize each mobile app review into BOW form, remove the common Arabic stopwords in addition to Egyptian stopword from [40]. Then transform each MASR review into TF-IDF feature vector. Finally, we suggest to employ Classifier Chains (CC) [41] approach to convert classifying multi-labeled data problem into one or more problems of single labeling, and utilizes the hybrid stack classification model [39] which combine Machine Learning (ML) and Deep Learning (DL) approaches which comprised of three classification techniques: Logistic Regression (LR) + Random Forest (RF)+ Multi-layer Perceptron Neural Network (MLP-NN) which accomplish high accuracy results 89.4% on classifying Egyptian MASR polarity sentiments (positive or negative or neutral).

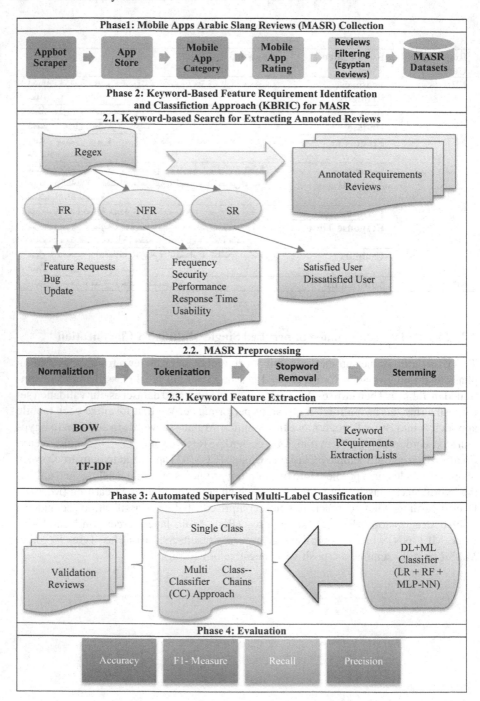

Fig. 1. Keyword-Based Feature Extraction Approach

Table 3. MASR preprocessing phases

Normalization	This step includes applying two tasks: removing and replacing. First: Removing punctuation marks, special characters, all diacritics, digit numbers, and non-Arabic words. Second: Replacing each final letter (ي) with (ى), Replace initial letter alef-hamza (أ ,إ ,آ ,ء) with (ا), and replace each final letter (ة) with (ه).
Tokenization	separate text by word or by sentence. This will allow deal with smaller groups of text that are still relatively significative regular outgoing of the context of the rest of the text.
Stop-word Removal	abstract all stop-words from apps reviews. In this research, Arabic stop word list used from various resources also specific Egyptian stop word [40].
Stemming	technique of reducing a word to its root. In this research, Snowball stemmer performs on MASR dataset.

Table 4. Feature Extraction Techniques

BOW	an operation of extracting features from text for utilize in modeling, such as with ML algorithms. BOW model assigns a corpus with word counts for every document
TF-IDF	a statistical method measure utilized to evaluate the importance of a word to a document in a corpus. The significance grows proportionally to the frequency of times a word represents in the document

3.4 Phase Four: Evaluation

To evaluate our proposed approach, we suggest to apply those performance evaluation measures [42]: Accuracy (ACC), F1-measure (F1), Precision (PRE), and Recall (REC) as mentioned in Table 6.

Table 5. Requirements Types and Categories for Egyptian MASR

Req.	Req.Type	Egyptian MASR	Translated Review	Pol.
FR	Feature Re-quests	حلو بس لو تضيفو مكالمة صوتية بس بدون فيديو	Nice, but if you add an audio call, but without a video	Pos.
	Bugs	لدي مشكلة في قسم فودافون كاش حيث دائمًا ما تعطيني خطأ داخلي في الخادم ، لا أعرف السبب	I have a problem in Vodafone cash section in which it always gives me internal server error, I don't know why	Neg.
	Update	الإصدار الجديد مليء بالأخطاء بحتاج للتعديل...	The new version is full of bugs and need update...	Neg.
NFR	Usability	تطبيق سهل فى التعامل وتفعيل والغاء الخدمات ومتابعة الاستهلاك	An easy application in dealing, activating and canceling services, and following up on consumption	Pos.
	Security	الابلكيشن دايما بيدينى خطأ بالرغم انى بدخل ويب من غير مشاكل نهائي.. ارجو افادتي بحل للمشكلة علشان اقدر اعيد التقييم تاني.	The application is always wrong password or user name in my hands, even though I am on a normal web income without a final problem .. Please advise me of a solution to the problem so that I can re-evaluate again	Neg.
	"Frequency", "Performance [Multi-Label]	لابد من ادخال تفاصيل بطاقتى فى كل مرة على الرغم من ان التطبيق يقول انه سيحفظ المعلومات. ايضا ، خدمة العملاء الخاصة بك هى الابطأ التى رايتها على الاطلاق. الدردشة المباشرة بطيئة للغاية ، و يستغرق الاشخاص وقت اطول للعودة ، فقط ليقولوا ان الطلب سيكون هنا خلال 10 الى 15 دقيقة فى كل مرة.	I have to enter my card details every time even though the app says it'll save the information. Also, your customer service is the slowest I've ever seen. Live chat is too slow, and your people take too long to get back, only to say the order will be here in 10 to 15 mins. Every. Single. Time.	Neg.
	Response Time	حلو جدا و ثقافي.؛ بس ممكن تخلو سريع	Very sweet and cultural.; You can just give up quickly	Pos.
SR	Satisfied users	كنت راضيه كل الرضا عن خدمة خطوطكم متألقين واتمنى لكم كل التوفيق و انصح باستخدام البرنامج	I was completely satisfied with the service of your lines shining and I wish you all the best and I recommend using the program	Pos.
	Dissatisfied Users	خدمة عملاء سيئة للغاية أنا مستاء	very bad customer service I'm upset	Neg.

4 Results and Discussion

For empirical research, we apply a hybrid ML, and DL stack Model [39] for classifying 600 random sample of Egyptian MASR user requirements datasets. Figure 2 displays Egyptian MASR requirements distribution as follow: FR [Feature Requests 7%, Bugs

Table 6. Evaluation Measures

ACC	evaluates the performance measure, and it represents a ratio of correctly predicted examination to the total examinations	$\frac{\sum TP+\sum TN}{\sum TP+FP+TN+FN}$ (1)
F1	a technique that illustrates the incorporated precision, while recall denotes the harmonic medium of recall and precision, and traditional F-measure	$\frac{2*Precision*Recall}{(Precision*Recall)}$ (2)
PRE	evaluates the number of True Positives (TP) divided by the number of True Positives (TP) and False Positives (FP)	$\frac{TP}{TP+FP}$ (3)
REC	refers to positive predictive value (PPV). It evaluates the true positive rate	$\frac{TP}{TP+FN}$ (4)

10%, Update 14%], NFR [Security 5%, Performance 2%, Response Time 6%, Usability 2%, Frequency 5%], SR [Satisfied Users 44%, Dissatisfied Users 3%], and Others 2%. We apply K-Fold Cross Validation (CV) with K = 10. And finally, we implement four evaluation measures: ACC, F1, PRE, RE for evaluating Egyptian MASR user require ments to assist mobile app developers to meet user requirements evolution as shown in Table 7.

Table 7. Evaluation Measures Results for Egyptian MASR User Requirements

		ACC	F1	PR	RE
FR	Feature Requests	97.4%	80%	85.7%	75%
	Bugs	86.9%	53.4%	43%	70.5%
	Update	94.6%	83.2%	76.2%	91.7%
NFR	Security	98.1%	81.4%	**92.3%**	72.7%
	Performance	**99.7%**	35%	33%	28%
	Response Time	94.1%	6%	50%	3%
	Usability	97.9%	13%	33%	9%
	Frequency	94.4%	11%	33%	7%
SR	Satisfied Users	91.5%	**91.4%**	86.1%	**97.4%**
	Dissatisfied Users	99.5%	15%	35%	9%
Others		98.8%	17%	37%	8%

Accuracy. Table 7 shows that the hybrid classification model accomplishes high accuracy (99.7%) for classifying Performance, (99.5%) for classifying Dissatisfied Users,

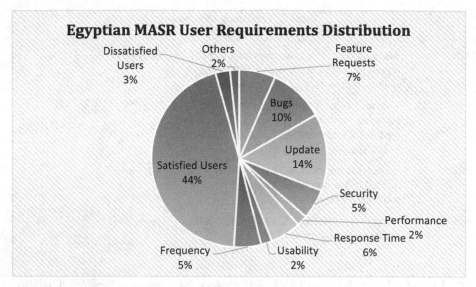

Fig. 2. Distribution of Egyptian MASR User Requirements

(98.8%) for classifying Others, (98.1%) for classifying Security, (97.9%) for classifying Usability, and (97.4%) for classifying Feature Requests.

F1-Measure. Table 7 shows that the hybrid classification model accomplishes high F1-measure (91.4%) for classifying Satisfied Users, (83.2%) for classifying Update, (81.4%) for classifying Security, and (80%) for classifying Feature Requests.

Precision. Table 7 shows that the hybrid classification model accomplishes high precision (92.3%) for classifying Security, (86.1%) for classifying Satisfied Users, (85.7%) for classifying Feature Requests, and (76.2%) for classifying Update.

Recall. Table 7 shows that the hybrid classification model accomplishes high recall (97.4%) for classifying Satisfied Users, (91.7%) for classifying Update, (75%) for classifying Feature Requests, and (72.7%) for classifying Security.

5   Conclusion and Future Work

In this paper, we aim to propose an automatic approach for identifying and classifying user requirements into FR, NFR and SR from Egyptian MASR. TF-IDF, BOW and NLP techniques utilized for extracting keywords. A keyword list was collected for FR consists of (Feature Request, Bug, and Update), NFR consists of (Response Time, Usability, Performance, Security, Frequency), and SR consists of (Satisfied Users, Dissatisfied Users). For multi-labeled problem, we suggest applying the CC approach to classify multi-labeled data problems into one or more problems of single labeling. We also suggest to utilizes the hybrid stack classification model which combines ML and DL approaches consist of LR, RF, and MLP-NN, and also evaluate our hybrid approach using

ACC, F1, PRE, RE measures, which accomplish high accuracy results for classifying Egyptian MASR user requirements as follow: (99.7%) for classifying Performance, (99.5%) for classifying Dissatisfied Users, (98.8%) for classifying Others, and (98.1%) for classifying Security, (97.9%) for classifying Usability, and (97.4%) for classifying Feature Requests.

In the future, we intend to apply different keyword feature extraction methods such as n-grams, word enrichment, and word embedding. We plan to apply Topic Modeling approach for extracting other topics that represent new requirements from Others requirements that cannot be classified as FR, NFR, and SR from Egyptian MASR.

References

1. Holzer, A., Ondrus, J.: Mobile application market: a developer's perspective. Telematics Inform. **28**(1), 22–31 (2011)
2. Bano, M., Zowgh, D.: User involvement in software development and system success: a systematic literature review. In: Proceedings of the 17th International Conference on Evaluation and Assessment in Software Engineering (ESEM) (2013)
3. Abelein, U., Sharp, H., Paech, B.: Involving users in software development really influence system success? IEEE Softw. **30**(6), 17–23 (2013)
4. Liang, P., Avgriou, P., He, K., Xu, L.: From collective knowledge to intelligence: pre-requirements analysis of large and complex systems. In: Proceedings of the 1st Workshop on Web 2.0 for Software Engineering (2010)
5. Saudy, R.E., Nasr, E.S., El-Ghazaly, A.E.D.M., Gheith, M.H.: Use of arabic sentiment analysis for mobile applications' requirements evolution: trends and challenges. In: Hassanien, A.E., Shaalan, K., Gaber, T., Tolba, M.F. (eds.) AISI 2017. AISC, vol. 639, pp. 477–487. Springer, Cham (2018). https://doi.org/10.1007/978-3-319-64861-3_45
6. Francese, R., Gravino, C., Risi, M., Scanniello, G., Tortora, G.: Mobile app development and management: results from a qualitative investigation. In: Proceedings of the 2017 IEEE/ACM 4th International Conference on Mobile Software Engineering and Systems (MOBILESoft) (2017)
7. Finkelstein, A., Harman, M., Jia, Y., Sarro, F., Zhang, Y.: Mining App Stores: Extracting Technical, Business and Customer Rating Information for Analysis and Prediction. Research Note RN/13/21 (2013)
8. Phong, M.V., The Nguyen, T., Viet Pham, H., Thanh Nguyen, T.: Mining user opinions in mobile app reviews: a keyword-based approach. In: Proceedings of the 2015 30th IEEE/ACM International Conference on Automated Software Engineering (ASE) (2015)
9. Di Sorbo, A., et al.: What would users change in my app? summarizing app reviews for recommending software changes. In: Proceedings of the 2016 24th ACM SIGSOFT International Symposium on Foundations of Software Engineering (2016)
10. Gao, C., Wang, B., He, P., Zhu, J., Zhou, Y., Lyu, M.R.: Paid: Prioritizing app issues for developers by tracking user reviews over versions. In: Proceedings of the 2015 IEEE 26th International symposium on software reliability engineering (ISSRE) (2015)
11. Guzman, E., El-Haliby, M., Bruegge, B.: Ensemble methods for app review classification: an approach for software evolution (N). In: Proceedings of the 30th IEEE/ACM International Conference on Automated Software Engineering, ASE'15 (2015)
12. McIlroy, S., Ali, N., Khalid, H., Hassan, A.E.: Analyzing and automatically labelling the types of user issues that are raised in mobile app reviews. Empirical Softw. Eng. **21**(3), 1067–1106 (2015). https://doi.org/10.1007/s10664-015-9375-7

13. Chen, N., Lin, J., Hoi, S.C.H., Xiao, X., Zhang, B.: AR-miner: mining informative reviews for developers from mobile app marketplace. In: Proceedings of the 36th International Conference on Software Engineering (ICSE), Hyderabad, India (2014)

14. Chandy, R., Gu, H.: Identifying spam in the iOS App Store. In: Proceedings of the 2Nd Joint WICOW/AIRWeb Workshop on Web Quality, WebQuality'12. ACM (2012)

15. Harman, M., Jia, Y., Zhang, Y.: App store mining and analysis: MSR for app stores. In: Proceedings of the 2012 9th IEEE Working Conference on Mining Software Repositories (MSR) (2012)

16. Zaidman, A., Van Rompaey, B., Demeyer, S., Van Deursen, A.: Mining software repositories to study co-evolution of production & test code. In: Proceedings of the 1st International Conference on Software Testing, Verification, and Validation (ICST) (2008)

17. Garba, S., Isyaku, B., Abdullahi, M.: A-driven model for non-functional requirements in mobile application development. Int. J. Comput. Sci. Inform. Technol. (IJCSIT) 11(2), 97–109 (2019)

18. Lu, M., Liang, P.: Automatic classification of non-functional requirements from augmented app user reviews. In: Proceedings of the 21st International Conference on Evaluation and Assessment in Software Engineering (2017)

19. Corbalán, L., et al: A study of non-functional requirements in apps for mobile devices. In: Proceedings of the Conference on Cloud Computing and Big Data, Cham (2019)

20. Tóth, L., Vidács, L.: Study of various classifiers for identification and classification of non-functional requirements. In: Proceedings of the International Conference on Computational Science and Its Applications, Cham (2018)

21. Ahmad, A., Feng, C., Li, K., Asim, S.M., Sun, T.: Toward empirically investigating non-functional requirements of iOS developers on stack overflow. IEEE Access 7, 61145–61169 (2019)

22. Wang, T., Liang, P., Lu, M.: What aspects do non-functional requirements in app user reviews describe?: an exploratory and comparative study. In: Proceedings of the 25th Asia-Pacific Software Engineering Conference (APSEC) (2018)

23. Saudy, R.E., Nasr, E.S., El-Ghazly, A.E.D.M., Gheith, M.H.: A comparative framework for Arabic sentiment analysis research. In: The 54thAnnual Conference on Statistics, Computer Sciences and Operation Research, Egypt (2019)

24. Villarroel, L., Bavota, G., Russo, B., Oliveto, R., Di Penta, M.: Release planning of mobile apps based on user reviews. In: Procedings of the 2016 IEEE/ACM 38th International Conference on Software Engineering (ICSE) (2016)

25. Guzman, E., Aly, O., Bruegge, B.: Retrieving diverse opinions from app reviews. In: Proceedings of the ACM/IEEE International Symposium on Empirical Software Engineering and Measurement, ESEM'15. IEEE (2015)

26. Al-Subaihin, A.A., Sarro, F., Black, S., Capra, L., Harman, M., Jia, Y., Zhang, Y.: Clustering mobile apps based on mined textual features. In: Proceedings of the 10th ACM/IEEE International Symposium on Empirical Software Engineering and Measurement (2016)

27. Panichella, S., Sorbo, A.D., Guzman, E.: How can i improve my app? classifying user reviews for software maintenance and evolution. In: Proceedings of the 31st IEEE International Conference on Software Maintenance and Evolution (2015)

28. Rastkar, S., Murphy, G.C., Murray, G.: Automatic summarization of bug reports. IEEE Trans. Software Eng. 40(4), 366–380 (2014)

29. Oh, J., Daehoon, K., Lee, U., Lee, J.-G., Song, J.: Facilitating developer-user interactions with mobile app review digests. In: Proceedings of the CHI'13 Extended Abstracts on Human Factors in Computing Systems, CHI EA'13, ACM (2013)

30. Yang, H., Liang, P.: Identification and classification of requirements from app user reviews. In: Proceedings of the 27th International Conference on Software Engineering and Knowledge Engineering (SEKE'15) (2015)

31. Hoon, L., Rodriguez-García, M.A., Vasa, R., Valencia-García, R., Schneider, J.-G.: App reviews: breaking the user and developer language barrier. In: Mejia, J., Munoz, M., Rocha, Á., Calvo-Manzano, J. (eds.) Trends and Applications in Software Engineering, pp. 223–233. Springer International Publishing, Cham (2016). https://doi.org/10.1007/978-3-319-26285-7_19

32. Gao, C., Xu, H., Hu, J., Zhou, Y.: AR-tracker: track the dynamics of mobile apps via user review mining. In: Proceedings of International Workshop on Internet based Virtual Computing Environment (IVCE), San Francisco, USA (2015)

33. Tian, Y., Nagappan, M., Lo, D., Hassan, A.E.: What are the characteristics of high-rated apps? a case study on free android applications. In: Proceedings of the 2015 IEEE international conference on software maintenance and evolution (ICSME) (2015)

34. Maalej, W., Nayebi, M., Johann, T., Ruhe, G.: Toward data-driven requirements engineering. IEEE Softw. 33(1), 48–54 (2015)

35. Galvis Carreño, L.V., Winbladh, K.: Analysis of user comments: an approach for software requirements evolution. In: Proceedings of the 2013 International Conference on Software Engineering, ICSE'13. IEEE Press (2013)

36. Wei, J., Courbis, A.-L., Lambolais, T., Xu, B., Bernard, P.L., Dray, G.: Towards a data-driven requirements engineering approach: automatic analysis of user reviews. In: Proceedings of the 7th National Conference on Practical Applications of Artificial Intelligence, Saint-Étienne (2022)

37. Yang, T., Gao, C., Zang, J., Lo, D., Lyu, M.R.: TOUR: dynamic topic and sentiment analysis of user reviews for assisting app release. In: Proceedings of the WWW'21. The Web Conference 2021, Ljubljana, Slovenia (2021)

38. Sany, M.M.H., Keya, M., Khushbu, S.A., Rabby, A.S.A., Masum, A.K.M.: An opinion mining of text in COVID-19 Issues along with comparative study in ML, BERT & RNN. In: Proceedings of the International Conference on Deep Learning, Artificial Intelligence and Robotics, Cham (2022)

39. Saudy, R.E., El-Ghazaly, A.E.D.M., Nasr, E.S., Gheith, M.H.: A novel hybrid sentiment analysis classification approach for mobile applications Arabic slang reviews. Int. J. Adv. Comput. Sci. Appl. 13(8), 423–432 (2022)

40. Medhat, W., Yousef, A., Korashy, H.: Egyptian dialect stopword list generation from social network data. The Egypt. J. Lang. Eng. 2(1), 43–55 (2015)

41. Read, J., Pfahringer, B., Holmes, G., Frank, E.: Classifier chains for multi-label classification. Mach. Learn. 85(3), 333–359 (2011)

42. Yamout, B., et al.: Predictors of quality of life among multiple sclerosis patients: a comprehensive analysis. Eur. J. Neurol. 20(5), 756–764 (2013)

A Comparative Study for Anonymizing Datasets with Multiple Sensitive Attributes and Multiple Records

Mona Mohamed Nasr[1], Hayam Mohamed Sayed[2], and Waleed Mahmoud Ead[2]([⊠])

[1] Information Systems Department, Faculty of Computers and Artificial Intelligence, Helwan University, Helwan, Egypt
[2] Information Systems Department, Faculty of Computers and Artificial Intelligence, Beni-Suef University, Beni-Suef, Egypt
`{hoyam.mohamed25,waleedead}@fcis.bsu.edu.eg`

Abstract. Today, there are many sources of data, such as IoT devices, that produce a massive amount of data, particularly in the healthcare industry. This microdata needs to be published, and shared for medical research purposes, data analysis, mining, learning analytics tasks, and the decision-making process. But this published data contains sensitive and private information for individuals, and if this microdata is published in its original format, the privacy of individuals may be disclosed, which puts the individuals at risk, especially if an adversary has strong background knowledge about the target individual. Owning multiple records and multiple sensitive attributes (MSA) for an individual can lead to new privacy leakages or disclosure. So, the fundamental issue is how to protect the privacy of 1:M with the MSA dataset using anonymization techniques and methods, as well as how to balance utility and privacy, for this data while reducing information loss and misuse. The objective of this paper is to use different methods and different anonymization algorithms, like the 1:m-generalization algorithm and Mondrian, and compare them to show which of them maintains data privacy and high utility of analysis results at the same time. From this comparison, we found that the m-generalization algorithm and the (p, k) angelization method perform well in terms of information loss and data utility compared to the other remaining methods and algorithms.

Keywords: Privacy · Anonymization · Healthcare · Data publishing · MSA · PPDP · IOT

1 Introduction

The IOT and storage technologies' rapid development results in the collection and integration of a flood of data and types of digital information available, as the data is being generated everywhere through various sources and organizations like healthcare, Biomedical, finance, social media, and so on. This collected data needs to be published, as medical data sharing is becoming a big demand for the purpose of analysis

© ICST Institute for Computer Sciences, Social Informatics and Telecommunications Engineering 2023
Published by Springer Nature Switzerland AG 2023. All Rights Reserved
R. Hou et al. (Eds.): BDTA 2021/2022, LNICST 480, pp. 38–57, 2023.
https://doi.org/10.1007/978-3-031-33614-0_3

and mining tasks in order to generate and process useful patterns. These patterns help managers and researchers make decisions about studying the characteristics of diseases and discovering new drugs. Besides this usefulness, the data may contain some sensitive information, which raises a privacy concern. As a result, determining how to protect privacy and prevent privacy leakage has been a significant challenge.

To address the trade-offs between data analysis and maintaining the privacy of specific information about individuals, such as their personally identifiable attributes or explicit attributes (like name, Zip code, address, social security number, and contact number), quasi-identifier attributes (like age, gender, and), and sensitive attributes (e.g. salary and disease), privacy-preserving data mining is proposed [8].

By using electronic health records (EHRs), numerous patient data records have been used in biomedical research projects. This data needs to be secure and protected from privacy disclosure, misuse, and exploitation. For example, in the era of IoT, new wearable devices like the Apple iWatch and Google Fit can give sensitive information about individuals like their location, health condition, and financial status by recording and analyzing their daily activities.

A specific person or group of persons can then be identified using this information, either alone or in combination. Especially when the attackers have strong background knowledge that helps them make correlation attacks and infer the privacy of individuals. For instance, many researches showed that a "linking attack" could identify almost 87% (Sweeney 2000) of the US population (i.e., connecting quasi identification properties with external information like a voter list) [?, 32]

To protect individual privacy, removing personally identifying information from databases is insufficient. As a result, to resolve these privacy concerns, many PPDP (privacy-preserving data publishing) algorithms are implemented by researchers. The most popular PPDP techniques are anonymization techniques because they have less information loss and high data utility. The requirements of the data miner and analyst are therefore taken into account for anonymization in order to produce anonymized data with significantly higher utility. Because maintaining privacy while increasing utility are two contradictory demands in data sharing, or contradictory goals, this means we have to lose one to gain the other. Further, the privacy preservation method is also dependent on the type or structure of the underlying dataset. At present, most privacy-preserving models for publishing data are applied to a dataset with just one record for each individual and a single sensitive attribute [15]. However, an individual may have multiple records and multiple sensitive attributes in a dataset. For instance, a user may post many status updates or messages using the same account on social networking sites (like Facebook and Twitter). In the same dataset, a patient may have records for more than one diagnosis. In this study, we employ 1: M generalization, a technique for anonymizing 1: M datasets. There are different models for preserving privacy, like l-diversity and SLAMS. However, the L-diversity model ignores the semantic relationship between sensitive values. So, there is a chance that the data may be disclosed. So we used different methods and anonymization algorithms to show which method did well in terms of privacy and utility, such as 1: M generalization, which performs SA anonymization first, followed by QID generalization. Use the Partition [30] for sensitive attribute anonymization and for QID generalization using the Mondrian [31]. Because semantic anonymization relies on semantic rules that lead to similarity attacks, we apply the appropriate anonymization process to such rules to avoid similarity attacks by checking each equivalence class of sensitive attributes. Other methods, such as Rating Privacy Preservation for MSA with Different Sensitivity Requirements, are made available in this manner, depending on the various sensitivity coefficients for various attributes [25]. This strategy preserves a lot of correlations between the microdata while also protecting the privacy of many sensitive variables.

(p-k) angelization for MSA, which uses the weight calculation to determine the correlation between sensitive attributes, the (p, k)-Angelization strategy decreases information loss while also protecting privacy by removing the risk of background join and non-membership attacks [15], but it takes more execution time (and has less accuracy) due to the complicated process of weight calculation.

We make use of two actual datasets. (heart disease, Informs), from uci –machine learning, (https://sites.google.com/site/informsdataminingcontest). Applying the mentioned methods to these datasets to show which method performs well due to privacy level and information loss. We found that each method has its limitations and advantages, so we need to combine the advantages of this method and propose a new approach that is effective in terms of privacy and data utility.

1.1 Our Main Contributions Are as Follows

1) We present a privacy framework for 1:M data publishing that makes use of (k, l)-diversity, as well as analytical results for the proposed model.By enforcing k-anonymity on the SA fingerprint and l-diversity on each equivalence class, (k, l)-diversity can protect QID and SA information during 1:M data publishing.
2) We develop an efficient method for 1: M-Generalization consisting of the combination of two algorithms: the Mondrian top-down greedy algorithm and the 1:M-Generalization algorithm, based on the (k, l)-diversity model, and compare the result between these algorithms according to information loss and efficiency according to execution time
3) applying the different methods to the two real-world datasets and comparing them to show which method performs well due to privacy level and information loss.

2   Related Work

Over the past several years, different techniques have been proposed to preserve privacy, and there are several techniques for privacy-preserving data publishing (PPDP) and privacy preserving data mining (PPDM).

We briefly discuss these methods and algorithms. Following are some novel works on privacy preservation. Since the introduction of the k-anonymity algorithm that was implemented by Sweeney in [1, 9, 10], many anonymization techniques [9, 13] and privacy models [11, 12] have been developed to prevent disclosure and privacy leakage during data publishing. To make sure that no record in the dataset can be distinguished from any other (k-1) record on QIDs, the author created k-anonymity. In [12], they discovered a k-anonymity barrier: a k-anonymized dataset is vulnerable to background knowledge and homogeneity attacks. They developed the L-diversity model with SA diversity chains to enhance privacy protection. In [11], they investigated the similarity and skewness attacks on l-diversity and proposed a t-closeness model with a distribution constraint to protect privacy. However, t-closeness cannot effectively protect the privacy of infrequent values, which are more vulnerable to privacy disclosure. In [18], they proposed the Mondrian multidimensional k-anonymization algorithm, which is based on top-down greedy approximation. In [24], they proposed a technique called Anatomy, which anonymizes microdata sets by damaging a relationship between QID and SA characteristics. But because Anatomy divulges specific QID values, it is susceptible to presence attacks. In [29], a proposed MNSACM method using clustering and multi-sensitive bucketization for anonymizing the datasets that contain both numerical and categorical sensitive attributes is described, but it is limited to numerical sensitive attributes only and has not been implemented on real datasets. Not suitable for incremental data sets. in [28] To anonymize set-valued data, a local differential privacy technique called LDPMiner was created. These techniques are only useful for publishing results; they cannot be used to publish secure data sets for sharing.

Privacy model (technique)	evaluation	Disclosure of Privacy	Utility of Data	references
Slicing	designed to handle high-dimensional data, although slicing can return the original tuples after random tuple permutation if separate tuples have the same QIDs and SAs	Attacks of Skewness and Similarity	loss of information	[33]
Anatomization + Slicing	The method takes a long time to complete and generates numerous tables. The solution is extremely intricate	Knowledge Attack Regarding Demography	loss of information	[26]
SLOMS	The suggested approach removed the link between MSA. As a result of generalization, it issued numerous tables with information loss	Knowledge Attack Regarding Demography	loss of information	[34]

(*continued*)

(*continued*)

Privacy model (technique)	evaluation	Disclosure of Privacy	Utility of Data	references
MSA (α, l)	Utilized suppression and generalization with anatomy, which reduced utility	------------	High information loss	[35]
LKC- privacy + slicing	For dynamic MSA data posting, the KC slice technique was offered; however, the authors did not give examples of numerous releases, thus I have just covered the entire technique for a single release	------------	High information loss	[27]
(p, k)-Anonymity + Angel	The suggested method keeps MSA's healthcare microdata private. The (p, k) angelization heuristic algorithm serves as its foundation This method, however, is susceptible to sensitive attribute correlation attacks and MSA quasi attribute assaults	Attacks with MSA correlation	Low Information loss	[15]
(p,l)-Angelization	The suggested method, which combines the 1 :M dataset and the MSA dataset, protects the privacy of healthcare microdata	generalization correlation attacks	Low Information loss	[36]

(*continued*)

(*continued*)

Privacy model (technique)	evaluation	Disclosure of Privacy	Utility of Data	references
G-Model	G-model protects against gender-specific SA attacks by maintaining separate groups and caches of male and female SAs. The G-model also stays away from generalization	Semantic correlation attacks	fail to provide optimal privacy protection	[37]

3 Problem Setting and Privacy Model

IOT devices generate a large amount of data, and this data may contain 1: m records or MSAs for each individual that lead to new privacy leaks due to different attacks such as similarity attacks, membership attacks, background knowledge attacks, and linking attacks. We consider 1: M-MSA dataset that can be faced many problems.

Two main problems are:

Problem 1: The majority of privacy models and techniques, such as K-anonymity, L-diversity, anatomization, and slicing, don't take the semantic relationship between sensitive values into account and are unable to process multiple attributes with various sensitivity requirements when simulating real-world privacy requirements for data publishing, which results in privacy disclosure.

Problem 2: (failure of Privacy model). Due to a dataset's many instances of a single individual, applying conventional 1:1 privacy methods to 1: M datasets and MSA may result in privacy exposure issues. K-anonymity, L-diversity, and SLOMS are examples of models. The key vulnerability information is that if an adversary is successful in identifying a single sensitive attribute, further sensitive qualities can be detected through co-relation.as the current framework falls short of ensuring data utility and protecting privacy for a number of sensitive characteristics.

We use the heart disease dataset to perform a comparative study between the different anonymization techniques for multiple sensitive attribute datasets. The dataset INFORMS consists of several attributes, such as month of birth, years of education, year of birth, marital status, race, income, diagnosis codes, sex, and disease. Heart Disease is a dataset with several attributes, including (gender: gender (1 = male; 0 = female), cp: chest pain type: Value 1: typical angina Value 2: atypical angina Value 3: non anginal pain Value 4: asymptomatic, trestbps: resting blood pressure (in mm Hg on admission to the hospital), fbs: (fasting blood sugar > 120 mg/dl) (1 = true; 0 = false), thalach: maximum heart rate achieved; resting electrocardiographic results). The original microdata as in Table 1.

4   Anonymization Algorithms and Methods

In this section, we discuss two algorithms and three methods to show which one performs well in terms of information loss, data utility, and execution time by comparing them.

Mondrian Algorithm on IT

The Mondrian algorithm is a popular one for relational data anonymization [18]. It can successfully anonymize QID in a top-down manner. Mondrian is the fastest local recording algorithm while retaining good data utility; categorical attributes have no generalization hierarchies. This operation results in lower information loss, but worse semantic results.

The main phases of Mondrian algorithm:

1. Use kd-tree to divide the raw dataset into k groups. Every group in a K-group consists of at least k records.
2. Ensure that each k-group has the same QID by generalizing each k-group.

5   1: M-Generalization Algorithm:

1M_Generalization is an anonymization algorithm for 1: M dataset. It contains two sub-algorithms: Mondrian (for the relational part) and Partition (for the transactional part). Both of them are straight forward based on (k, l)-diversity model by enforcing k-anonymity on the SA fingerprint and l -diversity on each equivalence class, (k, l)-diversity can protect QID and SA information during 1: M data publishing. This algorithm performs data partitioning twice. Perform SA anonymization first, followed by QID generalization. Use the Mondrian [18] for QID generalization and the Partition [22]. For SA anonymization. Following are the main stages of 1:M-generalization:

Step 1: Transformation convert 1:M microdata first to 1:1 microdata.
Step 2: SA fingerprint anonymization.
Step 3: QID anonymization and SA diversity.

Algorithm 1: Partition	**Algorithm 2:** Mondrian for data in 1: M Dataset

in relation to the partition with SA fingerprints.
Partition (partition, k)
Adding the partition to the global return list if the partition cannot be separated;
  else //
    The following steps are taken: / choose a node with the maximum information gain split_Node choose node (partition); // distribute records to sub partitions
Sub_ Partitions ← data distribution (partition, split_Node);
// deal with subp_artitions that have fewer than k records
balance partitions (sub Partitions);
  for sub_ Partition in sub _Partitions do
Partition (sub _Partition, k);
	Mondrian (partition, l)
	Add the partition to the global return list if the part's ion cannot be divided;
	else
	  /* It is best to choose the property with the widest (normaliZed) range of values. */
	dm ← Select the attribute (partition);
	  When dm is a number,
	    threshold ← Choose Threshold (dm, partition);
	IHS← {t ∈ partition: T [dm] ≤threshold};
	rHS← {t ∈ partition: T [dm] > threshold}; sub Partition ← {IHS} _ {rHS};
	else
	split_Node ← split (partition, dm);
	sub_ Partitions ← share information (partition, split Node);
	for sub Partition in sub Partitions do
	  Mondrian (sub _Partition, l) ;

Fig. 1. Anonymization Algorithms (Partition, Mondrian)

<table>
<tr><td>

Algorithm 3: 1: M-generalization.
Begin
Enter T, K, and L as input
Output: *T* ∗
T1 ◄──Transform *T* into 1:1 dataset;
T2 ◄── Partition (T, *K*);

T ∗◄── Mondrian (IT, l);
return T ∗;
end

</td><td>

Algorithm: algorithm for semantic extraction
L-diversity Table as an input (T)
Output: effective set of semantic guidelines
Clustering table into ECs;
While T isn't end do
For each equivalence class V from T do
Apply semantic rules on the sensitive attribute of EC;
If there is extracted data impacts on privacy resulted by a semantic rule, then
   a) Keep the semantic rule on file as a valid semantic rule.
   b) Assign this rule an anonymization action.
End while

</td></tr>
</table>

Fig. 2. 1: M-generalization Algorithm   **Fig. 3.** Semantic Anonymization algorithms [24]

A. Semantic Anonymization Method

The proposed method (Fig. 1) is based on the L-diversity approach and semantic extraction techniques. The semantic extraction is based on semantic rules that can be assigned by the owner of the data that will be published [24]. Describe the relationship between sensitive values. The semantic rules that produce data, which have an impact on privacy and lead to similarity attacks, are called "effective semantic rules."

The anonymizer determines the important pieces of information that need to be anonymized and then selects the effective semantic rules that produce these pieces of information. The approach consists of two main parts: Data extraction using effective semantic principles to determine the rules of anonymization Table 2 displays the ECs, the applicable semantic rule for them, and the suggested action for anonymization in accordance with the values of sensitive characteristics.

Our suggested rules:

In INFORMS dataset:

Rule 1: If "the bronchitis, lung cancer, cough, flu and bronchitis" then is Respiratory infection disease.
Rule 2: If "income with values 0 to 2000" then is very low salary.

In Heat disease dataset:

Rule 1: If "cp is typical angina or atypical angina" then is heart disease.
Rule 2: If "trestbps from 150 to 200" then is high resting blood pressure. Rule 3: If "fbs > 120" then blood sugar disease. Rule 4: If "thalach from 170 to 202" then is heart disease. Rule 5: If "restecg ST > .5" then is heart disease.

Table 3 demonstrates the ECs, the relevant semantic rule, and generates action for anonymization in accordance with the semantic similarity between sensitive attribute values, the red cells refer to the effective semantic rules (described above) that produce data, which have an impact on the privacy and lead to privacy disclosure, to solve this issue, we applying the anonymization, the data is shown in Table 4. It is noticed that the EC which has QI {[30, 40], F} is merged with EC which has QI {[40, 50], M} into one EC where become has QI {[30, 50], *} and contain all sensitive values that were in the two EC. Therefore, prevent attacker from discloser the privacy of SA (Figs. 2 and 3).

Table 1. Original microdata (the heart disease dataset before anonymization)

Age	Sex	cp	trestbps	fbs	thalach	Restecg
28	M	typical angina	145	108	150	0
29	M	asymptomatic	130	101	162	1
21	M	atypical angina	120	110	148	0
41	M	non-anginal pain	140	105	153	0
50	M	atypical angina	138	110	151	1
48	M	asymptomatic	120	110	114	1
36	F	typical angina	160	125	187	1
37	F	atypical angina	150	130	172	1
30	F	atypical angina	172	130	178	1

Table 2. Entropy 3_Diversity (the heart disease dataset after 3_Diversity)

Age	Sex	cp	trestbps	fbs	thalach	Restecg
[20, 30]	M	typical angina	145	108	150	0
[20, 30]	M	asymptomatic	130	101	162	1
[20, 30]	M	atypical angina	120	110	148	0
[30, 40]	F	atypical angina	172	130	178	1
[30, 40]	F	typical angina	160	125	187	1
[30, 40]	F	atypical angina	150	130	172	1
[40, 50]	M	non-anginal pain	140	105	153	0
[40, 50]	M	asymptomatic	120	110	114	1
[40, 50]	M	atypical angina	138	110	151	1

Table 3. The effective semantic rules and anonymization action

Age	Sex	cp	trestbps	fbs	thalach	Restecg	Rules	action
[20,30]	M	typical angina	145	108	150	0	....	....
[20,30]	M	asymptomatic	130	101	162	1	....	....
[20,30]	M	atypical angina	120	110	148	0	....	....
[30,40]	F	atypical angina	172	130	178	1	heart disease blood sugar disease high resting blood pressure	Generalization, Adding +10 Suppress Sex attributes
[30,40]	F	typical angina	160	125	187	1		
[30,40]	F	atypical angina	150	130	172	1		
[40,50]	M	non-anginal pain	140	105	153	0	....	....
[40,50]	M	asymptomatic	120	110	114	1	....	....
[40,50]	M	atypical angina	138	110	151	1	....	....

Table 4. 3_Diversity after anonymization

Age	Sex	cp	trestbps	fbs	thalach	Restecg
[20, 30]	M	typical angina	145	108	150	0
[20, 30]	M	asymptomatic	130	101	162	1
[20, 30]	M	atypical angina	120	110	148	0
[30,50]	*	atypical angina	172	130	178	1
[30,50]	*	typical angina	160	125	187	1
[30,50]	*	atypical angina	150	130	172	1
[30,50]	*	non-anginal pain	140	105	153	0
[30,50]	*	asymptomatic	120	110	114	1
[30,50]	*	atypical angina	138	110	151	1

B. Rating Privacy Preservation method

Rating method (Fig. 4) used to disseminate sensitive data The AT (Attribute Table) and IDT (ID Table) tables for rating releases are based on various sensitivity coefficients for various qualities. This approach preserves many microdata correlations while simultaneously safeguarding the privacy of numerous sensitive variables. [25]. Increase the usefulness of released data while meeting the privacy requirements for a variety of sensitive features. This technique calculates the (sensitivity coefficient SCi).

Table 5. Miodata used for rating method

Age	Sex	cp	trestbps	fbs	thalach	Restecg
28	M	typical angina	145	108	150	0
29	M	asymptomatic	130	101	162	1
21	M	atypical angina	120	110	148	0
30	M	atypical angina	172	130	178	1
36	M	non-anginal pain	160	125	187	0
37	F	atypical angina	150	130	172	1
41	F	non-anginal pain	140	105	153	0
48	F	asymptomatic	120	110	114	1
56	F	atypical angina	138	110	151	1
65	F	asymptomatic	150	105	148	0

```
Algorithm: AiIDj-Creation
input: T with SC1, SC2, SCd+1
Results: AiIDj
1: j=0 AiIDj=∅
2: For each property Ai, multiply by (1 ≤ i ≤ d + 1)
3: based on their values, hash the Aitk in Ai (each bin according to value)
/* The group-creation process is in lines 4–9. */
4: so long as at least SCi non-empty hash buckets exist;
/* lines 5 to 9 create a new AiIDj. */
5: j=j+1; AiIDj = ∅
6: S is the collection of SCi buckets with the largest size at the moment.
7: for each bucket in S
8: remove a random tuple Aitk from the collection
9: AiIDj = AiIDj U {Aitk}
/* The step of residue assignment is lines 10 to 13. */
10: for each non-empty bucket
/* There is just one value for this bucket; see Lemma 3. */
11: Ait'k = the bucket's sole remaining asset
12: S' = the collection of AiIDj without the Ait'k
13: pick a random AiIDj in S' to receive Ait'k.
```

Fig. 4. Rating method [25]

Table 6. Rating publishes AT with SC (3; 2; 2; 2; 2; 2; 2) for microdata in Table 5.

tk	Age (A1)	Sex(A2)	cp(A3)	Trestbps (A4)	Fbs (A5)	Thalach (A6)	Restecg (A7)
t1	A1ID1	A2ID1	A3ID2	A4ID1	A5ID1	A6ID1	A7ID1
t2	A1ID1	A2ID2	A3ID2	A4ID2	A5ID2	A6ID2	A7ID2
t3	A1ID1	A2ID3	A3ID1	A4ID3	A5ID3	A6ID3	A7ID3
t4	A1ID2	A2ID4	A3ID3	A4ID4	A5ID4	A6ID4	A7ID4
t5	A1ID2	A2ID5	A3ID5	A4ID5	A5ID5	A6ID5	A7ID5
t6	A1ID2	A2ID1	A3ID4	A4ID1	A5ID1	A6ID1	A7ID1
t7	A1ID3	A2ID2	A3ID4	A4ID2	A5ID2	A6ID2	A7ID2
t8	A1ID3	A2ID3	A3ID3	A4ID3	A5ID4	A6ID3	A7ID3
t9	A1ID3	A2ID4	A3ID5	A4ID5	A5ID5	A6ID4	A7ID5
t10	A1ID3	A2ID5	A3ID1	A4ID4	A5ID3	A6ID5	A7ID4

C. (p, k) angelization for MSAS data publication with weight calculation

Since each bucket contains entries that fall within the p categories, each bucket partitioning complies with the (p, k)-anonymity principle. This technique (Angelization)

Table 7. For microdata in Table 5, rating publishes IDT with SC (3, 2; 2; 2; 2). (aty = atypical angina, Ty = typical angina, asy = asymptomatic, non = non-anginal pain)

IDj	Age (A1)	Sex(A2)	cp(A3)	Trestbps (A4)	Fbs (A5)	Thalach (A6)	Restecg (A7)
ID1	21,28,29	M,F	aty, asy	108,130	108,130	150,172	0,1
ID2	30,36,37	M,F	Ty, asy	130,140	101,105	162,153	0,1
ID3	41,48,56,65	M,F	aty, asy	120,120	110,105	148,114	0,1
ID4	-	M,F	aty,non	172,150	130,110	178,151	0,1
ID5	-	M,F	non, aty	160,138	125,110	187,148	0,1

comprises the bucket and batch partitioning pairs. At least k tuples are present in each bucket, where k is the minimum group size to prevent linking attacks (Tables 6 and 7).

This approach uses weighted measurements of SA (sensitive attributes), as all of these sensitive attributes have different levels of sensitivity or weight. The weights of all sensitive attributes are calculated for the purpose of identifying the level of sensitivity of each attribute. Let W = {w1, w2,.............. wd} [15] w1 is the weight of s1, w2 is the weight of s2, as shown in Table 8 to indicate the set of weights assigned to each sensitive attribute., and so on. There are two published tables as a result (a generalized table and a sensitive batch table), as shown in Tables 9 and 10.

Table 8. Weight calculation

Sensitive attributes	Identified by	Dependency	Weightage
S1 = cp: chest pain type	S2,S3,S4	3	3
S2 = trestbps: resting blood pressure	---------	0	0
S3 = restecg: resting electrocardiographic results	S2,S5	2	2
S4 = thalach: maximum heart rate achieved	S1,S2,S5	3	3
S5 = fbs: fasting blood sugar	S2	1	1

A single table contains numerous, highly correlated attributes. For example, {cp, thalach} and {restecg, trestbps, fbs} as shown in Table 11 and Table 12. In order to ensure l-diversity in each bucket, horizontal partitioning is used (Fig. 5).

Using (p, k) angelization algorithm which the output consists of Generalized table and Sensitive batch Table (Table 13 and Table 14).

Table 9. QUASI-TABLE (QIT) (publish all quasi identifiers for each individual)

Tuple id	Age	Sex
P1	**28**	**M**
P2	29	M
P3	21	M
P4	30	F
P5	36	F
P6	37	F
P7	41	M
P8	48	M
P9	46	M

Table 10. Sensitive attribute table (ST) (publish all sensitive attributes for each individual)

cp	trestbps	fbs	thalach	Restecg
typical angina	145	108	150	0
asymptomatic	130	101	162	1
atypical angina	120	110	148	0
atypical angina	172	130	178	1
typical angina	160	125	187	0
atypical angina	150	130	172	1
non-anginal pain	140	105	153	0
asymptomatic	145	115	114	1
atypical angina	138	110	151	1

Table 11. Sliced sensitive attributes (CP, THALACH)

Tuple ID	cp	thalach	Group
P1	typical angina	150	1
P2	asymptomatic	162	
P3	atypical angina	148	
P4	atypical angina	178	2
P7	non-anginal pain	187	
P9	atypical angina	151	
P5	typical angina	153	3
P8	asymptomatic	114	
P6	atypical angina	172	

Table 12. Sliced sensitive attributes (RESTEC, TRESTBPS, FBS)

Tuple ID	restecg	trestbps	fbs	Group
P1	0	145	108	1
P2	1	130	101	
P5	0	160	125	
P4	1	172	130	2
P3	0	120	110	
P6	1	150	130	
P7	0	140	105	3
P8	1	145	110	
P9	1	138	115	

> **Input:**
> 1: micro dataset
>   A)   Explicit identifier(E)
>   B)   quasi – identifier attributes
>   C)   sensitive attributes
> **2: EX: (External factor)**
> **Output:**
>   A)   Generalized Table
>   B)   Sensitive Batch Table

Fig. 5. "(p, K) – Angelization": [15]

Table 13. Generalized table

Age	Sex	Batch ID
[20, 30]	Person	1
[20, 30	Person	
[20, 30	Person	
[30,38]	Person	2
[30,38]	Person	
[38,45]	Person	3
[38,45]	Person	
[45,50]	Person	4
[45,50]	Person	

Table 14. Sensitive batch table (SBT)

cp	trestbps	fbs	thalach	Restecg	Batch ID
typical angina, asymptomatic	145, 130	108, 101	150, 162	0,1	1
non-anginal pain, atypical angina	140, 172	105, 130	153, 178	0,1	2
atypical angina, asymptomatic	120, 145	110, 115	148,115	0,1	3
typical angina, atypical angina	160, 138	125, 110	187, 151	0,1	4

6   Experiments and Analysis Result

We use different algorithms and methods to anonymize the dataset and show the effects of each method due to data privacy, information loss, and computational efficiency. Execution time and the quality of anonymized data are measured. to compare 1: M-generalization algorithm, Mondrian algorithm. We use two actual datasets. (Heart disease, INFORMS) from UCI repository. By contrasting these techniques with l-diversity, we assess the effectiveness of these techniques., and we apply the method of semantic anonymization to solve the problem of similarity attack. In Informs, we select (sex, maternal status, and education) as QIA and (income, disease) as SA. We select $l = 5$ and $k = 10$ as the default values. The Heat Disease dataset: this dataset contains 75 attributes. We have taken 2 quasi-identifier attributes (sex and age) and (cp: chest pain type; trestbps: resting blood pressure, restecg: resting electrocardiographic results; thalach: maximum heart rate achieved; fbs: fasting blood sugar) as SAs.

6.1 Information Loss and Data Utility

We employed NCP (Normalized Certainty Penalty) [19] to quantify the information loss caused by anonymization. We calculate QIDNCP and SANCP with different parameters and present the results. We observed that QID–NCP increases when l grows because a larger l necessitates a larger size for each EC, which implies that QID values can be more broadly generalized; however, it provides more privacy guarantee because the criterion for l-diversity offers superior protection to the requirement for k-anonymity when l is larger than k. Meanwhile, both SA–NCP and QID–NCP of 1: M-generalization will increase slightly when k increases, and in other algorithms the NCP will increase slightly when k increases see Table 15.

The outcome demonstrates that the rating method enables data analysis that is substantially more efficient than l-diversity [23]. For categorization, rating performs better than Actually Rating performance for classification is comparable to that of microdata. In other words, the information about the original data is not significantly lost during the rating process. The (p, k)-Angelization strategy guards against non-membership attacks and demographic attacks on the rating method. Also decreases information loss, increasing the usefulness of the information that has been released publicly. But have more execution time due to the complicated process of weight calculation and the (p, k)-Angelization publication of numerous tables. The more release tables there are, the longer it takes to execute.

6.2 Efficiency

We calculate the entire execution time of our methods to evaluate their effectiveness (except for the pre-processing). Specifically, we tested our algorithms on several datasets (l and k). For k = 10, l = 5 as a default parameter, 1:M-generalization typically takes less than 28 s to execute. When k increases, the overall execution time of the 1:M-generalization is marginally reduced. This is due to the fact that a higher k suggests fewer partition splits. On the other hand, running time does not appear to change much with parameter l. The average execution time of the Mondrian algorithm is less than 20 s, and Mondrian_l_diversity is less than 10 s; see Table 16.

We tested the effect of the similarity attack on data after semantic anonymization. The results of the proposed method show enhancement in terms of privacy but decrease the utility of data due to information loss as a result of generalization and suppression in the anonymization process. We found that the balancing point between utility and privacy depends on the dataset and value of L. As the number of quasi-identifiers increases, the balancing point shifts downward and balances between Utility and privacy occur at a higher value of L, as shown in Fig. 6. Which plots the performance curves of anonymous data information loss over various L. The execution time of the (p, k)-Angelization is compared with the rating technique. The execution time has been measured while increasing the number of records. Since the rating technique publishes multiple tables, its execution time is larger than the (p, k)-Angelization as represented in Fig. 7. It has been calculated by varying the number of sensitive attributes from 1 to 6. The results are shown in Figs. 7 and 8 (Table 17).

Table 15. Evaluation of information loss in percentage

Algorithm name	k-value	l-value	NCP-percentage
1:M-generalization	10 20	5 5	QID–NCP = 11.68% SA–NCP = 6.70% QID NCP = 11.66% SA–NCP = 7.87%
Mondrian algorithm	10 20	......	NCP = 12% NCP = 15.03%

Table 16. Evaluation of efficiency based on execution time

Algorithm name	K-value	L-value	Actual Execution time
1:M-generalization	10 20	5 5	21.9 s 18.84 s
Mondrian algorithm	10 20	....	2 s 1. 2 s

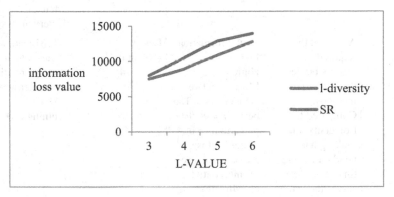

Fig. 6. Information loss for various l.

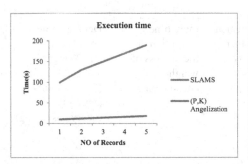

Fig. 7. Execution time when changing No of records

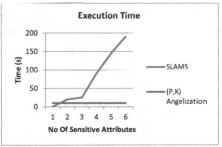

Fig. 8. Execution time when changing No of SA

As a result, the data publisher must strike a balance between the level of privacy required and the utility of the data (to minimize information loss). So we need to migrate

Table 17. Comparison between the different methods

Method or technique	Privacy requirement	Utility	Time execution	Method used for measurement of utility
Semantic rules	More enhancements to the term privacy. Than other methods Reduces of similarity attack	More information loss than other methods due to generalization and suppression decrease the utility	Less time Execution	(Entropy, recursive (c, L))-diversity with different values for L using the generalized loss metric, Discernibility Metric (query answering)
Rating	Achieved the required level of privacy but less than other two methods. Compared to l-diversity, that ranking has nearly a hundred times less ARE solves the "curse of dimensionality" issue	Low information loss High utility More effective data analysis. The performance the performance of rating is close to the performance of microdata for classification	Less time Execution	Classification measurement and average relative error measurement (ARE) (mining process)
(p,k) angelization	Provides enhanced privacy that Achieved the most required level of privacy Reduces of correlation attacks and prevents demographic attack and non-membership attacks	Low information loss than other two methods	more time Execution due to the process of weight calculation	Demographic error (DE) KL-divergence and DCP (Discernibility penalty) (query answering)

or combine the advantages of these methods and propose a new method that can achieve the target of balanced privacy and utility. From this comparison, we found that the 1: m-generalization algorithm and the (p, k) angelization method perform well in terms of information loss and data utility.

7 Conclusion and Future Work

This paper stands out a study and concept of multiple sensitive attributes (MSAs). 1: M records of an individual and MSAs in microdata separately is a topic that the majority of earlier studies address; the generalization of QID or MSAs, which results in significant information loss and low data value, are two major drawbacks of this strategy. While MSA privacy models make an effort to prevent privacy exposures, such strategies are either overly complex or lacking in some crucial components. Consequently, there is a need for an efficient solution for 1: M with MSA that strikes a balance between data utility and privacy. We apply different privacy methods to address this problem. Overall, experiments with real-world datasets point out that these methods outperform the most recent developments in terms of privacy, information loss, and execution time. Our work applied on MSAs in the future we seek to handle the dataset that contain also multiple records for each individual with MSA. Additionally, this approach assumes a static dataset will only be published once, as opposed to a dynamic dataset being repeatedly republished. It is yet unclear how 1: M with MSAs works across different re-publications of a dynamic dataset. Future research will also examine similar repeated publications of dynamic data rather than static data. (data streams).

References

1. Latanya, S.: k-anonymity: a model for protecting privacy. Int. J. Uncertain. Fuzziness Knowl.-Based Syst. **10**(05), 557–570 (2002)
2. Yaseen, S., Saba, T., Anjum, A.: Improved generalization for secure data publishing. IEEE Access **6**, 27156–27165 (2018)
3. Komishani, E.G., Abadi, M., Deldar, F.: PPTD: preserving personalized privacy in trajectory data publishing by sensitive attribute generalization and trajectory local suppression. Knowl.-Based Syst. **94**, 43–59 (2016). https://doi.org/10.1016/j.knosys.2015.11.007
4. Wang, J., Du, K., Luo, X., Li, X.: Two privacy-preserving approaches for data publishing with identity reservation. Knowl. Inf. Syst. **60**(2), 1039–1080 (2018). https://doi.org/10.1007/s10115-018-1237-3
5. Wang, R., Zhu, Y., Chen, T.S., Chang, C.C.: Privacy-preserving algorithms for multiple sensitive attributes satisfying t-closeness. J. Comput. Sci. Technol. **33**(6), 1231–1242 (2018)
6. Tao, Y., Tong, Y., Tan, S., Tang, S., Yang, D.: Protecting the publishing identity in multiple tuples. In: Atluri, V. (ed.) DBSec 2008. LNCS, vol. 5094, pp. 205–218. Springer, Heidelberg (2008). https://doi.org/10.1007/978-3-540-70567-3_16
7. Poulis, G., Loukides, G., Skiadopoulos, S., Divanis, A.J.: Anonymizing data with relational and transaction attributes. In: European Conference on Machine Learning and Knowledge Discovery in Databases. Springer, Berlin, Heidelberg (2013)
8. Anjum, A., Ahmed, T., Khan, A., Ahmad, N.: Privacy preserving data by conceptualizing smart cities using MIDR-Angelization. Sustain. Cities Soc. **40**, 326–334 (2018)
9. Ting, Y., Jajodia, S.: Secure data management in decentralized systems, vol. 33. Springer Science & Business Media (2007)
10. Li, N., Li, T., Venkatasubramanian, S.: t-closeness: Privacy beyond k-anonymity and l-diversity In:. IEEE 23rd International Conference on Data Engineering (2007)
11. Machanavajjhala, A., Gehrke, J., Kifer, D., Venkitasubramaniam, M.: l-diversity: Privacy beyond k-anonymity. In: 22nd International Conference on Data Engineering (ICDE'06). IEEE (2006)

12. Ercan Nergiz, M., Clifton, C.: Thoughts on k-anonymization. Data Knowl. Eng. **63**(3), 622–645 (2007). https://doi.org/10.1016/j.datak.2007.03.009
13. Jabeen, F., Hamid, Z., Wadood, A., Ghouzali, S.: Enhanced architecture for privacy preserving data integration in a medical research environment. IEEE Access **5**, 13308–13326 (2017)
14. Anjum, A., Ahmad, N., Malik, S.U.R., Zubair, S., Shahzad, B.: An efficient approach for publishing microdata for multiple sensitive attributes. The Journal of Supercomputing **74**(10), 5127–5155 (2018). https://doi.org/10.1007/s11227-018-2390-x
15. Lee, H., Kim, S., Kim, J.W., Chung, Y.D.: Utility-preserving anonymization for health data publishing. BMC Med. Inform. Decis. Mak. **17**, 104 (2017)
16. Majeed, A.: Attribute-centric anonymization scheme for improving user privacy and utility of publishing e-health data. J. King Saud Univ.-Comput. Inform. Sci. **31**, 426-435 (2018)
17. LeFevre, K., De Witt, D.J., Ramakrishnan, R.: Mondrian Multidimensional k-anonymity, vol. 6. ICDE (2006)
18. Xu, J.,Wang, W., Pei, J., Wang, X.: Utility-based anonymization using local recoding. In: Proceedings of the 12th ACM SIGKDD international conference on Knowledge discovery and data mining (2006)
19. Abdelhameed, S.A., Moussa, S.M., Khalifa, M.E.: Privacy-preserving tabular data publishing: a comprehensive evaluation from web to cloud. Comput. Secur. **72**, 74–95 (2018)
20. Anjum, A., Ahmad, N., Raza, B.: An efficient privacy mechanism for electronic health records. Comput. Secur. **72**, 196–211 (2018)
21. He, Y., Naughton, J.F.: Anonymization of set-valued data via top-down, local generalization. Proc. VLDB Endow. **2**(1), 934–945 (2009)
22. Lu, H., Setiono, R., Liu, H.: Effective data mining using neural networks. IEEE Trans. Knowl. Data Eng. **8**(6), 957–961 (1996)
23. Mubark, A.A., Elabd, E., Abdulkader, H.: Semantic anonymization in publishing categorical sensitive attributes. In: 8th International Conference on Knowledge and Smart Technology (KST). IEEE (2016)
24. Liu, J., Luo, J., Huang, J.Z.: Rating: privacy preservation for multiple attributes with different sensitivity requirements. In: IEEE 11th International Conference on Data Mining Workshops. IEEE (2011)
25. Susan, V.S., Christopher, T.: Anatomisation with slicing: a new privacy preservation approach for multiple sensitive attributes. Springerplus **5**(1), 1–21 (2016)
26. Onashoga, S.A., Bamiro, B.A., Akinwale, A.T., Oguntuase. J.A.: KC-Slice: A dynamic privacy-preserving data publishing technique for multisensitive attributes. Inform. Secur. J.: A Global Perspect. **26**(3), 121–135 (2017)
27. Zaman, A.N.K., Obimbo, C., Dara, R.A.: An improved data sanitization algorithm for privacy preserving medical data publishing. In: Mouhoub, M., Langlais, P. (eds.) AI 2017. LNCS (LNAI), vol. 10233, pp. 64–70. Springer, Cham (2017). https://doi.org/10.1007/978-3-319-57351-9_8
28. Liu, Q., Shen, H., Sang, Y.: A privacy-preserving data publishing method for multiple numerical sensitive attributes via clustering and multi-sensitive Bucketization. In: Sixth International Symposium on Parallel Architectures, Algorithms and Programming. IEEE (2014)
29. He, Y., Naughton, J.F.: Anonymization of set-valued data via top-down, local gen-eralization. In: Proceedings of the 35th International Conference on Very Large Data Bases(VLDB), VLDB Endowment (2009)
30. LeFevre, K., DeWitt, D.J., Ramakrishnan, R.: Mondrian multidimensional k-anonymity. In: Proceedings of the 22nd International Conference on Data Engineering(ICDE), p. 25. IEEE Computer Society (2006)
31. Li, T., Li, N., Zhang, J., Molloy, I.: Slicing: a new approach for privacy preserving data publishing. IEEE Trans. Knowl. Data Eng. **24**(3), 561–574 (2012)

32. Han, J., Luo, F., Lu, J., Peng, H.: SLOMS: a privacy preserving data publishing method for multiple sensitive attributes microdata. JSW **8**(12), 3096–3104 (2013)
33. Abdalaal, A., Nergiz, M.E., Saygin, Y.: Privacy-preserving publishing of opinion polls. Comput. Secur. **37**, 143–154 (2013)
34. Kanwal, T., Anjum, A.: Privacy-preserving model and generalization correlation attacks for 1: M data with multiple sensitive attributes. Inf. Sci. **488**, 238–256 (2019)
35. Albulayhi, Kh., Tosic, P.T., Sheldon, F.T.: G-model: a novel approach to privacy-preserving 1:M microdata publication. In: 7th IEEE International Conference on Cyber Security and Cloud Computing (CSCloud)/2020 6th IEEE International Conference on Edge Computing and Scalable Cloud (EdgeCom). New York, NY, USA (2020)

A Proposed Framework for Cloud Immunization Information System: Challenges and Opportunities

Lamia Aladel[1] and Heba M. Sabry[2($\boxtimes$)]

[1] Department of Computers and Information Systems, Sadat Academy, Cairo, Egypt
[2] Department of Computer Science, Faculty of Computers and Information, Sadat Academy, Cairo, Egypt
heba.ict@gmail.com

Abstract. Immunization and vaccination do not exactly mean the same thing. The term "vaccination" refers to receiving a vaccine, which includes receiving the injection or oral dose. Immunization is the process of receiving the vaccine and developing an immunity to the disease after receiving it. By compiling immunization information into a single trustworthy source, Immunization information systems (IIS) assist healthcare professionals, families, and public health officials. The data can then be utilized to enhance vaccination rates, direct patient treatment, and ultimately lower the incidence of diseases that are preventable by vaccination.

This paper seeks to identify the immunization information systems (IIS) concept its functions, clarify why it is important, propose a framework of cloud Immunization information systems, discuss the levels of this framework and its goals, challenges, and opportunities.

Keywords: Immunization Information System · Cloud Computing · Electronic Immunization Registries

1 Introduction

The gathering of complete population-level immunization data is fraught with difficulties. Immunization administration is spreading out more and more. People can now get vaccines from a variety of healthcare professionals, such as primary care doctors, public health officials, and pharmacists.

Additionally, the increased cross-border migration of people raises issues with the exchange of immunization data between public health jurisdictions. Therefore, to gather and aggregate immunization data, effective immunization programs are becoming more and more dependent on the involvement of citizens, healthcare professionals, and public health officials. A potential solution to some of these problems is offered by internet and mobile technology [1].

To increase and enhance vaccination distribution in Egypt, one tactic that might be used is the use of a Cloud Immunization Information System (CIIS).

R. Hou et al. (Eds.): BDTA 2021/2022, LNICST 480, pp. 58–63, 2023.
https://doi.org/10.1007/978-3-031-33614-0_4

Access to consolidated immunization history records, which include details on all immunizations a person has had from providers that report to the IIS, is made possible by IISs for authorized users, such as patients and clinicians.

Public health organizations often use aggregate IIS data to track and assess vaccination trends in specific regions. IISs can help with additional public health tasks like managing vaccination supplies, automating vaccine reminders, and responding to infectious disease outbreaks [2].

1.1 Distinction Between Electronic Immunization Registries (EIR) and IIS

EIR and IIS are frequently used interchangeably in the literature. It is necessary to make reference to other widely used phrases in order to differentiate them from one another and create clarity [3].

A recorded history of vaccinations is referred to as an immunization record. The following is a suitable definition of a vaccination record:

Records of vaccinations, often known as immunization records, give a history of all the vaccinations you or your kid have had. This record might be necessary for applying for specific jobs, travelling overseas, or enrolling in school. This is equivalent to a physical vaccination card for an individual, and it relates to paper-based nominal registers or records for a community. Any immunization program's foundation has always been its vaccination records, which enable the documentation of the vaccination event [4]. An electronic immunization record is a written record of immunization history that has been digitalized. Improving individual and societal vaccination is made possible by having immunization records in electronic form.

In a database, electronic immunization records are compiled. An electronic immunization registry is the term used to describe this collection of data [5]. Records and databases should not be confused with the range of possible functions that go along with them. Some of these features will also permit the registration of additional information about individuals, such as age, sex, profession, or risk factors, in addition to vaccination history, while other features permit the inclusion of additional information, such as a vaccine inventory function to simplify vaccine ordering. Then, an immunization information system could include electronic immunization registries.

Clinics, hospitals, pharmacies, schools, child care facilities and public health who uses IIS [7].

1.2 Purpose of Immunization Information System

The tangible advantages it offers to stakeholders and the abundance of chances it presents are the finest ways to illustrate an IIS's mission [8].

Immunization campaigns are intricate public health initiatives that have a significant positive impact on health. They are susceptible to shifts in public perception and confidence. Recent controversy surrounding vaccination programs has hindered vaccination uptake for some vaccines. It is necessary to quickly provide real-world evidence of the effectiveness and great safety profile of immunizations in order to resolve this issue. IIS are a crucial instrument for promptly documenting the advantages of immunization for health. When laws protecting data security and privacy are in place, technological advancements have made it possible to create an extensive national IIS.

The following are some examples of a comprehensive IIS's general goals are to offer data to help with operational decisions, to support the administration of the vaccination program at the point of administration, to enable instant access to personal immunization records, and to provide data that will help decision-makers make more informed strategic choices, and to preserve and make available access to reliable statistics on immunization and the general population [9].

1.3 The Need for an Immunization Information System

IIS development and design take into account both individual and societal demands.

IIS capabilities enable clinical decision assistance at the point of care, customized vaccination advice, and the creation of immunization reports at the individual level.

IIS supports supply chain management, safety monitoring, reporting, and monitoring of vaccine coverage at the population level (for instance, at the district or national level). This makes it possible to monitor and assess the success, impact, and effectiveness of services.

The capabilities of IIS are expanding beyond simply recording vaccinations and toward the inclusion of advanced features, such as personalized information on vaccination, a communication platform that enables targeted communication towards healthcare professionals and the general public, decision support systems for vaccine providers (such as automated protocols for vaccination catch-up), recording of reasons for vaccination refusal, and a communication platform [6, 10].

The Immunization Information System (IIS) Function outlines the operations, data quality, and technology required for IISs to serve vaccination programmes, vaccination providers, and other stakeholders in the field of vaccination. Some of the IIS's features such as: Provide Healthcare Effectiveness Data and Information; Exchange data with Medicaid programmes; Assess coverage by geographic region; Conduct centralised reminder/recall; Provide public access to IIS portal; Exchange data with other regions. Support patient look-up and vaccine tracking for mass vaccination. Use IIS to conduct emergency preparedness activities [11].

2 The Proposed Framework

In this section, we outline a proposed digital platform that would enable people to take control of own immunization data and share them with others via cloud computing. The framework under consideration is a cloud-based immunization record that could assist in bridging jurisdictional gaps in the flow of immunization data by giving people easily shareable, standardized digital copies of their records (Fig. 1).

As shown in the proposed framework, it consists of different phases as follows:

2.1 Cloud Infrastructure

These hardware and software components' characteristics and functionalities are covered by the cloud infrastructure. After that, a cloud service provider or, in the case of a private

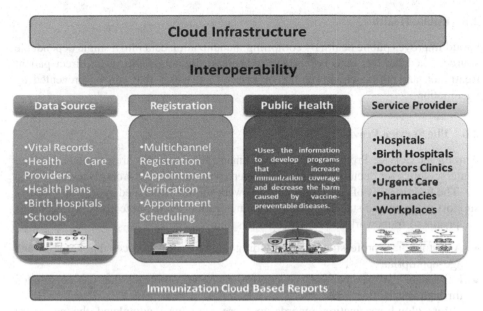

Fig. 1. A Proposed Framework of Cloud Immunization Information System

cloud, an information technology department hosts such virtualized resources and makes them available to users over a network or the internet. Virtual machines (VMs) and parts including servers, memory, network switches, firewalls, load balancers, and storage are examples of these resources.

2.2 Cloud Interoperability

The capacity of the systems to operate successfully and collaborate across various cloud platforms is referred to as cloud interoperability. Cloud interoperability addresses the following issues to help with data quality issues: Precision, promptness, and completeness.

2.3 Data Sources

Vital records, healthcare providers, health plans, birth hospitals, schools, and surveys are some of the places where data on immunizations can be found.

2.4 Registration

Before using the system's various services, citizens must complete CIIS' registration process.

2.5 Public Health

Cloud improves public health by compiling immunization data into a single dependable source. The data can then be utilized to increase immunization rates, direct patient treatment, and ultimately lower the incidence of diseases that can be prevented by vaccination.

2.6 The Service Providers

Among the Service Providers that offer immunization services are hospitals, birthing centers, clinics for doctors, urgent care centers, pharmacies, and workplaces.

The functionality of the suggested framework should be pursued in order to properly support program and stakeholder cloud immunization-related objectives. The goals of the proposed framework can be illustrated as follows:

- Assist medical professionals in providing immunization services that are risk- and age-appropriate.
- Encourage the management and control of disease outbreaks that can be stopped through vaccination.
- Offers cloud vaccination records to those who have completed the necessary authentication.
- Offers predefined and customized evaluation reports that customers may create on their own, independent of IIS employees.
- Supports the national Vaccine Tracking System's data exchange.
- Notifies provider sites of the status of vaccine orders filed in the IIS.
- Creates reports or statistics to enhance the management and responsibility of vaccination inventories [12].

3   Immunization Information System Challenges and Opportunities

The challenges that face IIS include: incomplete data reporting; varying performance levels across IIS; a variety of stakeholder standards, technologies, and regulations; and inconsistent standard implementation.

However, the IIS provide many opportunities such as: Improve IIS Performance, Encourage IIS Standards Adherence, Support the IIS Community, Influence and Monitor the Health IT Environment. Through projects that aim to improve infrastructure and functionality, such as the IIS Minimum Functional Standards and the IIS Annual Report, a self-reported data collection of IIS progress toward achieving the functional standards, the Centers for Disease Control and Prevention has made strides to help IIS move toward a nationwide network since the early 2000s. While these initiatives have helped vaccination programs reach higher functional standards, it is now time to move the emphasis from infrastructure and functionality enhancements to high data quality through critical outcome evaluation and objective measurement of IIS performance. Additionally, in order to achieve the goal of a national repository of high-quality immunization data, it is necessary to address the numerous issues that have an impact on data availability and quality, such as those relating to policy, data sharing, data use, ageing IIS technology, sustainability, and IIS participation [11].

4 Conclusion

This paper discussed the concept of Immunization Information System, and why the countries need to build this system. Its functions, clarify why it is important, propose a framework of cloud Immunization information systems, discuss the levels of this framework and its goals, challenges, and opportunities.

References

1. Centers for Disease Control and Prevention (CDC): About Immunization Information Systems (2019). https://www.cdc.gov/vaccines/programs/iis/about.html. Last accessed 25 Oct 2022
2. Department of Health and Human Services (HHS): HHS Awards Funds to Expand Immunization Information Sharing Collaboration. Press release 19 Jan 2021, https://www.hhs.gov/about/news/2021/01/19/hhs-awardsfunds-to-expand-immunization-sharing-collaboration.html and American Immunization Registry Association (AIRA), Literature Review: An Environmental Scan on Progress, Challenges, and Opportunities: Expanding Immunization Information Systems for Adults in the United States, Jul 2020. https://repository.immregistries.org/files/resources/60830f3e4ce88/iis_information_session_-_final.pdf
3. Atkinson, K.M., Mithani, S.S., Bell, C., Rubens-Augustson, T., Wilson, K.: The digital immunization system of the future. imagining a patient-centric, interoperable immunization information system. Ther. Adv. Vaccines Immunother. 8, 2515135520967203 (2020)
4. Jackson, M.L., Henrikson, N.B., Grossman, D.C.: Evaluating Washington State's immunization information system as a research tool. Acad. Pediatr. 14(1), 71–76 (2014)
5. Boom, J.A., Sahni, L.C., Nelson, C.S., Dragsbaek, A.C., Franzini, L.: Immunization information system opt-in consent: at what cost? J. Public Health Manag. Pract. 16(5), E18–E25 (2010)
6. Szilagyi, P.G., et al.: Effect of state immunization information system based reminder/recall for influenza vaccinations: a randomized trial of Autodialer, text, and mailed messages. The J. Pediatr. 221, 123-131.e4 (2020). https://doi.org/10.1016/j.jpeds.2020.02.020
7. AIRA: Using IIS to Support an Outbreak Response. https://repository.immregistries.org/files/resources/5e976b84c018b/outbreak_webinar.pdf. Accessed 14 Apr 2020
8. Derrough, T., et al.: Immunisation Information Systems – useful tools for monitoring vaccination programmes in EU/EEA countries, 2016. Eurosurveillance 22(17), 30519 (2017)
9. Consumers, Health, Agriculture and Food Executive Agency: Funding under the 3rd health programme 2014–2020 – actions co-financed with Member State authorities (Joint Actions). Brussels: CHAFEA (2014). http://ec.europa.eu/chafea/documents/health/hp-factsheets/joint-actions/factsheets-hp-ja_en.pdf
10. National Health Service England: eRedbook Your baby's digital health record [Internet]. NHS, London (2017). [cited 3 May 2018]. https://www.eredbook.org.uk/
11. Lynn, G.S., Rebecca, C., Kafayat A., et al.: Current challenges and future possibilities for immunization information systems. Acad. Pediatr. 21(4S), S57–S64 (2021); National Vaccine Advisory Committee: Protecting the Public's Health: Critical Functions of the Section 317 Immunization Program—A Report of the National Vaccine Advisory Committee, vol. 128. Public Health Reports, Mar 2013
12. Martin, D.W., Lowery, N.E., Brand, B., Gold, R., Horlick, G.: Immunization information systems: a decade of progress in law and policy. J. Public Health Manag. Pract. 21(3), 296 (2015)

The Role of Block Chain Technology in Reducing Corruption Within the Local Governance in Egypt

Aliaa Kamal Abdella[1], Mostafa M. Hamed[2], and Mai. A. Elnady[1(✉)]

[1] Department of Computers and Information Systems, Sadat Academy, Cairo, Egypt
aliaaabdella@yahoo.com, doctormaielnady@gmail.com
[2] Department of Public Administration, Sadat Academy, Cairo, Egypt
Mostafa77hamed@gmail.com

Abstract. One of the most challenging issues facing municipal governments is corruption. Numerous studies, reports, and analyses highlight the fact that since corruption is by definition hidden from the public's perspective, increasing the transparency and scrutiny of governmental acts can help prevent corruption. Therefore, increasing the transparency of government operations and decision-making should be the ultimate goal of an anticorruption campaign inside a democratic system. In the framework of local governance, we must strengthen the current audit mode, increase accountability effectiveness, further anticipate the trend of covert corruption, identify the traits of corruption as soon as feasible, and promptly regulate the corruption behaviors. The study's findings indicate that the more local executives have authority, the less transparent the information is, the less reliable the monitoring system is, and the more likely it is for covert corruption to proliferate. Only by enhancing audit mode, ensuring data quality, increasing audit efficiency, and reducing audit risk using blockchain technology can the corruption of executives of state-owned companies be effectively stopped.

Keywords: Blockchain Technology · local governance · corruption · transparency · accountability

1 Introduction

The fourth industrial revolution has led to a variety of next-generation technologies that can be applied in a range of industries, including the Internet of Things (IoT), artificial intelligence (AI), big data, and blockchain technology. Blockchain technology has drawn attention as the most important new technology because its core concept—which many academics have sought to implement—is to avoid hacking in different contexts. Studies on how to use it to enhance governance or communication, studies on how to protect transparency using distributed storage technologies, and studies on electronic voting systems using blockchain technology are all related fields of study. In this context, the most important strategies for reducing corruption at the local level

© ICST Institute for Computer Sciences, Social Informatics and Telecommunications Engineering 2023
Published by Springer Nature Switzerland AG 2023. All Rights Reserved
R. Hou et al. (Eds.): BDTA 2021/2022, LNICST 480, pp. 64–74, 2023.
https://doi.org/10.1007/978-3-031-33614-0_5

revolve around increasing accountability, transparency, and effective control. For this reason, blockchain applications are being studied as a way to improve local governance and reduce corruption.

Blockchain is a decentralized, dependable, and difficult technology to exploit for fraudulent purposes. Blockchain technology can therefore be used in a wide range of industries [1]. According to Christian Cachin et al., the four parts of the blockchain that are duplicated are the ledger, cryptography, consensus, and business logic [2].

Before adding the finished database to the blockchain as a whole, a block—the "current" component of a blockchain—keeps track of some or all of the most recent transactions. Every time a previous block ends, a new block is formed. The blockchain contains an endless number of such blocks. Each block contains a hash of the block before it and is linked together (like a chain) in a proper linear, chronological manner [3]. Blockchain is a term used to describe a distributed database of records, or public ledger, of all completed transactions or digital events that are disseminated among users. Most users of the system review each transaction on the public ledger twice. Information cannot be deleted once it has been entered. Every transaction that has ever been made is documented on the blockchain and is both verifiable and definite [4]. The reliability of the blockchain technology itself, which has applications in both the financial and non-financial sectors, is without question [3]. In contrast to a distributed database, users of a distributed ledger must independently verify transactions because they do not trust one another. A "distributed ledger" is a replica, decentralized, synchronized, and cryptographically secured record of data and transactions shared among parties to a contract [5].

Blockchain, for example, can be classified as a distributed ledger technology. All decentralized systems for storing transactions and sharing data across numerous servers, corporations, or countries fall under this category. Although a distributed ledger and a blockchain are both types of distributed ledgers, not all distributed ledgers are built on a blockchain [3]. Blockchain technology has a lot of potential for keeping government data safe and handling transactions in a way that is more effective, responsible, and transparent. Data from recent storage as well as data from prior data points are both present in blocks. As a result, by joining one block to the one before it, a chain of information and data points can be created. The way a block operates as a decentralized form of a public ledger is known as "distributed ledger technology" (DLT) [6]. Data in blocks is time-stamped and cryptographically sealed when new transactions are linked to prior blocks. This process ensures that every piece of data added to the blockchain can be tracked back to the precise instant it was uploaded, preventing any data from being later modified or removed [7]. At its foundation, DLT is a brand-new approach to data storage that offers both benefits and drawbacks. If anti-corruption measures are taken into account during the design phase, data storage on the blockchain can have advantageous benefits. Data audits must be included [6].

Transparency in transactions is required if accountability is to be encouraged. This needs to be taken into account during the application development process as well as the expectation management process. The public sector has a lot of room to improve data management with blockchain. It might be possible to boost public confidence in the government in areas where corruption is rife and confidence is low. On the other hand, there are difficulties in implementation [7]. Digital government goes a step further by emphasizing the provision of user-centric, adaptable, and innovative government services. Digital technology should be used to enable these services and delivery methods [5]. Blockchain technology has the potential to facilitate direct connections between governmental organizations, people, and commercial enterprises in the framework of digital governance. This suggests improved public services for the simplest forms of registration and information exchange. Governments may not necessarily need to establish information storage and sharing channels on their own in order to foster economic activity in societies [7]. Despite the fact that it is still in its early stages, blockchain technology has already had a big impact on a variety of enterprises and industries. The following list includes some of the most notable advantages of blockchain applications: [4, 7, 8]. • Transparency: A blockchain continuously keeps track of each transaction and simultaneously makes that information accessible to all network users. Transparency is improved since all participants in the transaction may observe any alterations made to any data or recent transactions. • Business Continuity: Every company needs to make sure that their services are provided and will continue to be provided. Because single points of failure are eliminated by blockchain technology, even if some components fail, the system remains operational, ensuring business continuity. Disintermediation: The complete decentralization of the blockchain technology allows for massive disintermediation. In cases where trust is lacking, technology protocols and components can be utilized to substitute intermediaries, increasing efficiency and lowering friction-related direct and indirect expenses for both individuals and organizations. • Trust: The development of a trustworthy record among dubious parties is the essential premise of blockchain technology. The robust architecture and cryptographic properties of the blockchain-integrated protocols support trust and ease verification. • Smart Contracts: The majority of blockchain systems allow the use of scripting languages, which enables the extension of ledger capabilities.

Local corruption can take on a variety of shapes and forms. Municipalities will have different policies. However, accepting or asking for bribes is the most typical form of corruption. Patronage, nepotism, theft of public property, political corruption, and clientelism are all frequently seen to varying degrees at the local level. When officials have extensive discretion and/or frequent face-to-face interactions with the public, corruption is most likely to occur. Even though greater discretion is frequently associated with seniority, it may also be a component of a particular task or function performed at junior levels. Decentralization has frequently increased the burden of revenue-raising, making it a particularly susceptible area. Local corruption in many emerging nations can no longer be considered a collection of individual incidents. The issue has grown and taken on a systemic nature. The study of what are known as "captured states" or "captured economies" has resulted from research to better understand the nature and causes of systemic corruption. This refers to the extent of the "rule of the game" that is established by policy and judicial decision-making that is influenced by private parties.

2   Literature Review

Oliver Meza and Elizabeth Pérez-Chiqués' study from 2021 [9] attempts to establish a comprehensive framework for examining how corruption is institutionalized in municipal administrations. The study's authors contend that by ignoring how corruption becomes the "rule of the game," policies to combat it have been developed that are ineffective because they focus only on dyadic and venal forms of corruption and are overly dependent on formal institutions. According to the findings, corrupt schemes are very adaptable and robust and can get beyond official anti-corruption measures. The findings of the study indicate that, although the amount of the effect is small, audited municipalities do better overall than unaudited towns. Funk, Kendall D. 2020's Erica Owen [10] the article discusses corruption pressures at the local government level using a novel method of empirically evaluating local councillors' subjective assessments of the corruption risks they have encountered. The article provides proof that each local councillor's perception of corruption risk is shaped by their unique personal characteristics, with educational attainment serving as the most important deterrent to corruption risk. Edo Rajh, Jelena Budak, and Sunana Slijepevi (2020), [11] describe the various forms of corruption that exist; it is generally believed that they can be diminished or eliminated in Mexico through effective blockchain management. Examples include public tenders or bids, government purchases and acquisitions (procurement), money embezzlement, and audits of businesses or governmental agencies. In comparison to the standard web-based E-Auction system, Praveensankar Manimaran and Dr. R. Dhanalakshmi's [12] proposed blockchain-based smart bidding system is quite robust and secure. The auction can be conducted even though some of the bidders are unreliable, thanks to the confidentiality and integrity provided by blockchain technology. Other electronic-based systems, including electronic voting, can use this strategy. Chunxiao Mu, Dan Wang, and Jindong Zhao, 2021 [13]. This study introduces a blockchain- and smart contract-based decentralised electronic bidding system. The system processes business logic using chaincode and replaces the conventional database with a blockchain. The anonymity of participants, the privacy of data transmission, and the traceability and verifiability of data are all improved in data interaction when encryption techniques like zero-knowledge proof based on graph isomorphism are applied. Yi-Hui Chen, Iuon-Chang Lin, and Shih-Hsin Chen (2018) [14]. In order to guarantee the anonymity, non-repudiation, and unchangeability of electronic seals, this study offers a blockchain-based e-auction method. Thomas Jensen, Jonas Hedman, Suprateek Sarker, and Stefan Henningsson Learn how to resist corruption through social, digital, and informational resources, including blockchain technology, by 2021 [15]. Produce model illustrates the intricate interactions between identity, institutional actors, technical and other resources, and practises by relying on prior research on corruption. According to Sarker, Henningsson, Jensen, and Hedman (2021), [16] it is possible to fight corruption by using both social and technological resources, such as blockchain technology. Our model, which is based on prior research on corruption, illustrates the intricate interactions between identities, institutional actors, technical resources, and practices. We also create conditions that could help reduce corruption by utilizing technology like blockchain.

3 Defining and Diagnosing Corruption at Local Level

A successful anti-corruption strategy requires a thorough understanding of the types and patterns of corruption that exist in a given area. On what constitutes corruption and how it should be measured, relevant parties (such as government representatives, members of civil society, and the business community) must agree. It is not an easy task. It is challenging to detect and accurately measure corruption. The severity and origin of the issue are frequently disputed. Any participatory and long-lasting anticorruption reform programme must start by reaching agreement among stakeholders on these issues.

3.1 Causes of Corruption

There are numerous and regionally specific causes of corruption. But generally speaking, they fall within the sociological and institutional groups [17].

- Negative opinions held by employees, citizens, corporations, and politicians against local or state government are societal causes of corruption.
- Weak civil society, inefficient media, and a lack of political will to combat corruption are all typical socioeconomic characteristics that foster an environment where corruption thrives.
- Within this category, there may be cultural concerns that contribute to corruption, such as a conflict between the principles of good government and those of the local culture.
- Institutional reasons for corruption typically result from a lack of accountability and transparency.
- Public officials can hide or mask corruption when there is a lack of openness and information available to the general public. The likelihood of corruption rises when government operations are not open to public inspection [17].
- When there is a lack of accountability, wrongdoing by public servants is rarely or never punished.
- Decentralization can be classified as one of the institutional reasons for corruption. If not effectively managed, decentralization can lead to new, unfavorable incentives in local organizations. Unrealistic or increased demands on officials to provide services within the constraints of their resources can have a detrimental effect on how people view the state.

3.2 Procurement Procedures in Local Governments

Local government entities use government procurement processes to carry out their strategies and satisfy the demand for public services. Egypt's Law No. 182 of 2018 governs the contracts that governmental entities enter into.

Figure 1 illustrates these procedures, which start with identifying the requirements of each local unit and end with the execution of the contract. Because so many people are involved in the implementation of these steps and have informal ties with businesses and suppliers, government procurement procedures are one of the most at-risk areas for corruption (as illustrated in the accompanying image).

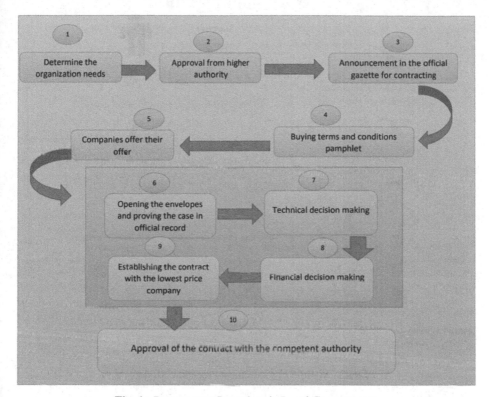

Fig. 1. Procurement Procedure in Local Governments

4 Improve Transparency and Accountability

Increasing the transparency of government operations and decision-making should be the main goal of an anti-corruption effort in a democratic society. A simplified blockchain approach for public procurement may only focus on using hash-function outputs recorded on distributed ledgers to permanently and tamper-resistant record documents and comments that are prone to corruption or removal.

Illegal trades are better known now. With the security of government data at its core, DLT provides an alternative form of data storage that has advantages and disadvantages. If anti-corruption measures are taken into account during the design phase, data storage on the blockchain can have advantageous benefits. Data audits must be included [18]. Initiatives to control land contain some of the most innovative concepts for using blockchain to store public data. Land registration records and land titles can be stored on the blockchain using DLT to protect them against fraud and corruption.

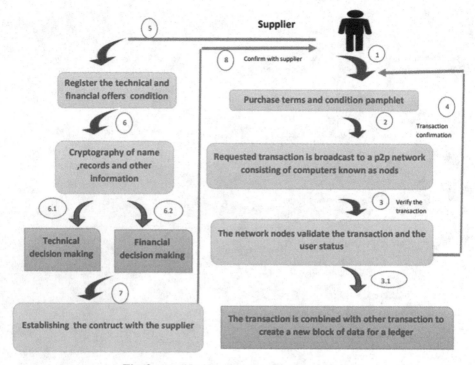

Fig. 2. Modified Procurement Procedure Model

After the supplier purchases the terms and conditions pamphlet, the requested transaction is broadcast to all business-to-business networks to validate the transaction, which is then merged with other transactions to build a new block. There are many sequences in Fig. 2 to increase transparency in the DLT. The supplier can register the technical and financial bids that are processed in cryptographic order once a fresh block has been established.

5   Applying Blockchain to Track Procurement Workflows:

Using blockchain to handle procurement would enable real-time traceability of anomalies, enhancing the immutability of audit trails (Fig. 3). The system will enable real-time auditing to detect corruption and simultaneous viewing of each stage by all stakeholders. Audits may gain credibility as a result of safeguards against unauthorized access and modification of data used for analysis.

Activities start with the provider, and higher authorities are in charge of every function. The first algorithm is used to verify the supplier name and ID associated with the contract that was confirmed by higher authority.

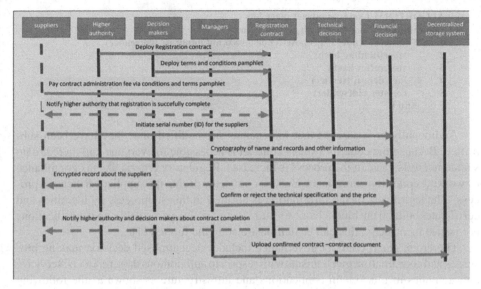

Fig. 3. Tracking Procurement Activities Workflow

6 ALGORITHM: Smart Contract Place Bid

Emerging technical tools like blockchain technology based smart contracts can be utilised as record-keeping systems and as a method to reduce some of the fraud affecting public procurement records. Several applications have already adopted smart contracts' immutability, transparency, dissemination, and automation features to prevent harmful human meddling [19].

Immutability, decentralization, transparency, representation of agreements, self-execution, and verifiability are the key benefits of blockchain-based smart contracts. A pre-written, impenetrable, and unchangeable computer programme that represents an agreement between two or more parties is what we refer to as a "smart contract." A smart contract can take control of and direct the movement of assets with blockchain titles and is stored, copied, and self-executed on a blockchain or distributed ledger. It is triggered by events or conditions that can be digitally verified.

In terms of information decentralization, block chain technology decentralizes the storage and management of all information, distributing it to all network users and reducing government and corporate control over information access [20].

Smart contracts take away a single person's authority from the entire procurement process. The secret entry of a bid is enabled during the bidding phase to prevent privileged access to information or its unwarranted publication. The idea for this came from anonymous auctions. As a result, it is hard for those participating to reveal their bids to rivals.The following algorithm1 illustrate the smart contract place bid [19].

ALGORITHM 1 smart contract place bid
Input :bidding hash offer hash ,tender , sender
1   If status of tender is propose(tender)AND not duplicate bid(sender)
2   store(bidding hash)
3   store(offer hash)
4   lock deposit(sender)
5   register bid(sender)
6   End if

Additionally, it is assured that bids cannot be modified once they have been submitted. Because the code of a smart contract is accessible to everyone and there are no vested interests, trust in the process is increased. Regulatory criteria like tax compliance or working condition compliance must be completed during the supplier verification process. The legitimacy of the information is ensured in this subprocess by identities and certificates built on the blockchain. An audit record is always available, so if certifications are issued incorrectly, this can be demonstrated in the future [21].

Therefore, smart contract governance includes decentralised decision-making processes and coordination mechanisms with respect to autonomous data, products, services, and activities in blockchain applications and infrastructure as shown as the following algorithms 2, 3 [21].

ALGORITHM2: SMART CONTRACT SUPPLIER
Input: product id ,quantity, supplier name
1   If sender is a higher authority then
2   If supplier name is registered in the registration smart contract then
3   Generate a new contract number
4   Generate a new supplier ID
5   Link new contract number to supplier name
6   Link new supplier ID to supplier name
7   Set contract status to new contract
8   Announce the availability of a new contract for examination
9   End
10   Else
11   Revert transaction
12   Endif

ALGORITHM3:smart contract order verification
Input :tender

1　Prerequisite: only verified supplier ID can execute
2　If status of tender is evaluate
3　　Repeat
4　　　Select supplier ID randomly
5　　　Wait for validation
6　　Until number of all validation reached
7　　If all validations correct
8　　　Release payment
9　　Else
10　　Terminate process
11　　End if
12 END IF

7　Conclusion

Corruption in public procurement is a worldwide appearance that causes immense financial and reputational damages. Especially in developing countries, corruption is a widespread issue due to secrecy and lack of transparency. An important instrument for transparency and account ability assurance is the record which is managed and controlled by recordkeeping systems. The discussion ended with the importance of utilizing technology to enhance local governance capabilities in eliminating forms of administrative corruption at local levels. Block chain technology can be used efficiently in limiting the various human interventions with the framework of government procurement carried out by local units, which control potential corruption opportunities. By improving the basic component of internal governance (transparency – accountability-oversight-audit) possible forms of corruption can be eliminated during government procurement processes in local unit and this can have done by using smart contract place bid.

References

1. Pinyaphat, T., Chian, T.: Blockchain: Challenges and Applications (2018)
2. Danda, B.R., Vijay, C., Ronald, D.: Blockchain technology: emerging applications and use cases for secure and trustworthy smart systems. J. Cybersecur. Privacy (2020)
3. Michael, C.N., Pradhan, P., Sanjeev, V., Vignesh, K.: Blockchain Technology Beyond Bitcoin, Sutardja. Center for Entrepreneurship & Technology: Technical Report (2015)
4. Wajde, B., Janet, L., Aniket, M.: Blockchain technology and its applications across multiple domains: a technology review. J. Int. Technol. Inf. Manag. (2021)
5. Exploring Blockchain Technology for Government Transparency. Blockchain-Based Public Procurement to Reduce Corruption, IDB (2020)
6. Niklas, K., Victoria, D.: Blockchain, bitcoin and corruption. A review of the linkages. Transparency International Anti-Corruption Helpdesk Answer (2018)
7. David, A.M., Sobolewski, L.V.: An Assessment of Pioneering Implementations in Public Services. Blockchain for Digital Government. Publications Office of the European Union, Luxembourg (2019)

8. Blockchain for Government Council – Cities Committee Taskforce. Big Innovation Centre (2020)
9. Oliver, M., Elizabeth, P.C.: Corruption consolidation in local governments: a grounded analytical framework. Public Admin. J. **99**, 530–546 (2021)
10. Kendall, D., Funk, E.O.: Consequences of anti-corruption experiment for local government performance in Brazil. J. Policy Anal. Manage. **39**(2), 444–468 (2020)
11. Sunčana, S., Edo, R., Jelena, B.: Determinants of corruption pressures on local government in the E.U. Economic Research-Ekonomska Istraživanja. **33**(1), 3492–3508 (2020)
12. García, H.C.E.: Blockchain innovation technology for corruption decrease in Mexico. Asian J. Innov. Policy. **1**(2), 177–194 (2021)
13. Praveensankar, M., Dhanalakshmi, R.: Blockchain-based smart contract for E-bidding system. In: 2nd International Conference on Intelligent Communication and Computational Techniques (ICCT), Manipal University, Jaipur, 28–29 Sep (2019)
14. Dan, W., Jindong, Z., Chunxiao, M.: Research on blockchain-based E-bidding system. Appl. Sci. **11**, 4011 (2021). https://doi.org/10.3390/app11094011 https://www.mdpi.com/journal/applsci
15. Chen, Y.-H., Chen, Y.-H., Lin, I.-C.: Blockchain based smart contract for bidding system. In: Proceedings of IEEE International Conference on Applied System Innovation. IEEE ICASI 2018- Meen, Prior & Lam (eds) (2018). https://doi.org/10.1109/ICASI.2018.8394569
16. Sarker, S., Henningsson, S., Jensen, T., Hedman, J.: The use of blockchain as a resource for combating corruption in global shipping: an interpretive case study. J. Manag. Inf. Syst. **38**(2), 338–373 (2021). https://doi.org/10.1080/07421222.2021.1912919
17. Maria, G.D.: Reducing Corruption at the Local Level. World Bank (2006)
18. Saikal, A.k., Gregory, J.D., John, A.S.: Chain and silk: alternative futures of blockchain governance in Kyrgyzstan. European J. Futures Res. 1–14 (2022)
19. Weingärtner, T., Batista, D., Köchli, S., Voutat, G.: Prototyping a smart contract based public procurement to fight corruption. Computers 10–85 (2021). https://doi.org/10.3390/computers 10070085
20. Myeong, S., Jung, Y.: Administrative reforms in the fourth industrial revolution: the case of blockchain use. Sustainability **11**, 39–71 (2019)
21. Lin, R., Wang, L., Li, B., Lu, Y., Qi, Z., Xie, L.: Organizational governance in the smart era: the implications of blockchain. Nankai Business Review International (2022)

A Data Brokering Architecture to Guarantee Nonfunctional Requirements in IoT Applications

Taha Mansouri[1(✉)] [iD], Julian M. Bass[1] [iD], Tarek Gaber[1] [iD], Steve Wright[2], and Benedict Scorey[3]

[1] University of Salford, Manchester, UK
t.mansouri@salford.ac.uk
[2] Invisible Systems Ltd, Manchester, UK
[3] Forsberg Services Ltd, Morecambe, UK

Abstract. IoT sensors capture different aspects of the environmental data and generate high throughput data streams. To harvest potential values from these sensors, a system fulfilling the big data requirements should be designed. In this work, we reviewed the important nonfunctional requirements, in particular big data-based ones. Moreover, we dug out a conventional IoT architecture to address these requirements. Finally, we designed a brokering based architecture which is flexible and scalable enough to cover big data requirements of high throughput data streams resulted from modern sensors. Evaluation results using quantitative comparisons on use case displayed that the proposed new architecture outperformed the conventional ones. The experiments showed that the proposed architecture can handle 32 times more load than the conventional.

Keywords: IoT · wireless sensors · software architecture · data brokering

1 Introduction

The Internet of Things is a network of various devices that exchange data and communicate with each other over the Internet based on a contract agreement (Yue and He 2018). This dynamic network is available almost anywhere (Poniszewska-Maranda and Kaczmarek 2015). IoT unify the physical and the virtual domains using the Internet (Balaji et al. 2019). Systems built using the concept of IoT are based not only on the simple sensors that transmit information to the systems but also operate primarily based on statistics and simple mathematical calculations. In IoT, data integrations over different environments are thus challenging and will be supported by modular, interoperable components. Therefore, architectures should be open and follow standards; they should not restrict users from using fixed, end-to-end solutions (Shah and Yaqoob 2016; Shanzhi Chen et al. 2014). Meanwhile, IoT architectures should consider big data requirements, including volume, velocity, value, variety, and veracity (Farhan et al. 2017).

Besides functional requirements coupled with any specific application, important non-functional requirements are common in most IoT applications. Security and privacy

© ICST Institute for Computer Sciences, Social Informatics and Telecommunications Engineering 2023
Published by Springer Nature Switzerland AG 2023. All Rights Reserved
R. Hou et al. (Eds.): BDTA 2021/2022, LNICST 480, pp. 75–84, 2023.
https://doi.org/10.1007/978-3-031-33614-0_6

encompass security mechanisms (Aksu et al. 2018) to preserve users' crucial data and ensure their integrity alongside the architecture. It includes maintaining confidentiality, access control, and policy enforcement such as encryption algorithms (Tunc et al. 2021). Scalability denotes how the architecture can handle the constant streams of new devices or changes in throughput of the existing ones (Aksu et al. 2018). Interoperability happens among different entities. It is critical for communicating information across devices, layers, functions, and applications (Shanzhi Chen et al. 2014). Fault tolerance denotes how resilient the architecture is in case of faults in constituent entities (Farhan et al. 2017). In other words, whether, if a failure occurred in one component of the architecture, the whole system would continue functioning or not. Availability identifies the number of computing resources available to implement IoT applications (Aksu et al. 2018). And finally fast response is how much latency end users experience before receiving a response to their request (Afzal et al. 2019).

Table 1 summarizes the most important non-functionals reported in the literature. The table implies that security and scalability are the most important ones. Moreover, IoT has all notions of big data, including volume of data, variety of data types, the velocity of data streams, and value of the stored data. In terms of the volume, the problem is with storing and managing huge amounts of received data for long periods. Regarding the need to handle variety, there is an increasing requirement to communicate through a growing number of platforms, a growing number of protocols, new sensors with cutting edge technologies, and some standards. This influences the data types and data structures being processed and stored. With the growth of the number of sensors, customers, applications, and more rapid networks, the throughputs of incoming data are increasing, making retrieving the same data from conventional databases and extracting added value increasingly challenging. These sensors sense different aspects of the environment; therefore, processing them to extract valuable knowledge and insight is more demanding. Therefore, real-time analytics is a serious requirement.

Table 1. Important non-functional requirements for designing an IoT architecture.

Requirement	References
Security and Privacy	(Afzal et al. 2019; Aksu et al. 2018; Balaji et al. 2019; Farhan et al. 2017; Shah and Yaqoob 2016; Shanzhi Chen et al. 2014; Tunc et al. 2021)
Scalability	(Afzal et al. 2019; Balaji et al. 2019; Farhan et al. 2017; Shah and Yaqoob, 2016; Shanzhi Chen et al. 2014; Tunc et al. 2021)
Interoperability	(Afzal et al. 2019; Balaji et al. 2019; Farhan et al. 2017; Shanzhi Chen et al. 2014; Tunc et al. 2021)
Fault tolerance	(Balaji et al. 2019; Farhan et al. 2017; Tunc et al. 2021)
Availability	(Shah and Yaqoob 2016; Tunc et al. 2021)
Fast response/Low latency	(Afzal et al. 2019; Balaji et al. 2019; Shah and Yaqoob 2016; Tunc et al. 2021)

There are other important requirements such as the expectations of customers to push data into other third-party platforms, varying from large players like Microsoft Azure and Amazon AWS to smaller bespoke systems over various APIs. This work aims to design a scalable IoT architecture to ensure the important non-functional requirements in particular big data requirements. Therefore, the research question is which architecture is more suitable to guarantee big data requirements. The rest of this paper will consider the existing multi-tier IoT architecture and the potential improvements. Then we describe the new architecture and explain how it will tackle the non-functional requirements.

2   Existing Architecture

IoT service providers usually adopt a generic architecture and evolve it over years. As time has gone on, the number of different sensors, their applications, and the breadth of wireless communication protocols used for this. In order to visualize the data, perform analysis, and provide event-based actions and notifications for their customers, these companies either develop their own platforms or use the existing cloud-hosted services. The conventional architecture includes a very large RDBMS backend database and a web front end. The components of this architecture are tightly coupled together to conduct the main functionalities. Which is to ingest data to the backend database and disseminate them through the web applications and third parties. Figure 1 highlights the main components of this architecture.

In this architecture device is primarily a wireless sensor to capture different aspects of the environment, such as humidity, temperature, state, vibration, and so on, and transmit them through a network. The devices communicate through different protocols, including LoRa, LoRaWAN, and NB-IoT. Devices with LoRa and LoRaWAN types use a gateway which is a connected appliance to connect to the other components. However, NB-IoT sensors send data directly to the uplink network. Therefore, the communication protocols and the data types are different. Due to the different devices, there is a heavy weighted and tightly coupled ingestion layer in this architecture, which is in charge of carrying out most receiving data packets, returning acknowledgment, decryption and decoding packet data, and storing them in a local RDBMS. Then other processes running in this layer extract data from the local database, transform them to give them applicable schemas and load them into the main database. Moreover, this layer processes data sharing requests raised by third parties, fetching data from the main database and sending them an agreed protocol.

The primary storage is an RDBMS containing a few transactional tables that grow fast regarding incoming data streams' throughput. Moreover, many dimensional tables depend on the changes of the incoming data structures and the web application requirements. Finally, the web front end and a core of APIs interact with this database to fetch and share data and save the related commands and configurations.

While the architecture denoted in Fig. 1 could cover the many functional requirements, changes in the business environment and the fast-growing non-functional requirements, there are some improvements to be considered to make the architecture more manageable. Based on the big data 4 Vs (Farhan et al. 2017), we have classified these improvements into the followings:

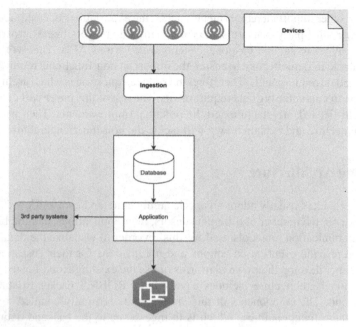

Fig. 1. A conventional IoT architecture containing a layer to gather data from different sources with different protocols, a database which is mostly a relational database, and an application as the serving layer.

2.1 Volume

Many companies, as time passes the number of customers and the period that data has been accumulated have both grown. Database changes over the years and upgrades to the database engine have all helped. It leads to a few very large tables for which guaranteeing the performance is becoming more challenging. Fast fetching data and parallel access are common problems in this environment. Moreover, managing this volume of concentrated data, such as running backups, is getting harder. Therefore, a solution needs to be more scalable, fault tolerant, with fast response and low latency data access.

2.2 Variety

In the common multi-tiered architectures, the backend data storage is still tied very heavily to the product range as it was in the early years of development. This has its consequences on the scalability and interoperability of the architecture. Early development focuses on a relatively narrow set of products. The main tables, stored in an RDBMS database, have a flat structure with a predefined number of fields for all sensors. For sensors that report less than this, it results in empty fields, whereas for sensors that report more, or where the values will not fit in the number and type available, an awkward arrangement involving several rows is required. Whilst traditional database management systems using Structured Query Languages guarantee non-functional requirements such as simplicity, consistency, availability, and performance, they suffer from static schemas and consequently limited applications for IoT (Rautmare and Bhalerao 2016).

With the development of sensors with several measurands, and the ingress of data from third-party sensors and platforms, the frequency of awkward workarounds grows, and the system becomes harder to maintain. Moreover, since all components, such as the heavily weighted ingestion layer, the database, and the web application, are tightly coupled, and any change is a radical refactor.

2.3 Velocity

With the evolution of technology, and the rise of powerful competing platforms – many developed by big names such as Microsoft in their Azure IoT platform – expectations have moved on. Expectations are now to see current 'live' data streamed to cloud platforms and dashboards, where live now means within a few seconds. Although technologies such as web-sockets could be used to deliver data to the user interface, it is difficult to see how the back-end structure could support this, given the current architecture and speed issues. To keep pace with evolving technologies, a new approach is needed to improve horizontal scalability, availability, fast response, and low latency.

Key to achieving high velocity delivery of data through the system is event driven data processing and handling. Modern transport layer technologies make continuous data streaming from/to many clients a viable option with little overhead. The common platform uses usually batching techniques which are not event driven, increasing latency and making the system unreactive to data changes.

2.4 Value Extraction

With the growing size of the data storage tables in the database comes the associated slowing down of queries that pull from this data. A general approach is to query and process stored data at the point of use. However, time taken to query data grows to such a length that it is impossible to display live real-time values of this aggregated data in some cases. And even where it is still possible, on sites with many such sensors, or where this is an overview of many customer sites, it becomes impossible. The above speed issues always restrict any further analytics of data. Therefore, the current architecture with one very large store of raw sensor data is starting to limit future possibilities and undermine system performance to the point where it becomes a serious business risk.

3 The Proposed New Architecture

In order to mitigate the mentioned challenges and to guarantee the important nonfunctional requirements, a new architecture is required. The main goal is to move the existing web platform from being at the heart of the system to becoming one of the potentially many subscribers to data in a brokered architecture and enabling big data requirements. The idea is to leverage a broker-based architecture. Figure 2 highlights the most important components of the new architecture which is based on a microservice architectural model. All existing data ingress from devices is seen as data feeders to the broker in this architecture. Future ingress from other devices, APIs, or elsewhere is further data feeders adhering to a well-defined protocol. Eexisting web applications are subscribers and sit alongside other cloud platforms or connectors subscribed to the broker; the exchange of information with the broker follows the same defined rules and protocols available to other platforms. Configuration and other such activities could be done by the web application but would not have to be done by it; other platforms could do the same via the broker and a well-defined protocol. Where data is only going to a third party, it would never touch the web application cloud platform; the data feeders and brokers only forward data to authenticated subscribers.

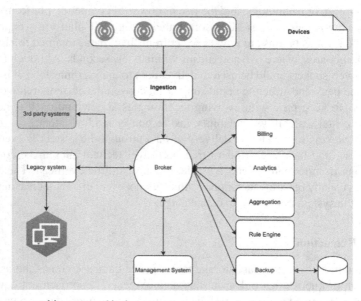

Fig. 2. The new architecture and its important components. In this architecture the ingestion layer is just a thin layer to fetch data from sources and import into the broker with no manipulation. The broker is the shared area which should be scalable enough to tolerate many concurrent accesses by different microservices to add values to data. Therefore, any entity should read from and write to this component.

In this architecture, the ingestion layer is again in charge of receiving and decoding data sent by devices. After this phase, it assigns a universal id to each received message and publishes them directly to the data broker. Ingestion publishes each stream into different buckets. Therefore, it is not a heavyweight layer anymore, and also it is not coupled with the structures of the upstream database. The broker is the heart of this archi-tecture. The main idea is that data will be stored in different parts to enable concurrent access. It makes the architecture horizontal scalable and guarantees its interoperability by storing it in a semi-structured way. Different microservices are in charge of granting the functional structure to the incoming data streams through stream processing services. This policy can run the microservices in parallel, so the solution is scalable. The model is widely based on publish-subscribe architecture.

After preparing data, other microservices go through conducting different functionality, such as aggregation, analytics, billing, rule engine, and so on. This architecture can also accept configurations from the user and carry out related functions on a specific schedule over the data broker. Since the data access in the data broker is distributed, the model is scalable. Data aggregation might be done in memory such that only aggregated data is stored. This would reduce data storage requirements and increase the speed of further analysis. Different security policies are available in this architecture.

4 Benefits of the New Architecture

Data ownership will be ensured by a flexible access control. Moreover, in transit and at rest encryptions are enforced. Eexisting web platforms simply become subscribers to the broker. The broker itself is a dedicated process that is standards-compliant, lightweight, secure and fast. It is fit for handling all mentioned Big Data requirements. In order to ensure easier integration with other third-party platforms and benefit from the robustness of a tried and tested platform, the broker would be built around a standards-compliant technology.

All data feeders that publish to the broker would do so under well-defined topics. Using this method, all other processes can get access to the incoming data streams in simultaneously. Therefore, the horizontal scalability is guaranteed, and data is much more accessible. There would be a clear demarcation between device data and diagnostic data. New data feeds, e.g., from new technology such as the NB-IoT devices or third-party platforms, would be easily on-boarded – they would simply be another publisher that supports defined schemas. Therefore, a wide variety of data structures can be considered.

By brokering data, the current application in the future would only receive relevant data. Its job would no longer involve the export of large amounts of data. This load would be picked up by the broker and additional microservices designed for the sole purpose of doing this. Moreover, most brokers support clustering by which there would be clear options such as adding redundancy as a disaster recovery option, adding off-site back-up, and moving brokers to other servers and sites.

This architecture through the publish-subscribe model facilitates the one-to-many relationship for sharing data streams with one or more subscribers. For example, data could be shared concurrently with the existing web platform and other platforms, but a data stream could also be shared with, e.g., an aggregator. For a data broker, data would not be stored long term. This reduces the impact of any security breach. Where data is held in short-term volatile storage (e.g., memory) or non-volatile (e.g., NoSQL databases), encryption at rest should be achieved if possible.

An analytics engine can be adopted simply as another microservice. It would be a more powerful version of the data aggregator in many ways. Analytics could vary from the simple to the more complex. It could even harness artificial intelligence (AI), e.g., to spot patterns in data.

The engine (or multiple engines) would subscribe to data streams on the broker and publish back processed data or event streams. Throughout IoT systems, there are many processes and devices that need configuring. These can vary widely from configuration data for devices (e.g., for a LoRa radio transmitter, transmit frequency, and high and low thresholds for edge intelligence), to gateways (e.g., upload frequency), to alarm processes (e.g., high and low thresholds, alarm delays) and more. The broker could handle the exchange of this configuration data, with all such data passing through the broker. It would be the responsibility of the client subscribing to this feed to handle the data. For example, in the use case company Invisible Systems LTD (ISL), the cloud platform already passes configuration data down to the Ingestion layer. Instead, this would be passed to the broker, and an independent microservice would subscribe to this to conduct the related processing over the given incoming data stream.

Moving to a central broker allow a standalone, clearly defined, maintainable and scalable process to be built for each export route. Moreover, where the existing platform does not require data, it would be pushed straight out to a third party, ensuring speed, reduced data storage, and capacity for Big Data. A new approach could be envisioned around the broker, including an API process subscribing to the broker for data stream topics it is interested in; fixed-term storage is used to keep a log of recent data (e.g., for the last month, according to agreed commercial terms); this could be stored in a separate database that is specific to the process or may be stored in a NoSQL database.

5 Discussion

Some quantitative experiments have been made to compare these two architectures regarding their related technologies in Invisible Systems Ltd' data. In the new architecture, Apache Kafka is an appropriate candidate as a data broker. And a candidate database to persist data streams is influxDB. During testing, we have achieved sustained throughput in excess of 30 k messages per second with 3 Kafka broker nodes and 1 client node (AWS t3.small, co-hosted in same data center as broker). Moreover, we have achieved sustained database write speeds of 32 k data points per second (unlimited influxDB resource, writing from 1 client node, different AWS data centres). The conventional architecture writes at up to 75 devices/second (empirically equivalent to around 75 $\times$ 5.3 = 400 data points), from minimum 2 ingest nodes (equivalent to 200 data points per node per second). Therefore, node for node, the new architecture is 32000/200 = 160 times faster.

The new architecture also offers additional processing, such as detecting alarms, which generate additional data points. Therefore, the load generated by the new architecture is arbitrarily larger, depending on user configuration. Based on an estimated 5 additional data points (alarms etc.) per measured data point, each node can handle 160/5 = 32 times more load than a current data node. This yields an estimated throughput per node of (200 $\times$ 32)/5.3 = 1200 devices per second. At standard transmit intervals of around 7.5 min, this equates to 540,000 devices in the field per node. The platform can scale horizontally, giving a capacity of many millions of devices. Table 2 summarizes the above findings to compare these two architectures.

Table 2. Comparison between the conventional and the proposed architectures.

Architecture	Write speed (datapoint per node)	Load number
Conventional architecture	200	5
The proposed architecture	32000	160

6 Conclusion

In this research we reviewed important non-functional requirements to design an IoT system. To this end a conventional system has been investigated, and the important requirements have been addressed. To overcome the important requirements, a new brokering-based architecture was designed and prototyped. In this research we discussed that how the new architecture could cover the non-functional requirements such as security, scalability, extensibility, resiliency and low latency. We also carried out some experiments by gathering data from ISL that showed the new architecture outperforms the existing ones.

Acknowledgement. This research has resulted from the Knowledge Transfer Partnership between the University of Salford and Invisible Systems Ltd (ISL) partially funded by Innovate UK "KTP011129".

References

Afzal, B., Umair, M., Asadullah Shah, G., Ahmed, E.: Enabling IoT platforms for social IoT applications: vision, feature mapping, and challenges. Futur. Gener. Comput. Syst. **92**, 718–731 (2019). https://doi.org/10.1016/j.future.2017.12.002

Aksu, H., Babun, L., Conti, M., Tolomei, G., Uluagac, A.S.: Advertising in the IoT era: vision and challenges. IEEE Commun. Mag. **56**(11), 138–144 (2018). https://doi.org/10.1109/MCOM.2017.1700871

Balaji, S., Nathani, K., Santhakumar, R.: IoT Technology, applications and challenges: a contemporary survey. Wireless Pers. Commun. **108**(1), 363–388 (2019). https://doi.org/10.1007/s11277-019-06407-w

Raza, U., Kharel, R.: A survey on the challenges and opportunities of the Internet of Things (IoT). In: 2017 Eleventh International Conference on Sensing Technology (ICST), pp. 1–5. https://doi.org/10.1109/ICSensT.2017.8304465

Poniszewska-Maranda, A., Kaczmarek, D.: Selected methods of artificial intelligence for Internet of Things conception, pp. 1343–1348. https://doi.org/10.15439/2015F161

Rautmare, S., Bhalerao, D.M.: MySQL and NoSQL database comparison for IoT application. In: 2016 IEEE International Conference on Advances in Computer Applications, ICACA 2016, pp. 235–238 (2016)

Shah, S.H., Yaqoob, I.: A survey: Internet of Things (IOT) technologies, applications and challenges. IEEE Smart Energy Grid Engineering (SEGE) **2016**, 381–385 (2016). https://doi.org/10.1109/SEGE.2016.7589556

Chen, S., Hui, X., Liu, D., Bo, H., Wang, H.: A Vision of IoT: applications, challenges, and opportunities with China perspective. IEEE Internet Things J. **1**(4), 349–359 (2014). https://doi.org/10.1109/JIOT.2014.2337336

Tunc, M.A., Gures, E., Shayea, I.: A Survey on IoT smart healthcare: emerging technologies, applications, challenges, and future trends. [Cs, Math]. http://arxiv.org/abs/2109.02042

Yue, Y.-G., He, P.: A comprehensive survey on the reliability of mobile wireless sensor networks: taxonomy, challenges, and future directions. Inf. Fusion **44**, 188–204 (2018). https://doi.org/10.1016/j.inffus.2018.03.005

Machine Learning and Big Data Applications

A Proposed Virtual Learning Model Based on Statistical Analysis of Educational Data of Egypt

Aliaa Kamal Abdella[1], Mai A. Elnady[1], Lamia Aladel[1], and Heba M. Sabry[2]([⊠])

[1] Department of Computers and Information Systems, Sadat Academy, Cairo, Egypt
[2] Department of Computer Science, Faculty of Computers and Information, Sadat Academy, Cairo, Egypt
heba.ict@gmail.com

Abstract. Current political and research agendas all around the world place artificial intelligence (AI) high on the list. Although the foundations for AI have existed for a number of decades, recent advanced directions are accelerating what AI could do. One of these directions is education; those in charge of reforming education must consider the effects of an AI-driven future on education. However, various risks and issues are unavoidably brought on by these quick technological advancements; they have so far outrun policy discussions and regulatory structures. This paper seeks to identify the impact of AI on teaching, learning, and education, by analyzing educational data in Egypt. The data set was downloaded from the ministry of education website. It contained information such as the number of schools, the number of classes, and the number of students per class of the general education and al-Azhar education for primary, preparatory, and secondary stages. In addition, this data set contained information regarding the correlation between different factors. The finding of this research can inform the future design and implementation of the virtual learning model.

Keywords: Stages of Learning in Artificial Intelligence · Correlation · Virtual Learning Environment · Education Data Analysis

1 Introduction

Since the beginning of the 1980s, and until recently, educational applications of AI have mainly focused on the knowledge-based approach. The most prominent line of research has been concerned with intelligent tutoring systems.

(ITS). In formal education, AI can have both positive and negative impact on learning. As AI is now high on the policy agenda, it should appear that AI should be applied in as many educational settings as possible. When a replacement promising technology emerges, and when the restrictions of technology and also the challenges of applying it are often not perfectly understood, technology could appear to open radically new possibilities for solving old problems.

R. Hou et al. (Eds.): BDTA 2021/2022, LNICST 480, pp. 87–96, 2023.
https://doi.org/10.1007/978-3-031-33614-0_7

This is what happens in the first phases of the life-cycle of general-purpose technologies, and it ends up in technology push. Visionary entrepreneurs and policymakers realize the potential of latest technology and see all the chances of how it could make a difference.

1.1 Stages of Learning in Artificial Intelligence

Artificial Intelligence can be defined as the development of computer systems that are capable of performing tasks that require human intelligence, such as decision making, Learning and education, object detection, solving complex problems and so on. There are different stages of learning in Artificial Intelligence as described below, and shown in Fig. 1.

1.1.1 Artificial Narrow Intelligence

Artificial narrow intelligence (ANI) is a goal-oriented subset of artificial intelligence (AI) that is designed to be better at a single task, such as keeping track of weather updates, creating data science reports by analyzing raw data, or playing games like chess, poker, etc. By utilizing data from a single dataset, artificial narrow intelligence systems are trained to focus on one task at a time. In other words, such systems stop at the duties that have been allocated to them. [1].

1.1.2 Artificial General Intelligence

A machine with Artificial General Intelligence (AGI) would have the same capacity to learn how to perform a wide variety of tasks and be able to comprehend the world on par with any human. Any work that a human could complete, and probably many that a human couldn't, could be completed by an artificial general intelligence. At the very least, an AGI could combine flexible, human-like thinking and reasoning with computational benefits, such as almost instantaneous recollection and split-second number crunching [2].

1.1.3 Artificial Super Intelligence

The idea of artificial super intelligence is a futuristic one that explores how AI can surpass human intelligence. Computing software must outperform human intellect in all metrics and situations if artificial super intelligence is to develop and become reality. Artificial super intelligence will be a reality once AI surpasses human intelligence [3].

Machines with super intelligence are able to consider potential abstractions and interpretations that are just not conceivable for people to consider. This is due to the human brain's limited capacity for thought, which is restricted to a small number of billion neurons [4].

1.2 Types of Artificial Intelligence

Based on the functionality of AI-based systems, AI can be categorized into the following types:

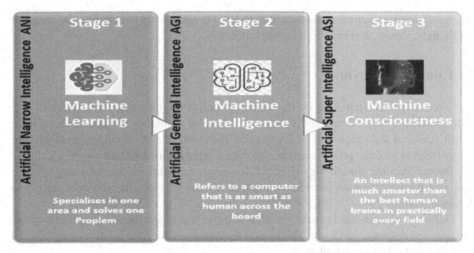

Fig. 1. Stages of learning in Artificial intelligence

1.2.1 Reactive Machines AI

The most fundamental forms of AI are entirely reactive; they lack the capacity to remember past events or draw conclusions about the present from them. This form of intelligence entails the computer directly observing the outside world and responding accordingly. It is independent of any personal worldview [5].

1.2.2 Limited Memory AI

Limited memory Similar to how the neurons in the human brain link, AI is distinguished by its capacity to assimilate new information and get better with practice. This type of AI is now in use and being improved. The AI environment is designed with low memory so that models are automatically trained and then updated based on the model behavior. AI with limited memory can solve challenging classification tasks and make predictions using past data [5].

1.2.3 Theory of Mind AI

All of the reactive AI systems in use today are categorized as narrow AI. According to theory of mind, machines are meant to represent the environment in which people think, feel, and make decisions. In the future, this is what needs to be accomplished [4].

An AI with a Theory of Mind would be aware that people have feelings, thoughts, and expectations regarding how they should be treated. It can then modify its reaction appropriately.

1.2.4 Self-Aware AI

The development of self-aware machines that can create representations of themselves is the last stage in AI research. It is a development and expansion of the Theory of Mind

AI. A self-aware machine possesses human-level consciousness, including the capacity for thought, desire, and emotional comprehension.

2 Literature Review

More research has been done on the effects of online learning since the SARS-CoV-2 virus pandemic led schools and colleges to close in a number of nations around the world. This has led to the crucial finding that the rising use of online learning is better categorized as an emergency reaction action than what online learning should ideally be [8]. Online learning should ideally be an alternative to traditional learning that is made available by digitalization in order to provide education to people who need access to distance learning [9].

Online education has become the standard method of instruction as a result of the pedagogical response to Covid-19-induced lockdowns, making education accessible to a sizable section of the population.

The difficulties encountered throughout the online learning stage are the elements that are anticipated. to make learning more difficult. As students, technology is a huge source of worry. Using out-of-date hardware may prevent you from downloading newer software that requires a higher computer specification, which hinders their ability to learn [8].

Research innovation is a big opportunity because online learning is a requirement for COVID-19. Research may focus on developing frameworks for approaches, adoptions, and improvements to online learning that permit individualizing instruction for students and reassessing the educational process [7]. An opportunity for educational institutions to further develop their IT infrastructure, which can then be used to guarantee business continuity [9].

A study by [10] looked at the digital disruptions in their research brought on by the Covid-19 shutdown and the difficulties UK educational institutions face while switching to online courses. This study, which involved 1148 participants, looked qualitatively at the main issues that experts from UK universities predicted would arise as a result of the move to online education.

3 Impact on Learning, Teaching, and Education

The knowledge-based approach has been the main focus of educational applications of AI since the early 1980s and up until recently. 61 The most well-known area of study has focused on intelligent tutoring systems, or ITS. The architecture of these systems is knowledge-based. A domain model that specifies the subject matter to be learnt is present in a typical ITS architecture, together with a student model that depicts the students' current level of understanding and learning. Through an adaptable and interactive user interface, an expert system or pedagogical model controls the introduction of learning materials to the learner [11].

These systems have historically employed the knowledge-based approach, and their success has mostly been shown in narrow and clear-cut fields like physics and mathematics. Intelligent tutoring settings have also been a significant source of data for learning research since student behavior and learning can be closely tracked in ITS environments. The challenge of creating ITS for wide learning domains has shifted attention to the more specific issue of leveraging AI and machine learning to produce teacher interfaces for student and learner monitoring, as well as learning diagnostics. This is often referred to as educational data mining and learning analytics (EDM).

4   Data Analysis of the Educational Data (Case Study of Education in Egypt)

For investors looking to establish a presence in the Middle East's education market, Egypt ranks among the most alluring locations.

The first grade in the Egyptian educational system is called pre-primary education. However, basic education is only required to be completed for six years before moving on to three years of preparatory school and three years of secondary education. Primary school has the largest enrollment of all educational levels, with more than 12.8 million students. In 2019–2020, there were about 5.2 million pupils enrolled in preparatory classes. After finishing their required schooling, almost 3.3 million students choose to continue their studies in higher education, mostly at public colleges.

There is also Al-Azhar, a separate religious education program that runs independently of the Ministry of Education. Downloads of Egypt's educational data sets are available on the website of the Ministry of Education [12].

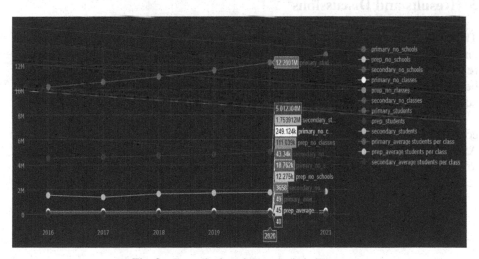

Fig. 2. General education analysis in Egypt

According to the general education analysis in Fig. 2, primary grade students make up the largest proportion of students, followed by prep students and secondary students, with the average number of students enrolled in classes, the number of schools, and the number of classes roughly equal across the three education phases.

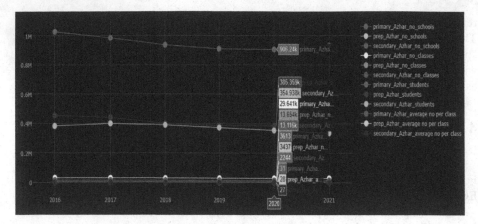

Fig. 3. Azhar education analysis in Egypt

Students in the primary grades make up a larger portion than prep students in the Azhar education study in Fig. 3. And secondary pupils who roughly equal the ratio of the number of schools, the number of students enrolled in classes, and the average number of students in each class. In recent years, fewer children across all stages have attended Azhar school.

5   Results and Discussions

The researchers determine the relationship between the average number of students enrolled in classes, the number of classes, and the number of schools in this area, as represented in the below figures from [4–9], which represent the correlation results between different factors. The Table 1 represent the percentages of correlation for general education, and Azhar education for different factors.

The general education students in primary and prep stages are strong positively correlated to the average number of students in classes and number of classes. While in Azhar education students in primary and secondary stages are strong positively correlated to no of students in schools and no of classes but is negative correlated with number of schools (Figs. 4, 5, 6, 7, 8 and 9).

Table 1. Correlation between students and number of students in classes, number of classes and number of schools.

		Average number of students	Number of classes	Number of schools
general education	primary students	0.9957	0.9981	0.9986
	prep.students	0.98865	0.9789	0.9918
	secondary students	0.5848	0.74689	0.6808
Azhar education	primary students	0.96412	0.97514	-0.79449
	prep.students	0.2988	0.5577	-0.80373
	secondary students	0.99125	0.90086	-0.948299

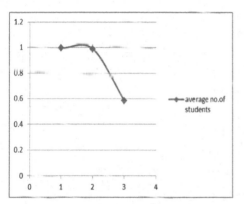

Fig. 4. Correlation between general primary no of students and average no of students in schools, no of classes and no of schools

Fig. 5. Correlation between general prep.no of students and average no of students in schools, no of classes and no of schools

6   A Proposed Virtual Learning Model

The researchers conclude from the previous data analysis that there is a need to build virtual model to apply virtual classrooms in schools to cope with the increasing numbers of students. This virtual learning system was built up from theories, principals and research in.

educational background. As described in Fig. 10.

The model begins with the phase1, which is a preparation of the learners to understand the virtual learning process, and then move to the second stage which is identifying goals of the teaching process and identify the ILO (institutional learning outcome),the next stage is searching facts that the learners need to know finding the ideas, and then move

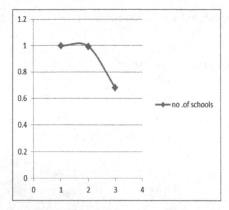

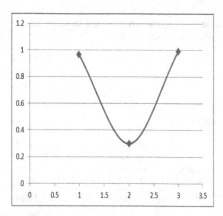

Fig. 6. Correlation between general secondary no of students and average no of students in schools, no of classes and no of schools

Fig. 7. Correlation between Azhar primary no of students and average no of students in schools, no of classes and no of schools

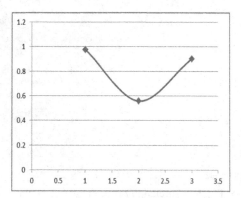

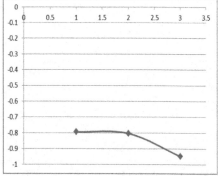

Fig. 8. Correlation between al-Azhar prep.no of students and average no of students in schools, no of classes and no of schools

Fig. 9. Correlation between al-Azhar secondary no of students and average no of students in schools, no of classes and no of schools

to the next stage which is prepared students to find problem solutions, then stage 6 is creating productivity and evaluate the results, and the final stage is accepting productivity.

The paper suggests to apply this model on the general education (primary, preparatory and secondary) schools of Egypt to cope with the increasing number of students in school and to improve the learning system of Egypt.

Fig. 10. A Proposed Virtual Learning Model

7 Conclusion

In this paper, the researchers seek to identify the impact of AI on teaching, learning, and education by discussing the stages of learning in Artificial Intelligence and also, mentioned the types of AI system. And then highlight the impact of Ai on learning process, finally, the paper analyzing data set about educational data in Egypt and measure correlation between number of schools, number of classes, and number of students per class for primary, preparatory, and secondary stages for general education and al-Azhar education and found that there is a positive correlation in the general education, which means that the number of students is increasing when number of school increases. While there is a negative correlation in al-Azhar education Which lead to the importance and the need of build virtual model to apply virtual classrooms in schools to cope with the increasing numbers of students.

References

1. Tzimas, T.: Legal and Ethical Challenges of Artificial Intelligence from an International Law Prespective. Springer Nature, Switzerland (2021)
2. Franz, A.: Artificial general intelligence through recursive data compression and grounded reasoning: a position paper. arXiv preprint arXiv:1506.04366 (2015)
3. Sajja, P.S.: Introduction to artificial intelligence. In: Sajja, P.S. (ed.) Illustrated Computational Intelligence: Examples and Applications, pp. 1–25. Springer, Singapore (2021). https://doi.org/10.1007/978-981-15-9589-9_1
4. Geiser, L.H., Patel-Weynand, T., Marsh, A.S., Mafune, K., Vogt, D.J.: Challenges and opportunities. In: Pouyat, R.V., Page-Dumroese, D.S., Patel-Weynand, T., Geiser, L.H. (eds.) Forest and Rangeland Soils of the United States Under Changing Conditions, pp. 189–198. Springer, Cham (2020). https://doi.org/10.1007/978-3-030-45216-2_10
5. Hassani, H., Silva, E.S., Unger, S., TajMazinani, M., Mac Feely, S.: Artificial intelligence (AI) or intelligence augmentation (IA): what is the future? Ai **1**(2), 143–155 (2020)
6. Chatila, R., et al.: Toward self-aware robots. Front. Robot. AI **5**, 88 (2018)
7. Yaseen, H., Alsoud, A., Nofal, M., Abdeljaber, O., Al-Adwan, A.: The effects of online learning on students' performance: a comparison between UK and Jordanian universities. Int. J. Emerg. Technol. Learn. **16**, 4–18 (2021)

8. Adedoyin, O.B., Soykan, E.: Covid-19 pandemic and online learning: the challenges and opportunities. Interact. Learn. Env. **31**, 863–875 (2020)
9. Manfuso, L.G.: How the remote learning pivot could shape Higher Ed IT. EdTech Magazine (2020)
10. Watermeyer, R., Crick, T., Knight, C., Goodall, J.: COVID-19 and digital disruption in UK universities: afflictions and affordances of emergency online migration. High. Educ. **81**, 623–641 (2020)
11. Ilkka, T.: The impact of artificial intelligence on learning, teaching, and education. European Union (2018)
12. https://emis.gov.eg/. Last accessed 10 Oct 2022

Diagnosis Hepatitis B Using Machine and Deep Learning: Survey

Gehad Ahmed Soltan Abd-Elaleem[1,2]([✉]), Fahad Elsheref[1,2], Rabab Maher[3],
Ahmed Elsayed[1], Doaa S. Elzanfaly[1], and Ahmed Sharaf Eldin[1,4]

[1] Faculty of Computers and Artificial Intelligence, Helwan University, Helwan, Egypt
eng.gehadahmed2013@yahoo.com
[2] Faculty of Computers and Artificial Intelligence, Beni Suef University, Beni Suef, Egypt
[3] Student's Hospital, Fellow of Tropical Medicine, Cairo University, Cairo, Egypt
[4] Faculty of Computers and Artificial Intelligence, Sinai University, Sinai, Egypt

Abstract. Machine Learning (ML) improves healthcare systems by helping to reach a proper diagnosis and reducing the diagnosis faults such as severe illness, cancer, inflammatory diseases, other diseases, and pathology. Many studies found that ML-based systems can be better than humans in more critical tasks. The study of liver disease diagnosis is very important, especially the diagnosis of hepatic virus diseases, which are among the most problems facing the liver, particularly Hepatitis B, as this virus is ranked by the World Health Organization (WHO) as the second most dangerous carcinogen in the world, after tobacco. Therefore, it is crucial to identify this harmful virus as soon as possible. As a result, the field of machine learning has focused on the early detection of Liver Hepatitis, particularly virus B. In this paper, we surveyed machine and deep-learning liver disease diagnosis, particularly hepatitis B, and we demonstrated the findings of previous experimental studies and results, as well as the limitations and future work that is suggested in this area.

Keywords: Artificial Intelligence · Hepatitis B · Liver Diseases · Machine Learning · Deep Learning · DL · AI · HBV · HCV · HCC · ML

1 Introduction

The new technology directed it's towards to medical field that is called recently Biomedical fields, the field of artificial intelligence is used widely today in medical diagnosis In all medical specialties; especially the field of machine learning; which reduced the mortality rate and the treatments waste time by more accuracy of classification in diagnosis, patients may need for reviewing consultation of specialists, the developed technology introduced automated detection and diagnosis systems of diseases or illnesses to facilitate the diagnosis for specialists. Humans are prone to error, so it is not surprising that a patient may have over-diagnosis or under-diagnosis. If such problems the patient may receive unnecessary treatment which will be impacting the individual's health and economy.

© ICST Institute for Computer Sciences, Social Informatics and Telecommunications Engineering 2023
Published by Springer Nature Switzerland AG 2023. All Rights Reserved
R. Hou et al. (Eds.): BDTA 2021/2022, LNICST 480, pp. 97–116, 2023.
https://doi.org/10.1007/978-3-031-33614-0_8

Machine learning is used in the diagnosis of Hepatitis diseases using various algorithms for the learning machine such as neural networks and Naive Bayes that solved many problems of diagnosis [1].

Among the human body's largest organs is the liver, Therefore, the study in diagnosing diseases of this organ has great importance. Inflammation of the liver which called Hepatitis [2, 3], and [4]. Hepatitis is the most widespread and virulent of liver diseases, as it affects negatively the liver and makes more problems after a long time of inflammation that may appear later after the liver has been damaged especially in viral infections such as viruses B and C.

Epidemiology. In 2019, the World Organization of Health (WHO) reported annual chronic diagnoses of hepatitis B of around 300 million and nearly 820 thousand deaths, a primary cause of this death is cirrhosis, followed by hepatocellular carcinoma [5].

Hepatitis B infection is most common in the African Region of the World Health Organization and the Western Pacific Region, where 81 million and 116 million people, respectively, are chronically infected. There are 60 million infected people in the WHO Eastern Mediterranean Region, 18 million in the WHO South-East Asia Region, 14 million in the WHO European Region, and 5 million in the WHO Americas Region [5].

Hepatitis B is a chronic infection that can be fatal due to serious liver damage [6, 7]. As a result, trustworthy techniques for hepatitis B virus infection diagnosis were developed [8].

In recent years, almost all researchers have used a variety of deep and machine learning techniques, including CNN, RF, Neural Networks, SVM, KNN, Decision Trees, etc., to detect liver diseases.

For all of these reasons, we focused on the work that had already been done in this area. As a result, this paper introduced the diagnosis using machine learning and deep learning Studies, discussions, and limitations. The sections of this paper are organized as follows: Sect. 2 presented the Background of Hepatitis B, Machine and Deep Learning, Sect. 3 introduced the explanation of Machine and Deep Learning in Disease Diagnosis, Sect. 4 is a survey of the machine and deep learning methodologies, algorithms, and techniques for diagnosing liver disease, particularly hepatitis B, Sect. 5 introduced the Discussion and Limitations of Deep and Machine Learning for Diagnosing Liver Disease, and Sect. 6 concluded the paper.

2 Background

2.1 Hepatitis B Definition and Structure

The DNA virus from the Family: Hepadnaviridae Orthohepadna virus, a type of virus that can cause hepatitis B, infects liver cells, and then causes hepatocellular necrosis and inflammation in humans. Figure 1 shows the structure of the hepatitis B virus. According to Fig. 1, there are four layers to hepatitis B. They are as follows.

- An external surface envelope: Its structure consists of a 27 nm core, and an icosahedral nucleocapsid (4 nm).

- The surface layer (or envelope): known as the "surface antigen" or "HBsAg," is primarily made up of lipids and proteins.
- The basic particles: inner protein shell, or "HBCAg," contains viral DNA and enzymes used in HBV replication as well as ("DNA polymerase").
- The HBV nucleocapsid: is closely related to the antigenic major factor known as HBeAg (hepatitis B envelope antigen). Additionally, it appears as a soluble protein in serum.

2.2 Hepatitis B (CHB) Stages

Hepatitis B has consequence phases, which are summarized in Table 1. The following phases are sorted according to the hepatitis case or the sequenced phases of treatment [9], and [10].

Phase 1: Immune Tolerant Phase
'Immune tolerance phase' HBV DNA, HBeAg, and HBsAg are all produced during active HBV replication and are detectable in serum. The immune response is confined to the formation of anti-HBc antibodies (first IgM, then IgG), but this does not function to neutralize infection [9], and [10].

Phase 2: HBeAg-Positive CHB (Immune Reactive Phase)
Serum ALT levels are elevated (greater levels indicate a more aggressive reaction and hence more hepatocyte destruction), and chronic active hepatitis is apparent on hepatic ultrasound (USS) or biopsy [9], and [10].

Phase 3: Low Replicative Phase
HBV replication is minimal in patients in the low replicative phase, and HBV DNA levels are low or undetectable. Although HBeAg is negative, HBsAg remains positive [9], and [10].

Phase 4: HBeAg-Negative CHB
HBeAg-negative CHB is caused by a form of the HBV virus that is unable to generate HBeAg while still actively replicating. HBeAg-negative CHB can arise after periods of low replicative or HBeAg-positive CHB and is usually at a later stage in disease development [9], and [10].

Phase 5: HBsAg-Negative Phase
The 'HBsAg-negative phase' refers to the progression to the elimination of both HBsAg and HBeAg. Although HBV viral replication may continue, it is unlikely to be detected in serum. Once in the HBsAg-negative phase, there is a better result and a lower chance of liver problems, while HBV may reactivate in immunocompromised persons and remains a concern for organ donation [9], and [10].

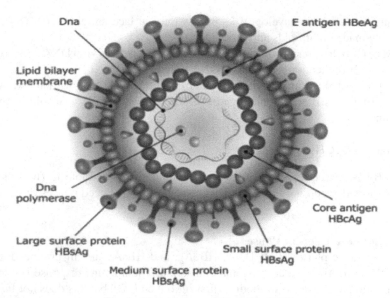

Fig. 1. The structure of Hepatitis B [4]

Table 1. The phases of Hepatitis B

	Acute HBV	Chronic HBV	Cleared HBV	Vaccination
HBcAb IgM	+	-	-	-
HBcAb IgG	+	+	+	-
HBsAg	+	+	-	-
Anti - HBs	-	-	+	+
HBeAg	+	-/+	-	-
Anti - HBe	-	-/+	-/+	-
HBV DNA	High/Low	Low/High	-	-

Stage	ALT	HBeAg	HBV DNA
Immune tolerant	Normal	Positive	High
Immune active	High	Positive/Negative	Low
Immune surveillance	Normal/Slightly raised	Mostly Negative	Low
Immune escape	High	Negative	High

2.3 Machine Learning

We have benefited from machine learning in several ways. Self-driving cars, Google Assistant, weather forecasting, image recognition, language translation, YouTube recommendation, and many other technologies have all benefited from it.

Supervised, unsupervised, and reinforcement learning are the three types of machine learning techniques; the following machine learning techniques and methods are summarized as follows: Linear Regression Methods, KNN Methods, Decision Tree Methods, K-Means Methods, Naive Classifier Methods, and Logistic regression analysis are used for regression, SVM (Support Vector Machine) techniques, Random Forest methods,

Dimensionality Reduction Algorithms, and Gradient boosting algorithms (XG Boost, GBM, Light GBM, and Cat Boost).

The most commonly used machine learning algorithms and approaches for identifying liver disease are SVM, K-Nearest Neighbor, Naive Bayes, and Decision Tree. Scientists and researchers strive to enhance machine learning techniques and procedures to achieve the highest level of categorization accuracy possible. The following is a definition of each method.

- Naive Bayes: This learning algorithm relies on the Bayes theorem and makes strong (naive) assumptions about independence. The metrics derived from training data essentially determine whether an object is related to a specific class.
- SVM (Support Vector Machine): This classifier technique assumes that there is a distinct difference between the data samples. Finding the best hyperplane to maximize the objective's class margin.
- K-Nearest Neighbor: This technique is used to resolve classification and regression issues. It measures all potential probabilities for data instances and then categorizes new ones using metrics for similarity as distance functions.
- Decision Tree: Used to create a training model that may be applied to learning straightforward decision rules produced from ad hoc data to forecast a trustworthy variable class. Trees are mainly composed of arcs and leaves. Each leaf represents a classification class, and each arc displays a feature taken from training data.

Additionally, machine learning finds that it is very beneficial in the fields of biology, health informatics, and medical sciences. Machine learning algorithms are now being taught to recognize cancer simply by examining an image. Such experiments are no longer just hypothetical; they are now a very real possibility. ML may be a good tool for predicting HCC recurrence. To provide a useful tool for the clinical care of HCC patients [11]. Also, ML algorithms seek to describe the strengths and limitations of ML, as well as its potential utility in prognostic prediction, following various HCC treatment regimens [12].

2.4 Deep Learning

Deep Learning (DL): is a machine learning subcategory in which an artificial neural network mimics the brain's ideas to process data, identify patterns, and reach conclusions. The core of the artificial neural network is interconnecting components called perceptron which is a simplified model of a functioning neuron. It has a way for input (of data) and output (of information). There are at least two input layers of a perceptron. In between these two layers, there can be many more layers sandwiched, these sandwiched hidden layers make up a 'deep' neural network. Deep learning is very good at finding a pattern and making predictions from analyzing huge amounts of data which can be incomprehensible to humans. The most crucial component of deep learning, which allows techniques and models to learn from training data and teach themselves, is the convolutional neural network. The procedures and algorithms outlined below are deep learning approaches.

1) Neural Network Convolutional
2) Long-Term Memory Network
3) RNN (Recurrent Neural Network)
4) Adversarial Generative Network
5) Network with Radial Basis Functions
6) Perceptron Multilayer
7) Self-Organization Model
8) Deep Belief Networks
9) Restricted Boltzmann Machine
10) Automatic encoders

3 Disease Diagnosis Using Deep Learning and Machine Learning

The medical sector is extremely complicated, particularly when identifying different diseases because many diseases may have symptoms that are similar and might result in an inaccurate diagnosis, and then fault Prescription is prescribed by doctors and may cause death for patients, Therefore, accuracy and clarity in diagnosis are crucial. The machine learning algorithms were based on the accuracy and precision in categorizing things and grouping comparable items in a proper method, as well as scientific equations generated by the machine learning algorithms.

To help clinicians and doctors overcome the constraints, and make wise, and accurate decisions in disease diagnosis, Methodologies of some disease diagnoses using machine learning (ML) algorithms have been recently reviewed [13]. Among these diseases is Liver disease which is the most important in diagnosis because of hidden almost symptoms and the lately almost symptoms that may lead to death. The examples listed below demonstrate how deep learning and machine learning have been applied to liver disease diagnosis and treatment.

3.1 Applying Machine Learning to Identify Liver Problems

In Liver Fibrosis Evaluation and Inflammation, a proprietary ML algorithm developed using a dataset of 2862 different biomarker clinical assessments was used to examine three major stages of liver lesions to detect fatty liver [14], even though other studies that used ML ideas for the detection of liver disease have been presented in a variety of ways [15].

Using Machine Learning in Hepatocellular Cancer

The most prevalent form of chronic liver disease worldwide is liver cirrhosis. The capacity to predict the start of liver cirrhosis disease is essential for effective treatment and the avoidance of grave health consequences. As a consequence, the researchers used machine learning to construct a prediction model to predict liver cirrhosis [16]. Although new machine-learning algorithms yielded accurate risk ratings for hepatocellular cancer in individuals with chronic viral hepatitis (HCC). The HCC ridge score was consistently more accurate than earlier HCC risk assessments. To develop efficient cancer monitoring strategies and reduce cancer-related mortality, new models might be used for electronic medical heath systems [17]. Although a very accurate HCC detection model has been built using individualized biological pathways analyses and machine learning methods. This model's outstanding interpretable performance and transferability make it ideal for customized medicine, assisting physicians in the identification of HCC patients. [18, 19].

3.2 Deep Learning for Liver Disease Prediction

Liver tumors have been divided into seven types using deep learning. The CNN approach performs effectively in separating benign from malignant liver tumors, unenhanced images are utilized (AUC, 0.95; 95% CI, 0.92–0.97 vs. 0.95; 0.92–0.98, P = 0.66). New CNN Combining clinical data with unassuming images significantly enhanced the efficacy of diagnosing cancers such as hepatocellular carcinoma [20]. Deep learning algorithms are also being used to forecast the long-term mortality serious risks of liver transplant recipients [21], and finally, a framework of deep learning is demonstrated for automatically predicting liver fibrosis, where the information has been provided by multiple ultrasound images for more accuracy [22].

4 Diagnosis Hepatitis B Using Machine and Deep Learning: Survey

The diagnosis of hepatitis B using machine and deep learning was presented in Sects. 4.1 and 4.2 respectively, to identify liver disorders, particularly hepatitis B, which have been sequenced from the oldest to the most recent order, the two following sections of 4.1, 4.2 summarized the previous studies that have been introduced in this area, and also presented in Table 2 and Table 3 respectively, where Table 2 summarizes studies in machine learning algorithms for hepatitis B diagnosis and Table 3 summarizes studies in deep learning algorithms for hepatitis B diagnosis, each table one and two contain authors and year of the study, techniques, and algorithms used, and finally results of each algorithm.

Table 2. Machine Learning Algorithms for Hepatitis

	Algorithm	Author	Year	Main Enhancements
NN Algorithms	MLP, RBF, CSFNN, C4.5, NB, TAN, BNND, BNNF	OZYILMAZ, L.,	2003	5. Fold cross-validation method outcomes are accuracy (81,3750 (average) 85, 90, 83,60 (max) 87,830 (max) 90,10 (max) 90 (max) 88,760 (max)) Respectively

(*continued*)

Table 2. (*continued*)

	Algorithm	Author	Year	Main Enhancements
	BPNN, RBFNN, PNN, GRNN	Panchal, D.,	2011	HBV is Positive IF (anti-VHD = Negative) AND (AgHBe = positive) AND (AgHBs = Positive)
	(MLNN)	Çetin, O.	2015	Classification accuracies for activation were 91.90% to 93.80% through 10-fold cross-validation
	ANFIS	Abtahi, S.,	2020	• The rapid, highly accurate estimation capability of the ANFIS observer • After each therapy session, the high ability of ANFIS can observe and predict the trend of safe and inflamed cells • The error rate is negligible. About 0.1% of errors are allowed at their maximum
DT and GB Algorithms	C4.5 Decision Tree	Shankarsowmien, V.,	2016	determining the abnormalities of the patient which resulted in 85.81% accuracy
	(J48), (LMT), (Random Forest), (Random Tree), (REP Tree), (Decision Stump) (Hoeffding Tree)	Nahar, N.,	2018	Classification Accuracy (65.69, 69.47, 69.30, 66.55, 66.13, 70.67, 69.75) Respectively

(*continued*)

Table 2. (*continued*)

	Algorithm	Author	Year	Main Enhancements
	GB-based	Wei, R.,	2018	In HBV and HCV cohorts. Consistent improvements compared to FIB-4
	(XG Boost), (RF), (DCT), And (LR))	Tian, X.,	2019	AUC (95% CI) [0.891 (0.889, 0.895), 0.829 (0.824, 0.834), 0.619 (0.614, 0.624), 0.680 (0.677, 0.683)] respectively
	SMOTE (XG Boost, RF, DT), XG Boost, RF, DT And (LR))	Wang, Y.,	2019	Accuracy (0.702, 0.681, 660, 0.711, 0.634, 0.719, 668) respectively
	Enhanced RF	Chen, S.,	2021	(AUC, 0.9660; 95% confidence interval, 0.9220–0.9890) with α-fetoprotein (0.7130; 6320– 7840)
	CART	Jameel, A.,	2022	CART with a sensitivity of 88%, an accuracy of 80%, and a specificity of 52%
	(GBM) algorithm	Kim, H.	2022	During an 8-year follow-up, the minimal-risk group (11.2% of the Korean cohort and 8.8% of the Caucasian cohort) had a risk of HCC of less than 0.5%
Support Vector Machine	A confusion matrix	Alamsyah, A.,	2021	The prediction accuracy for hepatitis was 93.55%

(*continued*)

Table 2. (*continued*)

Algorithm	Author	Year	Main Enhancements
SHAP	Obaido, G.,	2022	92% accuracy, 91% specificity, and 93% sensitivity, respectively. Meanwhile, both the decision tree and the SVM achieved 73% balanced accuracy

Table 3. Deep Learning Algorithms for Hepatitis

Algorithm	Author	Year	Main Enhancements
(SOM)	Uttreshwar, Gh. SH.,	2008	HBV is Positive If(AgHBs = Positive) and (anti-VHC = Negative) and (anti-VHD = Negative) and (AgHBe = Positive)
(DLRE)	Wang, K.,	2018	DLRE AUCs are 0.970 of F4 (95% CI 0.940 - 0.990), 0.980 of $\geq$ F3 (95% CI 0.960 - 1.000), and 0.850 (95% CI 0.810 - 0.890) of $\geq$ F2, which outperformed all other methods except 2D-SWE in $\geq$ F2
Pre-Trained Alex Net-CNN	Yu, Y.,	2018	Accurately and automatically score the stages of liver cirrhosis
(DLS) and LR	Choi, KJ.,	2018	AUROC For (F2–4), (F3–4), and (F4) are (0.960, 0.970, and 0.950), respectively, and an Accuracy of 79.40% (707 of 891)
DCNN Model	Yasaka K,	2018	The FDL score was related to the stage of fibrosis (correlation coefficient is 0.630; P, .001). The ROC curve of (F4, F3, and F2) are (0.840, 0.840, and 0.850), respectively

(*continued*)

Table 3. (*continued*)

Algorithm	Author	Year	Main Enhancements
SOM, ANFIS, DT	Nilashi, M.,	2019	Accuracy are K-NN = 71.410%, SVM = 81.170%, NN = 78.310%, ANFIS = 79.670%, NIPALS–SOM–ANFIS = 93.060%, PCA–LSSVM = 95.00%, PCA–AIRS = 94.120%, LFDA SVM = 96.770%, RES–ELM − 100%
(MLFFDNN)	Murty, S.,	2019	71.0%, 97%, 92%, 75.0%, 83%, and 98% for Nave Bayes, C4.5, AD Tree, SVM, RBF, and MLFFDNN, respectively
TL-ResNet101 model	Ali, S.,	2020	Accuracy, sensitivity, and AUC of 99.70%, 100%, and 98.70%, respectively, and compared with PCA-SVM and PCA-LDA and showed an increase in accuracy of more than 7.0%
HBSRS with DL Model	Guo, Z.,	2020	Accuracy GRU-MCNN SVM LDA KNN MLP CNN, 0.9680 ± 0.0060 0.9040 ± 0.0300 0.8150 ± 0.0940 0.7810 ± 0.0320 0.9350 ± 0.0070 0.9460 ± 0.0020 Precision is 0.9600 ± 0.0130 0.9420 ± 0.0220 0.8090 ± 0.1260 0.8710 ± 0.0310 0.9400 ± 0.0140 0.9400 ± 0.0090 Sensitivity is 0.9800 ± 0.0080 0.8390 ± 0.0630 0.8240 ± 0.0830 0.6460 ± 0.0750 0.9400 ± 0.0070 0.9590 ± 0.0030 Specificity is 0.9550 ± 0.0110 0.9610 ± 0.0380 0.8130 ± 0.0750 0.9250 ± 0.0540 0.9300 ± 0.0230 0.9310 ± 0.0070 AUC is 0.9500 ± 0.0100 0.9180 ± 0.0410 0.8090 ± 0.0530 0.8040 ± 0.0210 0.9250 ± 0.0130 0.9190 ± 0.0140

(*continued*)

Table 3. (*continued*)

Algorithm	Author	Year	Main Enhancements
Deep NN	Nam, J. Y.,	2020	cohort (PAGE-B [c-index 0.5700; 95% CI 0.5140–0.6260], CU-HCC [c-index 0.5480; 95% CI 0.4910–0.6040], HCC-RESCUE [c-index 0.5770; 95% CI 0.520–0.6320], ADRESS-HCC [c-index 0.5510; 95% CI 0.4950–0.6070
CNN	Wu, C.,	2021	The deep HBV With an AUROC of 0.9430 and an AUPR of 0.9310 after adding genomic features, the model significantly improved
METAVIR method	Zhu, Z.,	2021	the accuracy, sensitivity, specificity, precision, F1, MCC, and FMI were 88.13% ± 1.47% 81.45% ± 3.69%, 91.12% ± 1.72%, 80.49% ± 2.94%, 80.90% ± 2.39%, 72.36% ± 3.39%, and 80.94% ± 2.37%, respectively
Combined Mueller matrix	Pham, T.,	2022	As a consequence, five separate deep learning models—Xception, VGG16, VGG19, ResNet 50, and ResNet 150—take M22 and M33 as their inputs. The best classification accuracy (94.5%) is demonstrated to be achieved using the VGG19 model with element M22 as the input

4.1 Hepatitis B Using Machine Learning Algorithms

The following models and techniques of machine learning algorithms have been implemented for diagnosing hepatitis B, sorted from the oldest to the most recent, and grouped according to the unified machine learning techniques and summarized in Table 2.

Neural Network
In [23] A hybrid network has been applied successfully for the detection of hepatitis, it was introduced with the Results after standard feed-forward, and hybrid networks were both tested and proved that the hybrid network is more advanced than the feed-forward network (OZYILMAZ, L., 2003) [23]. Also in [24] The Hepatitis B virus has been

detected using the generalized neural network, which provided more effective results for determining whether the patient has Hepatitis B or not (Panchal, D., October 2011) [24].

Another form of NN algorithms is the approximations of the sigmoid function that have been applied as an activation function, This technique of hepatitis disease classification introduced an accuracy from 91.90% to 93.80% via ten-cross-validation using 10 folds that consist of a neural network with multiple layers and sigmoid activation functions, which are used to determine hepatitis disease (Çetin, O., 2015) [25].

The Adaptive Nero Fuzzy Integrated System (ANFIS) approach is implemented in [26] to generate a controller for the drug's dosage that is based on the number of viruses combined; the ANFIS system's superiority is reducing the required number of input variables to quantify the proper dosage; The ANFIS performs well in tracking the desired reducing virus replication (Abtahi, S., 2020) [26].

Decision Tree

The decision tree method is used for liver disease prediction where it constructs all possibilities of the disease's liver. The tree was built using the C4.5 algorithm, which used 19 features to diagnose liver diseases. These 19 attributes determined the abnormal results of the patient with 85.8% accuracy, Also To identify the early stages of liver disease, the author used classification tree algorithms (Shankar sowmien, V., Jun-Jul 2016) [27].

Different outcomes are produced via accuracy, precision, mean absolute error, kappa statistics, recall, and runtime; these study's findings, which evaluated and contrasted the performance of the methodologies utilized, showed that Decision Stump performed better than other algorithms (Nahar, N., Mar 2018) [28].

The author Used a random forest (RF) model, which takes into account (10 features) in [22], and illustrated the highest result for prediction accuracy both Cross-validation and independent validation resulted in accuracy, and AUC is 0.90, and 0.96, respectively, regardless of HBV genotypes or sequential depth. Moreover, HCC risk scores obtained from the RF model (confidence interval, 0.922–0.989 AUC, 0.96; 95%) performed better results in fetoprotein (0.713; 0.632–0.784) for categorizing HCC and CHB patients (Chen, S., June 2021) [29].

The prognosis of hepatitis disease classification is introduced by using the J48 decision tree algorithm. Where J48 predicted effective results with the highest classification rate and gives a better understanding regarding performance parameters as compared to CART with a sensitivity of 88%, an accuracy of 80%, and a specificity of 52% that will aid physicians (Jameel, A., 2022) [30].

Gradient Boosting

The study in [31] aimed to compare logistic regression (LR), decision tree (DCT), random forest (RF), and extreme gradient boosting (XGBoost), which are four well-known machine learning algorithms by regressing (HBsAg seroclearance), which is a substantial achievement for disease outcome of liver diseases during CHB treatment. The findings show that machine learning algorithms, specifically XGBoost, can predict exactly (HBsAg seroclearance) (Tian, X., Jun 2019) [31].

The author used machine learning for HBV and HCV-related hepatic fibrosis detection, he used gradient boosting (GB) to outperform other methods in addition to FIB-4 scores in the discovery data. The GB is based on the same parameters as FIB-4, and the GB prediction system produced consistent enhancements compared to FIB-4 in HCV and HBV cohorts with required values in different etiological groups (Wei, R., Sep 2018) [32].

Another study used Gradient Boosting to improve and validate models for recognizing communities at great risk that must be examined for hepatitis B surface antigen (HBsAg). The data were preprocessed using the borderline-synthetic minority oversampling technique (SMOTE), and four predictive models, including the extreme gradient boosting (X-GBoost), random forest (RF), decision tree (DT), and logistic regression (LR) algorithms, were developed in [33] (Wang, Y., December 2019)[33].

The GBM has the best predictive power for HCC risk in Korean and Caucasian patients with CHB and treated with entecavir or tenofovir. This model was used to develop and validate an artificial intelligence-based HCC risk prediction (Kim, H., February 2022) [34].

Support Vector Machine

A confusion matrix is used to assess classification performanc. The prediction accuracy for hepatitis was 93.55%. This result outperforms the results of support vector machine classification without the use of principal component analysis (Alamsyah, A., 2021) [35].

The predictions of machine learning models employed for hepatitis B diagnosis were explained and shown using Shapley Additive exPlanations (SHAP), a game-based theoretical method. The SHAP values revealed that bilirubin is the most important factor causing a greater death rate is bilirubin. As a result, elderly individuals with high bilirubin levels have a higher risk of passing away. The findings of this study can help medical professionals by providing an explanation of how machine learning models for health-related issues work (Obaido, G., 2022) [36].

4.2 Hepatitis B Using Deep Learning Algorithms

A self-organization map (SOM) is used to predict HBV accuracy; it's an efficacious tool for predicting normal hepatitis B based on lab results because it generates quicker and more accurate hepatitis prediction. (Uttreshwar, Gh. SH., 2008) [37].

The author improved the prognosis of chronic hepatitis B using Radiomics of shear wave elastography, by developing Deep Learn Radiomics elastography (DLRE), which outperforms two-dimensional shear wave elastography (2D-SWE) in terms of overall advancements in the prediction of the different stages of hepatic fibrosis (Wang, K., May 2018) [38].

Another deep learning study has been enhanced, that the author used deep learning for scoring liver fibrosis stages automatically, He evaluated several deep learning-based algorithms and machine learning algorithms and demonstrated that the pre-trained CNN's Alex Net-CNN by makes use of deep learning-based algorithms could automatically score stages of liver fibrosis with better accuracy comparable to non-linear MLR,

Conventional ANN (CNN), feature ranking-based RF algorithms, and linear SVM. (Yu, Y., Oct 2018) [39].

Another form of the deep learning algorithm is regression analysis which is implemented by using CT techniques and patient characteristics on the DLS staging accuracy in the liver, the author's objective was to validate and enhance a deep learning system (DLS) for trying to stage Fibrosis of the liver (Choi, KJ., Dec 2018) [40].

DCNN model has been used for more efficient results and differentiates between the stages of liver fibrosis and the fibrosis score [FDL score]; which was produced using the technique of deep learning (Yasaka K, April 2018) [41].

The author proposed employing ensemble learning to create an advanced, accurate way of diagnosing hepatitis, he used Iterative Non-linear using Partial Least Squares to duce data dimensionality, Clustering using the Self-Organizing Map technique, and Ensembles of Neuro-Fuzzy Inference Systems to predict the diagnosis of hepatitis disease; decision tree algorithms were also applied to select the most important attributes of the experimental input data. He implemented the technique to the test on a real dataset and compared the results to the most recent study results of previous research. The method of [34] outperforms ANFIS, K Nearest Neighbors (KNN), the Neural Network (NN), and the Support Vector Machine (SVM) (Nilashi, M., Feb 2019) [42].

A Deep Neural Network with Multiple Layers of Feed Forward (MLFFDNN) has been tuned to make more accurate prognostications concerning liver disease by trying to fit the appropriate number of hidden nodes and layers, and a function for dropping out after hiding each layer to remove overfitting, learning rate loss functions, activation functions, and bias should all be reduced to a minimum rate. (Murty, S., July 2019) [43].

A novel diagnostic technique for HBV diagnosis has been introduced by using the concept of transfer learning and deep neural networks with Images of Raman spectroscopy. The suggested technique was generated by implementing pre-trained neural networks with convolutions ResNet101 was trained on an actual HBV-infected blood plasma samples dataset that used transfer learning, and TL-ResNet101 was evaluated and achieved results with (100%, 99.70%, 98.70%, and 99.25%) classification sensitivity, accuracy, AUC, and specificity respectively were obtained. The recommended TL-ResNet101 method exceeded conventional methods like PCA-LDA and PCA-SVM with more than a 7% improvement in accuracy. The developed TL-ResNet101 model has high performance that has the potential to be used for HBV diagnosis (Ali, S., 2020) [44].

A newer method for detecting the Infection of the hepatitis B virus using human blood serum Raman spectroscopy in conjunction with a model of deep learning has been introduced, the principal component method was used to decrease the dimensionality of the data. The features of multiple scales were then prepared and fused using a multiscale fusion convolution operation. Time series features were extracted using a gated recurrent unit network and then the output was classified using a soft-max (Guo, Z., March 2020) [45].

The author developed deep learning architecture and introduced the SSAE algorithm for the diagnosis of three focal liver diseases in addition to the normal liver. The Unsupervised SSAE architecture can obtain high-level image features of input pixels. These characteristics enable the classifier to efficiently diagnose lesions from patient images.

In classification performance, the experimental findings showed that the softmax and SSAE classifier outperformed the KNN, Nave Bayes, and multi-SVM. (Hassan, T.M., Jan 2017) [46].

In [47], a new deep learning model for predicting HCC risk was presented; in patients with HBV- cirrhosis taking effective anti-viral, this model performed noticeably better than earlier models at predicting the risk of HCC [47] (Nam, J. Y., 2020).

The author introduced Deep HBV which predicts Sites for HBV integration that were discovered by automatically finding local genomic attributes. The Deep HBV model's efficiency improved after integrating genomic capabilities, the results of this study are 0.9430 for AUROC and 0.9310 for AUPR. Furthermore, the author used a convolution neural network to reinforce the transcription factors binding sites of proteins [48] (Wu, C., 2021).

For the automatic classification of liver fibrosis in chronic hepatitis B, the author proposed a 5-layer deep convolution neural network structure. There were three convolution layers and two fully connected layers in the 5-layer deep convolution neural network structure, and each convolution layer was connected with a pooling layer. 123 ADC images with Magnetic Resonance were collected, and it achieved more effective results (Zhu, Z., 2021) [49].

The detection of the hepatitis B (HB) virus using a combined Mueller matrix imaging technique and deep learning method, the Mueller matrix imaging polarimetry is applied to obtain 4×4 Mueller matrix images of 138 HBsAg-containing (positive) serum samples and 136 HBsAg-free (negative) serum samples. The kernel estimation density results show that, of the 16 Mueller matrix elements, elements M22 and M33 provide the best discriminatory power between the positive and negative samples (Pham, T., July 2022) [50].

The authors correctly highlight the accuracy of DL models for predicting severe fibrosis in CHB patients when compared to existing standards. We challenge them to assist us to take this knowledge to the next level. How can such models assist enhance patient care, how will they be used in real-time, and how will they help categorize patients at the bedside to avoid disease progression and change the natural history of CHB? (Verma, N., 2022) [51].

5   Discussion and Limitations (Future Work)

Hopefully, the ANFIS system will be able to work with scatter information (drug dosage) to only be used in diagnostic and therapeutic therapy as a treatment, assisting in how many drugs patients should be injected every day or every week. Doctors can also count the number of normal and inflamed cells after each drug injection. Non-incremental learning was also used to learn classification techniques in the ANFIS system. Furthermore, the developed ANFIS system does not support incremental learning and requires precomputing all of the training data to build the prediction models. It is proposed that the ANFIS system be designed to incrementally update the trained models as new data becomes available, making memory more efficient and accurate in memory requirements.

Hepatitis B will be diagnosed using diverse data samples from various sick people. The results of the experiments with diverse data will introduce good results using both neural networks and logical methodologies in the recognition of the hepatitis B Stage.

The advanced TL-ResNet101 model was contrasted to the most recent methods of (PCA – SVM) and (PCA – LDA), and it accomplished improvement in accuracy of 5.71% and 7.21%, respectively. The outcomes of the supervised classification suggest that it has to be used for low-cost clinical HBV diagnosis and treatment. This system can be expanded in the future to recognize other diseases.

The classification accuracy is low using MLP in some cases. MLP already does not provide relatively similar achievement for a single run as random weight initialization in training RBF, which presents good results. However, CSFNN has height accuracy for hepatitis diagnostic tests. For these results using a combination of RBF and MLP called hybrid network CSFNN is more reliable for the diagnosis than one only.

Classification accuracy obtained in some previously proposed models is 98%. In the future, it will try to improve accuracy even greater by using boosting methodologies and trying to deal with data sets with imbalances.

In the future, larger HBV cohorts may be used to train and learn machine learning models. It may be used to rebuild existing clinical scoring systems and could be implemented for different indicators in different disease cohorts.

In the future, deep learning-based algorithms will use irrelevant or weak image sources using a transfer learning approach to address the requirement of large datasets.

Although the method of using Raman spectroscopy tended to detect hepatitis B, it will believe that applicable to other spectroscopies and diseases by fine-tuning the proposed model, it may achieve this very efficiently.

Future research might focus on how to better combine the information from video and indicator images and how to fully encode the information from ultrasound video rather than just select frames.

Deep HBV, powerful deep learning for predicting HBV integration sites, was the first attempt to use CNNs for HBV integration prediction. Deep HBV's attention mechanism could be used to validate the genomic preference for HBV integration and provide a more comprehensive understanding of the mechanism underlying HBV-related cancer.

The future work of most papers is to expand research on the above algorithm and to bring the efficient discovery of emerging patterns.

6   Conclusion

In this paper we surveyed machine and deep-learning-based liver disease diagnosis focusing on hepatitis B, and we presented the findings and results of the last and earlier experimental studies, as well as the drawbacks and recommended future research in this field, and a summary of all studies has been provided in Tables 2 and 3, which verify the experimental results, authors, models, and years of the studies.

References

1. Karlik, B.: Hepatitis disease diagnosis using backpropagation and the Naive Bayes classifiers. J. Sci. Technol. 1(1), 49–62 (2011)
2. https://www.niddk.nih.gov/health-information/liver-disease/viral-hepatitis/hepatitis-b. Last accessed 22 Dec 2022

3. Frank, H. Netter, M.D.: Atlas of Human Anatomy, 3rd edition, Icon Learning Systems, 2002 ISBN 10: 1929007116 ISBN 13: 9781929007110

4. Young, B., O'Dowd, G., Woodford, Ph.: Wheatear's Functional Histology 4th edn. Churchill Livingstone (2000)

5. https://www.who.int/news-room/fact-sheets/detail/hepatitis-b. 27 Jul 2021

6. British Liver Trust: "Fighting liver disease", A professional's guide to Hepatitis B

7. Terrault, N., Lok, A., McMahon, B.: Update on prevention, diagnosis, and treatment of chronic Hepatitis B: AASLD 2018 Hepatitis B guidance. Hepatology 67(4), 1560–1599 (2018)

8. Villar, L., Cruz, H., Barbosa, J.: Update on Hepatitis B and C virus diagnosis. World J. Virol. 4(4), 323–342 (2015). https://doi.org/10.5501/wjv.v4.i4.323

9. Aspinall, E.J., Hawkins, G., Fraser, A., Hutchinson, S.J., Goldberg, D.: Hepatitis B prevention, diagnosis, treatment and care: a review. Occup. Med. 61(8), 531–540 (2011). https://doi.org/10.1093/occmed/kqr136

10. Liaw, Y.F., Chu, C.M.: Hepatitis B virus infection. Lancet 373(9663), 582–592 (2009). https://doi.org/10.1016/S0140-6736(09)60207-5. PMID: 19217993

11. Mega, A., et al.: Supervised machine learning techniques for the prediction of hepatocellular carcinoma recurrence. J. Surg. Res 05(02), 238–251 (2022)

12. Zou, Z.-M., Chang, D.-H., Liu, H., Xiao, Y.-D.: Current updates in machine learning in the prediction of therapeutic outcome of hepatocellular carcinoma: what should we know? Insights Imaging 12(1), 1–13 (2021). https://doi.org/10.1186/s13244-021-00977-9

13. Bhavsar, K.A., Singla, J., Al-Otaibi, Y.D., et al.: Medical diagnosis using machine learning: a statistical review. Comput. Mater. Continua 67(1), 107–125 (2021)

14. Aravind, A., Bahirvani, A., Quiambao, R., Gonzalo, T.L.: Machine learning technology for evaluation of liver fibrosis, inflammation activity and steatosis (LIVERFAStTM). J. Intell. Learn. Syst. Appl. 12, 31–49 (2020). https://doi.org/10.4236/jilsa.2020.122003. https://www.scirp.org/journal/journalarticles.aspx?journalid=102

15. Tanwar, N., Rahman, Kh.: Machine learning in liver disease diagnosis: current progress and future opportunities. IOP Conf. Series: Mater. Sci. Eng. 1022, 012029 (2021). https://doi.org/10.1088/1757899X/1022/1/012029

16. Jamila, G., Wajiga, G.M., Malgwi, Y.M., Maidabara, A.H.: A diagnostic model for the prediction of liver cirrhosis using machine learning techniques. Comput. Sci. IT Res. J. 3(1), 36–51 (2022). https://doi.org/10.51594/csitrj.v3i1.296

17. Wong, G., Hui, V., Tan, Q.: Novel machine learning models outperform risk scores in predicting hepatocellular carcinoma in patients with chronic viral Hepatitis. JHEP Reports 4, 100441 (2022). https://doi.org/10.1016/j.jhep.2022.100441

18. Cheng, B., Zhou, P., Chen, Y.: Machine-learning algorithms based on personalized pathways for a novel predictive model for the diagnosis of hepatocellular carcinoma. BMC Bioinform. 23, 248 (2022). https://doi.org/10.1186/s12859-022-04805-9

19. Kawka, M., Dawidziuk, A., Jiao, L.R., Gall, T.M.H.: Artificial intelligence in the detection, characterisation and prediction of hepatocellular carcinoma: a narrative review. Trans. Gastroenterol. Hepatol. 7, 41–41 (2022). https://doi.org/10.21037/tgh-20-242

20. Zhen, S., Cheng, M., Cai, X., et al.: Deep learning for accurate diagnosis of liver tumor based on magnetic resonance imaging and clinical data. Front. Oncol. 10, 680 (2020). https://doi.org/10.3389/fonc.2020.00680

21. Nitski, O., Azhie, A., Ali Qazi-Arisar, F., et al.: Long-term mortality risk stratification of liver transplant recipients: real-time application of deep-learning algorithms on longitudinal data. The Lancet Dig. Health 3(5), e295–e305 (2021). https://doi.org/10.1016/S2589-7500(21)000 40-6. www.thelancet.com/digital-health

22. Liu, J., Wang, W., Guan, T., Zhao, N., et al: Ultrasound Liver Fibrosis Diagnosis using Multi-indicator guided Deep Neural Networks. arXiv: 2009.04924v1 [eess.IV] 10 Sep 2020

23. Ozyilmaz, L., Yildirim, T.: Artificial neural networks for diagnosis of Hepatitis disease. In: Proceedings of the International Joint Conference on Neural Networks, vol. 1, pp. 586–589 (2003). https://doi.org/10.1109/IJCNN.2003.1223422
24. Panchal, D., Shah, S.: Artificial intelligence based expert system for Hepatitis B diagnosis. Int. J. Model. Optim. **1**(4), 362–366 (2011)
25. Çetin, O., Temurtaş, F., Gülgönül, Ş: An application of multilayer neural network on Hepatitis disease diagnosis using approximations of sigmoid activation function. Dicle Med. J. **42**(2), 150–157 (2015). https://doi.org/10.5798/diclemedj.0921.2015.02.0550
26. Abtahi, S., Sharifi, M.: Machine Learning Method to Control and Observe for Treatment and Monitoring of Hepatitis B Virus. arXiv. https://doi.org/10.48550/arXiv.2004.09751 (2020)
27. Shankar Sowmien, V., Sugumaran, V., Karthikeyan, C.P., et al.: Diagnosis of Hepatitis using Decision tree Algorithm. Int. J. Eng. Technol. (IJET) **8**(3), 1414–1419 (2016)
28. Nahar, N., Ara, F.: Liver disease prediction by using different decision tree techniques. Int. J. Data Min. Knowl. Manag. Process **8**(2), 01–09 (2018)
29. Chen, S., Zhang, Z., Wang, Y., Fang, M., et al.: Using Quasispecies patterns of Hepatitis B virus to predict hepatocellular carcinoma with deep sequencing and machine learning. J Infect Dis. **223**(11), 1887–1896 (2021). https://doi.org/10.1093/infdis/jiaa647. PMID: 33049037
30. Jameel, A., Bajwa, I., Ponum, M.: Prognosis of Hepatitis Disease Classification using Non-Linear Compound Algorithms. 14 Sep 2022. https://doi.org/10.21203/rs.3.rs-2022961/v1
31. Tian, X., Chong, Y., Huang, Y., et al.: Using machine learning algorithms to predict Hepatitis B surface antigen seroclearance. Comput. Math. Methods Med. **2019**, 6915850 (2019). https://doi.org/10.1155/2019/6915850
32. Wei, R., Wang, J., Wang, X., et al.: Clinical prediction of HBV and HCV-related hepatic fibrosis using machine learning. EBioMedicine **35**, 124–132 (2018)
33. Wang, Y., Du, Z., Lawrence, W.R., et al.: Predicting hepatitis B virus infection based on health examination data of community population. Int. J. Env. Res. Public Health **16**(23), 4842 (2019)
34. Kim, H., Lampertico, P., Nam, J.: An artificial intelligence model to predict hepatocellular carcinoma risk in Korean and Caucasian patients with chronic Hepatitis B. J. Hepatol. **76**(2), 311–318 (2022)
35. Alamsyah, A., Fadila, T.: Increased accuracy of prediction Hepatitis disease using the application of principal component analysis on a support vector machine. J. Phys.: Conf. Ser. **1968**(1), 012016 (2021)
36. Obaido, G., et al.: An interpretable machine learning approach for Hepatitis B diagnosis. Appl. Sci. **12**(21), 11127 (2022)
37. Uttreshwar, G.S., Ghatol, A.A.: Hepatitis B diagnosis using logical inference and self-organizing map. J. Comput. Sci. **4**(12), 1042–1050 (2008)
38. Wang, K., Lu, X., Zhou, H., et al.: Deep learning Radiomics of shear wave elastography significantly improved diagnostic performance for assessing liver fibrosis in chronic Hepatitis B: a prospective multicentre study. Gut **68**(4), 729–741 (2019). https://doi.org/10.1136/gutjnl-2018-316204
39. Yu, Y., et al.: Deep learning enables automated scoring of liver fibrosis stages. Sci. Rep. **8**(1), 1–10 (2018)
40. Choi, K.J., Jang, J.K., Lee, S.S., et al.: Development and validation of a deep learning system for staging liver fibrosis by using contrast agent-enhanced CT images in the Liver. Radiology **289**(3), 688–697 (2018). https://doi.org/10.1148/radiol.2018180763. Epub 2018 Sep 4 PMID: 30179104
41. Yasaka, K., Akai, H., Kunimatsu, A., Abe, O., Kiryu, S.: Liver fibrosis: deep convolutional neural network for staging by using gadoxetic acid-enhanced hepatobiliary phase MR images. Radiology **287**(1), 146–155 (2018). https://doi.org/10.1148/radiol.2017171928. Epub 2017 Dec 14 PMID: 29239710

42. Nilashi, M., Ahmadi, H., Shahmoradi, L., Ibrahim, O., Akbari, E.: A predictive method for Hepatitis disease diagnosis using ensembles of neuro-fuzzy technique. J. Infect. Public Health **12**(1), 13–20 (2019). https://doi.org/10.1016/j.jiph.2018.09.009

43. Murty, S.V., Kumar, R.K.: Enhanced classifier accuracy in liver disease diagnosis using a novel multi layer feed forward deep neural network. Int. J. Recent Technol. Eng. (IJRTE) **8**(2), 1392–1400 (2019). https://doi.org/10.35940/ijrte.B2047.078219

44. Ali, S., Hassan, M., Saleem, M., Tahir, S.F.: Deep transfer learning-based Hepatitis B virus diagnosis using spectroscopic images. Int. J. Imaging Syst. Technol. **31**(1), 94–105 (2021)

45. Guo, Z., Lv, X., Yu, L., Zhang, Z., Tian, S.: Identification of Hepatitis B using Raman spectroscopy combined with gated recurrent unit and multiscale fusion convolutional neural network. Spectrosc. Lett. **53**(4), 277–288 (2020). https://doi.org/10.1080/00387010.2020.1737944

46. Hassan, T.M., Elmogy, M., Sallam, E.S.: Diagnosis of focal liver diseases based on deep learning technique for ultrasound images. Arab. J. Sci. Eng. **42**(8), 3127–3140 (2017). https://doi.org/10.1007/s13369-016-2387-9

47. Nam, J.Y., Sinn, D.H., Bae, J., Jang, E.S., Kim, J.W., Jeong, S.H.: Deep learning model for prediction of hepatocellular carcinoma in patients with HBV-related cirrhosis on antiviral therapy. JHEP Rep. **2**(6), 100175 (2020)

48. Wu, C., Guo, X., Li, M., et al.: Deep HBV: a deep learning model to predict Hepatitis B virus (HBV) integration sites. BMC Ecol Evo **21**, 138 (2021). https://doi.org/10.1186/s12862-021-01869-8

49. Zhu, Z., Lv, D., Zhang, X.: Deep learning in the classification of stage of liver fibrosis in chronic Hepatitis B with magnetic resonance ADC images. Contrast Media Mol. Imaging **2021**, 2015780 (2021). https://doi.org/10.1155/2021/2015780

50. Pham, T.-T.-H., Nguyen, H.-P., Luu, T.-N.: Combined Mueller matrix imaging and artificial intelligence classification framework for He/patitis B detection. J. Biomed. Opt. **27**, 075002 (2022). https://doi.org/10.1117/1.JBO.27.7.075002

51. Verma, N., Asrani, S.K.: Deep learning and non-invasive assessment of significant fibrosis: does adding more toppings improve the flavor of prediction? Hepatol. Int. **16**, 492–494 (2022). https://doi.org/10.1007/s12072-022-10329-4

Using Grasshopper Optimization in Big Data

Asmaa G. Khalf[1(✉)] and Kareem Kamal A. Ghany[2]

[1] Faculty of Computers and Information, Beni-Seuf University, Beni Suef, Egypt
Asmaagaber95@fcis.bsu.edu.eg
[2] Faculty of Computers and Information, Sadat Academy, Cairo, Egypt

Abstract. From algorithms that have been popular and presently used in meta-heuristic is the grasshopper optimization method, which has made many theoretical breakthroughs and is widely applied in numerous optimization issues across different fields such as image processing, machine learning, engineering design, control over wireless networking, power systems, and other things. In this study, we review the literature that is currently accessible on the grasshopper optimization technique and its extensions to the chaotic, binary, multi-objective scenarios and hybrid. Finally, the grasshopper optimization algorithm has proven superior to other optimization algorithms in most literature.

Keywords: Grasshopper Optimization · Data Mining · Meta-heuristic Optimization

1 Introduction

Optimization determines the optimal value of a specific problem variable to reduce or increase the target function. There are optimal problems in all areas of the study. There are several steps you can take to resolve an optimization problem. First, the problem's parameters must be determined. The problems can be categorized as either discrete or continuous depending on the type of parameters. Second, it's important to understand the restrictions placed on the parameters. Restrictions separate unrestricted and restricted optimization problems. Third, it is necessary to look through and consider the supplied problem's objectives. In this instance, optimization issues are separated into issues with many objectives and issues with a single target. An appropriate optimizer should be chosen and used to solve the problem based on the number of targets identified, the types of parameters, and the limitations [1]. Examples of optimization are all areas such as business, personnel management, sophisticated engineering planning, transportation problems, winning proposals and industrial applications [2]. Before humans existed on this planet, nature used evolution to solve difficult problems all the time. In the field of optimization, the Netherlands proposed a revolutionary idea in 1977 when simulating evolutionary concepts in nature on a computer to solve optimization problems [3].

R. Hou et al. (Eds.): BDTA 2022, LNICST 480, pp. 117–136, 2023.
https://doi.org/10.1007/978-3-031-33614-0_9

Many optimization mechanisms have been used to solve many complicated problems in various fields, including engineering applications, machine learning, data mining, text mining, networks, economics, medicine, energy, and others. Optimization algorithms are mostly used to find the best solution by combining different ideal values to provide a candidate solution that solves the underlying problem. Typically, meta-heuristic optimization algorithms work by minimizing or maximizing the objective function to arrive at the ideal value and arrive at the optimum choice. Finding the best choice value from a range of feasible options is the main objective of decision-making. The ultimate objective of optimization methods is to identify the best decision value among all potential solutions.

Many research topics in optimization fields have recently remained interesting. They require promising solutions owing to their realism in life and nature, like problems with an industrial nature, problems with mathematics, problems with the real world, and other problems. These problems are referred to as hard optimization problems. [4]. Typically, utilizing the various optimization techniques available, the main purpose is to maximize or minimize the fitness function or objective function of a problem to find the optimum solution. Four categories can be used to classify optimization problems: the first group includes multi-objective or single problems, and the second category contains constrained and unconstrained problems. The third category contains dynamic or static problems. The fourth category explores discrete and continuous problems. The following steps describe steps for solving optimization problems.

1. Describe each variable separately. Create a diagram with all variables labeled, if applicable.
2. Determine the range of values for the other variables and the quantity that will be minimized or maximized (if at this time this can be set).
3. Making use of the variables, develop an formula to minimize or maximize the quantity. Multiple variables could be used in this formula.
4. The quantity that has to be minimized or maximized as one variable in this function should be written down using any equations find in step 3 in the formula relating the independent variables with these equations.
5. To solve the physical problem, choose the domain of consideration for the function in step 4.
6. From step 4, determine the maximum and lowest values of the function. Typically, this stage entails looking for important places and testing a function at endpoints.

Recently, a number of biologically or naturally inspired algorithms have been developed to locate nearly ideal answers to a variety of challenging optimization issues. These algorithms have demonstrated success in resolving actual optimization issues. Additionally, its superior searchability and ability to handle large instances make it a superior choice over other methods. In general, Optimization algorithms research things that happen in nature, like animals looking for food [3]. The four major categories of optimization algorithms are human-based, swarm-based, evolution-based, and physics-based. Evolutionary algorithms (EAs) use methods like recombination that are inspired by biological evolution, mutation, crossover, and the inheritance of traits in offspring [5]. When solving optimization problems, potential solutions are represented as members of a population, and the answers' quality depends on the fitness function. Differential evolution (DE) [6] and the genetic algorithm [7] are two major EAs inspired by biological evolution.

The swarm optimization algorithms are algorithms that mimic the mass behavior of living creatures. The best mass behaviour is achieved through interaction between living things [8]. An offshoot is particle swarm optimization [9], which mimics the hunting behavior of groups of fish and birds, we use physics in physics-based algorithms to create variables that facilitate the search for the ideal answer within the search scope [10,11]. Some of the most popular categories in this branch are electromagnetism optimization (EMO) [12] and the gravitational search algorithm [13]. Human-based algorithms are inspired by human gregarious demeanor. The main algorithms in this branch are the election campaign algorithm [14], the heap-based optimizer (HBO) [15] and teaching-learning-based optimization.

The main goal of this paper is to survey previously published articles using the GOA. This paper has carried out a comprehensive study of all the perspectives of the GOA as well as the researcher's viewpoints. In addition, we investigate how interesting academics employ grasshopper optimization algorithms to tackle a variety of optimization problems in complicated applications.

2   Grasshopper Optimization Algorithm

The Grasshopper Algorithm (GA), which is inspired by honey badger behavior in nature, is described in this section along with its mathematical model.

A new metaheuristic algorithm called GOA was created by Saremi et al. based on a productive population that was inspired by nature. To promote grasshopper insects' in the wild exhibiting their ideal, polite demeanour in 2017. For global unlimited/unlimited optimization and different practical jobs, this algorithm can deliver enhanced results and scientific understanding. The baseline GOA was utilised to determine the optimal proton exchange (PEMFC) parameters, and the results highlighted the viability of GOA-based rhythm while dealing with steady-state models and dynamic [16]. 2016 Wu et al. [17] a GOA was suggested to streamline the UAV distribution path in an urban environment. They showed that this algorithm could achieve satisfactory satisfaction paths and improved results. The basics GOA are developed with multiple objectives by Tharwat et al. Restricted and Mirjalili et al. [18] and the proposed algorithm can solve multiple reference problems more efficiently and effectively in terms of the optimal distribution and accuracy of individual solutions.

The grasshoppers move slowly and take small steps, which is the most distinguishing feature of the swarm of larvae. On the other hand, the adult swarm's key trait is long-term, abrupt movement. The locusts' quest for a food supply is another significant aspect of them. As was explained in the introduction session, nature-inspired algorithms logically divide the research process into two trends:

exploitation and exploration. During operations, search agents although they often move locally during an operation, sudden movement is encouraged. These two capabilities are incorporated, as well as the trainees' ability to search for a certain part of the course. So, if we can find out a mathematical way to do it, we can come up with a new algorithm inspired by nature. This is exactly what we do. There are three stages in a grasshopper's life cycle: The three stages of development are the egg, the nymph, and the adult. At any time throughout the swarm, you can find a grasshopper. From nymph to adulthood, it goes through all stages of its life cycle [19]. Figure 1 shows The life, in general, is depicted.

Fig. 1. The grasshopper's life cycle [1].

The mathematical model that was applied to replicate the behavior of a swarm of grasshoppers is as follows: The mathematical model that was utilized to replicate the behavior of swarms of grasshoppers is shown in the table below:

$$X_i = G_i + S_i + A_i \tag{1}$$

where X_i determines the position of the i-th grasshopper, A_i depicts wind addiction, S_i represents the gravitational pull on it, and G_i represents social interaction. Be aware that the equation $X_i = v_1 G_i + v_2 S_i + v_3$ can be written to produce random behavior. A_i, where [0, 1] random integers v_1, v_2, and v_3 are used.

$$G_i = \sum_{\substack{J=1 \\ J \neq 1}}^{N} g(d_{ij})\widehat{d_{ij}} \tag{2}$$

between the ith and jth grasshoppers, there is a distance of d_{ij} and can be calculated as $d_{ij} = |X_j - X_i|$. In Eq. 1, The social force's strength is denoted by

G and determined by Eq (3) by using

$$\widehat{d_{ij}} = \frac{x_j - x_i}{d_{ij}}$$

The unit vector between the ith and j-th grasshoppers can be calculated The function that calculates the social forces is determined as:

$$g(v) = fe^{\frac{v}{l}} - e^{-v} \tag{3}$$

where the density of attraction is exemplified by f and the attractive length scale is referenced by l. The S component in Eq. (1) is calculated as:

$$S_i = -s\widehat{e_s} \tag{4}$$

Here the gravitational constant is represented by s and and the vector pointing toward the centre of the earth is denoted by the letter $\widehat{e}_s$. (1)'s A component is calculated as:

$$A_i = \widehat{ue_w} \tag{5}$$

In this case, u stands for the continuous drift and $\widehat{e}_g$ is the unity vector for the wind direction. The equation changes when G. S. and A are substituted in Eq. (1).

$$x_i = \sum_{j=1,j\neq i}^{N} s(|x_j - x_i|)\frac{x_j - x_i}{d_{ij}} - g\widehat{e_g} + u\widehat{e_w} \tag{6}$$

N then stands for the number of grasshoppers. Because Eq. (6) inhibits the program from exploring and taking advantage of the search space close to a solution, it is not used in the optimization method. This model of a grasshopper nymph represents an open-air grasshopper swarm. Furthermore, the swarm doesn't congregate at a single location because the grasshoppers reach their comfort zone fast, the optimization issues were not immediately addressed by this mathematical model. In order to address optimization issues, a modified version of Eq. (6) is applied:

$$X_i^d = c_1\left(\sum_{j=1,j\neq 1}^{N} c_2\frac{ub_d - lb_d}{2}g([x_j^d - x_i^d])\frac{x_j - x_i}{d_{ij}}\right) + \widehat{T_d} \tag{7}$$

Here are appeared the lower and upper borders by lb_d and ub_d, respectively, the aimed value and the best solution are represented by T_d, whereas c_2 and c_1 are the coefficients to shrivel the repulsion zone, attraction zone, and comfort zone. It is assumed in this equation that the wind always blows in the direction of a target T_d and that the gravity component is not used. The target's position, its present location, and the locations of every other grasshopper are used to determine the grasshopper's subsequent location.

The next position of a grasshopper is determined based on its current position, global best, and the positions of all other search agents, as shown in Eq. (7). In other words, GOA mandates that all search agents participate in determining each grasshopper's future position. It is important to note that the initial part of Eq. (7) decreases the agent's motions around the target. In contrast, the second portion of the equation allows for the direction of the existing grasshopper to other grasshoppers in the area. In particular, the parameter c_1 is in charge of limiting grasshopper moves around the target, which means that c_1 balances the swarm's widespread exploitation and exploration. On the other hand, the parameter c_2 decreases the attraction zone, comfort zone, and repulsion zone between grasshoppers, i.e., c_2 linearly decreases the space to guide the grasshoppers to find the optimal solution in the search space. A related point to consider is that the adaptive parameter c_1 contributes to the reduction in repulsion or attraction forces among grasshoppers proportional to the number of iterations, while the c_2 reduces the search coverage around the target as the number of iteration increases. To maintain a balance between exploration and exploitation, c_1 is dropped proportionally as the amount of iterations rises. With the help of this strategy, GOA was able to carry out efficient exploitation in the optimization's final stages.

Similar to this, the values of c_2 are dropped to reduce the comfort level about a rise in the number of iterations. The arguments c_1 and c_2 are treated as one parameter for the following modification:

$$c = c\max - I\frac{c\max - c\min}{N} \tag{8}$$

where I denotes the number of current iterations and N denotes the total number of iterations. The highest and lowest values of c are denoted by cmax and cmin, respectively. The mature swarm is distinguished by abrupt, distant movements. In contrast, In the nymph phase, the swarm moves slowly and with small cricket steps. A crucial characteristic of grasshoppers is their constant quest for food sources. The two primary stages of nature-inspired algorithms exploitation and exploration are designed to speed up convergence and/or prevent local optima from forming when the algorithm is looking for a target. Search agents frequently move in the search space locally while operating. Nevertheless, during the exploratory process, they are urged to move quickly. Both of these actions are carried out by locusts in a natural manner in search of their prey (food source). The authors conducted in depth tests to examine the behaviour of grasshoppers with various values of the attractive length scale and the intensity of attraction, and they discovered that repulsion occurs between any two grasshoppers if their distances fall within the range [0, 2.079]. Grasshoppers enter their comfort zones when they are 2.079 units apart from one another. The conceptual model of the comfort zone and the forces that draw grasshoppers together and away from each other are shown in Fig. 2. The swarm in the nymph stage is a characteristic of slow movements with small cricket levels. Revenge, the swarm, and a phase maturity characterize the sudden and distant movements. Discover the grasshoppers' unique characteristics and their sources of nourishment. When

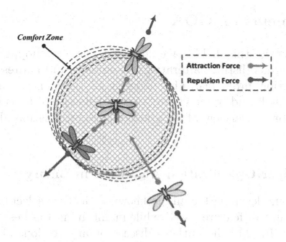

Fig. 2. The comfort zone of grasshopper [20].

searching for a goal, algorithms that are inspired by nature typically go through two stages: exploration and exploitation. These two steps aim to speed up convergence and/or prevent local optimization. During the activation phase, search agents frequently relocate locally inside the search region. While the review is taking place, feel free to move suddenly. Both of these actions are equally carried out by locusts in a natural manner.

Beginning with a sequence of initial random solutions (grasshoppers), GOA determines the applicability of each of these solutions. Locust updates its positions based on the equations many researchers in this field have modified the grasshopper optimization method for numerous distinct alterations to manage and handle different challenging problems of optimization. Modifications are mostly in (binary, hybridized, adjusted, and variants that are listed beneath) will now be covered, nevertheless not comprehensive. A brief overview of all grasshopper optimization algorithm types and vers. The best grasshopper (target) location is updated for each iteration. Additionally, the normalizing of the grasshopper distances from 1 to 4 and the calculation of the current position is done with each iteration. Iteratively updating the grasshopper's location until the stop condition is satisfied. The best estimation of the total optimal is then returned, known as the good goal(target) [20].

When there is a distance of [0, 2.079] between two locusts, there is a repulsive force, and when there is a distance of 2.079 between the two locusts, there is neither an attraction nor a repulsion to create a comfortable area. The gravitational force progressively increases and diminishes by 4 for distances greater than 2.079. To address this issue, the distance between the locusts is specified in [1, 4]. If the distance between the two locusts is larger than 10, the function cannot have force between the locusts. The study shown above demonstrates the grasshopper optimization algorithm's suitability for problems with illogical optimal solutions.

3 Developments on GOA

Many researchers in this field have modified the grasshopper optimization method for numerous distinct alterations to manage and address various challenging optimization problems. The majority of these modifications (binary, hybridized, modified, and other variants listed below) will be covered, but not exhaustively. A brief overview of all grasshopper optimization algorithm types and versions.

3.1 Grasshopper Optimization Algorithm in Binary

A complex machine learning technique known as feature selection (FS) is used to limit the amount of features used while maintaining the best level of classification accuracy. In [20], the authors discuss binary versions of the technique of the Grasshopper optimization for choosing the ideal subset of classification to features for goals inside of an envelope-based framework. The sigmoid model (transfer function) is the first strategy used to produce an algorithm for binary locust optimization, and function of V-shaped (transfer function) is the second technique, which is referred to as BGOA-V and BGOA-S, respectively.

3.2 Grasshopper Optimization Algorithm Modifications

In [21], improved Grasshopper optimization method is presented to handle optimization problems such as financial stress prediction (prediction) problems and continuous optimization. Grasshopper is a recently developed optimization method inspired by the clustering process of the grasshopper in real life. This approach has been proven to be beneficial for solving numerous global problems of optimization (unconstrained and constrained). Nonetheless, The original Grasshopper optimization process has several weaknesses, for example, becoming stuck in optimum, slowing its the velocity of convergence. To overcome these issues, an enhanced Grasshopper optimization method has been presented, three search strategies (operators) are combined to improve the balance of search strategies like exploration and exploitation.

3.3 Chaotic Grasshopper Optimization Algorithm

To accelerate global convergence, chaos theory systems are incorporated into the optimization techniques of the Grasshopper optimization algorithm [22]. Chaotic system maps are employed in optimization procedures to create a fair and efficient balance between exploring and exploiting search techniques, as well as to lessen the operative forces of attraction and repulsion (discord) between grasshoppers. The results revealed that chaotic system mappings are typically beneficial in improving performance. Especially, the circular map is thought to be the optimum map for the best outcomes when running the grasshopper optimization method.

3.4   Grasshopper Optimization Algorithm Hybridizations

In [19], Two main optimization issues are addressed by a hybrid Grasshopper optimization method with opposition-based learning (OBL). Namely technical optimization problems and benchmark test functions. This hybridization is known as OBLGOA. There are two phases in the suggested Grasshopper optimization technique. In the first phase, the opposing learning process is used to produce the initial solution approaches and their opposite. Opposition-based learning is incorporated into the population of the Grasshopper optimization algorithm in the second phase as a new step in each generation. However, opposition-based learning is used in a balanced population to reduce lead times. The GOA-SVM approach was published in [23] as a hybrid classification strategy for computational seizure exposure in EEG that uses a support vector machine and a Grasshopper optimization algorithm. Several fitting parameters are chosen and used as leaders in the radial support function kernel function classification strategy to train support vector machines. To acquire a good EEG classification, The subset of valuable features and the best support vector machine parameter values are chosen using the Grasshopper optimization procedure. The test results showed that the suggested approach is capable of detecting the start of epileptic seizures in healthy individuals, and as a result, it might enhance the study of epilepsy with a high accuracy rate (100%).

4   Applications of Grasshopper Optimization Algorithm

The GOA algorithm is able to outperform other methods and get beyond the challenges of multi-goal research space. Additionally, the computational complexity of this optimization strategy is less difficult than many others described in the literature. Our efforts to develop certain applications and strategies that employed GOA to tackle their challenges were motivated by these potent capabilities.

Data clustering, also known as the division of a huge data set into discrete groups of comparable structure, is a crucial issue in data analysis and study. Several clustering strategies that use either mathematical or heuristic methods can be used to tackle this data clustering challenge. The main components of heuristic approaches often consist of a wide range of instruments that are helpful in nature's active optimizers. The potential application of a novel optimization method, the Grasshopper optimization algorithm, is discussed in [24], to produce more accurate data clustering results is investigated. The Calinski-Harabasz index, which is based on the cluster validation test, is used as a metric to generate solutions. To tackle the data clustering challenge, the researchers used the Grasshopper optimization method and ran experimental testing on several reference data sets. In the context of this investigation, it was found that, in comparison to other conventional k-means approaches, the clustering methodology with the suggested algorithm attained a high accuracy rate.

Autism Spectrum Disorder (ASD) is a neurodevelopmental disorder whose late diagnosis has made addressing the severity of patients' problems difficult.

Patients with ASD have difficulty communicating and interacting with others. They also engage in constrained and repetitive behavior patterns. ASD affects roughly 62 million people worldwide. ASD is 3–4 times more common in males than in girls. ASD is statistically detectable between the ages of one and two, Some situations, nevertheless, can take a very long time to be detected. To effectively treat ASD, it is imperative to appropriately and promptly identify it. Used the Modified Grasshopper Optimization Algorithm (MGOA) to identify Autism Spectrum Disorder at all stages of life in the study [25]. By making this change, researchers hoped to improve upon the limitations of the conventional GOA and enable the early diagnosis of sickness. Three ASD screening datasets for distinct age groups adults, adolescents, and children are subjected to the algorithm, and the findings are contrasted with those from cutting-edge methods. The proposed algorithm's Random Forest classifier was able to predict ASD at every stage of life with a specificity and sensitivity that was about equal to 100.

Cloud computing is a novel computing technique that keeps data and apps operating by utilizing the internet and central remote servers. Users can access database resources from anywhere via cloud computing, removing the need to manage physical resources. Almost every industry, including healthcare, can benefit from this notion. Data mining and successful inquiry from the cloud are more difficult in such circumstances due to the privacy involved in data preservation. As a result, security attacks such as the Known Cipher Text Attack (CTA) and the Plain Text Attack (KPA) represent a serious threat to the information system's privacy and security (CPA). To solve these issues and offer a privacy-preserving solution for protecting medical data through data restoration and cleaning. Researchers presented a hybrid system called Grasshopper Optimization with Genetic Algorithm for the data restoration and cleaning procedure (GOAGA) [26]. In addition, the success of the hybrid approach's restoration and sanitization, statistical analysis, convergence, and key sensitivity analysis are compared to those of other traditional ways, validating the advanced approach's governance. Finally, this hybrid approach has proven to be superior to other conventional approaches.

Text mining involves the employment of complex procedures for dealing with multiple text documents, which necessitates the use of text analysis. Text clustering is one of the most successful text mining, pattern recognition, and machine recruitment techniques. Using a suitable text-clustering technique, computers can start to arrange a corpus document into a specific organisational structure of conceptual clusters. Noise, irrelevant, and extraneous elements can be found in both informative and non-informational text documents. Unsupervised text feature selection is the primary method for identifying a brand-new subset of informative feats for each document. Reduce the quantity of uninformative features and increase the dependability of the text clustering algorithm are the two objectives of the functional selection technique. The suggested method is imprisoned in local minima in a low-dimensional space, has a mature convergence rate, and takes little processing effort. The document pre-processes the text data that it receives as input. Then, using a hybrid GWO-GOA algorithm, the text feature selection is completed by first identifying the local optima from the text content. [27], choosing from the local optimum the finest global optimum. The Fuzzy c-means (FCM) clustering algorithm is also used to group the selected optima. With this technique, dependability is improved while computation time is decreased. The proposed algorithm makes use of eight datasets and has proven superior when compared to other algorithms, text clustering evaluation and Text feature selection measures include specificity, precision, sensitivity, F-measure, accuracy, recall, and demonstrate higher quality. The proposed methodology is 87.6% more effective than GOA, the proposed hybrid GWO-GOA algorithm, and GWO.

Using irrelevant features with powerful classifiers can result in over-fitting and models that do not perform as well as when these features are not utilized, hence feature selection strategies are crucial in predictive modeling. It's particularly essential when it comes to sickness datasets because many of the factors in these data may not be related to a disease's diagnosis and a variety of characteristics or traits are accessible through patient medical records. In this circumstance, inaccurate models can be fatal, resulting in misdiagnosis and, in the worst-case scenario, death. We used a wrapper-based feature selection technique to do this. In recent years, the Grasshopper Optimization Algorithm (GOA) has proven to be superior to other optimization algorithms in a range of study areas. Researchers propose (LAGOA) [28], an improved version of GOA that uses Learning Automata (LA) for adaptive adjusting GOA parameters and two-phase mutation to improve the algorithm's exploitation capability. In the swarm, every grasshopper has its parameters individually adjusted using LA. The two-phase mutation's first stage reduces the amount of chosen characteristics while retaining highly accurate results, and the second stage introduces pertinent features that raise classification accuracy. Data from the UCI Repository, including Breast Cancer (Diagnosis), Breast Cancer (Wisconsin), Lung Cancer, Statlog (Heart), Hepatitis, and SpectF Heart, were subjected to the LAGOA method. Results of experiments demonstrate that it performs better than cutting-edge techniques comparison.

Researchers suggest a modified grasshopper optimization technique to handle the optimal power flow (OPF) problem (MGOA). In [29], the traditional GOA is a relatively new optimization technique based on grasshopper movement and migration in their native habitat. The MGOA avoids entrapment in local optima by altering the mutation process in the standard GOA. The suggested optimization method is used to solve various multi-objective and single functions. Active power loss minimization, quadratic fuel cost and active power loss minimization, quadratic fuel cost minimization, voltage profile improvement, emission cost minimization, quadratic fuel cost and voltage stability improvement, quadratic fuel cost and power loss minimization, quadratic fuel cost, quadratic fuel cost and emission minimization, voltage stability improvement and voltage profile, are some of these objective functions. The proposed technique is validated with thirteen case studies using standard IEEE 118-bus, IEEE 57-bus, and IEEE 30-bus test systems. The simulation results present that the proposed technique outperforms and outperforms well-known evolutionary optimization techniques in solving various OPF problems.

4.1 GOA in Medical Domain

There are many diseases in which GOA contributed to obtaining better results, early detection of diseases, and prescribing the appropriate medication, which led to reducing the risk to the patient through early detection and reducing the death rate resulting from various diseases. In [30], through the application of several machine learning approaches, GOA is utilized to develop a better classifier and increase the accuracy of diabetic type II testing. A promising accuracy of 97% was achieved in the study using the Support-Vector Machine (SVM) technique. To show that the grasshopper algorithm is superior at choosing characteristics and improving the accuracy of diabetes testing. [31], the MGOA was influential in identifying Parkinson's disease with a detection rate of 99.4%, a calculated accuracy of 95.37%, and a false alarm rate of 15.78%. The results of the MGOA presented on The sets of data were assessed and compared with the results of the modified squid optimization algorithm and the modified gray wolf optimizer. Experience has shown that the results indicate that modifying the GOA can improve accuracy and reduce the number of selected features. [32], to aid clinicians in the detection of cardiac illness, the algorithms Bi-Hybrid Grasshopper Optimization (BGO) and K-Nearest Neighbors (KNN) were used. Feature selection (FS) is done with the BGO method, and classification is done with the KNN algorithm. The sensitivity was 89.61%, the accuracy was 89.82%, and the specificity was 90.41%, which is acceptable when compared to previous cardiology investigations. [33], the diagnostic model was developed using an upgraded GOA-based support vector machine to discriminate complex appendicitis (CAP) from uncomplicated appendicitis (UAP). The best model has average values for sensitivity, accuracy, Matthews correlation coefficients, and specificity of 81.71%, 83.56%, and 85.33%. The intelligent diagnosis paradigm that has been proposed is quite trustworthy, because it is based on commonly available markers. [34], Grasshopper algorithm improvement aims to provide a new method for diagnosing lung cancer using (GOA) high-dimensional feature identification and uses (KNN) to classify these features. The results indicate that This technique performs wonderfully, with an efficiency of 98.65, a specificity of 96.7, and a sensitivity of 94.10, which indicates the distinction of this method from others. [35], the process of diagnosing breast cancer can be sped up using GOA, a new technique that does so by using fewer features. In the last stage, a classifier is used to choose the best features and optimise the parameters (SVM). For the datasets from the WDBC, WBC, and WPBC, respectively, this technique yields high accuracy values of 99.51, 98.83, and 91.38. The outcomes revealed that the proposed strategy performs better when compared to other methods. [36], improved Linear Factor depend on GOA with Ensemble Learning (ILFGOA with EL) for covid-19 forecasting. The optimal features are then chosen using the Improved Linear Factor-based Grasshopper Optimization Algorithm (ILF-GOA) algorithm to improve prediction accuracy. The analysis results show that the introduced method outperforms the previous system in terms of error rate, accuracy, error rate, recall, precision, and f-measure. In [37], the GOA technique is used to analyse the type 1 diabetes mellitus system's performance, and modifying the controller parameters to boost control performance is also covered. The simulation results showed that the suggested approach performed significantly better than other standard controllers like PSO-PID and EHO-PID [38], with better outcomes. Artificial Neural networks are based on error estimations that use the GOA and Gradient Descent. Deep neural networks (DNNs) powered by Grasshopper Optimization-based (GOA-based) are designed to classify cancer more accurately. A 0.0769 FAR, a 0.9666 detection rate, and a 0.9534 accuracy rate are achieved by the suggested classification approach employing gene expression data.

4.2   GOA in Industry Domain

There are many improvements and problems in which the government contributed to obtaining better results and reaching a faster solution at a lower cost to reach a higher benefit, which led to a reduction in industrial risks. IN [39], Using an enhanced grasshopper optimization technique, the hidden units in the bidirectional LSTM (long short-term memory) layer of the AlexNet are selected (IGOA). The accuracy, specificity, sensitivity, recall, and precision of the suggested technique were found to be 2.4%, 0.3%, 1.01%, and 0.97%, respectively. Considering the findings, the proposed algorithm is found to be more efficient than the existing algorithm. [40], ESN based on an IGOA. To improve performance, The new solution representation used by the proposed method has streamlined mechanisms for attraction and repulsion. The RUL (Remaining Useful Life) of turbofan engines The original GOA, conventional ESN, deep ESN, LSTM, Particle Swarm Optimization (PSO), Binary PSO (BPSO), Differential Evolution (DE), Cuckoo Search (CS), Particle Swarm Optimization (PSO), and Binary PSO (BPSO) are all surpassed by this approach. [41], The GOA-ELM is a combination of the GOA and Harris hawks optimization (HHO) for foretelling ground vibrations brought by mine blasting. The error values of the GOA-ELM model were 2.8551and 2.0239 for the testing dataset and training dataset, respectively. And the coefficients of determination for the GOA-ELM model 0.9410 for the training and 0.9105 testing datasets, which produced more accurate ground vibration values. [42], the problems of grain train design and pressure vessel are used to evaluated the performance of original GOA algorithm as benchmark engineering design. To achieve the best feasible economic structures using these structures with the smallest design weights while meeting structural behavior limitations like strength, displacement, stability, and drift derived from the American Institute of Steel Construction-Load and Resistance Factor Design specifications. [43], a novel multi-objective model's optimization to enhance voltage profiles, maximise energy transfer between peak and off-peak hours, and reduce DG and BESS costs. The Multi-Objective Grasshopper Optimization Algorithm (MOGOA) is used to solve. Using two Pareto optimality indices, the other heuristic optimization algorithms is compared to that of

MOGOA algorithm's performance. [44], standard GOA performance has been improved with a new clutter strategy and velocity perturbation mechanism. CV-CAVA outperforms the other variants in terms of accuracy and rate of convergence. The results show that the structural weight is excellently designed. CV-GOA outperforms the other variants in terms of accuracy and rate of convergence. Furthermore, CV-GOA optimizes three structural weight design problems: the cantilever beam design problem, the pressure vessel design problem, and the speed reducer design problem. [45], in the automotive industry, there is a growing interest in designing lightweight, low-cost vehicles to solve shape improvement problems. One of the first experiments used in the literature is the use of HHO, SSA, GOA, and DA to form design optimization problems. The results demonstrate the ability of HHO, SSA, GOA, and DA to design the most optimal components. [46], an automated voltage regulator (AVR) system's optimal controller settings can be determined using a unique approach, which has given. The performance index is called the integral of time-weighted squared error (ITSE). The proposed technique, when compared with the differential evolution (DE), artificial bee colony (ABC) tuning methods, and PID controllers based on Ziegler-Nichols (ZN), is robust and highly effective. [47], the hybrid GA-GOA algorithm does indeed improve performance, with a 1.45% increase in optimum weighted efficiency at a computation cost of 63.7 h. The proposed hybrid GA-GOA algorithm is a useful tool for optimising heliostat field layouts and reducing their land footprint. [48], system that reliably optimizes energy demand based on Power Supply Potential (DPSP) and Cost of Energy (COE). The results show that GOA outperforms its peers, CS and PSO, in terms of system size. The system capital cost is reduced by 14% and 19.3%, respectively.

[49], GOA-based VMD method for analysing vibration signals from rotating machinery. The method works well for analysing machinery vibration signals for fault diagnosis. In comparison to the traditional VMD and fast kurtogram methods. [50], the problem of traffic light optimization to minimise cars' waiting time and maximise the cars arriving at the destination within a specified time period GWGHA performance is evaluated using different data experimental cases. The results show that the algorithm outperforms other optimization algorithms when compared to CTLP. [51], a new approach to predict monthly volatility of iron ore prices. In terms of mean square error, the chaotic grasshopper optimization algorithm (CGOA)-NN model outperforms GOA-NN, PSO-NN, GA-NN, and classic NN models by 38.71 %, 16.49 %, 32.18 %, and 60.82 %, respectively. [52], the problem of big data sonar classification. According to the results, FGOA has the highest accuracy for both training and generalised datasets, with 96.43% and 92.03%, respectively. [53], a novel enhanced version of (GOA) for solving the optimal chiller loading (OCL) problem while minimizing power consumption. The outcomes demonstrated that the shown chaos GOA produces better (or comparable) outcomes than the other methods investigated. [54], the new GOA improves the factors for reducing power loss and voltage stability by optimizing the allocation of (BSS) and distributed generation (DG). GOA outperforms in terms of convergence characteristics and system performance. EV users, BSS

developers, and the power and utility grid benefit from the optimized DG-BSS placement in the system.

4.3 GOA in Agriculture Domain

For many people, agriculture is a key and significant field, and its advancement aids in the progress of the entire population. GOA has aided in the development of several agricultural solutions and enhancements, such as, [55], a classification model for cadmium stress in lettuce leaves was developed using VISA-GOA-SVM. The calibration and forecast accuracies were both 100% and 98.57%, respectively. The most effective techniques were found to be RTD (initial fusion of three data input layers) combined with SVM mixed with grasshopper optimization support vector machine and vis-NIR spectra. In [56], the authors enhanced the GOA to optimize the model of the Non-linear Muskingum flood routing. The results of GOA proved superior compared with HS and GA in the problem of the optimal flood routing river, and values of optimal solutions obtained by the GOA, Harmony search (IIS), and Genetic Algorithm (GA) were 3.53, 5.69, and 5.29, respectively. [57], it is proposed to use a hybrid GOA with invasive weed optimization (IWGOA). The grouping strategy improves the IWGOA algorithm's exploration and exploitation capabilities. The optimal solutions obtained by the IWGOA algorithm proved superior in most test functions. [58], the suggested IGOA utilized for optimizing the parameters of HAPF topologies. To replace the target in the original GOA, a learning technique is added, and an exemplar pool is established, which can avoid drop into local optima and enhance global search ability. In [59], the GOA's intelligence is used for optimizing the PI controller parameters. The results produced from compared GOA with WOA and PSO proved that the GOA is fastest and best solution, resulting in less frequency and voltage, less Total Harmonic Distortion (THD), and less output current.

4.4 GOA in Education Domain

Education is the foundation for any society's progress, and one of the most significant aspects is its development, progress, and improvement across all fields. Assisted GOA with this assignment and submitted numerous models, including [60], the genetic algorithm (GA) and GOA are used to solve the nonlinear equations system: GOA-GA-hybrid (SNLEs). The GOA-GA-hybrid algorithm outperforms the other algorithms. GOA-GA-hybrid is efficient in resolving SNLEs in terms of accuracy. [61], the grid search is compared to a hybrid approach based on the GOA, the common technique for tuning SVM parameters. In terms of classification accuracy, it outperforms all compared methods in most databases. In [62], the results of the constrained and unconstrained test functions solved utilizing the GOA can validate that the algorithm produces reliable results. The algorithm can also be utilized for solving various problems of engineering in reality. In [28], the authors enhanced a version of GOA by utilizing Learning Automata (LA) called LAGOA to adjust the parameters of GOA adaptively, and is implemented for Lung Cancer, Breast Cancer disease (Diagnosis or Wisconsin), Starlog (Heart), and Spector Heart, and demonstrates its superiority. GOA algorithm performance is enhanced in [63] by incorporating a novel mutation factor into the standard GOA algorithm. It is the EGOA that seeks to solve the problems in optimization such as trapping in the local optima and slow convergence, by striking a good balance between the exploration phase and exploitation phase, EGOAs is superior to the original GOA algorithm. [64], a strategy for quantifying the quality of work-life through the elimination of human resource hazards. It is carried out using the enhanced GOA. The GOA and the bees algorithm make up this algorithm. The newly proposed method outperforms the traditional method and produces more accurate findings.

5   Conclusion and Future Work

This article provided and summarized the most popular Optimization methods used in machine learning and data mining, as well as examined their applications in various fields. First, we discuss the theoretical foundation's First-class, high-level optimization methods, Derivative-free perspectives, as well as recent research progress. Then, in the supplementary material, we describe the applications of optimization methods in various Machine learning scenarios, data mining, and treatment of many diseases and in the fields of industry, agriculture, and education, as well as approaches to improve their performance. Finally, most Of the previous literature has proven that the optimum grasshopper algorithm is superior to other metaheuristic optimization algorithms in data mining and machine learning problems. Therefore, we expect that if we integrate Archimedes' optimization algorithm using the grasshopper algorithm for reduce national computing time and avoid baiting in the local optima, this hybrid will give more performance than other algorithms, according to previous studies.

Acknowledgement. We acknowledge that this paper is not part of a MSc or Ph.D. thesis.

References

1. Saremi, S., Mirjalili, S., Lewis, A.: Grasshopper optimisation algorithm: theory and application. Adv. Eng. Softw. **105**, 30–47 (2017)
2. Saxena, A., Shekhawat, S., Kumar, R.: Application and development of enhanced chaotic grasshopper optimization algorithms. Model. Simul. Eng. **2018** (2018)
3. Merrikh-Bayat, F.: The runner-root algorithm: a metaheuristic for solving unimodal and multimodal optimization problems inspired by runners and roots of plants in nature. Appl. Soft Comput. **33**, 292–303 (2015)
4. Arora, S.: Approximation schemes for NP-hard geometric optimization problems. Math. Program. **97**, 43–69 (2003)
5. Zitzler, E., Thiele, L.: Multi-objective Optimization Using Evolutionary. Wiley, Hoboken (2001)

6. Storn, R., Price, K.: Differential evolution–a simple and efficient heuristic for global optimization over continuous spaces. J. Global Optim. **11**, 341–359 (1997)
7. Holland, J.H.: Genetic algorithms. Sci. Am. **267**, 66–73 (1992)
8. Eberhart, R.C., Shi, Y.: Comparison between genetic algorithms and particle swarm optimization. In: Porto, V.W., Saravanan, N., Waagen, D., Eiben, A.E. (eds.) EP 1998. LNCS, vol. 1447, pp. 611–616. Springer, Heidelberg (1998). https://doi.org/10.1007/BFb0040812
9. Eberhart, R., Kennedy, J.: A new optimizer using particle swarm theory. In: Proceedings of the Sixth International Symposium on Micro Machine and Human Science, MHS 1995, pp. 39–43. IEEE (1995). https://doi.org/10.1109/MHS.1995.494215
10. Hashim, F.A., Houssein, E.H., Mabrouk, M.S., Al-Atabany, W., Mirjalili, S.: Henry gas solubility optimization: a novel physics-based algorithm. Futur. Gener. Comput. Syst. **101**, 646–667 (2019)
11. Qais, M.H., Hasanien, H.M., Alghuwainem, S.: Transient search optimization: a new meta-heuristic optimization algorithm. Appl. Intell. **50**(11), 3926–3941 (2020). https://doi.org/10.1007/s10489-020-01727-y
12. Birbil, Ş.İ., Fang, S.C.: An electromagnetism-like mechanism for global optimization. J. Glob. Optim. **25**, 263–282 (2003)
13. Rashedi, E., Nezamabadi-Pour, H., Saryazdi, S.: GSA: a gravitational search algorithm. Inf. Sci. **179**, 2232–2248 (2009)
14. Lv, W., He, C., Li, D., Cheng, S., Luo, S., Zhang, X.: Election campaign optimization algorithm. Procedia Comput. Sci. **1**, 1377–1386 (2010)
15. Askari, Q., Saeed, M., Younas, I.: Heap-based optimizer inspired by corporate rank hierarchy for global optimization. Expert Syst. Appl. **161**, 113702 (2020)
16. Topaz, C.M., Bernoff, A.J., Logan, S., Toolson, W.: A model for rolling swarms of locusts. Eur. Phys. J. Spec. Top. **157**, 93–109 (2008)
17. El-Fergany, A.A.: Electrical characterisation of proton exchange membrane fuel cells stack using grasshopper optimiser. IET Renew. Power Gener. **12**, 9–17 (2018)
18. Wu, J., et al.: Distributed trajectory optimization for multiple solar-powered UAVs target tracking in urban environment by Adaptive Grasshopper Optimization Algorithm. Aerosp. Sci. Technol. **70**, 497–510 (2017)
19. Ewees, A.A., Abd Elaziz, M., Houssein, E.H.: Improved grasshopper optimization algorithm using opposition-based learning. Expert Syst. Appl. **112**, 156–172 (2018)
20. Mafarja, M., Aljarah, I., Faris, H., Hammouri, A.I., Ala'M, A.Z., Mirjalili, S.: Binary grasshopper optimisation algorithm approaches for feature selection problems. Expert Syst. Appl. **117**, 267–286 (2019)
21. Luo, J., Chen, H., Xu, Y., Huang, H., Zhao, X.: An improved grasshopper optimization algorithm with application to financial stress prediction. Appl. Math. Model. **64**, 654–668 (2018)
22. Arora, S., Anand, P.: Chaotic grasshopper optimization algorithm for global optimization. Neural Comput. Appl. **31**, 4385–4405 (2019)
23. Hamad, A., Houssein, E.H., Hassanien, A.E., Fahmy, A.A.: Hybrid grasshopper optimization algorithm and support vector machines for automatic seizure detection in EEG signals. In: Hassanien, A.E., Tolba, M.F., Elhoseny, M., Mostafa, M. (eds.) AMLTA 2018. AISC, vol. 723, pp. 82–91. Springer, Cham (2018). https://doi.org/10.1007/978-3-319-74690-6_9
24. Łukasik, S., Kowalski, P.A., Charytanowicz, M., Kulczycki, P.: Data clustering with grasshopper optimization algorithm. In: 2017 Federated Conference on Computer Science and Information Systems (FedCSIS), Czech Republic, pp. 71–74. IEEE (2017). https://doi.org/10.15439/2017F340

25. Goel, N., Grover, B., Gupta, D., Khanna, A., Sharma, M.: Modified grasshopper optimization algorithm for detection of autism spectrum disorder. Phys. Commun. **41**, 101115 (2020)
26. Alphonsa, M.A., MohanaSundaram, N.: A reformed grasshopper optimization with genetic principle for securing medical data. J. Inf. Secur. Appl. **47**, 410–420 (2019)
27. Purushothaman, R., Rajagopalan, S.P., Dhandapani, G.: Hybridizing Gray Wolf Optimization (GWO) with Grasshopper Optimization Algorithm (GOA) for text feature selection and clustering. Appl. Soft Comput. **96**, 106651 (2020)
28. Dey, C., Bose, R., Ghosh, K.K., Malakar, S., Sarkar, R., Kulkarni, O.: LAGOA: learning automata based grasshopper optimization algorithm for feature selection in disease datasets. J. Ambient. Intell. Humaniz. Comput. **13**, 3175–3194 (2022)
29. Taher, M.A., Kamel, S., Jurado, F., Ebeed, M.: Modified grasshopper optimization framework for optimal power flow solution. Electr. Eng. **101**(1), 121–148 (2019). https://doi.org/10.1007/s00202-019-00762-4
30. Kamel, S.R., Yaghoubzadeh, R.: Feature selection using grasshopper optimization algorithm in diagnosis of diabetes disease. Adv. Eng. Softw. **26**, 100707 (2021)
31. Sehgal, S., Agarwal, M., Gupta, D., Sundaram, S., Bashambu, A.: Optimized grass hopper algorithm for diagnosis of Parkinson's disease. SN Appl. Sci. **2**, 1–18 (2020)
32. DezhAloud, N.: Diagnosis of heart disease using binary grasshopper optimization algorithm and K-nearest neighbors. J. Health Adm. **23**, 42–54 (2020)
33. Xia, J., et al.: Performance optimization of support vector machine with oppositional grasshopper optimization for acute appendicitis diagnosis. Comput. Biol. Med. 105206 (2022)
34. Rahmani, A.I., et al.: Diagnosing lung cancer using grasshopper optimization algorithm and K-nearest neighbor classification. Journal **6**, 69–75 (2019). http://iieta. org/journals/rces
35. Rahmani, A., Katouli, M.: Breast cancer detection improvement by grasshopper optimization algorithm and classification SVM. Rev. d'Intelligence Artif. **34**, 195–202 (2020)
36. Algamal, Z.Y., Qasim, M.K., Lee, M.H., Ali, H.T.M.: QSAR model for predicting neuraminidase inhibitors of influenza A viruses (H1N1) based on adaptive grasshopper optimization algorithm. SAR QSAR Environ. Res. **31**, 803–814 (2020)
37. Belmon, A.P., Auxillia, J.: An adaptive technique based blood glucose control in type-1 diabetes mellitus patients. Int. J. Numer. Methods Biomed. Eng. **36**, e3371 (2020)
38. Tumuluru, P., Ravi, B.: GOA-based DBN: grasshopper optimization algorithm-based deep belief neural networks for cancer classification. Int. J. Appl. Eng. Res. **12**, 14218–14231 (2017)
39. Ghulanavar, R., Dama, K.K., Jagadeesh, A.: Diagnosis of faulty gears by modified AlexNet and improved grasshopper optimization algorithm (IGOA). J. Mech. Sci. Technol. **34**(10), 4173–4182 (2020). https://doi.org/10.1007/s12206-020-0909-6
40. Bala, A., Ismail, I., Ibrahim, R., Sait, S.M., Oliva, D.: An improved grasshopper optimization algorithm based echo state network for predicting faults in airplane engines. IEEE Access **8**, 159773–159789 (2020)
41. Yu, C., et al.: Optimal ELM-Harris Hawks optimization and ELM-Grasshopper optimization models to forecast peak particle velocity resulting from mine blasting. Nat. Resour. Res. **30**, 2647–2662 (2021)
42. Aydogdu, I., Ormecioglu, T.O., Tunca, O., Carbas, S.: Design of large-scale real-size steel structures using various modified grasshopper optimization algorithms. Neural Comput. Appl. 1–24 (2022)

43. Ahmadi, B., Ceylan, O., Ozdemir, A.: Distributed energy resource allocation using multi-objective grasshopper optimization algorithm. Electr. Power Syst. Res. **201**, 107564 (2021)
44. Ye, Y., Xiong, S., Dong, C., Chen, Z.: The structural weight design method based on the modified grasshopper optimization algorithm. Multimed. Tools Appl. 1–29 (2022)
45. Yıldız, B.S., Yıldız, A.R.: The Harris hawks optimization algorithm, salp swarm algorithm, grasshopper optimization algorithm and dragonfly algorithm for structural design optimization of vehicle components. Mater. Test. **61**, 744–748 (2019)
46. Hekimoğlu, B., Ekinci, S.: Grasshopper optimization algorithm for automatic voltage regulator system. In: 2018 5th International Conference on Electrical and Electronic Engineering (ICEEE), Turkey, pp. 152–156. IEEE (2018) https://doi.org/10.1109/ICEEE2.2018.8391320
47. Arrif, T., Hassani, S., Guermoui, M., Sánchez-González, A., Taylor, R.A., Belaid, A.: GA-Goa hybrid algorithm and comparative study of different metaheuristic population-based algorithms for solar tower heliostat field design. Renew. Energy **192**, 745–758 (2022)
48. Bukar, A.L., Tan, C.W., Lau, K.Y.: Optimal sizing of an autonomous photovoltaic/wind/battery/diesel generator microgrid using grasshopper optimization algorithm. Sol. Energy **88**, 685–696 (2019)
49. Zhang, X., Miao, Q., Zhang, H., Wang, L.: A parameter-adaptive VMD method based on grasshopper optimization algorithm to analyze vibration signals from rotating machinery. Mech. Syst. Signal Process. **108**, 58–72 (2018)
50. Teng, T.C., Chiang, M.C., Yang, C.S.: A hybrid algorithm based on GWO and GOA for cycle traffic light timing optimization. In: 2019 IEEE International Conference on Systems, Man and Cybernetics (SMC), Italy, pp. 774–779. IEEE (2019). https://doi.org/10.1109/SMC.2019.8914661
51. Ewees, A.A., Abd Elaziz, M., Alameer, Z., Ye, H., Jianhua, Z.: Improving multilayer perceptron neural network using chaotic grasshopper optimization algorithm to forecast iron ore price volatility. Resour. Policy **65**, 101555 (2020)
52. Saffari, A., Zahiri, S.H., Khishe, M.: Fuzzy grasshopper optimization algorithm: a hybrid technique for tuning the control parameters of GOA using fuzzy system for big data sonar classification. Iran. J. Electr. Electron. Eng. **18**, 2131 (2020)
53. Wenhan, X., Yuanxing, W., Di, Q., Daneshvar Rouyendegh, B.: Improved grasshopper optimization algorithm to solve energy consuming reduction of chiller loading. Energy Sources 1–14 (2019)
54. Sultana, U., Khairuddin, A.B., Sultana, B., Rasheed, N., Qazi, S.H., Malik, N.R.: Placement and sizing of multiple distributed generation and battery swapping stations using grasshopper optimizer algorithm. Energy **165**, 408–421 (2018)
55. Zhou, X., Sun, J., Tian, Y., Wu, X., Dai, C., Li, B.: Spectral classification of lettuce cadmium stress based on information fusion and VISSA-GOA-SVM algorithm. J. Food Process. Eng. **42**, e13085 (2019)
56. Khalifeh, S., Esmaili, K., Khodashenas, S., Akbarifard, S.: Data on optimization of the non-linear Muskingum flood routing in Kardeh River using Goa algorithm. Data Brief **30**, 105398 (2020)
57. Yue, X., Zhang, H., Yu, H., Akbarifard, S.: A hybrid grasshopper optimization algorithm with invasive weed for global optimization. IEEE Access **8**, 5928–5960 (2020)
58. Huang, J., Li, C., Cui, Z., Zhang, L., Dai, W.: An improved grasshopper optimization algorithm for optimizing hybrid active power filters' parameters. IEEE Access **8**, 137004–137018 (2020)

59. Jumani, T.A., Mustafa, M.W., Md Rasid, M., Mirjat, N.H., Leghari, Z.H., Saeed, M.S.: Optimal voltage and frequency control of an islanded microgrid using grasshopper optimization algorithm. Energies **11**, 3191 (2018)
60. El-Shorbagy, M.A., El-Refaey, A.M.: Hybridization of grasshopper optimization algorithm with genetic algorithm for solving system of non-linear equations. Cogn. Comput. **10**, 478–495 (2020)
61. Aljarah, I., Al-Zoubi, A.M., Faris, H., Hassonah, M.A., Mirjalili, S., Saadeh, H.: Simultaneous feature selection and support vector machine optimization using the grasshopper optimization algorithm. IEEE Access **8**, 220944–220961 (2018)
62. Neve, A.G., Kakandikar, G.M., Kulkarni, O.: Application of grasshopper optimization algorithm for constrained and unconstrained test functions. Int. J. Swarm Intell. Evol. Comput. **6**, 1–7 (2017)
63. Ghaleb, S.A.A., Mohamad, M., Syed Abdullah, E.F.H., Ghanem, W.A.H.M.: Integrating mutation operator into grasshopper optimization algorithm for global optimization. Soft. Comput. **25**(13), 8281–8324 (2021). https://doi.org/10.1007/s00500-021-05752-y
64. Doudaran, A.J., Ghousi, R., Makui, A., Jafari, M.: Development of a method to measure the quality of working life using the improved metaheuristic grasshopper optimization algorithm. Math. Probl. Eng. **2021** (2021)

A Semi-supervised Learning Application for Hand Posture Classification

Kailiang Nan[1], Shengnan Hu[1], Haozhe Luo[1], Patricia Wong[1],
and Saeid Pourroostaei Ardakani[1,2(✉)] (iD)

[1] School of Computer Science, University of Nottingham Ningbo China,
Ningbo 315100, China
{scykn1,scysh1,scyhl2,omyww1,saeid.ardakani}@nottingham.edu.cn
[2] School of Computer Science, University of Lincoln, Lincoln Ln6 7TS, UK
spourroostaei@lincoln.ac.uk

Abstract. The rapid growth of HCI applications results in increased data size and complexity. For this, advanced machine learning techniques and data analysis solutions are used to prepare and process data patterns. However, the cost of data pre-processing, labelling, and classification can be significantly increased if the dataset is huge, complex, and unlabelled. This paper aims to propose a data pre-processing approach and semi-supervised learning technique to prepare and classify a big Motion Capture Hand Postures dataset. It builds the solutions via Tri-training and Co-forest techniques and compares them to figure out the best-fitted approach for hand posture classification. According to the results, Co-forest outperforms Tri-training in terms of Accuracy, Precision, recall, and F1-score.

Keywords: Semi-supervised learning · Big data Analysis · Co-forest · Tri-training · hand posture classification

1 Introduction

Human-computer-Interaction (HCI) data classification is a research field that has attracted computer scientists and researchers during the past decades. For this, Machine Learning (ML) techniques are widely used to learn HCI data patterns and classify the datasets [18]. However, traditional ML approaches are usually unable to offer benefits to modern HCI applications especially if the dataset is huge [3]. This is because the ML models should fit a huge dataset into limited and expensive working memories [6]. It results in increased ML model/memory failures and data processing costs.

Big data analysis applications are increasingly being popular as they have the capacity to automate the processing of huge and complex data [5]. However, ML-enabled Big data solutions usually suffer from the lack of labelled data [7]. This is because manual data labelling is expensive and requires complex data domain knowledge analysis especially if the dataset is big [2]. By this, a combination of

R. Hou et al. (Eds.): BDTA 2022, LNICST 480, pp. 137–148, 2023.
https://doi.org/10.1007/978-3-031-33614-0_10

unsupervised and supervised learning techniques is used to form Semi-supervised learning (SSL) approaches for data classification and/or prediction. Indeed, SSL refers to supervised learning with additional unlabelled data or unsupervised learning with labelled data [10]. SSL techniques have the capacity to additionally label the unlabelled data points using the knowledge learned from a small number of labelled data samples. However, the cost of SSL techniques can be sharply increased depending on the dataset size and the ratio of labelled data over unlabelled samples.

This paper aims to propose an SSL-enabled Big data analysis solution to classify and analysis hand postures. A data pre-processing approach is proposed to clean (i.e., missing and noise value removal) and prepare (i.e., feature extraction and data normalisation) a massive Motion Capture Hand Postures dataset [4] with 78095 records. In turn, two advanced SSL techniques inducing *Co-forest* [19] and *Tri-training* [1] are used on an Apache Spark framework [32] to build a data classification model. The former is a co-training-style Random Forest algorithm, while the latter utilises three classifiers to learn data labels. The results of the two ML algorithms are evaluated and compared to figure out the best-fitted solution. The key contributions of this research are outlined below:

- To deploy a data pre-processing approach for cleaning and preparing a hand posture big dataset.
- To train and test two SSL machine learning approaches for hand posture classification.
- To analyse and evaluate the performance of the SSL solutions and find the best-fitted approach.

This paper is organized as follows: Sect. 2 reviews self-labelling and SSL techniques and highlights their similarities, differences, and superiorities. Section 3 introduces the research methodology, while Sect. 4 presents and discusses the experimental results. Section 5 summarises the research's key findings and refers to future works.

2   Literature Review

This section outlines the state-of-the-art literature on self-labelling and SSL techniques. This is not a statistical analysis, however, it surveys the relevant state-of-the-art solutions to highlight their similarities and differences and outline the existing research gaps.

SSL Classification techniques are categorised as transductive and inductive learning classes [9]. The former takes both training and test datasets to train a classification model, while the latter uses only the training dataset to classify the unseen data samples. Self-training is a well-known SSL technique that trains the classifier(s) using the labelled samples to predict the label values for the unlabelled samples [8]. However, limited or low-quality labelled data results in an inaccurate self-training prediction and consequently false labelling and misclassification [21].

SSL approaches can be used in HCI data classification/prediction [15], Computer Vision [17], and Natural Language Processing [16]. They can be deployed on large-scale data analysis frameworks (e.g., Apache Spark) to build parallel classification models and process big and complex datasets [12–14]. It offers distributed processing, fault tolerance, and scalability benefits [24]. However, the cost of SSL approaches is still an existing drawback in this field of research especially if the dataset is big and complex. For example, graph-based semi-supervised learning takes cubic time complexity $O(n^3)$ [11].

There are two advanced and widely used SSL algorithms including Tri-training and Co-forest [19]. They are commonly used in semi-supervised classification due to their performance and accuracy [23]. Tri-Training aims to train three classifiers for labelling the unlabelled samples [1]. The classifiers are refined, and the final label prediction is made via a majority voting technique [22]. Co-forest is well-known ensemble learning based on a Random Forest technique. It amplifies the power of ensemble modelling and extends the Tri-training technique with additional classifiers to achieve a better result. Ensemble learning is a method that uses multiple machine learning algorithms and builds several classifiers instead of a single classifier [19]. Co-forest requires neither a dataset with rich attributes/features nor a cross-validation analysis to pick up high-confidence unlabeled samples. Hence, it has the capacity to offer real-time classification applications such as financial anomaly detection or speech pattern recognition.

This literature review summarises the key factors of SSL techniques. However, it is still required to investigate the performance of the SSL techniques once they are used to classify big and complex HCI datasets. For this, SSL approaches need to be adapted to support Big data analysis and parallel data processing, and model training. This paper aims to build, tune and parallelise two SSL approaches on Apache Spark and test and evaluate their performance for a data-driven hand posture classification application.

3   Methodology and Implementation

This section presents the research methodology that focuses on proposing a data pre-processing approach to clean and prepare a big hand posture dataset, and Tri-training and Co-forest SSL deployment to predict and classify the dataset samples.

3.1   Dataset Selection and Pre-processing

The Motion Capture Hand Postures dataset [4] by Louisiana Tech University is used in this research to build and evaluate the SSL models. It contains 5 static hand postures (78095 records) including 1) Fist with thumb out, 2) Stop (hand flat), 3) Point1 (using pointer finger), 4) Point2 (using both pointer and middle fingers), and 5) Grab (fingers curled to grab). The postures are captured via a Vicon motion capture camera system with markers attached to a left-handed glove. Table 1 outlines the dataset attributes and descriptions, while Fig. 1 shows these five postures including fist, stop, pointing with one finger, pointing with two fingers, and grab (fingers curled).

Table 1. Dataset Attributes and Description

Attribute	Description	Datatype
Class	Class value (1 to 5)	integer
User	User ID	integer
Xi	x-coord of the i-th marker position	double
Yi	y-coord of the i-th marker position	double
Zi	z-coord of the i-th marker position	double

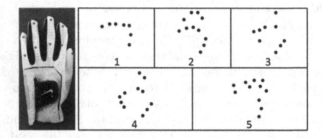

Fig. 1. The data collection glove and hand postures [4].

Data preprocessing is built via Apache Spark DataFrame API (e.g., select, filter, join, and aggregate functions) and MLlib [27,28]. Apache Spark provides MLlib (Machine Learning library) which is a scalable library to build machine learning models [25]. It allows large-scale machine learning settings to benefit from model/data parallelism and build a scalable machine learning infrastructure [26]. The Spark-CSV package is used to read the CSV file and convert them into Spark DataFrame. In addition, SparkSQL operations are used to uncover the data characteristics. According to Table 2, the dataset has a balanced class labelling distribution. It is key to include balanced datasets in ML analysis as imbalanced datasets lead to misclassification especially if the dataset is big.

Data normalization and data cleaning techniques are used to prepare the dataset. *StandardScaler* library on Spark is used to normalize data features, while two approaches are used to handle missing data including 1) removing columns with more than 80% of missing values and 2) mean imputation (MI) technique to impute the missing data. According to Bennett [29], missing values can likely result in statistical bias. For this, a data cleaning approach is used to remove columns with 80% of missing values. Then, feature selection and missing value imputation techniques are used to replace missing values with substituted ones.

Table 2. The Distribution of Dataset Class Labelling

Class	Data Samples
1	16265
2	14978
3	16344
4	14775
5	15733

3.2 Tri-training

Tri-training uses three classifiers which not only allows for easy handling of the labelled confidence estimation problem and the prediction of unlabelled data samples but also improves generalization via ensemble learning. According to the original Tri-training algorithm, an unlabelled sample gives high labelling confidence if it has the same classification results using two classifiers. In turn, the third classifier gives a label value and adds the unlabelled data sample to the labelled set. A voting method is used to integrate the results of the three classifiers and achieve a better and faster classification [1].

Tri-training approach is built via $RandomForestClassifier()$ which forms three Random Forest classifiers. The training dataset is randomly partitioned as labelled (L_train) and unlabelled (U_train) samples using randomSplit() function. Data features are stored as a vector DataFrame (label: Double, features: Vector) using Spark's $VectorAssembler$ transformer, and the columns are assembled into a single vector called 'features'. The Tri-training algorithm takes samples from the L_train dataset using a bootstrap approach. It forms three sub-datasets as h_i, h_j, and h_k to train the Random Forest classifiers. Each classifier calculates the classification error rate of the hypothesis $e[i]$, which is derived from the combination of the other two classifiers, using the $measure\_error()$ function during a Tri-training round.

The classification error rate is used in this approach to find the best-fitted unlabelled samples that should be added to the labelled set. Classifiers h_j and h_k aim to predict U_train and select data samples with the same predictions as the newly labelled data. Let's assume $e[i]$ is the error rate upper bound of h_j and h_k in the classification round of t. Hence, unlabelled sample$i$ is a labelling candidate if $e[i]$ in round t is less than the previous round $(e[i]_{t-1})$. Equation 1 [1] shows the range of accepting an unlabelled sample, where $|L_t|$ and $|L_{t-1}|$ are the sample size during round t and $t-1$.

$$0 < \frac{e[i]_t}{e[i]_{t-1}} < \frac{|L_{t-1}|}{|L_t|} < 1 \tag{1}$$

The unlabelled samples (U) are labelled and added to L_train for further processing and updating the model if their $|L_t|$ is larger than $|L_{t-1}|$ and $e[i] \times |L_t|$ is less than $e[i]_{t-1} \times |L_{t-1}|$. Otherwise, a subsampling method is required to randomly select $|L_t - S|$ samples as L_t where $|L_t|$ stays larger than $|L_{t-1}|$ and Eq. 2 works. Equation 3 is used to calculate the value of s and ensure that $e[i] \times |L_t|$ is still less than $e[i]_{t-1} \times |L_{t-1}|$ after subsampling. It is repeated for each of the three classifiers until all the high-confidence unlabelled data samples are selected and no further update is left. Finally, the results of the three classifiers are combined via a voting approach [1].

$$|L_{t-1}| > \frac{e[i]_t}{e[i]_{t-1} - e[i]_t} \tag{2}$$

$$S = \left[\frac{e[i]_{t-1} |L_{t-1}|}{e[i]_t} - 1 \right] \tag{3}$$

Table 3 shows the initialisation parameters in Tri-training.

Table 3. Tri-training Training: Parameter Initialization

label_ratio	0.05
numTrees	2
maxDepth	12
bootstrap	False
seed	99999
max_iter	10000

3.3   Co-forest

Co-forest is an enhanced version of co-training that builds an ensemble model to classify unlabelled samples. It utilises diverse learners aiming to add unlabelled data to the labelled dataset when the voting ratio for a certain label is larger than a predefined threshold. Indeed, Co-forest selects new unlabelled data for each separated learner based on the ratio of voting in an ensemble model and excludes the learners that use the data to train the new classifiers.

The dataset is automatically partitioned into several parts according to the number of available working nodes/threads on the Apache Spark framework [30]. However, it can be manually partitioned using *repartition* or *partitionBy* methods which are available on Spark DataFrame/RDD [20]. In turn, *VectorAssembler* and *StringIndexer* methods are used to form training and testing datasets. To support inductive learning, the training set is further divided into the labelled set and unlabelled set, while the testing set is used to evaluate the proposed model.

To deploy Co-Forrest, first, the model's parameters including error rates, the weighted sums of confidence, and base classifiers are initialised. Then, the algorithm measures the error rate of a classifier (C_i) for the labelled data. It uses the *sample* method in Apache Spark to subsample some unlabelled data if the error rate is lower than the previous classifier. However, it terminates the model training if it gives a larger error rate than the previously trained classifier. In turn, the classifiers aim to predict the labels based on an ensemble learning fashion. By this, the unlabelled data are labelled using the classifiers' voting if the labelling confidence is greater than the predefined threshold. The labelling confidence is measured as the number of voter classifiers over the total number of all available classifiers. Finally, the classifier C_i is trained using the new dataset and it is repeated until no classifier needs an update. Table 4 shows the Co-forest's initialisation parameters.

Table 4. Co-forest Training: Parameter Initialization

num of classifiers	6
seed	99999
threshold	0.75
max iter	10000

4   Results and Discussions

This section presents and discusses the experimental results to evaluate the performance of the proposed approach for hand posture classification.

4.1   Evaluation Metrics

This research uses Accuracy, F1_score, Precision, and Recall metrics to evaluate the performance of the SSL techniques including Co-forest and Tri-training [31].

Accuracy is the number of correct predictions according to all the predictions. It is computed using Eq. 4, in which True Positive (TP), False Positive (FP), True Negative (TN), and False Negative (FN), are respectively true prediction as positive, false prediction as positive, true prediction as negative, and false prediction as negative.

$$Accuracy = \frac{TP + TN}{TP + TN + FP + FN} \tag{4}$$

Precision is measured as the proportion of true positive samples over all positive predictions using Eq. 5.

$$Precision = \frac{TP}{TP + FP} \tag{5}$$

Recall refers to the proportion of correctly predicted positives over all positive labels. It is calculated using Eq. 6.

$$Recall = \frac{TP}{TP + FN} \tag{6}$$

F1_score uses Eq. 7 to take both precision and recall into account and study the performance of the prediction model.

$$F1\_Score = 2 \cdot \frac{Precision \cdot Recall}{Precision + Recall} \tag{7}$$

Tri-Training Results. Table 5 shows the performance of a basic Tri-training model which is trained using the initial parameters (Table 3) and according to variously labelled data ratio. The labelled data ratio changes from 0.05% to 95%. The accuracy of the model is increased when the ratio of the labelled data is increased. However, the model's performance is reduced due to the model over-fitting when the labelled data ratio is too high. The Tri-training model is tuned based on tree depth ($maxDepth$) and the number of trees ($numTrees$).

Table 5. Tri-training Performance Based on Labelled Data Ratio

Labelled ratio	0.05(base)	0.10	0.20	0.30	0.50	0.60	0.95
Accuracy	0.7269	0.7846	0.8070	0.8254	0.8398	0.8605	0.8578
f1_score	0.7264	0.7849	0.8067	0.8257	0.8394	0.8604	0.8577
precision	0.7270	0.7858	0.8074	0.8265	0.8399	0.8612	0.8585
recall	0.7269	0.7846	0.8070	0.8254	0.8398	0.8605	0.8578

Table 6 highlights the performance of Tri-training according to the tree depth parameter. For this, a base model ($RandomForestClassifier$) is built based on seven different tree depths ($maxDepth$) to find the best-fitted model. According to the results, the performance of Tri-training is increased when tree depth is increased. This stems from the fact that deeper trees build more accurate classifiers. However, the results show over-fitting and accuracy reduction when the tree depth is greater than 12.

Table 6. Tri-training Performance Based on the Depth of Trees

Tree depth	2	4	8	10	12 (base)	16	20
Accuracy	0.4237	0.5373	0.7139	0.7408	0.7987	0.7649	0.7423
f1_score	0.3346	0.5289	0.7127	0.7402	0.7982	0.7585	0.7302
precision	0.3403	0.5255	0.7127	0.7408	0.7994	0.7918	0.7878
recall	0.4237	0.5373	0.7139	0.7408	0.7987	0.7649	0.7423

The performance of Tri-training model is studied if the number of trees ($numTrees$) changes. Table 7 shows the model performance according to five scenarios. According to it, a better Tri-training performance is achieved when the number of trees is increased. Hence, the best Tri-training model works with a labeling ratio of 0.05, and 30 decision trees each of which in the depth of 12.

Table 7. Tri-training Performance Based on the Number of Trees

Number of trees	2	4	10	20	30
Accuracy	0.7625	0.8144	0.8508	0.8569	0.8604
f1_score	0.7600	0.8145	0.8507	0.8559	0.8601
precision	0.7632	0.8167	0.8515	0.8587	0.8608
recall	0.7627	0.8144	0.8508	0.8564	0.8605

Co-forest Results. Table 8 shows the performance of the proposed Co-forest algorithm according to variously labelled data ratio. According to it, the accuracy of Co-forest algorithm is enhanced as the ratio of labelled data is increased. SSL uses the labelled dataset to predict new labelled data. Hence, it enhances the model performance if a greater number of labelled data are included in model training. However, the model accuracy drops when the labelled data ratio reaches 95%. It is because of the model over-fitting. According to Tables 8 and 5 Co-forest outperforms Tri-training especially if the labelled data ratio is low.

Table 8. Co-forest Performance Based on Labelled Data Ratio

Labelled ratio	0.05(base)	0.10	0.20	0.30	0.50	0.60	0.95
Accuracy	0.7987	0.8339	0.8583	0.8757	0.8793	0.8864	0.8761
f1_score	0.7981	0.8332	0.8580	0.8751	0.8789	0.8860	0.8760
precision	0.7993	0.8354	0.8614	0.8790	0.8812	0.8884	0.8787
recall	0.7987	0.8339	0.8583	0.8757	0.8794	0.8865	0.8761

According to Table 9, Co-forest gives better performance if the tree depth is increased. It is because deeper trees build more accurate base classifiers to accurately classify the data. According to it, the best results are achieved if the tree depth is 16. However, it leads to over-fitting and accuracy reduction if the tree depth is increased to greater than 16.

The performance of Co-forest algorithm is analysed based on the number of trees/classifiers. As Table 10 shows, the model's accuracy is increased when the classifiers increase until having 6 trees. However, the accuracy drops when the number of base classifiers goes behind 6. Hence, the best-fitted Co-forest model should be trained with a 5% labelled data ratio, 6 classifiers, and a tree depth of 20.

Table 9. Co-forest Performance Based on the Depth of Trees

Tree depth	2	4	8	12 (base)	16	20
Accuracy	0.4323	0.5683	0.7060	0.7987	0.8217	0.8092
F1_score	0.3714	0.5680	0.7080	0.7982	0.8216	0.8093
precision	0.3380	0.5791	0.7176	0.7994	0.8232	0.8100
recall	0.4323	0.5683	0.7060	0.7987	0.8217	0.8092

Table 10. Co-forest Performance Based on the Number of Trees

Number of trees	2	4	6 (base)	8	10	12
Accuracy	0.6684	0.7716	0.7987	0.7975	0.7823	0.7761
F1_score	0.6641	0.7707	0.7982	0.7967	0.7805	0.7761
precision	0.6768	0.7717	0.7994	0.7986	0.7840	0.7786
recall	0.6684	0.7716	0.7987	0.7975	0.7823	0.7761

5   Conclusion and Future Work

Large-scale hand posture data classification needs to take benefit of Big data-enabled machine learning techniques and Semi-supervised Learning approaches. They offer benefits as compared to classic supervised learning due to the cost of hand posture data labelling in big and complex datasets.

This research aims to propose a data pre-processing approach and build two advanced semi-supervised learning algorithms including Tri-training and Co-forest for a classification problem. It uses Spark MLlib to support model training parallelism. The semi-supervised learning approaches are evaluated and tuned via an extensive experimental plan to find the best-fitted models according to the given dataset. According to the results, Co-forest model outperforms Tri-training in terms of Accuracy, F1-score, Precision, and Recall.

The performance of the semi-supervised learning on the Apache Spark framework is improved if a Federated Learning method is used. Federated Learning provides a distributed framework for collaborative model training and has the capacity to offer benefits -mainly model training parallelism with minimised data sharing/leakage. It results in reduced model training delay, especially in Big data applications.

The performance of the SSL approaches can be improved if a multicomputer platform. This allows true parallelism resulting in enhanced performance and more accurate outputs. However, this research utilises a hyper-threading method to build and test the proposed algorithms due to the cost and lack of resources. Hyper-threading is unable to simultaneously run threads due to the restriction of CPU scheduling algorithm and computing resources (e.g., number of CPU cores).

References

1. Zhou, Z.H., Li, M.: Tri-training: exploiting unlabeled data using three classifiers. IEEE Trans. Knowl. Data Eng. **17**(11), 1529–1541 (2005)
2. Triguero, I., García, S., Herrera, F.: Self-labeled techniques for semi-supervised learning: taxonomy, software and empirical study. Knowl. Inf. Syst. **42**(2), 245–284 (2015)
3. Zhou, L., Pan, S., Wang, J., Vasilakos, A.V.: Machine learning on big data: opportunities and challenges. Neurocomputing **237**, 350–361 (2017)
4. Gardner, A., Duncan, C. A., Kanno, J., Selmic, R.: 3D hand posture recognition from small unlabeled point sets. In: 2014 IEEE International Conference on Systems, Man and Cybernetics (SMC), pp. 164–169 (2014)
5. Elgendy, N., Elragal, A.: Big data analytics: a literature review paper. In: Perner, P. (ed.) ICDM 2014. LNCS (LNAI), vol. 8557, pp. 214–227. Springer, Cham (2014). https://doi.org/10.1007/978-3-319-08976-8_16
6. L'heureux, A., Grolinger, K., Elyamany, H.F., Capretz, M.A.: Machine learning with big data: challenges and approaches. IEEE Access **5**, 7776–7797 (2017)
7. Chawla, N.V., Karakoulas, G.: Learning from labeled and unlabeled data: an empirical study across techniques and domains. J. Artif. Intell. Res. **23**, 331–366 (2005)
8. Zhu, X., Goldberg, A.B.: Introduction to semi-supervised learning. Synth. Lect. Artif. Intell. Mach. Learn **3**(1), 1–130 (2009)
9. Chen, K., Wang, S.: Semi-supervised learning via regularized boosting working on multiple semi-supervised assumptions. IEEE Trans. Pattern Anal. Mach. Intell. **33**(1), 129–143 (2010)
10. Reddy, Y.C.A.P., Viswanath, P., Reddy, B.E.: Semi-supervised learning: a brief review. Int. J. Eng. Technol. **7**(1.8), 81 (2018)
11. Sawant, S.S., Prabukumar, M.: A review on graph-based semi-supervised learning methods for hyperspectral image classification. Egypt. J. Remote Sens. Space Sci. **23**(2), 243–248 (2020)
12. Kacheria, A.: Semi-Supervised Learning Algorithm for Large Datasets Using Spark Environment (Doctoral dissertation, University of Cincinnati) (2021)
13. BalaAnand, M., Karthikeyan, N., Karthik, S., Varatharajan, R., Manogaran, G., Sivaparthipan, C.B.: An enhanced graph-based semi-supervised learning algorithm to detect fake users on Twitter. J. Supercomput. **75**(9), 6085–6105 (2019). https://doi.org/10.1007/s11227-019-02948-w
14. Melo-Acosta, G.E., Duitama-Munoz, F., Arias-Londono, J.D.: Fraud detection in big data using supervised and semi-supervised learning techniques. In: 2017 IEEE Colombian Conference on Communications and Computing (COLCOM), pp. 1–6. IEEE (2017)
15. Rosenberg, C., Hebert, M., Schneiderman, H.: Semi-supervised self-training of object detection models (2005)
16. Riloff, E., Wiebe, J., Phillips, W.: Exploiting subjectivity classification to improve information extraction. In: AAAI, pp. 1106–1111 (2005)
17. Xia, Y., et al.: 3D semi-supervised learning with uncertainty-aware multi-view co-training. In: Proceedings of the IEEE/CVF Winter Conference on Applications of Computer Vision, pp. 3646–3655 (2020)
18. Maeireizo, B., Litman, D., Hwa, R.: Co-training for predicting emotions with spoken dialogue data. In: Proceedings of the ACL Interactive Poster and Demonstration Sessions, pp. 202–205 (2004)

19. Li, M., Zhou, Z.H.: Improve computer-aided diagnosis with machine learning techniques using undiagnosed samples. IEEE Trans. Syst. Man Cybernet.-Part A: Syst. Hum. **37**(6), 1088–1098 (2007)
20. Aziz, K., Zaidouni, D., Bellafkih, M.: Leveraging resource management for efficient performance of Apache Spark. J. Big Data **6**(1), 1–23 (2019). https://doi.org/10. 1186/s40537-019-0240-1
21. Kostopoulos, G., Kotsiantis, S., Pintelas, P.: Estimating student dropout in distance higher education using semi-supervised techniques. In: Proceedings of the 19th Panhellenic Conference on Informatics, pp. 38–43 (2015)
22. Hady, F.A.M., Schwenker, F.: Combining committee-based semi-supervised learning and active learning. J. Comput. Sci. Technol. **25**(4), 681–698 (2010)
23. Li, K., Zhang, W., Ma, X., Cao, Z., Zhang, C.: A novel semi-supervised SVM based on Tri-training. In: 2008 Second International Symposium on Intelligent Information Technology Application, vol. 3, pp. 47–51. IEEE (2008)
24. Penchikala, S.: Big data processing with apache spark (2018). https://www.lulu. com
25. Meng, X., et al.: MLlib: machine learning in apache spark. J. Mach. Learn. Res. **17**(1), 1235–1241 (2016)
26. Armbrust, M., et al.: Scaling spark in the real world: performance and usability. Proc. VLDB Endow. **8**(12), 1840–1843 (2015)
27. López, V., Fernández, A., García, S., Palade, V., Herrera, F.: An insight into classification with imbalanced data: empirical results and current trends on using data intrinsic characteristics. Inf. Sci. **250**, 113–141 (2013)
28. García, S., Ramírez-Gallego, S., Luengo, J., Benítez, J.M., Herrera, F.: Big data preprocessing: methods and prospects. Big Data Anal. **1**(1), 1–22 (2016)
29. Bennett, D.A.: How can I deal with missing data in my study? Aust. N. Z. J. Public Health **25**(5), 464–469 (2001)
30. Zhang, J., Yang, Z., Benslimane, Y.: Exploring and evaluating the scalability and efficiency of apache spark using educational datasets. In: 2019 International Conference on Machine Learning and Cybernetics (ICMLC), pp. 1–6. IEEE (2019)
31. Grandini, M., Bagli, E., Visani, G.: Metrics for multi-class classification: an overview. arXiv preprint arXiv:2008.05756 (2020)
32. Spark. Apache Spark (2022). https://spark.apache.org/ Accessed Aug 2022

Explore the Relationship Between Procedural Score Feedback and Subsequent Time Allocation and Learning Outcomes of Learners in a Massive Open Online Course (MOOC)

Zongjun Wang[1] and Changsheng Chen[2]([⊠])

[1] Shandong Youth University of Political Science, Jinan 250103, China
[2] Shandong Women's University, Jinan 250300, China
chen.changsheng@hotmail.com

Abstract. Procedural feedback is considered to be one of the most powerful educational interventions. Procedural feedback attempts to help learners improve their future performance by providing information about past performance. However, little is known about the impact of processual feedback on learners' subsequent performance. This study aims to uncover the relationship between procedural score feedback, time allocation, and learning outcome, for which a conceptual model was constructed. The model was validated by collecting clickstream data from 7924 MOOC learners in a Chinese MOOC. Partial least squares structural equation modeling (PLS-SEM) was used to test the various hypotheses of the model above. The results found that: (1) procedural score feedback has a significant positive effect on learning outcomes. (2) time allocation for evaluative tasks partially mediates the relationship between procedural score feedback and learning outcome. (3) time allocation for non-evaluative tasks does not mediate the relationship between procedural score feedback and learning outcome. The study suggests some potentially effective measures for MOOC teachers and developers to provide learners with procedural support and to ensure that they achieve good learning outcomes. It also hopes to inspire future research and advance the theory and practice of online education.

Keywords: MOOC · Procedural Score Feedback · Study Time Allocation · Learning Process Analysis · Behavioral Analysis

1 Introduction

Feedback is the transmission of information about the 'outcome' of learning behavior (Tanes et al. 2011). In contrast to final feedback, procedural feedback is an opportunity to provide feedback early in the learning process, before the teacher formally assesses and provides feedback on the outcome (i.e. teacher intervention) (Sedrakyan 2016). Procedural feedback is prominent in supporting learners' behavioral performance in learning. Sedrakyan et al. argue that it is important for course instruction to know whether low

R. Hou et al. (Eds.): BDTA 2021/2022, LNICST 480, pp. 149–168, 2023.
https://doi.org/10.1007/978-3-031-33614-0_11

performance is influenced by misunderstandings of questions, tasks, or concepts or by procedural aspects of learning (e.g., not putting enough effort into validating a solution) to distinguish whether cognitive or behavioral types of feedback are needed (Sedrakyan and Snoeck 2017; Sedrakyan 2016). Therefore, procedural feedback becomes a necessary part of supporting learners' problem inquiry, goal focus, and continuity, and it should receive extra attention from course instructors and administrators.

The application of a new generation of information technology in the field of education has triggered huge changes in educational concepts, teaching and learning styles, and management mechanisms. Currently, open learning spaces express a break from convention and routine through a school-less form, and MOOCs are rapidly emerging worldwide as a form of self-help online learning source. MOOCs are regrouping teaching conditions and learning elements, and are promoting changes in teaching content, model of instruction, and management mechanisms, bringing new opportunities to the reform and development of teaching and learning. However, as a weakly supervised form and self-regulation, MOOCs tend to induce psychological and behavioral problems such as anxiety, procrastination, disorientation, and attention deficit in some learners. Actually, technology-enhanced procedural feedback offers a number of possibilities for addressing these issues, such as providing motivation, engaging participation, and improving retention. However, it has also been found that providing appropriate feedback through digital teaching and learning is not easy, due to the fact that much digital feedback still lacks the support of educational theory and has to be adapted to learners' reading levels to recognize the feedback.

Additionally, procedural feedback is considered to be one of the most powerful educational interventions. Procedural feedback attempts to help learners improve their future performance by providing information about previous performance. Score feedback provides a very effective learning strategy for distributed exercises in MOOCs (Dunlosky et al. 2013). If tests are done well, feedback can be given to students to help them identify areas and key signals that they should focus on (Smith and Lipnevich 2018; Bjork et al. 2010). Generally, when feedback is delivered appropriately and students are able to use it, it can improve teaching and learning (Lipnevich and Smith 2008; Smith and Lipnevich 2018). Slavin explored the value of feedback through the reward structure, arguing that the frequency, size, and sensitivity with which learners receive rewards affect their performance, and there is a correlation between improved performance and increased rewards (Slavin 1980). This illustrates that learner behavior is reinforced by positive outcomes and that rewards provide positive feedback and reinforcement of individual outcomes (Eisenberger and Rhoades 2001). The score feedback provides learners with the information they need to guide their subsequent decisions. Firstly, it provides an informative guide for learners to evaluate their experience, certain extent, and the effectiveness of the endeavor. Moreover, it also provides a controlled guide for learners to engage in self-regulation. However, fewer studies have examined the impact of procedural feedback on adult learners who take informal online courses and have never been face-to-face. This study attempts to fill this gap by focusing on the relationship between procedural score feedback and subsequent time allocation and final outcomes in a MOOC.

2   Theoretical Foundation

2.1   Feedback and Score Feedback

Much research has focused on the design and application of instructional feedback to test its effectiveness. Researchers have been interested in the impact of feedback on students' outcomes and how to provide appropriate feedback in a way that inspires students to regulate, arguing that procedural tests have the value of encouraging distributed exercises, identifying areas of expertise, identifying points of focus, and are effective learning strategies to help learners enhance their self-concept and self-direction (Dunlosky et al. 2013; Smith and Lipnevich 2018; Bjork et al. 2010). The effects of score feedback on memory and learning outcomes have been explored. For example, Beckman investigated the effects of pretesting in a sample of undergraduate students taking a science course, and students reported that pretesting motivated them to monitor their own learning (Beckman 2008). Janelli and Lipnevich conducted an experimental study of 399 students enrolled in the American Museum of Natural History's (AMNH) Climate Change MOOC course and found no effect of pre-test and feedback on learning outcomes among all students. Nevertheless, there was evidence that successful recall of information made students more likely to successfully recall the same information in the future (Janelli and Lipnevich 2021).

MOOCs have currently built mechanisms for publishing academic results through the development of system features and assessment modules such as unit tests, forums, and tasks, resulting in visual feedback in the form of learning dashboards and lists (van Den Hurk 2006; Misra and McKean 2000). MOOC unit tests are a non-face-to-face basic means of testing students' knowledge acquisition in an interactive context (van Den Hurk 2006; Misra and Mckean 2000). In order to answer a question or manipulation, the quiz or exam forces students to generate information through knowledge coding and then reuse these coding processes when the test is administered again. And in the view of Bjork et al. (2010), the use and reuse of coding processes have the potential to provide advantages in future examination attempts.

2.2   Study Time Allocation

Study time allocation is a typical decision-making behavior of learners who make item choices under metacognitive monitoring (Slavin 2012), and learners allocate their attention and subjective effort in a way that reflects their understanding of the task and their ability to selectively engage (Misra and McKean 2000; Eilam and Aharon 2003). Thus, learners' perceptions of reward structures cannot directly influence learning outcomes but are subject to metacognitive modulation.

Current research on the thesis has focused on the factors that influence it and its relationship to the various elements of teaching and learning. In terms of factors influencing study time allocation, Bloom characterizes study time allocation in terms of time spent on work, arguing that time spent on work varies with students' cognitive characteristics, affective characteristics, and quality of instruction (Bloom 1976). Vroom's expectancy theory provides a perspective on time allocation research, arguing that the amount of time individuals actively devote to learning is influenced by a combination of goal validity and expectancy (Vroom 2019).

In terms of the utility of time allocation on learning outcomes, an experimental study by Koriat et al. found that time allocation for learning reflects the fluency with which learners encode learning items and predicts the outcome of learners' recall of learning items (Koriat et al. 2005). van Den Hurk's study showed that students with good time management skills not only scored higher on cognitive. Carroll has used the practical time to evaluate learning output, arguing that learning effectiveness is a function of the amount of time students actually put in divided by the amount of necessary time they should put in (Carroll 1963). Misra and Mckean argue that time management is an effective strategy for reducing academic stress and anxiety and that effective time management can improve learning performance (Misra and Mckean 2000).

In terms of the relationship between study time allocation and behavior, Koriat argues that time management, the allocation of content phases, and behavioral sequences during activities are temporal dimensions of learners' metacognitive control (Koriat et al. 2006). Studies by Hristova and Kim et al. confirm that the number of times learners gaze at a learning item or the duration of gaze can reflect learners' attentional bias (Hristova and Grinberg 2009; Kimet al. 2012).

In addition, according to Self-Determination Theory (SDT), factors such as guidance, rules, feedback, evaluation, and rewards in the social environment influence the satisfaction of individual psychological needs. What's more, learners tend to construct agendas for study time allocation based on elements such as task difficulty, reward structure, and time constraints in the learning situation, directed by learning goals, in conjunction with individual characteristics such as achievement motivation, domain knowledge, and self-efficacy, and perform the agendas under the monitoring of a central executive system for study time allocation (Ariel et al. 2009). It is thus evident that study time allocation provides a pathway for the influence of learners' metacognitive monitoring on their engagement and outcomes.

2.3 Learned Industriousness Theory

Eisenberger's Learned Industriousness Theory (LIT) suggests that individual behavior is reinforced by positive outcomes and that individuals whose effort experiences are characterized by secondary rewards will tend to have the most rewarding responses (high effort operations) in their subsequent behavior; rewards provide positive feedback and reinforcement mechanisms for individual behavior, making them willing to invest more effort (e.g., time and frequency) in learning and acquiring the skills necessary to solve the challenges encountered during the task, and to generalize this learning to new tasks (Eisenberger et al. 1999). It follows that learning is a process in which effort and reinforcement interact, and that diligence is an integral response to engagement and self-efficacy regulation (Eisenberger and Rhoades 2001).

Moreover, it has been shown that learners' commitment to learning can be predicted by perceived task value, competence beliefs, motivational regulation, and perceived teacher support (Zhang and Liu 2019; Korlat et al. 2021). In addition to learning according to the rhythm of the course (instructional design, task requirements, etc.), learners also draw on perceptions of reward structure to fulfill learning commitments and increase engagement (Slavin 2012). Reward strategies can be used as an element of motivation for student progress and achievement, encouraging them to track their learning and performance (Codish and Ravid 2014).

In the context of the new generation of learning management systems, MOOC has developed a clear reward structure based on value-based rewards, supplemented by honor-based rewards, which are informative and controlled in terms of learning criteria (e.g., instructions, achievement requirements, etc.) that can guide and regulate the learner's process, thus influencing their study time allocation (Mazzoni and Cornoldi 1993).

3 Hypotheses Development

3.1 Procedural Score Feedback (PSF) and Learning Outcomes (LO)

Learners usually follow the pacing and task requirements of the course design and regulate their pace in MOOCs, driven by internal motivation, and learning experience, to continuously meet the outcome and performance expectations (Slavin 1980). In the MOOC context, feedback following learning inputs, such as grades, points, and badges, constitute procedural score feedback (PSF), which provides learners with important material to perceive their status and outcomes. In fact, when exploring the dynamics of learning outcomes, studies have found a correlation between outcome rewards and learners' fulfillment of commitment and retention of engagement as one of the factors influencing collaborative learning outcomes (Slavin 2012). As a result, the following hypothesis was therefore proposed.

H1: There is a positive effect of procedural score feedback on the final learning outcome.

3.2 Study Time Allocation (STA) and Learning Outcomes (LO)

Study time allocation is a process of cognitive engagement and regulation of the learning process and learning sources by MOOC learners. In order to adapt to the semi-supervised, self-regulated context of the MOOC, learners need to monitor and regulate their cognitive sources, motivational goals, and emotional states in a timely manner, with the necessary social support, in order to achieve their learning goals. There are two main types of objects that MOOC learners engage in, namely evaluative tasks such as quizzes, exams, and non-evaluative tasks such as viewing courseware and notifications. Thus, the corresponding study time allocation (STA) dimensions are time allocation for evaluative tasks (TAET) and time allocation for non-evaluative tasks (TANET). Therefore, this study proposes the hypothesis as follows.

H2: There is a positive effect of time allocation for evaluation tasks on learning outcomes.
H3: There is a positive effect of time allocation for non-evaluation tasks on learning outcomes.

3.3 Procedural Score Feedback (PSF) and Study Time Allocation (STA)

Procedural score feedback provides a scaffold for learners to understand their personal decisions and learning outcomes. In line with previous studies, Learners plan their time allocation based on the perceived value of the task and the perceived value of the reward. The informative and controlled nature of procedural score feedback can provide cues to guide and optimize the learning process and influence the learner's subsequent time allocation (Mazzoni and Cornoldi 1993). Furthermore, recent research has found that teachers' perceived task value positively predicts their online learning engagement in online professional learning communities and that teachers' motivational moderation partially mediates the ability of perceived task value to predict learning engagement (Zhang and Liu 2019). Therefore, both hypotheses are proposed.

H4: There is a positive effect of procedural score feedback on time allocated for evaluation tasks.
H5: There is a positive effect of procedural score feedback on time allocation for non-evaluation tasks.

As mentioned above, the research model constructed in this paper is shown in Fig. 1. It is hypothesized that the learning outcomes (LO) of MOOC learners are influenced by the time allocation of evaluative tasks (TAET), time allocation of non-evaluative tasks (TANET), and procedural score feedback (RSP). Likewise, the two types of study time allocation variables mediate the process by which procedural score feedback influences learning outcomes.

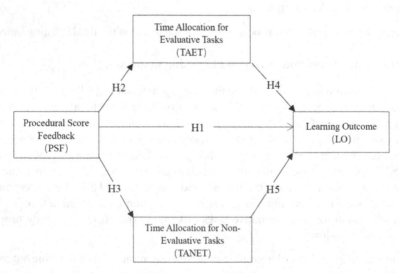

Fig. 1. Research model

4 Methodology

4.1 Research Context and Participants

In this study, 7924 learners' clickstream data in the course "How Teachers Do Research" on the Chinese university MOOC platform (https://www.icourse163.org) were collected. Due to the content of the course, the learners were mostly educational researchers and teacher-training students. Considering score as a classification criterion, 4,197 failures (<60), 595 passers (60–69), 949 moderators (70–79), and 2,183 excellenters (80–100). The data for the study were collected from 4 March 2016 to 29 January 2018, and the clickstream data extracted were mainly the record fields of information browsing, resource interaction, and evaluation participation generated by the learners. Besides, data pre-processing, cleaning, and integration were performed prior to data analysis.

4.2 Research Design

The research design consists of three segments. Session 1: Analyse the distribution of the variables through descriptive statistics of the independent and dependent variables to provide a basis for selecting an effective evaluation method for the research model; Session 2: Conduct an in-depth analysis of the research question with the structural equation modeling (SEM), mainly completing measurement model evaluation, structural model evaluation, and mediation analysis; Session 3: On the basis of quantitative analysis, generalize the strategies for MOOC procedural evaluation and feedback design.

In Session 2, along with the results of the statistical test, it was found that many of the variables had large skewness or kurtosis, indicating that the latent variables were mostly non-normally distributed. Therefore, using the maximum likelihood method that emphasizes the multivariate normal distribution of the variables would yield biased misinterpretations, and thus this study chooses to use a partial least squares (PLS) based method for the parameter estimation method.

4.3 Coding Scheme

Four latent variables were used in the study: procedural score feedback (PSF), time allocation for evaluative tasks (TAET), time allocation for non-evaluative tasks (TANET), and learning outcomes (LO). Firstly, three indicators were used to measure the procedural score feedback: assignment score, unit quiz score, and forum score, which are full of information about the effectiveness of the learner's engagement and potential guidance, and thus may convey developmental incentives or 'remedial' warnings. Secondly, five variables were used to measure learners' time allocation for tasks: time spent on participation in forums, completion of assignments, participation in quizzes, viewing quiz lists, and viewing exam lists. The time allocation for non-evaluative tasks was measured by three indicators: time spent on viewing announcements, watching micro-videos, and viewing assessment instructions. Furthermore, in order to observe learners' behavior under the influence of procedural score feedback, learners' time allocation was used to quantify the indicators above. Learning outcomes are measured by final exam scores. The coding scheme is shown in Table 1.

Table 1. Coding scheme

Latent variables	Observed variables	Coding	Explanation
Time allocation for non-evaluative tasks (TANET)	Time spent browsing course announcements	tanet1	The time allotted for learners to view information such as course announcements and bulletins
	Time spent on viewing videos and courseware	tanet2	The time allotted for learners to view the course videos and the accompanying courseware
	Time spent browsing assessment information	tanet3	Time allocation for learners to browse the course assessment information
Time allocation for evaluative tasks (TAET)	Time spent on checking examination lists	taet1	The time allocated for learners to browse information such as exam lists
	Time spent on participating forums	taet2	The time allocated for learners to participate in the forums
	Time spent on completing the assignments	taet3	Learners view assignment requirements and time allocation for assignments
	Time spent on the quizzes	taet4	The time allocated for learners to participate in the unit quizzes
	Time spent on checking the unit-quiz list	taet5	Time allocation for learners to browse the list of unit quizzes
Procedural Score Feedback (PSF)	Quiz scores	psf1	The learner's score on the unit quizzes
	Assignment scores	psf2	The learner's score on the assignments
	Forum scores	psf3	The learner's score on forum participation
Learning Outcome (LO)	Final score	lo1	The learner's score on final exam

5 Data Analysis and Results

5.1 Sample

Before starting the study, it was confirmed whether the sample of individuals followed a distribution within the parameters of normality. The values of kurtosis and Skewness were found for the selected indicators. With kurtosis and skewness, values lower than |3.00| indicate a normal distribution (Kline 2010, cited in Wu and Cheng 2019). In this study, KS values were found within an interval of |0.81| to |76.36| and SK values between |0.01| and |6.56|, which suggests that there is no serious deviation, from normality in the distributions (see Table 2). Therefore, the study needs to consider using statistical methods for analysis that is not limited by the distribution of variables to reduce bias in the study results.

Table 2. Descriptive statistical analysis of variables (N = 7924)

Variable	Min	Max	M	SD	KS	SK
tanet1	0.00	13354.63	753.08	1224.40	10.89	2.84
tanet2	0.00	198332.28	17618.53	21381.40	4.53	1.77
tanet3	0.00	46231.41	2140.29	3627.81	17.63	3.40
taet1	0.00	7299.72	513.36	956.93	5.92	2.31
taet2	0.00	68298.70	1009.80	2805.12	76.36	6.56
taet3	0.00	20778.59	933.70	1665.28	14.07	2.96
taet4	0.00	38889.42	3562.42	4309.12	4.50	1.75
taet5	0.00	18165.41	1078.87	1752.31	10.62	2.73
psf1	0.00	50.00	27.10	18.24	−1.69	−0.22
psf2	0.00	15.00	5.71	6.51	−1.81	0.33
psf3	0.00	100.00	31.33	37.01	−0.81	0.85
lol	0.00	20.00	8.60	8.16	−1.83	0.01

Min, minimum value; Max, maximum value; M, Mean; SD, Standard Deviation; KS, Kurtosis Statistic; SK, Skewness Statistic.

5.2 Measurement Model Evaluation

In this paper, measurement models and structural models are assessed using partial least squares (PLS), which does not require consideration of the distribution of the variables. Reliability, two tests were applied (Hair et al. 2019): Cronbach's Alpha (α) and composite reliability (CR). Cronbach's alpha (α) is a popular measure of internal consistency, which is generally considered to be good when the value is greater than 0.7, and fair when it is between 0.5 and 0.7 (Jum and Ira 1978). All constructs included in the proposed model satisfied these conditions and thus all possess reliable internal consistency as Cronbach's alpha values ranged from 0.766 (TANET) to 1 (LO) and CR values ranged from 0.851 (TAET) to 1 (LO), as displayed in Table 3.

Table 3. Reliability and validity tests

Variable	PSF	TAET	TANET	LO	α	CR	AVE
tanet1			0.803		0.766	0.865	0.681
tanet2			0.870				
tanet3			0.800				
taet1		0.663			0.781	0.851	0.537
taet2		0.575					
taet3		0.761					
taet4		0.833					
taet5		0.663					
psf1	0.918				0.876	0.924	0.801
psf2	0.904						
psf3	0.862						
lo1				1.00	1.00	1.00	1.00

The validity of the measurement model includes two items: convergent validity and discriminant validity. Firstly, convergent validity is assessed using factor loading (FL), composite reliability (CR), and average variance extracted (AVE) (Werts et al. 1974). In this study, the factor loadings of all variables were greater than 0.5 (recommended value greater than 0.5), CR was greater than 0.850 (recommended value greater than 0.7) and AVE was greater than 0.536 (recommended value greater than 0.5), indicating that the measurement model has good convergent validity. Moreover, the discriminant validity of the measurement model is assessed by AVE, cross-loading, and related indicators. (Chin 1998). As shown in Tables 3 and 4, the factor loadings of each indicator on the corresponding latent variables are all greater than 0.7 (recommended value is greater than 0.7), and the factor loadings of the same variable are higher than those of other variables; the square root of the AVE of each latent variable is higher than the correlation coefficient with other latent variables, indicating that the measurement model has good discriminant validity.

Table 4. Discriminant validity test (Fornell and Larcher criterion)

	AVE	PSF	TAET	TANET	LO
PSF	0.801	0.895			
TAET	0.681	0.640	0.733		
TANET	0.537	0.557	0.731	0.825	
LO	1.000	0.865	0.584	0.497	1.000

Note: The values on the diagonal line in the table represent the square root of the corresponding dimension AVE

Given the high correlation between the independent variables, various problems may arise in interpreting the fitness results of the regression model (Meloun et al. 2002). Therefore, it is also necessary to check for the presence of multi-collinearity. The variance inflation factor (VIF) was assessed to identify the presence of multi-collinearity (Hair et al. 2019). The presence of more severe multi-collinearity was demonstrated when the VIF coefficients of the respective variables in the study model exceeded 5. The results in Table 5 show that the VIF values of all independent variables are less than 5, indicating that there is no multi-collinearity between the independent variables.

Table 5. Multi-collinearity test

Independent variable	Dependent variable	VIF value
LO	PSF	1.723
	TAET	2.928
	TANET	2.508

5.3 Model Fit Indices

Before evaluating the structural model, it is essential to assess the performance of the studied model using the fit metrics. As shown in Table 6, all the fit metrics satisfy the acceptable values advocated by Henseler et al. (2016), indicating that the proposed model is able to adequately fit the dataset.

Table 6. Model fit indices

Fit index	Recommended value/condition	Actual values
SRMR (Standardized Root Mean Square Residual)	<0.08	0.069
NFI (Normed Fit Index)	>0.9	0.883
d_ULS (Unweighted Least Squares)	"d_ULS < bootstrapped HI 95% of d_ULS and d_G < bootstrapped HI 95% of d_G"	0.373
d_G (Geodesic Discrepancies)		0.206
GoF (Goodness of Fit)	<0.1 (small) 0.25 (medium) >0.36 (large)	0.608
rms Theta	<0.12	0.109

Note: GoF = sqrt(average(AVE)* average(R^2))

5.4 Structural Model Evaluation

In this stage, the significance of the path coefficients (β values) of the relationships (proposed hypotheses) among constructs was evaluated. Accordingly, the bootstrapping procedure (with 5000 bootstrap resampling) was applied. Both T-statistics and p-values were employed to determine the Both T-statistics and p-value were employed to determine the significance of path coefficients (β); specifically, a significance level of 5% (p value < 0.05) and a t value higher than 1.96. The PLS-SEM analysis indicates the estimation and evaluation of proposed hypotheses, as presented in Fig. 2. The results demonstrate that four out of the five hypotheses are These are H1 (PSF->LO), H2 (PSF->TAET), H3 (PSF->TANET) and H4 (TAET->LO). This implies that PSF and TAET have significant and direct positive effects on LO, with PSF acts as the strongest predictor (($\beta = 0.833$, p-value < 0.001). Further, H2 (PSF->TAET) is also supported as PSF ($\beta = 0.640$, p-value = 0.000 < 0.001) has a significant positive influence on TAET, H3 (PSF->TANET) is also supported as PSF ($\beta = 0.557$, p-value = 0.000 < 0.001) has a significant positive influence on TANET.

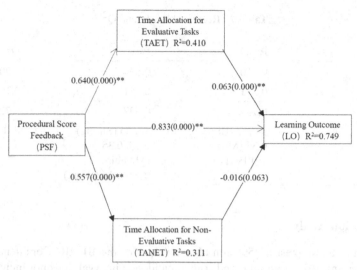

Fig. 2. Structural model analysis. Note: Numbers between brackets represent p value. **p value < 0.01, *p value < 0.05

Also, during this stage additional measures were evaluated, namely the determination coefficient (R^2), effect size (f^2), and predictive relevance (Q^2) (Hair et al. 2019). R^2 measures the predictive power of the research model by assessing the degree to which the independent variables explain the variance among the results in Table 7 indicate that the value of R^2 for LO (the key target construct) is 0.749, demonstrating that PSF, TAET, and TANET explain 74.9% of the variance among the dependent variables. Such predictive power is considered substantial (>0.67) (Chin 1998). TAET also explains 41% ($R^2 = 0.41$) of the variance in PSF. Additionally, TANET explains 31.1% ($R^2 = 0.311$) of the variance in PSF, indicating moderate TAET also explains 41% ($R^2 = 0.41$) of the variance in PSF.

Q^2 measures (only calculated for dependent variables) were obtained by running the blindfolding procedure (applying the omission distance of D = 7). All values of Q^2 (see Table 7) are above zero (Geisser 1975), indicating that the research model possesses high predictive relevance (Cohen 1988). Finally, the effect size (f^2) values for PSF, TAET and TANET on LO, and for PSF on TAET and TANET are displayed in Table 7. Based on Cohen (1988), the results suggest that the effect sizes for PSF, TAET, and TANET on LO are large, and PSF on TAET and TANET are large too.

Table 7. Results of R^2, f^2 and Q^2

Variables	R^2	f^2	Q^2
TAET	0.410	0.694	0.203
TANET	0.311	0.451	0.196
LO	0.749	0.537	0.728
Recommended value /condition	>0.67 (High) 0.33 (Medium) <0.19 (Low)	>0.35 (Strong) 0.15–0.35 (Medium) 0.02–0.15 (Weak)	0–1

5.5 Mediation Analysis

MacKinnon et al. suggest a 95% confidence value for the BI (BC Confidence Level) when performing Bootstrapping, and if the confidence interval does not include 0, the mediating effect is present; if the confidence interval includes 0, the mediating effect is not present (MacKinnon et al. 2007). If the confidence interval does not include 0, a mediating effect exists; if the confidence interval includes 0, a mediating effect does not exist (MacKinnon et al. 2007). The results of the study are shown in the Table 8. 95% confidence intervals for the indirect effect of procedural score feedback (PSF) via time allocation for evaluation tasks (TAET) on learning outcomes (LO) were [0.043,0.083], with confidence intervals excluding 0 indicating a significant mediating effect, corresponding to an indirect effect value of 0.04. However, the indirect effect of procedural score feedback (PSF) via time allocation for non-evaluation tasks (TANET) of time allocation (TANET) had a 95% confidence interval of [−0.031, 0.001] for the indirect effect of influencing learning outcomes (LO), with confidence intervals including 0, indicating a non-significant mediating effect.

Table 8. Intermediary Effect

Path	2.5%	97.5%	Results	Value
RSP->AST-PET->LO	0.043	0.083	Significant	0.04
RSP->AST-PNET->LO	−0.032	0.001	Not Significant	-

6 Discussion

The role of task value and academic emotion on learning engagement has been widely recognized by academics (Artino 2008), but the impact of procedural score feedback on learning time allocation has rarely been discussed in previous research. This study uses an empirical approach to analyze the mechanisms by which procedural feedback affects the allocation of learning time. The results show that procedural score feedback (PSF) significantly affects learners' subsequent allocation of learning time and has a stronger effect on the allocation of time to evaluative tasks (TAET) than to non-evaluative tasks (TANET). This result is consistent with previous research (Lei et al. 2017). Procedural score feedback (PSF) as a motivational mechanism for the course with embedded cues, and task value tendencies can help learners to form and adjust their personal learning pace. When learners experience learning gains and task values from learning, they can evaluate the effectiveness of their own learning inputs based on the gap between their effort state and expectations, and thus adjust the time allocation of learning tasks and learning resources. Those behavioral inputs that have met learning expectations will be reinforced and transferred, otherwise, they will be adjusted, eventually forming habitual learning behaviors and relatively reasonable time allocation. Thus, the results of procedural score feedback will lead to differences in learners' time allocation.The role of course-cued information on learning outcomes has received academic attention (Lamb et al. 2018), but there have been no consistent research findings. The present study shows that procedural score feedback (PSF) positively predicts learning outcomes (LO). This finding is similar to Webb and Johnson's research (Webb 1982; Jonassen et al. 2008), which validates the behavioral school's basic view of the utility of rewards, that extrinsic motivation is an enabler of intrinsic motivation, helping to guide individuals to enhance their self-competence around task goals or reward criteria, which in turn enhances the self-efficacy required to complete the task and psychological motivation.

According to the MOOC context, procedural score feedback provides a quantifiable and perceptible developmental scaffolding of learning for the learner's stage-by-stage commitment to learning. This is very similar to the reward structure of a course. Deci et al. argue that the informational nature of course rewards activates individual competency needs (Deci et al. 1999), provides cues and monitors learners' behavior, and can provide pacing guidance and process regulation for learners. Specifically, the types and modules in the reward structure of a catechism can guide learners to plan their own cognitive resources, make flexible pacing changes to reduce cognitive load, and enhance the sense of presence in online learning; the frequency and acceptability of rewards can facilitate learners' metacognitive monitoring and thus adjust paths to keep learners in an effective learning state.

Besides, Learning engagement levels can represent learner diligence, and this study examines the role of two types of learning time allocation on learning outcomes. The results indicate that time allocation to evaluative tasks (TAET) positively predicted learning outcome (LO) and it also had a mediating effect on the path of procedural score feedback (PSF) affecting learning outcome (LO), however, time allocation to engage in non-evaluative tasks (TANET) was weaker in predicting learning outcome (LO). This finding is in line with previous research findings (Broadbent 2017; van Den Hurk 2006). Study time allocation is a component of metacognitive control, where learners focus first on the way learning as whole proceeds and then on the allocation of time to individual items (Thiede and Dunlosky 1999). The allocation of learning time during learning reflects how well learners follow explicit or implicit learning rules (Kovanovic 2016), and there is a wide variation in learners' time commitment to task engagement and resource preferences. The metacognitive monitoring of learners in MOOC learning enables learners to focus more on tasks related to the evaluation of the course phase, and to allocate more time to this, often leading to good learning outcomes.

7 Implications for Theory and Practice

The above findings have some reference significance for MOOC feedback design and platform development. On the one hand, teachers can optimize the reward structure of the MOOC based on procedural score feedback and establish a clear and perfect reward mechanism to guide learners to increase their learning commitment. The main work includes two aspects: firstly, teachers should optimize the reward design and build a scientific and reasonable reward structure. In terms of reward types, in addition to increasing the number of points for resource access and behavioral participation, additional forms of honors such as ranking segments and points can be added to improve the single reward and comprehensive honor mechanisms; in terms of reward targets, reward mechanisms for learning groups can be designed in line with the needs of collaborative learning tasks to enhance learners' enthusiasm and sense of efficacy in collaborative learning; in terms of reward frequencies, they should be combined with course attributes and task In terms of the frequency of rewards, they should be planned in accordance with the attributes of the course and the characteristics of the tasks, and a reasonable frequency can motivate learners' progress; in terms of the acceptability of rewards, the design of direct and indirect rewards should be balanced, so as to play a comprehensive role of direct motivation and potential spur. Secondly, teachers and developers need to strengthen evaluation feedback mechanisms and build fully functional reward information push and visualization platforms. It has been shown that the behavior of learners to check the course progress and evaluation results in a timely manner can facilitate learners to adjust their learning pace (Gašević et al. 2016). Therefore, it is recommended that catechism platforms should be designed to provide vivid and real-time feedback on rewards, so that learners can clearly identify their progress and learning outputs, and receive 'external motivation' and learning references from the performance of their peers so that they can adjust and optimize their learning pace.

On the other hand, course teams and platform developers should guide learners' behavioral paths in conjunction with instructional design to help them allocate their learning time appropriately. This can be achieved through three tasks. First of all, teachers need to direct learners to devote more cognitive resources to more valuable learning activities. Given that procedural score feedback contains clear information about the value of the task, process management should focus on guiding learners' behavioral pathways by setting up reference learning times, progress dashboards, and resource indices to guide learners in planning their learning time allocation and carrying out in-depth learning. Moreover, the interaction between the pace of learning and the pace of teaching is facilitated through pedagogical activities. Research has shown that the allocation of learning time under the influence of groups of learners leads to a greater degree of structure in unstructured learning environments (online open environments) (Elvers et al. 2003). Along with the learning in a MOOC, the reward structure, the layout of resources, and the allocation of tasks are all reflections of the teaching rhythm, while the learning behavior and its time allocation are reflections of the learning rhythm. The course team can use the interaction between learning and teaching rhythms to assess the effectiveness of the design and inform the construction of the course. In addition, the course team can use this to personalize teaching and learning, guiding struggling learners to learn at the pace of their peers, adapt to the pace of teaching, and master the focus of their learning.

Furthermore, protocols should be signed between teachers and students to reduce the frequency of learners' 'disengagement' from the platform. Due to the learning environment, MOOC learners are prone to browse irrelevant websites and operate desktop software and other non-authentic learning states, which seriously interfere with learners' attention and learning continuity. Therefore, it is recommended that the course team should guide learners to actively commit to the learning behavior protocol by means of information prompts or access restrictions, blocking irrelevant websites, and restricting desktop software operations so that learners can focus on their tasks and thus improve their learning outcomes.

8 Conclusion and Future Work

The main aim of this study was to explore the latent relationship between procedural score feedback and study time allocation and learning outcomes. The empirical results indicate that the positive impact of procedural score feedback and time allocation for evaluative tasks on learning outcomes is mainly due to the fact that the reward structure of the MOOC acts as a 'vane' for learners' behavioral inputs and time allocation, which can provide an external value reference for their cognitive behavior, and that behavioral results and experiences trigger learners' learning motivation and behavioral rhythm regulation, thus facilitating the emergence of good learning outcomes for them.

The current study has a number of limitations that need to be addressed in future research. For example, the study was conducted through learners' feedback data and performance data over 8 weeks, which is considered cross-sectional data analysis, without phased data collection and validation, which may make it difficult to reflect the precise relationship between variables. Therefore, the subsequent study needs to conduct a comparison under multiple division results to test the validity of the research model in this paper. In addition, the data collected for this study only includes students from a MOOC in China, which limits the generalizability of the findings. Hence, further research is recommended to validate the research model using a larger sample size that includes students from a variety of MOOCs.

Acknowledgements. Thanks to the course team and MOOC platform (https://www.icourse16 3.org) for providing the data for this study.This work is funded by Shandong Province Higher Educational Research Program of China [Grant No. J18RA144], Shandong Social Science Planning Project of China[Grant No. 22CJYJ32], and Research Project of Shandong Youth University of Political Science[Grant No. XXPY20035].

References

Ariel, R., Dunlosky, J., Bailey, H.: Agenda-based regulation of study-time allocation: when agendas override item-based monitoring. J. Exp. Psychol. Gen. **138**(3), 432–447 (2009)

Artino, A.R.: Understanding satisfaction and continuing motivation in an online course: an extension of social cognitive, control-value theory. In: Annual Meeting of the American Educational Research Association, New York (2008)

Beckman, W.S.: Pre-testing as a method of conveying learning objectives. J. Aviation/Aerosp. Educ. Res. **17**(172), 61–70 (2008)

Bjork, E.L., Storm, B.C., de Winstanley, P.A.: Learning from the consequences of retrieval: another test effect. In: Benjamin, A.S. (ed.) Successful Remembering and Successful Forgetting: A Festschrift in Honor of Robert A. Bjork, 1st edn. Psychology Press (2010)

Bloom, B.S.: Human Characteristics and School Learning. McGraw-Hill (1976)

Broadbent, J.: Comparing online and blended learner's self-regulated learning strategies and academic performance. Internet High. Educ. **33**, 24–32 (2017)

Carroll, J.B.: A model of school learning. Teach. Coll. Rec. **64**(8), 1–9 (1963)

Chin, W.W.: The partial least squares approach to structural equation modeling. Mod. Methods Bus. Res. **295**(2), 295–336 (1998)

Codish, D., Ravid, G.: Academic course gamification: the art of perceived playfulness. Interdisc. J. E-Learn. Learn. Objects **10**(1), 131–151 (2014)

Cohen, J.: Statistical Power Analysis for the Behavioural Sciences. Lawrence Erlbaum (1988)

Deci, E.L., Koestner, R., Ryan, R.M.: A meta-analytic review of experiments examining the effects of extrinsic rewards on intrinsic motivation. Psychol. Bull. **125**(6), 627–668 (1999)

Dunlosky, J., Rawson, K.A., Marsh, E.J., Nathan, M.J., Willingham, D.T.: Improving students' learning with effective learning techniques: promising directions from cognitive and educational psychology. Psychol. Sci. Public Interest **14**(1), 4–58 (2013)

Eilam, B., Aharon, I.: Students' planning in the process of self-regulated learning. Contemp. Educ. Psychol. **28**(3), 304–334 (2003)

Eisenberger, R., Rhoades, L.: Incremental effects of reward on creativity. J. Pers. Soc. Psychol. **81**(4), 728–741 (2001)

Eisenberger, R., Pierce, W.D., Cameron, J.: Effects of reward on intrinsic motivation—negative, neutral, and positive: comment on Deci, Koestner, and Ryan (1999)

Elvers, G.C., Polzella, D.J., Graetz, K.: Procrastination in online courses: performance and attitudinal differences. Teach. Psychol. **30**(2), 159–162 (2003)

Gašević, D., Dawson, S., Rogers, T., Gasevic, D.: Learning analytics should not promote one size fits all: the effects of instructional conditions in predicting academic success. Internet High. Educ. **28**, 68–84 (2016)

Geisser, S.: The predictive sample reuse method with applications. J. Am. Stat. Assoc. **70**(350), 320–328 (1975)

Hair, J.F., Risher, J.J., Sarstedt, M., Ringle, C.M.: When to use and how to report the results of PLS-SEM. Eur. Bus. Rev. **31**(1), 2–24 (2019)

Henseler, J., Hubona, G., Ray, A.: Using PLS path modelling in new technology research: updated guide-lines. Ind. Manag. Data Syst. **116**(1), 2–20 (2016)

Janelli, M., Lipnevich, A.A.: Effects of pre-tests and feedback on performance outcomes and persistence in Massive Open Online Courses. Comput. Educ. **161**, 1–13 (2021)

Jonassen, D., Spector, M.J., Driscoll, M., Merrill, M.D., van Merrienboer, J., Driscoll, M.P.: Handbook of Research on Educational Communications and Technology: A Project of the Association for Educational Communications and Technology. Routledge (2008)

Jum, N., Ira, H.B.: Psychometric Theory. McGraw-Hill, New York (1978)

Kim, B.E., Seligman, D., Kable, J.W.: Preference reversals in decision making under risk are accompanied by changes in attention to different attributes. Front. Neurosci. **6**, 1–10 (2012)

Koriat, A., Ma'ayan, H.: The effects of encoding fluency and retrieval fluency on judgments of learning. J. Mem. Lang. **52**(4), 478–492 (2005)

Korlat, S., et al.: Gender differences in digital learning during COVID-19: competence beliefs, intrinsic value, learning engagement, and perceived teacher support. Front. Psychol. **12**, 1–13 (2021)

Kovanovic, V., Gašević, D., Dawson, S., Joksimovic, S., Baker, R.: Does time-on-task estimation matter? Implications on validity of learning analytics findings. J. Learn. Anal. **2**(3), 81–110 (2015)

Lamb, R.L., Annetta, L., Firestone, J., Etopio, E.: A meta-analysis with examination of moderators of student cognition, affect, and learning outcomes while using serious educational games, serious games, and simulations. Comput. Hum. Behav. **80**, 158–167 (2018)

Lipnevich, A.A., Smith, J.K.: Response to Assessment Feedback: The Effects of Grades, Praise, and Source of Information, Princeton (2008)

MacKinnon, D.P., Fritz, M.S., Williams, J., Lockwood, C.M.: Distribution of the product confidence limits for the indirect effect: program PRODCLIN. Behav. Res. Methods **39**(3), 384–389 (2007)

Mazzoni, G., Cornoldi, C.: Strategies in study time allocation: why is study time sometimes not effective? J. Exp. Psychol. Gen. **122**(1), 47–60 (1993)

Meloun, M., Militký, J., Hill, M., Brereton, R.G.: Crucial problems in regression modelling and their solutions. Analyst **127**(4), 433–450 (2002)

Misra, R., McKean, M.: College students' academic stress and its relation to their anxiety, time management, and leisure satisfaction. Am. J. Health Stud. **16**(1), 41 (2000)

Sedrakyan, G.: Process-oriented feedback perspectives based on feedback enabled simulation and learning process data analytics. Ph.D. thesis. KU Leuven (2016)

Sedrakyan, G., Snoeck, M.: Cognitive feedback and behavioral feedforward automation perspectives for modeling and validation in a learning context. In: Hammoudi, S., Pires, L.F., Selic, B., Desfray, P. (eds.) MODELSWARD 2016. CCIS, vol. 692, pp. 70–92. Springer, Cham (2017). https://doi.org/10.1007/978-3-319-66302-9_4

Sedrakyan, G., De Weerdt, J., Snoeck, M.: Process-mining enabled feedback: "tell me what I did wrong" vs. "tell me how to do it right." Comput. Hum. Behav. **57**, 352–376 (2016)

Slavin, R.E.: Cooperative learning. Rev. Educ. Res. **50**(2), 315–342 (1980)

Slavin, R.E.: Educational Psychology. Theory and Practice, 10th edn. Pearson, Upper Saddle River (2012)

Smith, J.K., Lipnevich, A.A.: Instructional feedback: analysis, synthesis, and extrapolation. In: Lipnevich, A.A., Smith, J.K. (eds.) The Cambridge Handbook of Instructional Feedback. Cambridge University Press (2018)

Tanes, Z., Arnold, K.E., King, A.S., Remnet, M.A.: Using signals for appropriate feedback: perceptions and practices. Comput. Educ. **57**(4), 2414–2422 (2011)

Thiede, K.W., Dunlosky, J.: Toward a general model of self-regulated study: an analysis of selection of items for study and self-paced study time. J. Exp. Psychol. Learn. Mem. Cogn. **25**(4), 1024–1037 (1999)

van Den Hurk, M.: The relation between self-regulated strategies and individual study time, prepared participation and achievement in a problem-based curriculum. Act. Learn. High. Educ. **7**(2), 155–169 (2006)

Vroom, V.H.: Some Personality Determinants of the Effects of Participation. Routledge (2019)

Webb, N.M.: Peer interaction and learning in cooperative small groups. J. Educ. Psychol. **74**(5), 642–655 (1982)

Werts, C.E., Linn, R.L., Jöreskog, K.G.: Intraclass reliability estimates: testing structural assumptions. Educ. Psychol. Measur. **34**(1), 25–33 (1974)

Wu, J.Y., Cheng, T.: Who is better adapted in learning online within the personal learning environment? Relating gender differences in cognitive attention networks to digital distraction. Comput. Educ. **128**, 312–329 (2019)

Zhang, S., Liu, Q.: Investigating the relationships among teachers' motivational beliefs, motivational regulation, and their learning engagement in online professional learning communities. Comput. Educ. **134**, 145–155 (2019)

DoS Attacks Detection in the Network of Drones: An Efficient Decision Tree-Based Model

Tarek Gaber[1,2]([envelope]) [iD], Xin Fan Guo[3], and Said Salloum[1] [iD]

[1] School of Science, Engineering, and Environment, University of Salford, Salford, UK
t.m.a.gaber@salford.ac.uk
[2] Faculty of Computers and Informatics, Suez Canal University, Ismailia 41522, Egypt
[3] Faculty of Natural, Mathematical and Engineering Sciences, Department of Informatics,
King's College London, London, UK

Abstract. This study examines the detection of the denial of service (DoS) attacks on Wi-Fi-based unmanned aerial vehicles (UAV). The paper proposed an efficient DoS attack detection method based on Decision Tree classifier. The method consists of preprocessing, feature extraction, and DoS attack detection. The preprocessing was proved to save drones' resources and improve the detection rate. The investigation of different classifiers, i.e., KNN, Random Forest, Logistic Regression, and Decision Tree, the latter was concluded to be the best in detecting DoS attacks of types of De-authentication and UDP/TCP flood within the shortest runtime. The evaluation further showed that proposed DoS detection method is better than the most related work where it achieved detection with F1-score of 0.989 and with the shortest latency.

Keywords: DoS attack · Smart cities · Machine learning · Decision Tree · Algorithm Latency

1 Introduction

In large-scale and interconnected urban residences, a smart city offers convenient and better-quality services [1]. A smart city may be considered a convergence of a large amount of information and communication technologies to offer services like logistics, traffic management, and goods delivery [2]. This ensures that citizens are offered intelligent, automated, and adaptive services. The smart city worldwide market was found to be around USD 741.6 billion during the COVID-19 crisis in 2020 and was expected to reach USD 2.5 Trillion by 2026 [3]. The rapid increase in digitally-enabled services during the COVID-19 crisis may have occurred because of the ready adoption of technology that allowed the masses to access services remotely [2]. However, such adoption could be hindered if the most common cybersecurity attacks such DoS [4] and phishing [5] are not detecting.

Various traditional services may be included in a smart city, which can be automated and delivered using Artificial Intelligence (AI)-based decision-making [6]. For example,

R. Hou et al. (Eds.): BDTA 2021/2022, LNICST 480, pp. 169–178, 2023.
https://doi.org/10.1007/978-3-031-33614-0_12

real-time traffic data that is obtained from different localities within a smart city can be provided to a traffic light, which leads to intelligence and adaptive signal transition timings and thus, improved traffic flow and reduced possibility of a traffic jam. In the same way, it is possible to transform a conventional electricity grid into a smart electricity grid that provides real-time energy usage information to both the grid operators and end users. It is expected that by 2026, the smart energy segment will attain a global market value of USD 652.9 billion [2, 3].

Various operations can be carried out by Unmanned Aerial Vehicles (UAV), which is an enabling technology, such as agriculture, rescue, delivery, inspection and, catastrophe response. Popularly known as drones, UAVs are a developing facilitator of various smart city services. A ground controller unit is used to control UAVs that usually offer services like observing weather phenomena, product delivery, aerial photography, and surveillance. UAVs also include remotely operated and unmanned flights, like the S-100 Camcopter, that carry defense service payloads to remote and hard-to-reach areas [7]. There is clearly a rapid spread of drones in the commercial markets, with its market share expected to become USD 58.4 billion by 2026 [2, 7]. Though it was used as a military vehicle initially, at present, it is increasingly used in commercial and consumer machines. Ensuring secure and reliable functioning is a key issue for the universal presence of UAVs. Cyber threats (such as GPS spoofing, data leakage, and flight disruption) exist, which can have an impact on these vehicles, generating unexpected situations that may be dangerous for stakeholders (such as operators, ground stations, and the general public) that are part of the operational environment [4, 7, 8].

As explained previously, there are several advantages of incorporating drones within a smart city. However, no universal and comprehensive model is developed for determining, avoiding, or even identifying cyber threats that are faced when drones are introduced in a smart city's airspace. Public safety is compromised when drones enter into no-fly zones, putting a secure premise at risk, such as entering an airport's airspace and putting aircraft and airport operations at risk, as well as the dropping of illegal products (such as delivering unlawful goods to prisons). Recent years have seen considerable developments in research and development in this field [2, 4, 9]. An AI-enabled portable drone detection unit (tower) has been presented by Dedrone for identifying unlawful drone intrusions into no-fly zones by installing monitoring towers in particular areas [2, 10].

Though there is a rapid development in the existing research about cyber-attacks involving drones, it is still needed to investigate drone-based cyber-attacks, evaluate the kinds of threats faced by a smart city's airspace, and how a city's economy is affected by a drone-based attack. For example, Denial of Service (DoS) attack could lead to operational disruption in a network of drones. One of the widely used platform controlling Wi-Fi-based UAVs is the Parrot AR Drone 2.0 as its documentation is extensively available and not expensive [11].

The authors in [4] proposed a DoS attack detection model using machine learning with high accuracy results reaching 99. However, from analyzing the dataset used in [4], it was noticed that there are duplicates of 32.17%, Fig. 2 shows an example of duplicate entries. Such duplication would lead to unreliable outcome, i.e., unreliable DoS detection rate which could have massive loss, e.g., unresponsive drone. This also leads to more power consumption which is limited in drone's environment. This paper aims to address these problems by proposing an efficient DoS attack detection with high detection rate.

The structure of the rest of the paper is as follows. The related work is discussed in Sect. 2 which is followed by an overview of the Denial of Service (DoS) attack in Sect. 3. The proposed method is presented in Sect. 3. In Sect. 4, the results and discussion are given. Finally, conclusions and some further work are highlighted in Sect. 5.

2 Related Work

As one of the widely available commercial quadcopter platform for controlling UAVs [11], the Parrot AR. Drone 2.0 has been subject to various security investigation studies which identified many security flaws. This platform is for many UAV activities including packet inspection, operating system assessment to identify active programs and file readers, as well as port scanning to look for accessible services. As reported by Hooper et al. [12] Buffer overflow, DoS, and ARP cache poisoning were effective attacks against the platform. To protect Wi-Fi-based commercial UAVs, it also proposes a multi-layer security method to tackle flaws on the so-called aerial computers, however, it does not offer any prevention for the breakthroughs or the subsequent actions to protect the existing susceptible system.

Pleban et al. [13] proposes a fortification process for the UAV to address the flaws. For instance, it advises altering the Wi-Fi communication protocol to include encryption and authentication. But this moderation does not address DoS attacks. The Parrot AR. Drone contains security issues, according to Pleban et al. [13], who also add that this UAV platform is widely used because of its affordable price point.

Gudla et al. [14] have novel suggestions for Parrot AR. Drone's. They proposed a layer between the controller and the UAV called single-board computer (SBC), particularly a Raspberry Pi 3. This SBC provides communication encryption and shifting target protection strategies in addition to a Kismet IDS. Nonetheless, there are no indications of how to apply their findings to protect against DoS in that scenario. As prevention for the security flaws which is a legacy system update, Astaburuaga et al. [15] propose a security evaluation for Parrot AR. Drone 2.0. However, the DoS is not resolved considering the excellent protection provided for other weaknesses.

The computational cost of traditional IDSs makes them impractical in UAVs context. Machine learning (ML) based approaches proved be effective in detecting different sort of attacks [16, 17]. Given the complex and dynamic nature of UAV systems' security domain, which is comparable to that of the intrusion detection system (IDS) sector, a lot of data analysis is necessary to categorize these security-related occurrences.

According to Sommer & Paxson [18], there are certain difficulties with using ML to IDS. Due to its inherent capacity to train from data and make judgments based on that learning, ML has been employed in a variety of disciplines in the past, including spam detection and object detection [19]. It contrasts the traditional employment of machine learning (ML) for classification issues with instances of misuse and anomaly identification needed for cyberattacks. Anomalies are deviations from regular conduct, while misuse is predicated on known malevolent conduct. It must be noted that ML outperforms in classifying recognized attacks (already trained - misuse) than it does in detecting unidentified malicious occurrences (anomalous). According to Sommer & Paxson [18], the enormous influence of untrue events in the security sectors, taken as not malicious can result in cataclysmic events for our application, as opposed to the influence on more traditional ML systems such as spam classifiers, where a false-negative will merely be bothersome.

The authors in [4] proposed a DoS attack detection model using machine learning with high accuracy results reaching 99. However, from analyzing the dataset used in [4], it was noticed that there are duplicates of 32.17%, Fig. 2 shows an example of duplicate entries. Such duplication would lead to unreliable outcome, i.e., unreliable DoS detection rate which could have massive loss, e.g., unresponsive drone. This also leads to more power consumption which is limited in drone's environment. So, his paper aims to address these problems by proposing an efficient DoS attack detection with high detection rate.

3   Overview of Denial of Service Attack

The reliability of the systems, e.g., UAV's systems, is hampered by Denial of Service (DoS) attacks. An effective DoS attack causes a communication or control failure on the target UAV systems causing major consequences.

- **TCP and UDP Flood**

TCP (Transmission Control Protocol) and UDP (User Datagram Protocol) are two widely employed protocols for data transfer via networks. The primary distinction between them is that TCP employs feedback packets to ensure error correction, packet ordering, and data transmission between transmitter and receiver. On the other side, UDP lacks TCP-specific "reliability" characteristics. Since there is no need for communication cost, UDP has benefits above TCP in terms of the velocity of communication between the controller and the system.

On port 5555 for streaming video and port 5559 for optional control and crucial data, the TCP protocol is employed. Just on Parrot AR. Drone 2, the UDP protocol is employed to transmit navigational data (status, location, speed, engine rotation speed, among others) on port 5554 and control data (referred to as AT commands) on port 5556. Delivering many packets using both transfer protocols to one of these ports is a flood attack. This enormous number of packets overwhelms the UAV's computing power and causes it to become inaccessible, which is known as a Denial of Service (DoS) Attack.

- **De-authentication Attack**

To conserve computing services, this sort of frame enables the point of access or the client linked to the access point to ask for its de-authentication. De-authentication is a feature of the IEEE 802.11 standard that belongs to the group of control packets. Malicious agents have taken advantage of this feature by pretending to be a valid client and asking for a de-authentication to the access point.

Consequently, a security technique that can recognize and disregard these malicious packets without removing their usefulness is needed. The IEEE 802.11 protocol offers no security protection against these spoofing attacks. Due to the absence of connectivity between the controller and the UAV throughout this de-authentication attack on the Parrot AR. Drone, a devastating collision into external obstructions while the flight is likely to occur.

4 Proposed DoS Attack Detection Method

The proposed method consists of three phases as given in Fig. 1: preprocessing, feature extraction, and DoS attack detection. In the preprocessing, from analyzing the dataset [4], it was noticed that there are duplicates of 32.17%, Fig. 2 shows an example of duplicate entries. Such duplication would lead to unreliable outcome, i.e., unreliable DoS detection rate. Table 1 shows a summary of the dataset after cleaning it where it can be noticed that 32.17% has been removed thus minimizing the processing time.

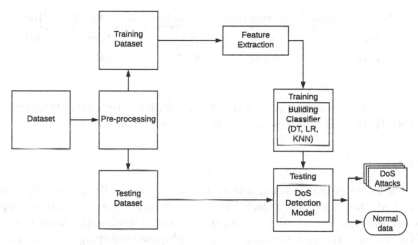

Fig. 1. DoS Detection Model in Drones.

The data was cleaned, i.e., deleting duplicates, using the Python function– *TimeDelata and Bytes(size)*. In the feature extraction phase, as reported by [4], it was tested that the best features to distinguish between DoS data and normal traffic are *Time delta from the previously captured frame (seconds)*, and *Frame Length (bytes)*. In this paper, we also used these two features in the classification phase. In the third phase, ML-based models were trained and tested using the dataset cleaned and built in this first and second phases. In this phase, different classifiers ware evaluated to build the most efficient one addressing the environment of the network of drones. Namely, the Decision Tree (DT) [2], Logistic Regression (LR) [3], KNN and Random Forest were used. Also, like [4], the test/train ratio was 4/6.

5 Results and Discussion

In this section, we discuss how the proposed model was evaluated. It starts with describing the dataset, then discussing the results of the scenarios under which the model was tested and finally the latency analysis of the model. All the experiments of this study were

	Protocol	Bytes	TimeDelta	DestPort	SrcPort	Class
340800	tcp	129	0.000001	NaN	NaN	normal
361715	tcp	129	0.000001	NaN	NaN	normal
319743	tcp	129	0.000001	NaN	NaN	normal
343401	tcp	129	0.000001	NaN	NaN	normal
316110	tcp	129	0.000001	NaN	NaN	normal

Fig. 2. Example of duplicate entries.

Table 1. Data statistics before and after cleaning.

	Number of entries	Normal traffic	De-auth attack	UDP flood	DoS TCP
Before	474311	459839	8576	5493	403
After	321744	307607	8282	5478	377

conduct under the following specifications: MacPro with Intel(R) Core(TM) i9-9980HK CPU 2.40GHz and the code was written using Python Python 3.10.2.

5.1 Dataset

To evaluate the proposed DoS detection method, the dataset, collected and described in [4], was used. The dataset was collected under the setting that Parrot AR.Drone 2.0 platform was controlling Wi-Fi UAVs. The attacks (De-Authentication Attack and TCP/UDP Flood) data were collected using aircrack-ng tool [20] used and hping3 tool [21] respectively. The normal data were collected under three scenarios: landing and takeoff command, UAV handshakes and Controller, and aleatory flight (multiple non-deterministic routes). The total number of rows of the dataset is 474311 (459839 of normal traffic, 8576 of De-auth attack, 5493of UDP floodand 403 of TCP flood). The evaluation of the proposed DoS detection method was evaluated using three main scenarios as follows.

5.2 Scenario 1: Impact of Data Cleaning on Performance

The aim of this experiment is to investigate whether cleaning the dataset would improve the performance of the modules used in the most related study [4]. So, the Decision Tree (DT) [2] and Logistic Regression (LR) [3] were used. Also, like [4], the test/train ratio was 4/6. The runtime was measured by 7 runs (100 loops each). The parameters values of DT were Criterion = Gini, Max depth = 3. From the results presented in Table 2, it can be noticed that cleaning the data improved the results of DT while only taking 3.81 ms instead of 4.9 for original dataset. It also improved the runtime of LR but not its results.

Table 2. Performance of DT and LR after cleaning the original dataset.

	F1-score	Recall	Precision	Runtime
DT on original dataset	96.8%	99.4%	94.3%	4.9 ms ± 195 μs
DT on cleaned dataset	**96.9%**	**99.4%**	**94.5%**	**3.81 ms** ± 101 μs
LR on original dataset	66.9%	59.5%	76.3%	2.02 ms ± 75.5 μs
LR on cleaned dataset	66.8%	**59.7%**	75.9%	**1.68 ms** ± 147 μs

5.3 Scenario 2: Best Value of the DT Parameter "Max-Depth"

In [4], the parameters for the Decision Tree was found using trial and error. The aim of this experiment is to use a more scientific approach to find the optimal max_depth parameter of the Decision Tree which was proven to better than LR in scenario 1 above.

To achieve the desired objective, we have tried different numbers of max_depth while using Gini as the criterion for the cleaned dataset. A summary of the results is given in Table 3 from which it can be seen that the best results (F1-score 98.89%, Precision 98.42%, and Recall 99.36%) were achieved when max_depth was 9 while keeping Criterion = Gini. These results are further improved than the ones in [4] with nearly 2% in F-score.

Table 3. Best value of the DT parameter "max-depth".

Max_depth of DT	F1-score	Recall	Precision
3	96.87%	99.36%	94.50%
5	98.67%	99.84%	97.53%
7	98.87%	99.58%	98.17%
9	98.89%	99.36%	98.42%
10	**98.94%**	**99.49%**	**98.39%**
11	98.87%	99.36%	98.39%

5.4 Scenario 3: Investigating Other Classifiers (KNN and Random Forest)

In this scenario, two more classifiers (KNN and Random Forest, RF) were applied on the cleaned dataset to investigate whether we can get better results. The KNN, as a non-parametric model, was chosen to compare its results with the parametric models such LR. The RF was chosen as it almost has the same parameters as the decision tree. The parameters of LR and DT were the same as the experiments in scenario 1 and 2 where the parameters of KNN and RF were K = 3 and max_depth = 8. Table 4 summarizes the results of Scenario 3.

From this table, it can be seen that the RF results are slightly better than that of DT ones but the later took very long runtime, 472 ns comparing with DT one which is only 3.29 ms. This is expected as the RF needs many trees to get the classification results. So, RF would not be the best algorithm to use in DoS detection in drones' environment which is characterised with limited resources (computation and power).

Table 4. Comparison among DT, LR, KNN, and RF.

	F1-score	Recall	Precision	Runtime
Logistic Regression	66.8%	59.7%	75.9%	1.68 ms ± 147 µs
Decision Tree	**98.94%**	**99.49%**	**98.39%**	**3.29 ms ± 60.6 µs**
KNN	99.0%	99.5%	98.4%	3.5 s ± 103 ms
Random Forest	98.9%	99.5%	98.3%	472 ms ± 30 ms

5.5 Analysis of Model Latency

Because of their embedded nature, UAV applications face the challenges of limited computational capacity and time-sensitive requirements. Thus, unlike the conventional machine learning measures discussed before, latency is an important consideration for these embedded and real-time applications. Therefore, Table 4 displays runtime of the predictions made by each algorithm on a test dataset. It's crucial to note that the testing Latency estimates come from a general-purpose computer, not an embedded one, thus these numbers need to be carefully evaluated. The results show that Logistic Regression is superior to all other algorithms, but its F1-score, recall, and precision are the lowest results. On the other hand, KNN and LR would not be good choices as they took longer time although they produced slightly better results than DT. So, the DoS detection model based on DT is the best choice as it need the lowest latency while still achieve over than 98% in all metrics (i.e., F1-score, recall, and precision). The DT is also good when small dataset is used and all features of this dataset is fed to the classification as in our case explained in the previous sections (Fig. 3).

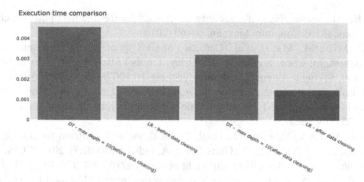

Fig. 3. Execution time comparison.

6 Conclusions and Future Works

The availability of the drones is one of the key issues which should be ensured. DoS attacks are the main threat of the availability services. This paper proposed an efficient and yet accurate DoS attack detection method based on Decision Tree for the Wi-Fi-based unmanned aerial vehicles (UAV). The preprocessing was showed to be very important in minimizing the runtime and algorithm latency which is crucial given the limited resources of UAV-based systems. The experimental results showed that Decision Tree is the best among KNN, Random Forest, and Logistic Regression. The Decision Tree showed to be accurate with F1-score of 0.989 in detecting DoS attacks of types of De-authentication and UDP/TCP flood within the shortest runtime. In the future work, it is planned to collect data for different type of DoS attacks such as spoofing, Sybil and ICMP (Ping) attack.

References

1. Al-Turjman, F., Zahmatkesh, H., Shahroze, R.: An overview of security and privacy in smart cities' IoT communications. Trans. Emerg. Telecommun. Technol. **33**, e3677 (2022)
2. Baig, Z., Syed, N., Mohammad, N.: Securing the smart city airspace: drone cyber attack detection through machine learning. Futur. Internet **14**, 205 (2022)
3. GlobeNewswire: Global Smart Cities Market to Reach $2.5 Trillion by 2026. In: Rep. Link. https://www.reportlinker.com/p05485940/Global-Smart-Cities-Industry.html. Last Accessed 25 Nov 2022
4. de Carvalho Bertoli, G., Pereira, L.A., Saotome, O.: Classification of denial of service attacks on Wi-Fi-based unmanned aerial vehicle. In: 2021 10th Latin-American Symposium on Dependable Computing (LADC). IEEE, pp. 1–6 (2021)
5. Salloum, S., Gaber, T., Vadera, S., Shaalan, K.: Phishing email detection using natural language processing techniques: a literature survey. Procedia Comput. Sci. **189**, 19–28 (2021)
6. Srihith, I.V.D., Kumar, I.V.S., Varaprasad, R., et al.: Future of smart cities: the role of machine learning and artificial intelligence. South Asian Res. J. Eng. Tech. **4**, 110–119 (2022)
7. Valente, J., Cardenas, A.A.: Understanding security threats in consumer drones through the lens of the discovery quadcopter family. In: Proceedings of the 2017 Workshop on Internet of Things Security and Privacy, pp 31–36 (2017)

8. Lin, C., He, D., Kumar, N., et al.: Security and privacy for the internet of drones: challenges and solutions. IEEE Commun. Mag. **56**, 64–69 (2018)
9. Liang, C., Miao, M., Ma, J., et al.: Detection of GPS spoofing attack on unmanned aerial vehicle system. In: Chen, X., Huang, X., Zhang, J. (eds.) ML4CS 2019. LNCS, vol. 11806, pp. 123–139. Springer, Cham (2019). https://doi.org/10.1007/978-3-030-30619-9_10
10. Dedrone Rolls Out Portable AI-Powered Drone Detection Unit. In: Res. Rep. https://www.verdict.co.uk/de%0Adrone-rolls-out-portable-ai-powered-drone-detection-unit/ (2022). Last Accessed 25 Nov 2022
11. Krajník, T., Vonásek, V., Fišer, D., Faigl, J.: AR-drone as a platform for robotic research and education. In: Obdržálek, D., Gottscheber, A. (eds.) EUROBOT 2011. CCIS, vol. 161, pp. 172–186. Springer, Heidelberg (2011). https://doi.org/10.1007/978-3-642-21975-7_16
12. Hooper, M., Tian, Y., Zhou, R., et al.: Securing commercial WiFi-based UAVs from common security attacks. In: MILCOM 2016–2016 IEEE Military Communications Conference, pp. 1213–1218. IEEE (2016)
13. Pleban, J.-S., Band, R., Creutzburg, R.: Hacking and securing the AR. Drone 2.0 quadcopter: investigations for improving the security of a toy. In: Mobile Devices and Multimedia: Enabling Technologies, Algorithms, and Applications 2014, pp 168–179. SPIE (2014)
14. Gudla, C,. Rana, M.S., Sung, A.H.: Defense techniques against cyber attacks on unmanned aerial vehicles. In: Proceedings of the International Conference on Embedded Systems, Cyber-Physical Systems, and Applications (ESCS). The Steering Committee of the World Congress in Computer Science, Computer, pp. 110–116 (2018)
15. Astaburuaga, I., Lombardi, A., La Torre, B., et al.: Vulnerability analysis of ar. drone 2.0, an embedded linux system. In: 2019 IEEE 9th Annual Computing and Communication Workshop and Conference (CCWC), pp. 666–672. IEEE (2019)
16. El-Sayed, R., El-Ghamry, A., Gaber, T., Hassanien, A.E.: Zero-day malware classification using deep features with support vector machines. In: 2021 Tenth International Conference on Intelligent Computing and Information Systems (ICICIS), pp. 311–317. IEEE (2021)
17. Applebaum, S., Gaber, T., Ahmed, A.: Signature-based and machine-learning-based web application firewalls: a short survey. Procedia Comput. Sci. **189**, 359–367 (2021)
18. Sommer, R., Paxson, V.: Outside the closed world: on using machine learning for network intrusion detection. In: 2010 IEEE symposium on security and privacy, pp. 305–316. IEEE (2010)
19. Abu-Mostafa, Y.S., Magdon-Ismail, M., Lin, H.T.: Learning from Data, vol. 4. New York. NY, USA, AMLBook (2012)
20. Aircrack-ng (2021). Last accessed 25 Nov 2022
21. Hping – active network security tool. In: Hping.org. http://www.hping.org (2021). Last accessed on 25 Nov 2022

Deep Learning Applications
and Bio-inspired Optimization

Detecting Fake News Spreaders on Twitter Through Follower Networks

Smita Ghosh[1], Juan Manuel Zuluaga Fernandez[1], Isabel Zuluaga González[2], Andres Mauricio Calle[1], and Navid Shaghaghi[1(✉)] (iD)

[1] Ethical, Pragmatic, and Intelligent Computing (EPIC) Research Lab, Santa Clara University (SCU), Santa Clara, CA 95053, USA
{sghosh3,jzuluga,aclle,nshaghaghi}@scu.edu
[2] Universidad Pontificia Bolivariana, Medellín, Antioquia, Colombia
isabel.zuluaga@upb.edu.co
https://www.scu.edu, https://www.upb.edu.co/es/home

Abstract. Obtaining news from social media platforms has become increasingly popular due to their ease of access and high speed of information dissemination. These same factors have, however, also increased the range and speed at which misinformation and fake news spread. While machine-run accounts (bots) contribute significantly to the spread of misinformation, human users on these platforms also play a key role in contributing to the spread. Thus, there is a need for an in-depth understanding of the relationship between users and the spread of fake news. This paper proposes a new data-driven metric called *User Impact Factor (UIF)* aims to show the importance of user content analysis and neighbourhood influence to profile a fake news spreader on Twitter. Tweets and retweets of each user are collected and classified as 'fake' or 'not fake' using Natural Language Processing (NLP). These labeled posts are combined with data on the number of the user's followers and retweet potential in order to generate the user's impact factor. Experiments are performed using data collected from Twitter and the results show the effectiveness of the proposed approach in identifying fake news spreaders.

Keywords: Bidirectional Encoder Representations from Transformers (BERT) · Fake News Detection · Misinformation Spread · Natural Language Processing (NLP) · Social Media · Twitter · User Impact Factor (UIF)

1 Introduction

The past decade has seen an increase in the public's reliance on social media as a source not only of entertainment, but also of news and commentary on current affairs. Unlike traditional media sources, social media provides extremely low barriers of entry to anyone seeking to disseminate information. These new sources of news also benefit from their platforms being not specifically news focused, allowing them to capture the attention of a wider audience who might

R. Hou et al. (Eds.): BDTA 2022, LNICST 480, pp. 181–195, 2023.
https://doi.org/10.1007/978-3-031-33614-0_13

have originally logged on for a different reason but were recommended the post by an advertising algorithm. In January 2019, Pew Research Center announced that 59% of Twitter's users get their news from the social media platform regularly [6]. Despite it's advantages, the quality of news on social media is however considered lower than that of traditional media [13].

The same low barriers of entry to disseminating news also result in the ability to spread much lower quality and even fake information to billions of users. Spreading of fake news has a detrimental effect on society. For example, during the initial outbreak of the COVID-19 pandemic, social media applications were heavily used in order to spread false information on the pandemic, prevention measures, and treatments [2]. During the 2016 presidential elections, a popular fake news story known as 'Pizzagate' was retweeted over 1 million times in November 2016 [7]. Thus it is not only important to detect fake news but also be able to find ways to anticipate their spreaders.

Detecting fake news spreaders involves detecting fake news and analyzing the pattern of the spread of such information. The former is achieved through analyzing the content of misinformation posts, which tend to invoke sensationalist tropes and often partisan language to attract and mislead their audience. The latter involves understanding the role of users in the propagation of misinformation on social media platforms [12,15,28].

This paper focuses on new solutions for detecting fake news spreaders through follower networks. This is done by understanding the relationship between users and their influence on not only their followers, but the followers of their followers. A new data-driven metric called *User's Impact Factor (UIF)* is proposed which combines a user's activity of posting and the influence of people they follow. These two properties help profile fake news spreaders. The aim of this novel metric is to highlight the interconnected nature of Twitter, and how a user's influence can extend past their immediate followers to have a greater impact on the spread of misinformation within a larger network.

The main contributions of this paper are:

1. Creating a repository of user's data by collecting tweets and follower data from Twitter.
2. Training a highly accurate and reliable fake news classifier to label the tweets and retweets as 'fake' or 'not fake'.
3. Proposing and formulating a new data-driven metric called *User's Impact Factor* to help profile fake news spreaders on Twitter.

This paper is organized as follows: Sect. 2 describes the background and related work. Section 3 describes the phases of the proposed approach and Sect. 4 talks in detail about the first two phases. Sections 5 and 6 describe the formulation of the new proposed UIF metric and show the results of utilizing it on gathered Twitter data. Section 7 provides concluding remarks and lastly, Sect. 8 describes the future directions for this work.

2 Background and Related Work

2.1 Fake News

The COVID-19 pandemic has served to amplify concerns regarding misinformation and fake news, as it has suddenly become capable of significantly effecting the health outcomes of a nation. Exposure to fake news regarding the pandemic and vaccines among people with poor skills at detecting misinformation unsurprisingly lead to increased vaccine hesitancy [21] and subsequently has increased mortality during the COVID-19 pandemic [11].

In addition to purely health related negative impacts, fake news has also resulted in many negative societal outcomes. While the scapegoating of minority groups during a pandemic has no end of examples in human history, social media allows for fake news in this vein to travel much further and faster than it would have been possible before. Previous studies have shown a connection between the consumption of misinformation and the physical assault and harassment of people of Asian origin as well as healthcare professionals [26]. Fake News Detection is a very popular area of research. Recent literature focuses on deep learning and machine learning methods for the detection of fake news [18,20].

2.2 Fake News Spreaders

Current literature focuses on analysing the content of the posts to detect fake news [19,22,24,25]. In order to combat the spread of misinformation we must not only look into the content of the tweet, but also the users who are retweeting them. Identifying 'influential' users is a very popular research area. It has also been studied that 'influential' accounts on different social media platforms tend to have an impact in information propagation. Authors of [1] study that the influence of users on their friends can increase or decrease sales, so businesses are interested in finding influential people and encouraging them to create positive influence. They propose a method that uses interaction between social network users to detect the most influential among them. Literature also shows that user's in general contribute towards the spread of misinformation [5,16].

The reach of misinformation can vary significantly based on what user is spreading it, showing the importance of the users themselves in the spread of information on social media [3]. User profile analysis has become significantly important in identifying spreaders. Given this, it becomes critical to not only be able to detect fake news, but to also be able to identify super-spreader users.

Most of the existing literature focuses on profiling fake news spreaders by analyzing the content that they post [24,28,30]. Recent works have started focusing on analyzing the network structure and the neighbourhood of the social media users to profile spreaders. For instance, in [15], the author's proposed a novel machine learning based approach for automatic identification of the users spreading rumors based on the trust measures of users in Twitter's retweet network. Authors of [32] analyzed different features for such as bot usage, patterns and emotions in tweets posted by bots, heterogeneity among the spreaders, and geographic as well as demographic characteristics to profile fake news spreaders. In [9] the authors analyze how news spreads in social networks, simulating a simple information-spreading process in various network topologies and demonstrating that news spreads much more quickly in existing social-network topologies than in other network topologies. Another paper [34], addresses the complications as well as challenges encountered when measuring message propagation and social influence on OSNs. These works indicate that social-interaction among user's on the platform play a pivotal role in spreading information.

This paper introduces a data-driven metric called User's Impact Factor(UIF) which draws inspiration from [9,15] and combines two important features that profile a fake news spreader 1) their own probability of tweeting fake news 2) Retweeting fake news by being influenced by the people they follow who tweet high number of fake news tweets. This metric aims to show the importance of content analysis and neighbourhood influence, to help profile a fake news spreader.

2.3   Twitter

Among different social media platforms, Twitter was chosen for this study due to it's inherent structure. All activity on Twitter is publicly available and consists of four basic actions: A post, a retweet or quote tweet of a post, a reply to a post, and a like of a post. All activity of a user is publicly available on their account, and unlike other social media platforms like Facebook, on Twitter a user can only either be public or protected. A user cannot customize the level of privacy their account has, it is either entirely public, or private and viewable only by approved followers. This simple structure allows for much simpler data collection and analysis, as well as making the construction of a Twitter ecosystem much more feasible.

2.4   Influence/Trust Network

Trust networks comprise of influential accounts that have built trust with their audiences over time [8]. Studies have found that Trust networks play an important role in impacting the spread of information on social media [4]. Trust networks can be used to examine how a particular user spreading fake news may have a larger impact than another [27]. For example, during the COVID-19 pandemic, a famous Bollywood actor had tweeted about houseflies playing a role in the spread of the virus, resulting in a sharp spike in the number of web searches for the term 'houseflies' [10]. Users with a strong trust network have more impact in the diffusion of information. In this paper, a trust network is represented as a follower network which is built by scraping data from Twitter. Section 4.2 explains this process in detail.

2.5   BERT Transformer

The model chosen for fake news detection was the Bidirectional Encoder Representations from Transformers (BERT), which was developed by Google in 2018. While experiments were also conducted using bidirectional long short term memory networks and non-Deep Learning based classifiers, the BERT model was found to significantly out-preform these models. While previously, the best attempts to accomplish this classification have used bidirectional long short term memory networks [33], and the authors have had experience with the use of these models [29], the development of the BERT model provided a new tool for research. BERT-based fake news classification models provided the critical step forward in providing a robust, reliable model for fake news detection. Whether trained on detecting fake headlines or specifically attempting to identify fake news relating to the COVID-19 pandemic, the BERT models have consistently produced results at or above 90% accuracy in determining the trustworthiness of the news [14,17]. As a transformer based model, BERT consists of stacks of encoder and decoder layers. The model is capable of performing different Natural Language Processing (NLP) tasks, including being trained on a large corpus to classify misinformation tweets. One of the basic advantages that BERT provides compared to other models is bidirectionally. Instead of simply reading the tweet sequentially, from left to right in English, BERT reads the input from both directions to provide it with a better comprehension of the input.

3   Proposed Approach

The proposed approach in this paper is divided into the following four phases:

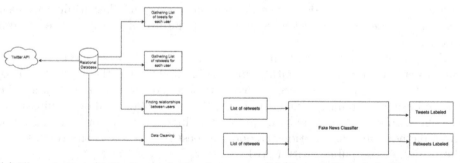

(a) Phase 1: Data Collection and Cleaning   (b) Phase 2: Data Labelling

Fig. 1. Phases

- **Phase 1: Data scraping and collection from Twitter** - In this phase, a Twitter API is used to scrape and collect data from Twitte. Two lists of information is gathered, one list being a collection of tweets and retweets of a user and the other being a list of each user's followersr (Fig. 1a).

- **Phase 2: Building the fake news classifier** - In this phase a BERT Transformer is trained to label the tweets and retweets from phase 1, as fake news or real newsr (Fig. 1b).
- **Phase 3: Building the graph** - In this phase, a graph is built to represent a Twitter follower network based on the list of followers of each user obtained in Phase 1. This also represents a trust network among users. The follower network is represented as a graph $G(V, E)$ where V represents the users scraped from Twitter and E represents the set of edges depicting the followers of that user who retweet. So if node A follows node B and retweets a tweet authored B, then there is an edge between them. Section 4.2 describes this process in detail.
- **Phase 4: Formulating and Calculating UIF** - After the tweet and retweets are labelled in phase 2, the UIF is calculated for each user by traversing the graph built in Phase 3. Section 5 describes the formulation in detail.

4   Data Gathering and Pre-processing

4.1   Twitter Scraping

There are four primary ways to obtain Twitter data: Retrieve the data using the Twitter public Application Programming Interface (API), find an existing dataset, purchase access from Twitter, or purchase access from a Twitter service provider.

Twitter provides APIs in order to search and post tweets, get a list of users and their likes and see relationships between users. However, this public twitter API has a number of limitations. The standard API only allows retrieval of tweets up to 7 days old and is rate limited, only allowing the scraping of 18,000 tweets per a 15 min window. The dataset must contain relationships between accounts to identify the followers along with the list of tweets, retweets, and who they retweeted from.

Purchasing the datasets from either Twitter or a Twitter service provider like PowerTrack requires a monthly subscription and are mostly oriented to businesses. Other services like DiscoverText have access to old tweets that cannot be scraped using the public Twitter API, and the cost will depend on requirements like the number of tweets and the periods of time gathered from. Taking all of these methods in consideration the one that best fits the needs and resources of the project is the public twitter API.

The first step was retrieving the tweets and some of the followers of four seed accounts. Based on the importance of influential users described Sect. 2.2, the initial users were chosen because of their popularity and the role they play in politics. After getting seed nodes and their group of followers, it was identified which ones among them are common retweeters, i.e, they re-post many tweets from the account they follow. A list of tweets, retweets for each user, and who they follow were recorded. The process was then repeated on the followers of the seed accounts, creating a new level of users with data associated to their accounts who also had followers to be recursively scraped from. A total of 222 user's accounts were scraped and a combined total of 393 followers were recorded. The dataset collected consists of the user's id, the user handle, the text of their tweets, and a list of their followers.

It was important to identify the users relationships and the post that are involved in a retweet chain. Retweeting is the fastest way in twitter to spread a post and was used in order to measure the influence of a user on the network. The more a user's tweets tended to be retweeted by their followers, the more influence they would have on the nodes following them. The Retweet Probability(RTP) in Sect. 5 describes this in detail.

4.2   Building the Twitter Follower Network

In this paper, the follower network was built by scraping information from Twitter using the Twitter API. The resulting dataset is a list of users who are related by a follower relationship who retweet from the person they follow. In the network each user is a node and the relationships between two nodes is represented as edges. A user 'A' has an edge with user 'B' if 'B' follows 'A' and have retweeted a tweet whose author was 'A'. Figure 2 shows an example of this graph. The seed nodes were selected from a list of the influential people in politics. Section 2.2 cites literature that indicate that influential nodes tend to play a vital role in the spreading of fake news. Of the selected seed users a list of followers were obtained and for this list it was critical to identify which users are not only followers but also retweeters. Each follower who was also a retweeter, was added as a node to the graph by adding an edge between the two nodes. For the users in the rest of the levels the same classification was done. The retweets posted were also recorded for each user. This was needed to calculate the influence between the nodes.

The Twitter follower network was represented as a directed graph $G = (V, E)$, where V represents the users on Twitter and the edges represented users who follow other users and retweet their authored posts. In Fig. 2, the list of followers is represented as a Node $-¿$ List of Nodes where the List of Node represents the list of followers of the Node. For example, directed edges are built between Node A and Nodes B,C and D, because the latter follow Node A and retweet posts authored by Node A. Figure 2 elaborates the graph building process from the list of followers. A total of 222 users were collected with a combined total of 392 followers. Thus the follower network comprised of 222 nodes and 392 edges.

4.3   Fake News Data Labeling

While many tweets were collected as a part of this project, the fake news identifier was not trained off of any of the user tweets that were gathered. In part, this was due to the fact that there were simply not enough tweets in that pool to properly train a NLP model, however, that was not the only reason. It was important to the creation of the model that all data points within it be new to the BERT fake news classifier, in order to better represent the reality of its use. To have the fake news detection model assign probabilities of fake news generation on users

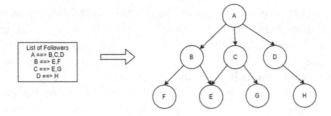

Fig. 2. Building the Twitter Follower Network from a List of Followers

who's tweets it was trained on would result in accuracy that could not properly be verified.

In order to train the fake news detection model, tweets from two major datasets were acquired. These two major datasets each focused on a different speciality, one consisting of true or false labels of political content, and the second focusing on COVID-19 related fake news. The political content dataset was aquired from the previously published FakeNewsNet which labeled its data with assistance from politifact [31]. The COVID-19 dataset was compiled and submitted at the CONSTRAINT 2021 workshop, and while the dataset included both English and Hindi language entries, only the English language tweets were used [23]. Together, the datasets accounted for 9615 unique items of true and fake news, off of which the model was trained on 90% of the dataset, with another 5% serving as a validation set and the last 5% serving as the testing set.

5   User's Impact Factor Formulation

In this paper, a new data-driven metric called User's Impact Factor (UIF) is proposed to identify potentially fake news spreaders. Current literature focuses on analyzing the content of the tweets that a user posts to classify them as spreaders. In this paper, UIF aims to highlight the importance of neighborhood influence in the dissemination of information in a network. It integrates the two characteristics of the user that form what content appears on their Twitter page: original content they tweeted, and content by others that they have chosen to retweet. By measuring both their activity of posting fake news content, and the fake news content of others they have retweeted, the total level of fake news spread by their account can be obtained, which is indicated by UIF. UIF helps in identifying nodes in the network that have a high impact in spreading fake news content. A high value of UIF indicates a high impact on the user in the propagation of fake news. Every user with a non-zero UIF value is considered as a potential fake news spreader. The value of UIF indicates the degree of their potential, instead of juts categorising users on a binary scale of 'spreaders' or 'non-spreaders'. One major significance of this metric is identifying fake news spreaders who do not post fake news content themselves but tend to retweet a lot of fake news due to influence from people they follow, thus highlighting the importance of influential neighborhood of users. UIF is formulated in the following steps:

1. **Fake Tweet Probability(FTP)** calculates the user's probability of posting fake news content. It is defined as the ratio of the number of tweets a user posts that are fake to the total number of posts that the user makes.

$$\text{FTP(U)}\& = \frac{-\text{Fake\_News\_Tweets(U)}}{-\text{Tweets(U)}-} \tag{1}$$

where U represents a user on the network. A high value of FTP(U) indicates that the user U has a high potential of posting fake news content themselves.

2. **Retweet Probability(RTP)** calculates the user's probability of re-posting fake news content posted originally by people they follow.

$$\text{RTP(U,V)}\& = \frac{-\text{Retweets(U,V)}-}{-\text{Retweets(U)}-} \tag{2}$$

where V represent a neighbour of U, i.e, U follows V. $|Retweets(U,V)|$ is the count of retweets made by U whose author was V and $|Retweets(U)|$ is the total number of retweets made by U. A high value of RTP(U,V) indicates V has a high influence on U.

3. **Fake Retweet Influence(FRI)** is a value assigned to a user that combines the RTP between them and all the people they follow on the network and the FTP of the people they follow.

$$\text{FRI(U)} = (\frac{\sum_{V \in Neighbors(U)} RTP(U,V) * FTP(V)}{-\text{Neighbors(U)}-}) \tag{3}$$

4. **User's Impact Factor (UIF)** is calculated as the sum of two metrics of each user 1) the FTP of the user (their own probability of tweeting fake news) and FRI (the retweets that they make as a result of following users who have a high probability of tweeting fake news.

$$\text{UIF(U)} = (\frac{FRI(U) + FTP(U)}{2}) \tag{4}$$

6   Results

6.1   BERT Classifier

The BERT Classifier was selected due to the reasons mentioned in Sect. 2.5. The performance of the BERT model can be seen in Fig. 3 which shows the final confusion matrix generated by the model.

With an accuracy of **96.26%**, the BERT model was able to provide the highly reliable predictions it was reputed to have. The weights for the best performing version of the model were saved, and could be then loaded in whenever predictions would need to be made on the twitter users.

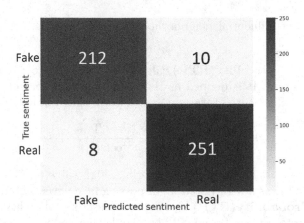

Fig. 3. Fake News Confusion Matrix

6.2   User's Impact Factor

For each user in the graph built in Sect. 4.2, their FTP, RTP and FRI were calculated to find their UIF by following the formulation mentioned in Sect. 5. Figure 4 shows the FTP and the UIF of 10% of users in the dataset. FTP indicates the probability of the user posting false tweets themselves and UIF is the probability that incorporates the neighbourhood influence of the user in retweeting. The comparison between these two metrics indicates the importance of influential neighborhood of a user.

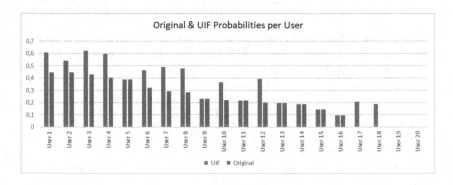

Fig. 4. Fake Tweet Probability (Original) VS User's Impact Factor

For privacy purposes, the names and handles of the users have been anonymized by replacing them with unique numbers. As seen in the Fig. 4, the UIF score analysis can be categorised as following

– **Case 1 (Increase in UIF from a zero FTP value):** This case indicates that the user originally did not post any fake news content by themselves, but were following and retweeting people who have a high tendency of posting fake news content. This increase in value indicated the user had a high impact in fake news propagation due to the high influence from their neighbors. In Fig. 4, users 17 and 18 are examples of this case.

- **Case 2 (Increase in UIF from a non-zero FTP value):** This case indicates that the user posts some fake news content themselves and additionally retweets fake news content posted by people they follow. Depending on the degree of fake news content posted by the user's neighbors, the increase would be small in some situations (User 2 in Fig. 4, and larger for others (User 1 in Fig. 4).
- **Case 3 (No change in UIF and FTP values):** This case indicates the user is not influenced by anybody they follow. However a non-zero value does indicate that the user still contributes to fake news propagation by posting fake news content themselves. Users 9, 11, 13 through 16 are some examples of this case.
- **Case 4 (Both UIF and FTP values are zero):** This case indicates that the user does not post any fake news content themselves and also does not retweet any fake news content from people they follow. User 19 and 20 is an example of this case.

The objective of the UIF metric was to highlight the impact of influential users on the fake news spreading potential of their followers, such as in User 4. Originally they had a FTP of 0.4, indicating that 40% of the tweets they made were classified as fake. However, User 4 followed popular nodes on the network and would retweet a high number of posts that were authored by the influential node. This influential node also had a high probability of making fake news posts. Thus, UIF(User 4) increased to a value of 0.6, indicating a high impact in spreading fake news. Also the aim of UIF is to weed out users who have an FTP value of '0' (i.e., they do not tweet any fake news content) however, they have a non-zero UIF value, indicating that they retweet fake news significantly. Among the 222 users in the dataset, the following table shows the categorisation of people into the different cases as mention above.

Table 1. UIF Score Categorization of Users

UIF Analysis	#Users
Case 1: FTP = 0, UIF != 0	87
Case 2: FTP != 0, UIF > FTP	32
Case 3: FTP = UIF	24
Case 4: FTP = 0, UIF = 0	79

From the Table 1, it is observed that 65% of users are categorised as potential fake news spreaders and 35% of users are classified as 'non-spreaders'. They are also not classified on a binary scale of 'spreader' and 'non-spreader', instead the

UIF value indicates the impact of the user in spreading fake news on a scale of 0 to 1. Among the 65%, almost 40% of the users were those who did not tweet any fake news content but would follow people who had a high influence on them and would also post fake tweets that user would be influenced to retweet. Without the UIF metric, chances are that the 40% of the users would not be profiled as fake news spreaders. The UIF metric weeds out these user's who would have otherwise gone unnoticed. 15% of users have an increase in the value from FTP to UIF. In addition to posting fake news content themselves, these users are also influenced by people who tweet fake news that these users retweet. 10% of users were those who were not influenced by their neighbors, but still posted fake news content themselves.

7   Conclusion

In this paper, a new data-driven metric called 'User's Impact Factor (UIF)' was proposed to help identify fake news spreaders. This metric aimed to highlight the impact of influential users on the dissemination of misinformation by their followers. This metric also representing the categorisation of users on a scale of 0 to 1, instead of a binary scale of 'spreader' and 'non-spreader'.

A BERT Transformer was trained to classify fake news tweets with 96% accuracy. The results show that UIF helps in identifying users that have a high impact in spreading fake news. Experimentation was performed on real world data and 65% of the users in the dataset was found to be potential fake news spreaders based on the UIF score. This metric helped in weeding out nodes that appear 'non-threatening' as they do not post any fake news tweets themselves, but tend to be highly influenced by the people they follow. The UIF scores show that analyzing content of the tweets posted by a user isn't enough and neighbourhood influence needs to be incorporated when analyzing patterns of fake news dissemination.

8   Future Steps

For future steps, many of the project phases can be explored further. For phase 1, more data is intended to be collected to expand the Twitter network of users and their followers. In phase 2, more state-of-the-art fake news detection models will be explored. For phase 4, variations of UIF like time-based or content-based UIF will be explored. Content-based UIF would analyse the change in retweet probability of a user based on the topic of the tweet. Other social media platforms like Reddit and Facebook are also intended to be explored. Another future direction is to detect and model the spread of different types of malicious content like hate speech, click-bait, scam links etc.

Acknowledgement. Many Thanks are due to the department of Mathematics & Computer Science (MCS) of the College of Arts & Sciences (CAS), the department of Computer Science & Engineering (CSEN) and the Frugal Innovation Hub (FIH) of the

School of Engineering (SoE), and the department of Information Systems & Analytics (ISA) of the School of Business at Santa Clara University in California, USA; as well as, the Computer Engineering department of the school of Engineering at Universidad Pontificia Bolivariana in Medellín, Colombia for their continued support of the project. Also thanks to Mubashir Hussain another member of the research team who worked on UIF graphs.

References

1. Afrasiabi Rad, A., Benyoucef, M.: Towards detecting influential users in social networks. In: Babin, G., Stanoevska-Slabeva, K., Kropf, P. (eds.) MCETECH 2011. LNBIP, vol. 78, pp. 227–240. Springer, Heidelberg (2011). https://doi.org/10.1007/978-3-642-20862-1_16

2. de Barcelos, T., Muniz, L.N., Dantas, D.M., Cotrim Junior, D.F., Cavalcante, J.R., Faerstein, E.: Analysis of fake news disseminated during the covid-19 pandemic in brazilanálisis de las noticias falsas divulgadas durante la pandemia de covid-19 en brasil. Revista Panamericana de Salud Publica= Pan Am. J. Public Health **45**, c65 c65 (2021)

3. Bodaghi, A., Oliveira, J.: The theater of fake news spreading, who plays which role? A study on real graphs of spreading on Twitter. Expert Syst. Appl. **189**, 116110 (2022)

4. Buskens, V.: Spreading information and developing trust in social networks to accelerate diffusion of innovations. Trends Food Sci. Technol. **106**, 485–488 (2020)

5. Carchiolo, V., Longheu, A., Malgeri, M., Mangioni, G., Previti, M.: Mutual influence of users credibility and news spreading in online social networks. Future Internet **13**(5), 107 (2021)

6. Center PR: News use across social media platforms in 2020 (2021). https://www.pewresearch.org/journalism/2021/01/12/news-use-across-social-media-platforms-in-2020/

7. Courier-Tribune: Religious zeal drives N.C. man in 'pizzagate' (2016). https://www.courier-tribune.com/story/news/state/2016/12/06/religious-zeal-drives-nc-man-in-8216pizzagate8217/24407347007/

8. Data, Society: Why influence matters in the spread of misinformation (2018). https://points.datasociety.net/why-influence-matters-in-the-spread-of-misinformation-fc99ee69040e

9. Doerr, B., Fouz, M., Friedrich, T.: Why rumors spread so quickly in social networks. Commun. ACM **55**(6), 70–75 (2012). https://doi.org/10.1145/2184319.2184338

10. First Draft: Online influencers have become powerful vectors in promoting false information and conspiracy theories (2020). https://firstdraftnews.org/articles/influencers-vectors-misinformation/

11. Dyer, O.: Covid-19: Moderna and Pfizer vaccines prevent infections as well as symptoms, CDC study finds. BMJ: Br. Med. J. (Online) **373** (2021)

12. Fernández, J.L., Ramírez, J.A.L.: Approaches to the profiling fake news spreaders on Twitter task in English and Spanish. In: CLEF (Working Notes) (2020)

13. Flick, D.: Combatting fake news: alternatives to limiting social media misinformation and rehabilitating quality journalism. SMU Sci. Tech. L. Rev. **20**, 375 (2017)

14. Heidari, M., et al.: BERT model for fake news detection based on social bot activities in the Covid-19 pandemic. In: 2021 IEEE 12th Annual Ubiquitous Computing, Electronics & Mobile Communication Conference (UEMCON), pp. 0103–0109. IEEE (2021)

15. Huang, Q., Zhou, C., Wu, J., Wang, M., Wang, B.: Deep structure learning for rumor detection on Twitter. In: 2019 International Joint Conference on Neural Networks (IJCNN), pp. 1–8. IEEE (2019)
16. Imaduwage, S., Kumara, P., Samaraweera, W.: Importance of user representation in propagation network-based fake news detection: a critical review and potential improvements. In: 2022 2nd International Conference on Advanced Research in Computing (ICARC), pp. 90–95. IEEE (2022)
17. Kula, S., Choraś, M., Kozik, R.: Application of the BERT-based architecture in fake news detection. In: Herrero, Á., Cambra, C., Urda, D., Sedano, J., Quintián, H., Corchado, E. (eds.) CISIS 2019. AISC, vol. 1267, pp. 239–249. Springer, Cham (2021). https://doi.org/10.1007/978-3-030-57805-3_23
18. Liu, Y., Wu, Y.F.B.: FNED: a deep network for fake news early detection on social media. ACM Trans. Inf. Syst (TOIS) $\mathbf{38}$(3), 1–33 (2020)
19. Luo, M., Hancock, J.T., Markowitz, D.M.: Credibility perceptions and detection accuracy of fake news headlines on social media: effects of truth-bias and endorsement cues. Commun. Res. $\mathbf{49}$(2), 171–195 (2022)
20. Mishra, S., Shukla, P., Agarwal, R.: Analyzing machine learning enabled fake news detection techniques for diversified datasets. Wirel. Commun. Mob. Comput. $\mathbf{2022}$ (2022)
21. Montagni, I., et al.: Acceptance of a Covid-19 vaccine is associated with ability to detect fake news and health literacy. J. Public Health $\mathbf{43}$(4), 695–702 (2021)
22. Nassif, A.B., Elnagar, A., Elgendy, O., Afadar, Y.: Arabic fake news detection based on deep contextualized embedding models. Neural Comput. Appl. $\mathbf{34}$, 16019–16032 (2022). https://doi.org/10.1007/s00521-022-07206-4
23. Patwa, P., et al.: Overview of CONSTRAINT 2021 shared tasks: detecting English COVID-19 fake news and Hindi hostile posts. In: Chakraborty, T., Shu, K., Bernard, H.R., Liu, H., Akhtar, M.S. (eds.) CONSTRAINT 2021. CCIS, vol. 1402, pp. 42–53. Springer, Cham (2021). https://doi.org/10.1007/978-3-030-73696-5_5
24. Pizarro, J.: Using N-grams to detect fake news spreaders on Twitter. In: CLEF (Working Notes) (2020)
25. Raza, S., Ding, C.: Fake news detection based on news content and social contexts: a transformer-based approach. Int. J. Data Sci. Anal. $\mathbf{13}$, 335–362 (2022)
26. Rocha, Y.M., et al.: The impact of fake news on social media and its influence on health during the Covid-19 pandemic: a systematic review. J. Public Health 1–10 (2021)
27. Ruan, Y., Durresi, A., Alfantoukh, L.: Using Twitter trust network for stock market analysis. Knowl.-Based Syst. $\mathbf{145}$, 207–218 (2018)
28. Saeed, U., Fahim, H., Shirazi, F.: Profiling fake news spreaders on Twitter. In: CLEF (Working notes) (2020)
29. Shaghaghi, N., Calle, A.M., Manuel Zuluaga Fernandez, J., Hussain, M., Kamdar, Y., Ghosh, S.: Twitter sentiment analysis and political approval ratings for situational awareness. In: 2021 IEEE Conference on Cognitive and Computational Aspects of Situation Management (CogSIMA), pp. 59–65 (2021). https://doi.org/10.1109/CogSIMA51574.2021.9475935
30. Shahid, W., Li, Y., Staples, D., Amin, G., Hakak, S., Ghorbani, A.: Are you a cyborg, bot or human?—a survey on detecting fake news spreaders. IEEE Access $\mathbf{10}$, 27069–27083 (2022)
31. Shu, K., Mahudeswaran, D., Wang, S., Lee, D., Liu, H.: FakeNewsNet: a data repository with news content, social context and spatialtemporal information for studying fake news on social media. arXiv preprint arXiv:1809.01286 (2018)

32. Singh, M., Kaur, R., Iyengar, S.R.S.: Multidimensional analysis of fake news spreaders on Twitter. In: Chellappan, S., Choo, K.-K.R., Phan, N.H. (eds.) CSoNet 2020. LNCS, vol. 12575, pp. 354–365. Springer, Cham (2020). https://doi.org/10. 1007/978-3-030-66046-8_29
33. Wang, W.Y.: "Liar, liar pants on fire": a new benchmark dataset for fake news detection. arXiv preprint arXiv:1705.00648 (2017)
34. Ye, S., Wu, S.F.: Measuring message propagation and social influence on Twitter.com. In: Bolc, L., Makowski, M., Wierzbicki, A. (eds.) SocInfo 2010. LNCS, vol. 6430, pp. 216–231. Springer, Heidelberg (2010). https://doi.org/10.1007/978-3-642-16567-2_16

NODDLE: Node2vec Based Deep Learning Model for Link Prediction

Kazi Zainab Khanam⑩, Aditya Singhal⁽✉⁾⑩, and Vijay Mago⑩

Lakehead University, Thunder Bay, ON P7B 5E1, Canada
{kkhanam,asinghal,vmago}@lakeheadu.ca

Abstract. Computing the probability of an edge's existence in a graph network is known as link prediction. While traditional methods calculate the similarity between two given nodes in a static network, recent research has focused on evaluating networks that evolve dynamically. Although deep learning techniques and network representation learning algorithms, such as node2vec, show remarkable improvements in prediction accuracy, the Stochastic Gradient Descent (SGD) method of node2vec tends to fall into a mediocre local optimum value due to a shortage of prior network information, resulting in failure to capture the global structure of the network. To tackle this problem, we propose NODDLE (integration of NOde2vec anD Deep Learning mEthod), a deep learning model which incorporates the features extracted by node2vec and feeds them into a four layer hidden neural network. NODDLE takes advantage of adaptive learning optimizers such as Adam, Adamax, Adadelta, and Adagrad to improve the performance of link prediction. Experimental results show that this method yields better results than the traditional methods on various social network datasets.

Keywords: Graph learning · Social networks · Link prediction · Web information systems

1   Introduction

Link prediction is a fundamental problem of network analysis, mainly because of its importance in social network applications such as designing recommendation systems for social media platforms and e-commerce websites, identification of credit card fraud, and even locating terrorist groups based on their criminal activities [3,10,12,32,37,44]. The field of bioinformatics often uses link prediction for predicting protein-protein interactions containing important information about biomolecular behavior. Such interactions can reveal answers about diseases and cures [4], and therefore, predicting such upcoming links is a crucial component of graph mining.

This research is funded by NSERC Discovery Grant (RGPIN-2017-05377), held by Dr. Vijay Mago.

The main objective of the link prediction problem is to predict the unseen edges that will emerge in a graph. Based upon the *snapshot assumption*, when a snapshot of a graph $G(t)$ at time t is given, link prediction is used to compute which new upcoming links will emerge in the future graph $G(t')$ within the time period $[t, t']$, where $t' = t + n$ (n is the sequence of snapshots) [34]. Link prediction is implemented on real-world network graphs, which are often too massive and *dynamic*, as such graphs are evolving at an extremely high speed. In addition, link prediction uses proximity-based measures, such as the Jaccard coefficient, Resource Allocation, and Adamic Adar metric, to measure the probability of the upcoming links in the network [8]. The features extracted are based on the local nodal properties as these functions use the information available only from the local proximity of the nodes. Although these metrics are used widely in multiple applications because of their simplicity and interpretability, the problem arises when social network graphs become large with numerous users. As a result, predicting future links with these measures becomes a very challenging task. Most importantly, hidden and meaningful knowledge lies between the nodes and edges of networks [4], and analyzing these graphs is extremely difficult when large-scale network data comprises billions of nodes and edges [42].

Traditional approaches calculated link prediction statically by using only a single network snapshot to predict future links. However, the prediction task is a time-dependent problem, where a network evolves over time [38]. Hence, the dynamic network concept was initiated in which the structure of the network is captured in multiple snapshots over a span of time [50]. Dynamic-link prediction is considered more valuable and challenging than static link prediction. The evolvement of the network structure offers much more information that adds a whole new dimension in network analysis and helps achieve a better link prediction performance [39]. The problem arises when the number of edges and nodes increases at a faster rate as it becomes very challenging to extract or infer any reasoning and information from the whole network [19]. Dimensional reduction techniques have been used to solve this issue, which transform the nodes of a graph into lower-dimensional latent representations [6]. These representations can be used as features for executing tasks in graph mining, such as clustering and link prediction [45]. Similarly, network representation learning algorithms such as node2vec have also been used to tackle this issue. Node2vec conducts high order proximity by escalating the probability of finding successive neighboring nodes within a fixed length of random walk [19]. This method can efficiently find the equilibrium position between breadth-first search (BFS) and depth-first search (DFS) graphs by developing random biased walks. As a result, it can succeed in embedding rich quality data, enabling node2vec to preserve the structural balance of the node communities.

Although node2vec has successfully achieved high link prediction performance, it still has many shortcomings [14]. Firstly, it follows a local approach that takes short random walks to get exposed to only the local neighborhood of nodes [13] and hence ignores the global relationship of nodes that might have longer distances. Due to this, the learned representation may be unable to comprehend the essential global structure of the model. Secondly, node2vec uses the Stochastic Gradient Descent (SGD) method to resolve non-convex optimization problems, where the non-convex constraints may have various regions and many locally optimal points within each region [7,23]. The algorithm repeatedly gets updated when SGD is used to optimize the objective function. This causes the optimal points to oscillate frequently and possibly causes them to get stuck in a local minima. Due to the complexity of the growing networks, recent research has focused on applying deep learning techniques to evaluate the complex relationships that exist in graphs and visualize the hidden patterns [43]. To tackle these problems we propose NODDLE (integration of **NO**de2vec an**D** **D**eep **L**earning m**E**thod), a deep learning model that combines the features extracted by node2vec algorithm and feeds them into four layers of hidden neural network. It optimizes the performance by using different types of optimizers, which include Adaptive Moment Estimation (Adam), Adamax, An Adaptive Learning Rate Method (Adadelta), and Adaptive Gradient Algorithm (Adagrad). We have compared our approach with the benchmark methods that include Adamic Adar, Jaccard coefficient, and Preferential Attachment [17,27,47].

The rest of the paper is organized as follows. Section 2 presents background on the previous studies conducted on link prediction of social networks with heuristic-based, machine learning, and deep learning approaches. Section 3 introduces our proposed approach in detail, including our data preparation method and the method for combining node2vec with the deep learning model. Later, in Sect. 4, we validate our approach on real-world social network data and analyze the results. Finally, Sect. 5 concludes the paper.

2   Related Work

2.1   Heuristic Similarity Metrics

Liben-Nowell and Kleinberg proposed a link prediction problem for social networks using multiple heuristic functions [32]. They found that topological features can be used to predict a future edge between two nodes that showed high "similarity" or "proximity" between the target nodes. Furthermore, their findings conveyed that the heuristics such as Adamic/Adar and Katz centrality measure notable correlation with the predicted future links [2,24].

Many research works emphasized enhancing the performance of heuristic functions by increasing the neighbor-based attributes to second, third, or higher adjacency degrees. For instance, Yao et al. presented an improved common neighbors heuristic algorithm that includes nodes with a distance of two hops and used time-decay for recent snapshots to have a greater weight [46]. Kaya et al. used progressive events to calculate the possibility of future links in a time-weighted fashion [25], and Deylami and Asadpour proposed a community detection algorithm to identify high activity clusters [15]. Similarity metrics have also been used to detect social and cognitive radio network events for common link prediction problems [21,22,49].

2.2   Machine Learning and Deep Learning

Both supervised and unsupervised techniques have been employed to predict links in the network. Unsupervised methods comprise developing the heuristic approaches to determine the score for the likelihood of each upcoming link [41]. Similarity metrics are most commonly used to measure the intensity of the relationship between the nodes. Topological features of the nodes such as common neighbors and graph distances are used to measure the strength of the interaction between the nodes [5]. Conversely, supervised methods involve treating the link prediction problem as a binary classification task in which the edges and non-edges of a network model are employed for training a classifier [29].

Compared to heuristic-based approaches, machine learning techniques have proven better at link prediction tasks as these models have received higher accuracy. Yet, the major problem with them is representing the graphical features, since it is impossible to use the large-scale graphs as input into the machine learning models. As a result, researchers have attempted to extract features. For example, Hasan et al. have extracted multiple graph features and implemented the features with various machine learning algorithms such as Decision trees, Naive Bayes, and k-Nearest Neighbors [5]. Similarly, Bechettara et al. have implemented topological-based features of bipartite graphs with decision trees [9], and Doppa et al. proposed a supervised feature vector-based approach with k-means classifier for link prediction [16]. Even though machine learning techniques have been shown to achieve better prediction accuracy, these methods rely highly on features developed by human intelligence. Thus, engineering such features is extremely tedious and slow. As a result, most state-of-art link prediction techniques utilize deep neural networks for their exceptional learning ability.

A deep neural network model is defined as a group of models in machine learning consisting of multiple connected layers. The layers generate output-yielding nodes where the parameters of the neural network layers are tuned in continuous iterations to reduce the error between the final output and the original value [11]. Li et al. have explored a neural network structure as a conditional temporal Restricted Boltzmann Machine (ctRBM), which expands on the architecture of an RBM to integrate the temporal elements of a dynamic changing network [31]. Furthermore, Zhang et al. suggested the neural network model as a means of feature representation by using the term Social Pattern and External Attribute Knowledge (SPEAK); these features are used as input in deep neural network models [48]. Ozcan A has proposed a link prediction algorithm that extracts multi-variable features from heterogeneous networks and is based upon non-linear autoregressive neural networks [36]. This method was tested on various datasets and has outperformed the existing algorithms that focus on only single variable features. Zhang et al. proposed a framework that uses graph neural networks to learn general graph features for link prediction [48]. Graph neural networks are defined as a message-passing algorithm, in which the message represents the features extracted from each node in a graph, and their effects on the edges and nodes are learned by neural networks [35]. Their framework has also shown promising results in the online social networking Stanford Facebook dataset [48]. Therefore, state-of-the-art research has mainly focused on learning multiple features from graphs at an extensive level as such features contain hidden and meaningful insights into link probability. With the rise of complex growing networks, deep learning techniques have produced highly accurate results. Besides, deep learning can model the complex relationships hidden in the network data and can reveal unseen patterns hidden beneath the billions of nodes and edges [38].

Further research is being conducted to improve link prediction performance by applying both supervised, unsupervised, as semi-supervised approaches [33, 52]. Semi-supervised learning combines a small proportion of labeled data with a large pile of unlabeled data during the training process. As mentioned earlier, a semi-supervised approach such as node2vec has outperformed existing supervised approaches since it can maintain the community structure and embed better quality information [19]. In addition, neural networks are also currently being used to enhance link prediction performance. These novel methods have proven to be highly effective [30]. Such methods can produce promising link prediction results in large complex networks. Even so, a primary disadvantage to such approaches is that the training and prediction process is highly time-consuming.

3   Proposed Approach

This section explains the strategy of solving the problem with the deep learning method. Algorithms 1 and 2 provide insights into how we have aggregated the connected and unconnected pairs from the network used to build the training dataset. The overall steps for preparing a graph with connected and unconnected pairs from the raw network graph are explained in Algorithm 3. Then, we present the node2vec model for extracting the features from the training network dataset. Finally, we show how we have developed the deep neural network model with improved optimizers for executing AUC scores for the link prediction of the network. Figure 1 provides the overview of our proposed approach.

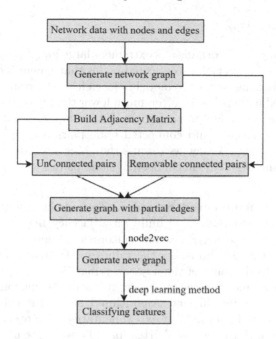

Fig. 1. Overall structure of the proposed approach

3.1   Problem Statement

A sequence of snapshots in time from t to $t+n$ is defined as a dynamic network in which the set of edges in each snapshot depicts the links present at time t. The link prediction problem is that given snapshots from t to $t+n$, return the score for the possibilities of edges at time $t+n$. Figure 2 and Fig. 3 show a dynamic network with two snapshots. Given the information at time t, we would like to predict the likelihood of link prediction at time $t+n$.

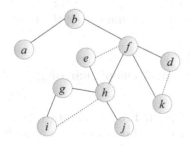
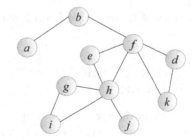

Fig. 2. At time t, the dotted lines represents the future links

Fig. 3. At time $t+n$, the new links have formed

3.2   Data Preparation

In real-time scenarios, network data is extremely large and highly imbalanced as it contains a higher number of unconnected nodes than connected nodes. Therefore, it is always challenging for the model to learn features from connected nodes since the connected node pairs are often much fewer than the unconnected nodes. Hence, we provide a way for preparing the data computationally economically to extract the unconnected and connected node pairs from a large number of imbalanced network data. Below we discuss the process of sampling the positive (connected) and the negative (unconnected) node pairs.

Aggregation of Unconnected Samples. To find the negative sample that depicts the unconnected nodes, we build an adjacency matrix with the aid of the *networkx* library. The connected and unconnected nodes are represented as rows and columns for each node. As the values in the matrix are the same for above and below the diagonal of the adjacency matrix, we only focus on finding the positions of the unconnected nodes from above the diagonal to make the approach computationally efficient. Algorithm 1 shows the complete steps for finding the unconnected nodes. After experimentation with other configurations, we use *networkx* library to find the shortest path between the unconnected nodes and only select the ones within distance 3. The unconnected node pairs were labeled as '0', as the unconnected node pairs represent the negative links.

Aggregation of Connected Samples. Some of the edges from the graph will be randomly removed and labelled '1' since, these edges connect the nodes and show the presence of links. Thus, when training the model, it will predict such potential links at time $t + n$. However, it is essential to ensure that the graph's nodes do not become completely isolated when dropping the edges since taking such a step can misrepresent data, and the model will be trained poorly. Thus, when removing an edge, we ensure this does not lead to splitting the graph, and the number of connected nodes is ≥ 1. If the removed edge satisfies both of the conditions, only then the edge is dropped, and the process is repeated for the next pairs of nodes. Algorithm 2 shows the steps for accumulating the positive samples.

3.3   NODDLE (Integration of NOde2vec and Deep Learning mEthod)

Given that node2vec is a local approach that is limited to the structure around the node, it uses a short random walk to find the local neighborhood of nodes. Such attention to local structure implicitly overlooks the long-distance relationship in the whole network, and the representation may not reveal the important global structure model [19]. We propose NODDLE, a deep learning model in which features extracted from the node2vec are fed into a 4 layer hidden neural

---

Algorithm 1: Finding all Unconnected pairs

Input: Adjacency Matrix as $AdjM$, Graph $G = (N, E)$
Output: All unconnected pairs as UCP

1 $UCP \leftarrow \phi$ // empty dataframe for all unconnected pairs
2 **for** *each row in AdjM* **do**
3   **for** *each column in AdjM* **do**
4   **if** *row.index ≠ column.index* **then**
5   **if** *FindShortestLength (G, row, column) ≤ 3* **then**
            /* using networkx for shortest length function   */
6   **if** *AdjM [row, column] == 0* **then**
7   Append *N.row, N.column* to *UCP*

8 **Return** UCP

Algorithm 2: Finding all Connected pairs

Input: Graph $G = (N, E)$
Output: Connected Pairs as CP

1 CP $\leftarrow \phi$ // Empty set of connected pairs
2 **for** *each e in E* **do**
3     $G' \leftarrow RemoveEdge(G)$ // remove edge from a node pair and generate
      a new graph as G'
4   **if** *the new nodes are not completely isolated* **then**
5        $CP \leftarrow$ Append(G'.node, G'.edge)

6 **Return** CP

---

network. The prediction performance is enhanced by applying various optimizers, including Adaptive Moment Estimation (Adam), Adamax, An Adaptive Learning Rate Method (Adadelta), and Adaptive Gradient Algorithm (Adagrad), respectively. We illustrate a brief description of node2vec, its limitations, and explain the need for this deep learning model.

Node2vec. Node2vec algorithm is a feature extraction method used to generate vector representations of nodes on a graph. It is mainly a local approach that uses random walk to search for the local neighborhood of nodes. The algorithm uses direct encoding and a product-based decoder. Therefore, node2vec embedding is defined as such:

$$DE(s_i, s_j) \cong \frac{e^{z_i^T z_j}}{\sum_{v_k \in V} e^{z_i^T z_k}} \approx (P, R(v_j|v_i)) \tag{1}$$

In this Eq. (1), $DE(s_i, s_j)$ represents the decoded product based proximity value, the probability of visiting to node target node v_j from the source node v_i with fixed length of random walk R, denoted by $(P, R(v_j|v_i))$. $(P, R(v_j|v_i))$ can be calculated for both random and undirected graphs. Cross entropy loss for node2vec is calculated by the following formula:

Algorithm 3: Data Preparation for generating Model

Input: Node as N and Edge as E
Output: New Graph as G'

1 G ← ϕ // Graph
2 AdjM ← ϕ // Adjacency Matrix
3 UCP ← ϕ // Empty set of unconnected pairs
4 CP ← ϕ // Empty set of connected pairs
5 **for** *each n, e in N, E* **do**
6 │ G ← (n, e) // Creating network Graph with networkx library
7 │ AdjM ← AdjacencyMatrix (G) /* Create Adjacency Matrix from nodes
│   and edges with networkx   */
8 │ UCP ← UnconnectedPairs $(AdjM, G)$ // Algorithm 1
9 │ CP ← ConnectedPairs (G) // Algorithm 2
10 └ G' ←Create NewGraph *(UCP, CP)*

11 **Return** df

$$Loss = \sum_{(v_i, v_j) \in Deno} -\log(DE(s_i, s_j)) \tag{2}$$

The training set is generated by collecting random walks from a source node v_i in which the N pairs of v_i for each node are collected from the probabilistic distribution of $(v_i, v_j) \sim (P, R(v_j|v_i))$. However, it is extremely expensive to calculate the cross entropy loss because of the high computational costs for evaluating $O(|Deno||V|)$, as $O(|V|)$ has a high time complexity when computing the denominator $Deno$ of (1). As a result, node2vec uses various optimization and approximation methods for computing the cross entropy loss. It uses the "Negative sampling" approximation method to evaluate (2). The node2vec takes a random set of negative samples for approximately calculating the normalization factor instead of letting the entire set of vertices be normalized [19]. Additionally, it applies two hyper parameters p and q. The probability of going back to a previous node after visiting a new node is controlled by p. The hyper parameter q controls the possibility of exploring the graph's new nodes. When these hyper parameters are employed, node2vec can interpolate between the walks much more smoothly, and the approach becomes similar to BFS and DFS. Grover et al. also demonstrated that when the two hyper parameters are well-adjusted, it enables node2vec to preserve the structural balance between the nodes [19]. However, node2vec still has its drawbacks. It uses SGD method for solving the non-convex optimization problem [18,28]. The algorithm constantly updates when SGD is used as the objective function, which causes the optimal points to oscillate frequently, leading the optimal points to dismount into the local minimum range.

Besides, SGD keeps the learning rate constant when the parameters are updated. As a result, SGD cannot adapt the learning rate and adjust it for carrying out greater updates on lower frequency features [40]. Hence, Adam, Adamax, and Adadelta optimizers have been introduced to resolve this issue. These optimizers can incorporate different learning rates with different parameters.

Compared to SGD, these optimizers are more compatible for large network datat-sets in high dimensional spaces and, most importantly, non-convex optimization objective functions. Furthermore, deep learning techniques are also applied to study the complex relationships with the growing networks. Hence, we are focus-ing on improving the performance of link prediction by fusing node2vec with a deep learning model, in which the model is supported with improved optimizers.

Algorithms 4 and 5, show the steps of the node2vec algorithm. The algorithm first learns the representations of the nodes by generating a random walk with a length of l, which starts from each of the nodes. When the step is taken in each of the walks, sampling is conducted with the transitional probability of θ_{vx}. The transitional probability θ_{vx} of the second order Markov chain is at first calculated so that node sampling can be computed efficiently by using the alias method in $O(1)$ time. In the final phase, the transitional probability preprocessing is conducted sequentially, and optimization of SGD is used.

Algorithm 4: Node2Vec Algorithm

Input: Graph $G' = (N, E)$, dimension dim, Walks per node r, Walk Length l,
Context size h, Return p, In-out q
Output: final Stochastic gradient descent function as f
1 θ = PreprocessModifiedWeights(G, p, q) $G' = (V, E, \theta)$ Initialize $walks$ to empty
2 **for** $iter$ 1 to r **do**
3   **for** all nodes $u \in V$ **do**
4          $walk$ = node2vecWalk $(G\prime, u, l)$
5   Append $walk$ to $walks$

6 f = Stochastic gradient descent $(h, dim, walks)$
7 **Return** f

Algorithm 5: node2vecWalk Algorithm

Input: Graph $G' = (N, E)$, Start node u, Length l, Walk Length l, Context size
h, Return p, In-out q
Output: $walk$
1 **node2vecWalk**(Graph $G' = (N, E)$, Start node u, Length l, Walk Length l,
Context size h, Return p, In-out q) Initialize $walk$ to $[u]$
2 $G' = (V, E, \theta)$
3 Initialize $walks$ to empty
4 **for** $walk$ from 1 to l **do**
5      $curr = walk[-1]$
6      $V_{current}$ = GetNeighbours$(Current, G')$
7   s = AliasSample $(V_{current}, \theta)$
8   Append s to $walk$

9 **Return** $walk$

Deep Learning Model. In the final step, we build a deep learning network in which the features extracted from node2vec are fed into a four layer hidden neural network. As mentioned earlier, the SGD optimization function of node2vec has limited capabilities to adapt to different learning rates. As a result, for boosting up the performance of the link prediction task, we built the deep learning model with adaptive learning rate optimizers: Adam, Adamax, Adadelta, and Adagrad, respectively. This approach is treated as a supervised classification problem, where the network aims to yield a single value representing the probability for a given edge. Thus, we end the deep learning model with a sigmoid activation function to score between 0 and 1.

Optimizers. Below we have discussed the different types of optimizers that were used with the model.

- Adagrad: Adaptive gradient, or AdaGrad, divides the learning rate by the square root of v, which is mainly the cumulative sum of current and past squared gradients up to time t [17]. Moreover, the gradient component is unchanged just like in SGD. The Adagrad is defined as such:

$$w_{t+1} = w_t - \frac{\rho}{\sqrt{v_t + \epsilon}} \cdot \frac{\partial L}{\partial w_t} \tag{3}$$

In Eq. (3), w_t is the current weight at time step t that needs to be updated, ρ represents the learning rate and $\frac{\partial L}{\partial w_t}$ denotes the gradient descent to update the weight at w_t and ϵ is a constant value.

- Adadelta: Adadelta is a much more powerful extension of Adagrad that emphasizes the learning rate component [47]. The optimizer is based on updating gradient using the sliding window technique instead of aggregating all the previous gradients. In Adadelta, the difference between the current and updated weights is denoted by 'delta'. Furthermore, the learning rate parameter is replaced by T, the exponential moving average of squared deltas and is defined in 4).

$$w_{t+1} = w_t - \frac{\sqrt{T_{t-1} + \epsilon}}{\sqrt{v_t + \epsilon}} \cdot \frac{\partial L}{\partial w_t} \tag{4}$$

- Adam: Adaptive moment estimation, or Adam, focuses on the gradient component by using $\hat{s}$, which estimates the exponential average of the moving gradients [27]. In addition, the learning rate component is calculated by dividing the learning rate ρ by the square root of v, which is the exponential moving average of squared gradients. The equation is defined as below:

$$w_{t+1} = w_t - \frac{\sqrt{T_{t-1} + \epsilon}}{\sqrt{v_t + \epsilon}} \cdot \hat{s}_t \tag{5}$$

- Adamax: AdaMax is a variation of the Adam optimizer, which uses infinity norms [27]. The infinity norm is used to calculate the absolute values of the v components in a vector space ('max'), and $\hat{s}$ refers to the estimated value of the exponential average of moving gradients, and v is the exponential moving average of previous p-norm of gradients, that is approximately the max function as defined below:

$$w_{t+1} = w_t - \frac{\rho}{v_t} \cdot \hat{s}_t \tag{6}$$

4 Experiment

This section will evaluate the proposed model on real-world data network datasets and examine how it is more effective than the existing benchmark methods, including Adamic Adar, Preferential Attachment, and Jaccard Coefficient.

4.1 Datasets

We evaluate our model on Facebook[1] and Twitter[2] datasets that consists of nodes and edges. Table 1 shows the overview of the five network datasets. The first four of these datasets were collected from the SNAP website. Also, with the aid of Twitter API we have extended a Twitter dataset of around 7,000 users who have followed Twitter medical accounts [26]. The extended dataset contains the follower and following IDs of the users working in the medical profession. Public biographical contents of the users were used for finding the occupation of the users.[3].

Table 1. Details of the datasets

Dataset	Number of nodes	Number of edges
Twitter	81,306	1,768,149
Facebook1	4,039	88,234
Facebook2	1,046	27,794
Facebook3	546	5,360
Occupation	6,754	470,168

4.2 Experimental Results and Discussions

Our proposed model was implemented in Python 2.8.6, and the experiment was conducted on HPC (High Configuration GPU enabled PC)[4]. In our model, we have used four layer fully connected deep neural network with 1024 ReLU neurons in each of the hidden layers. Then, we developed our model using Adagrad,

---

[1] https://snap.stanford.edu/data/egonets-Facebook.html.
[2] https://snap.stanford.edu/data/egonets-Twitter.html.
[3] https://github.com/ZainabKazi22/occupation_twitter.
[4] https://github.com/ZainabKazi22/link_prediction_with_gbm.

Adadelta, Adam, and Adamax optimizers to improve the performance of the link prediction task.

We calculate the Area Under ROC Curve (AUC) scores to evaluate the performance of our approach of combining node2vec and deep learning model with each of the optimizers, respectively. The AUC score is defined in (7):

$$AUC = \frac{D_0 - n_0(n_0 + 1)/2}{n_0 n_1} \tag{7}$$

In Eq. (7), n_0 and n_1 denotes the number of positive and negative class links, respectively and $D_0 = \sum r_i$, where r_i represents the rank of the index i in the positive class link in terms of similarity index. Also, $AUC \in [0, 1]$, in which the higher the value of AUC, the higher the link prediction accuracy of the algorithm. We have compared the performance of our approach with the traditional link prediction benchmark methods: Adamic Adar (AA), Jaccard Co-efficient (JC), and Preferential Attachment (PA).

In AA, the association between two neighboring nodes with a smaller degree may occur more than a node with a higher degree [51]. For instance, two celebrity fans are likely not to know each other. Yet, if two users follow someone who has fewer fans, then those two users will have a higher chance to have similar interests or tend to be in the same social circle. JC believes that the probability of the presence of links is proportional to the number of two nodes' neighbors [20]. If any two Twitter users tend to have similar interests, they have a higher chance of having some type of connections with each other. Research has shown that the rate of an edge to be connected to a node is proportional to the degree of the node [1]. Thus, PA states that the chances of a new edge to be connected to a node are related to the degree of the node. Two popular celebrities will have a higher chance to know each other since they have a higher degree compared

Table 2. AUC Scores of the Link Prediction Algorithms

Link Prediction Algorithm	AUC Score				
	Twitter	Occupation	Facebook1	Facebook2	Facebook3
Node2vec	0.895	0.876	0.938	0.873	0.861
Node2vec + DL (Adam)	0.902	0.931	0.934	0.862	0.855
Node2vec + DL (Adamax)	0.916	**0.945**	**0.941**	**0.879**	0.882
Node2vec + DL (Adagrad)	0.911	0.911	0.932	0.845	0.851
Node2vec + DL (Adadelta)	**0.924**	0.932	0.908	0.871	**0.863**
Adamic Adar	0.897	0.711	0.898	0.878	0.734
Jaccard Co-efficient	0.897	0.748	0.901	0.856	0.699
Preferential Attachment	0.891	0.803	0.835	0.801	0.76

to two ordinary persons. The equations of the following algorithms are stated in (8), (9), and (10):

$$s_{AA} = \sum_{x \in \Gamma(i) \cap \Gamma(j)} \frac{1}{\log k_x} \tag{8}$$

$$s_{JC} = \frac{|\Gamma(i) \cap \Gamma(j)|}{|\Gamma(i) \cup \Gamma(j)|} \tag{9}$$

$$s_{PA} = k_x \cdot k_y \tag{10}$$

Table 2 shows the AUC scores obtained from the link prediction algorithms. Overall, node2vec and the node2vec optimized algorithm (Node2Vec+DL) have performed better than the traditional benchmark methods. This might be because node2vec algorithms can learn high-level features from the network data [19]. Moreover, as high-end robust computational engines like GPU are readily available, it is possible to execute the deep learning models. Whereas predicting future links from large network data is challenging for the existing benchmark methods. Node2vec with Adamax optimizer has received the highest AUC score in Occupation and Facebook1 and Facebook2 datasets among the deep learning models. The node2vec with Adadelta optimizer has performed best in Twitter and Facebook3 datasets. The model with Adamax optimizer has performed better than the rest of the optimizers across three datasets, proving that the Adamax optimizer modified over Adam optimizer performs better than the Adam optimizer. Similarly, the model with the Adadelta optimizer has performed better for Twitter and Facebook3 datasets than the Adagrad optimizer. This has demonstrated that the Adadelta optimizer, an improved version of Adagrad optimizer, has achieved a better performance score than the Adagrad optimizer. Thus, from the results in Table 2, we can see that optimizers of the DL model have increased the performance of the node2vec algorithm. The model proposed in this paper has acquired higher AUC scores than the existing benchmark and node2vec method. Also, the AUC scores of the node2vec with improved optimizers of the DL model are highest across all the datasets.

5   Conclusion

In this paper, we explored the drawbacks of the node2vec algorithm when boosting up non-convex functions. In other words, the likelihood of falling into a local minimum due to lack of network knowledge and SGD optimizer's incapabilities to execute adaptive adjustment of the learning rate. Hence, such a scenario makes it extremely difficult for node2vec to process sparse social networks. As a result, we proposed NODDLE, a deep learning model where we have merged the features aggregated by the node2vec algorithm and used them as inputs into a multi-layer neural network optimizing its performance by using different types of improved optimizers such as Adam, Adamax, Adadelta, and Adagrad. Compared to the various baselines, the results of experiments on real-world social networks proved that our approach enhances the prediction accuracy and is much more effective and efficient.

Acknowledgements. The authors thank DaTALab members & Lakehead University's HPC (High Configuration GPU enabled PC) for executing the models, and Punardeep Sikkha, Arunim Garg, Bart, and Abhijit Rao for proofreading and reviewing the manuscript.

References

1. Abbasi, A., Hossain, L., Leydesdorff, L.: Betweenness centrality as a driver of preferential attachment in the evolution of research collaboration networks. J. Informet. **6**(3), 403–412 (2012)
2. Adamic, L.A., Adar, E.: Friends and neighbors on the web. Soc. Netw. **25**(3), 211–230 (2003)
3. Aiello, L.M., Barrat, A., Schifanella, R., Cattuto, C., Markines, B., Menczer, F.: Friendship prediction and homophily in social media. ACM Trans. Web (TWEB) **6**(2), 1–33 (2012)
4. Airoldi, E.M., Blei, D.M., Fienberg, S.E., Xing, E.P.: Mixed membership stochastic blockmodels. J. Mach. Learn. Res. **9**(Sep), 1981–2014 (2008)
5. Al Hasan, M., Chaoji, V., Salem, S., Zaki, M.: Link prediction using supervised learning. In: SDM06: Workshop on Link Analysis, Counter-terrorism and Security, vol. 30, pp. 798–805 (2006)
6. Al-Rfou, R., Perozzi, B., Zelle, D.: DDGK: learning graph representations for deep divergence graph kernels. In: The World Wide Web Conference, pp. 37–48 (2019)
7. Amari, S.I.: Backpropagation and stochastic gradient descent method. Neurocomputing **5**(4–5), 185–196 (1993)
8. Ayoub, J., Lotfi, D., El Marraki, M., Hammouch, A.: Accurate link prediction method based on path length between a pair of unlinked nodes and their degree. Soc. Netw. Anal. Min. **10**(1), 1–13 (2020). https://doi.org/10.1007/s13278-019-0618-2
9. Benchettara, N., Kanawati, R., Rouveirol, C.: Supervised machine learning applied to link prediction in bipartite social networks. In: 2010 International Conference on Advances in Social Networks Analysis and Mining, pp. 326–330. IEEE (2010)
10. Bressan, M., Chierichetti, F., Kumar, R., Leucci, S., Panconesi, A.: Counting graphlets: space vs time. In: Proceedings of the Tenth ACM International Conference on Web Search and Data Mining, pp. 557–566 (2017)
11. Canziani, A., Paszke, A., Culurciello, E.: An analysis of deep neural network models for practical applications. arXiv preprint arXiv:1605.07678 (2016)
12. Chen, H., Perozzi, B., Hu, Y., Skiena, S.: HARP: hierarchical representation learning for networks. arXiv preprint arXiv:1706.07845 (2017)
13. Chen, H., Perozzi, B., Hu, Y., Skiena, S.: HARP: hierarchical representation learning for networks. In: Proceedings of the AAAI Conference on Artificial Intelligence, vol. 32 (2018)
14. Chen, J., et al.: N2VSCDNNR: a local recommender system based on node2vec and rich information network. IEEE Trans. Comput. Soc. Syst. **6**(3), 456–466 (2019)
15. Deylami, H.A., Asadpour, M.: Link prediction in social networks using hierarchical community detection. In: 2015 7th Conference on Information and Knowledge Technology (IKT), pp. 1–5. IEEE (2015)

16. Doppa, J.R., Yu, J., Tadepalli, P., Getoor, L.: Learning algorithms for link prediction based on chance constraints. In: Balcázar, J.L., Bonchi, F., Gionis, A., Sebag, M. (eds.) ECML PKDD 2010. LNCS (LNAI), vol. 6321, pp. 344–360. Springer, Heidelberg (2010). https://doi.org/10.1007/978-3-642-15880-3_28
17. Duchi, J., Hazan, E., Singer, Y.: Adaptive subgradient methods for online learning and stochastic optimization. J. Mach. Learn. Res. **12**(7) (2011)
18. Goldberg, Y., Levy, O.: Word2vec explained: deriving Mikolov et al'.s negative-sampling word-embedding method. arXiv preprint arXiv:1402.3722 (2014)
19. Grover, A., Leskovec, J.: node2vec: scalable feature learning for networks. In: Proceedings of the 22nd ACM SIGKDD International Conference on Knowledge Discovery and Data Mining, pp. 855–864 (2016)
20. Gupta, A.K., Sardana, N.: Significance of clustering coefficient over jaccard index. In: 2015 Eighth International Conference on Contemporary Computing (IC3), pp. 463–466. IEEE (2015)
21. Hu, W., Wang, H., Peng, C., Liang, H., Du, B.: Retracted: an event detection method for social networks based on link prediction (2017)
22. Hu, W., Wang, H., Qiu, Z., Nie, C., Yan, L., Du, B.: An event detection method for social networks based on hybrid link prediction and quantum swarm intelligent. World Wide Web **20**(4), 775–795 (2017)
23. Jain, P., Kar, P.: Non-convex optimization for machine learning. arXiv preprint arXiv:1712.07897 (2017)
24. Katz, L.: A new status index derived from sociometric analysis. Psychometrika **18**(1), 39–43 (1953)
25. Kaya, M., Jawed, M., Butun, E., Alhajj, R.: Unsupervised link prediction based on time frames in weighted–directed citation networks. In: Missaoui, R., Abdessalem, T., Latapy, M. (eds.) Trends in Social Network Analysis. LNSN, pp. 189–205. Springer, Cham (2017). https://doi.org/10.1007/978-3-319-53420-6_8
26. Khanam, K.Z., Srivastava, G., Mago, V.: Identifying health related occupations of twitter users through word embedding and deep neural networks. In: Proceedings of The 19th Asia Pacific Bioinformatics Conference Accepted. In press (2021)
27. Kingma, D.P., Ba, J.: Adam: a method for stochastic optimization. arXiv preprint arXiv:1412.6980 (2014)
28. Le, Q., Mikolov, T.: Distributed representations of sentences and documents. In: International Conference on Machine Learning, pp. 1188–1196 (2014)
29. Li, J.C., Zhao, D.l., Ge, B.F., Yang, K.W., Chen, Y.W.: A link prediction method for heterogeneous networks based on BP neural network. Phys. A: Stat. Mech. Appl. **495**, 1–17 (2018)
30. Li, T., Zhang, J., Philip, S.Y., Zhang, Y., Yan, Y.: Deep dynamic network embedding for link prediction. IEEE Access **6**, 29219–29230 (2018)
31. Li, X., Du, N., Li, H., Li, K., Gao, J., Zhang, A.: A deep learning approach to link prediction in dynamic networks. In: Proceedings of the 2014 SIAM International Conference on Data Mining, pp. 289–297. SIAM (2014)
32. Liben-Nowell, D., Kleinberg, J.: The link-prediction problem for social networks. J. Am. Soc. Inform. Sci. Technol. **58**(7), 1019–1031 (2007)
33. Liu, D., Li, Q., Ru, Y., Zhang, J.: The network representation learning algorithm based on semi-supervised random walk. IEEE Access **8**, 222956–222965 (2020)
34. Liu, H., Kou, H., Yan, C., Qi, L.: Link prediction in paper citation network to construct paper correlation graph. EURASIP J. Wirel. Commun. Netw. **2019**(1), 1–12 (2019). https://doi.org/10.1186/s13638-019-1561-7

35. Maron, H., Ben-Hamu, H., Serviansky, H., Lipman, Y.: Provably powerful graph networks. In: Advances in Neural Information Processing Systems, pp. 2156–2167 (2019)
36. Ozcan, A., Oguducu, S.G.: Link prediction in evolving heterogeneous networks using the NARX neural networks. Knowl. Inf. Syst. **55**(2), 333–360 (2018)
37. Pezeshkpour, P., Tian, Y., Singh, S.: Investigating robustness and interpretability of link prediction via adversarial modifications. arXiv preprint arXiv:1905.00563 (2019)
38. Rahman, M., Hasan, M.A.: Link prediction in dynamic networks using graphlet. In: Frasconi, P., Landwehr, N., Manco, G., Vreeken, J. (eds.) ECML PKDD 2016. LNCS (LNAI), vol. 9851, pp. 394–409. Springer, Cham (2016). https://doi.org/10.1007/978-3-319-46128-1_25
39. Rahman, M., Saha, T.K., Hasan, M.A., Xu, K.S., Reddy, C.K.: Dylink2vec: effective feature representation for link prediction in dynamic networks. arXiv preprint arXiv:1804.05755 (2018)
40. Ruder, S.: An overview of gradient descent optimization algorithms. arXiv preprint arXiv:1609.04747 (2016)
41. Tabakhi, S., Moradi, P., Akhlaghian, F.: An unsupervised feature selection algorithm based on ant colony optimization. Eng. Appl. Artif. Intell. **32**, 112–123 (2014)
42. Tang, J., Qu, M., Wang, M., Zhang, M., Yan, J., Mei, Q.: LINE: large-scale information network embedding. In: Proceedings of the 24th International Conference on World Wide Web, pp. 1067–1077 (2015)
43. Wang, H., Shi, X., Yeung, D.Y.: Relational deep learning: a deep latent variable model for link prediction. In: AAAI, pp. 2688–2694 (2017)
44. Wang, P., Xu, B., Wu, Y., Zhou, X.: Link prediction in social networks: the state-of-the-art. Sci. China Inf. Sci. **58**(1), 1–38 (2015)
45. Xu, L., Wei, X., Cao, J., Yu, P.S.: Interaction content aware network embedding via co-embedding of nodes and edges. In: Phung, D., Tseng, V.S., Webb, G.I., Ho, B., Ganji, M., Rashidi, L. (eds.) PAKDD 2018. LNCS (LNAI), vol. 10938, pp. 183–195. Springer, Cham (2018). https://doi.org/10.1007/978-3-319-93037-4_15
46. Yao, L., Wang, L., Pan, L., Yao, K.: Link prediction based on common-neighbors for dynamic social network. Procedia Comput. Sci. **83**, 82–89 (2016)
47. Zeiler, M.D.: ADADELTA: an adaptive learning rate method. arXiv preprint arXiv:1212.5701 (2012)
48. Zhang, C., Zhang, H., Yuan, D., Zhang, M.: Deep learning based link prediction with social pattern and external attribute knowledge in bibliographic networks. In: 2016 IEEE International Conference on Internet of Things (iThings) and IEEE Green Computing and Communications (GreenCom) and IEEE Cyber, Physical and Social Computing (CPSCom) and IEEE Smart Data (SmartData), pp. 815–821. IEEE (2016)
49. Zhang, L., Zhuo, F., Bai, C., Xu, H.: Analytical model for predictable contact in intermittently connected cognitive radio ad hoc networks. Int. J. Distrib. Sens. Netw. **12**(7), 1550147716659426 (2016)
50. Zhang, Z., Wen, J., Sun, L., Deng, Q., Su, S., Yao, P.: Efficient incremental dynamic link prediction algorithms in social network. Knowl.-Based Syst. **132**, 226–235 (2017)
51. Zhou, T., Lü, L., Zhang, Y.C.: Predicting missing links via local information. Eur. Phys. J. B **71**(4), 623–630 (2009)
52. Zhu, J., Zheng, Z., Yang, M., Fung, G.P.C., Tang, Y.: A semi-supervised model for knowledge graph embedding. Data Min. Knowl. Disc. **34**(1), 1–20 (2020)

Hybrid Coral Reef Optimization Algorithm Employed Local Search Technique for Job Shop Scheduling Problems

Chin-Shiuh Shieh[1] (iD), Thanh-Tuan Nguyen[1,2](✉) (iD), Dinh-Cuong Nguyen[1] (iD), Thanh-Nghia Nguyen[3] (iD), Mong-Fong Horng[1] (iD), and Denis Miu[4]

[1] Department of Electronic Engineering, National Kaohsiung University of Science and Technology, Kaohsiung, Taiwan
`tuannt@ntu.edu.vn`
[2] Department of Electronics and Automation Engineering, Nha Trang University, Nha Trang, Vietnam
[3] FPT University HCMC, Ho Chi Minh City, Vietnam
[4] Genie Networks, Taipei, Taiwan

Abstract. The JSSP (job shop scheduling problem) is a crucial problem in operational research with certain real-world applications. Due to the fact that the JSSP is an NP-hard (nondeterministic polynomial time) issue, approximation techniques are frequently employed to solve it. This paper introduces a novel biologically-inspired metaheuristic algorithm called Coral Reef Optimization (CRO) in combination with local search strategies Simulated Annealing (SA) significantly improves performance and solution-finding speed. The performance of hybrid algorithms is examined by solving various instances of JSSP. The results indicate that local search methods greatly improve the search efficiency of the hybrid algorithm in comparison to the original algorithm, which was used to assess the improvement. Moreover, comparative findings with five state-of-the-art algorithms from the literature demonstrate that the proposed hybrid algorithms have advantageous search capabilities.

Keywords: Job-shop scheduling · coral reef optimization · local search · hybrid approach

1 Introduction

Scheduling production is essential in product manufacture and directly impacts system efficiency and overall manufacturing productivity [1]. In several businesses, production scheduling has become a significant challenge. To enhance production efficiency, dozens of innovative strategies are being evaluated, with an emphasis on schedule optimization [2]. Consequently, both the scientific and industry communities are focusing on production schedule optimization [3]. Since the 1950s, industrialization has considered production schedules as an important topic, and the job shop scheduling problem

© ICST Institute for Computer Sciences, Social Informatics and Telecommunications Engineering 2023
Published by Springer Nature Switzerland AG 2023. All Rights Reserved
R. Hou et al. (Eds.): BDTA 2021/2022, LNICST 480, pp. 213–231, 2023.
https://doi.org/10.1007/978-3-031-33614-0_15

(JSSP) is a fundamental production scheduling model [4]. Since Johnson's (1954) first two-machine scheduling system [5] the JSSP's complexity has expanded in direct proportion to the number of devices and workloads. The JSSP is classified as NP-hard (non-deterministic polynomial time) due to its tremendous complexity [6]. Solving large-scale JSSP in a sensible time frame has been studied for decades. JSSP is evolving into a variety of new forms with distinct features and characteristics for the rising workloads. It responds in various ways to variations in the fundamental JSSP [7]. According to a study by Xiong et al. [8], hundreds of studies and combinatorial optimization of individual aspects of JSSP and its implementations in the stated sectors were conducted and provided throughout five years period from 2016 to 2021.

In computer science and operations research, JSSP is classified as a multi-stage, static, deterministic task scheduling issue, and its solution strategies vary at each level of research development. The basis of JSSP consists of:

- A set of n jobs $J = \{J_i | i = 1, 2, ...n\}$, where J_i denotes ith job ($1 \leq i \leq n$).
- A set of m machines $M = \{M_j | j = 1, 2, ...m\}$, and Mj denotes jth machine.
- Each job Ji has a specific set of operations $O = \{O_{i1}, O_{i2}, ..., O_{ik}\}$, where k is the total operations in job Ji.
- Operation O_{ij} will be processed only once the operation O_{ij-1} has been completed in job Ji.

Scheduling distributes shared resources to concurrent tasks during processing. The system entails allocating and structuring restricted resources according to the problem's limits, such as activity sequence and time consumption, and provides a strategy for reaching optimization goals. The following are the fundamental JSSP requirements [9]:

- Each operation is executed separately from the others.
- No job operation can commence until all prior operations are finished.
- Once a processing operation has started, it will not be halted until the process is completed.
- It is impossible to perform numerous operations of the same work at one time.
- Job operations must queue until the next suitable machine becomes available.
- Single machine can only carry out one operation at a time.
- The machine will be idle throughout the unallocated period.

Notably, the set of constraints in real-world problems is more complex, including multiple objective scheduling issues in a job shop, processing times that can be either deterministic or probabilistic, and idle time requests that are restricted to no more than two subsequent machines or none at all. Any adjustment to the problem's constraints might result in a new problem variant. Therefore, JSSP problem-solving procedures differ with each study development stage [10]. One of the practical techniques to JSSP, metaheuristic optimization can deliver a good optimization solution in a sensible amount of time [11]. Enabling the speedy creation of high-quality solutions, metaheuristic algorithms apply unique search techniques to explore the solution space and avoid becoming trapped in local optima by directing the viable solution with a bias. Modern metaheuristic algorithms additionally use several mathematical models [12] and analytical operating processes [13] to improve performance.

The coral reef optimization approach (CRO) is one of the complicated bio-inspired computer techniques utilized to address engineering and scientific issues by modeling the "formation" and "reproduction" of corals in coral reefs. In 2014, Salcedo-Sanz et al. were the first to propose the method [14]. Since then, it has been applied to a number of relevant problems, such as optimum mobile network deployment [15], improved battery scheduling of microgrids [16], and wind speed prediction systems with success in "Offshore Wind Farm Design" [17]. This paper contributes by offering improved coral reef optimization strategies using local search techniques for the JSSP function. On the basis of the original coral reef optimization (CRO) approach, a hybrid algorithm, CROLS, which combines CRO with the Simulated Annealing (SA) strategy methodology, has been created and presented. Moreover, comparative findings with five state-of-the-art algorithms from the literature to demonstrate that the proposed hybrid algorithms have advantageous search capabilities.

The rest of this paper is organized as follows: Sect. 2 provides a summary of related work. Section 3 describes the rationale for the proposed method. The experimental results are described in Sect. 4. Section 5 concludes this research.

2 Related Work

Since its beginning, operation research has emphasized accurate techniques for tackling combinatorial problems with numerous variables. Exact algorithms are defined as those that ensure correct optimization problem answers. Almost every constrained combinatorial optimization problem might be solved using precise algorithms by finding all feasible solutions in a short amount of time [18]. However, it has been argued that when precise algorithms are used to solve combinatorial optimization problems, the time necessary to determine the optimal method increases exponentially with the problem's complexity. Branch and bind algorithms and mixed integer programming are the most often used accurate algorithms for tackling JSSP problems [19]. Small-scale JSSP seldom depicts production environments in actual production; thus, it is essential to analyze more complicated issues involving several works and resources. Due to resource constraints and lengthy execution periods, however, the exact approaches are seldom applied to large-scale scenarios.

Numerous approaches based on artificial intelligence were first suggested and opened a new area in the study of problem-solving strategies [20], and approximation algorithms are one of the most investigated solutions for large-scale combinatorial optimization problems. Although approximation algorithms are not guaranteed to uncover an ideal solution, they are guaranteed to identify a near-optimal solution in a reasonable period of time. Consequently, it has become a new area of study for addressing complicated and large-scale issues. There are two sorts of approximation algorithms: heuristic algorithms and metaheuristic algorithms [21].

Heuristic methods exist in two regions: constructive and local search strategies [22]. In normal constructive algorithms, solutions are constructed piecemeal until they are dependent on the problem's original limitations or predetermined priorities; in scheduling issues, solutions are often produced through operations. These algorithms may "construct" individual processes using "Dispatching Rules," such as programming to discover a workable solution within the limits of a priority hierarchy. Then, solutions are generated rapidly while preserving their quality. While with local search techniques, the originally created keys are gradually replaced by characteristics learned from a set of surrounding solutions, regardless of whether they originate with a random collection of initial solutions or employ building algorithms [23]. These approaches allow for a more efficient analysis of neighboring solutions in a problem space. These algorithms have the problem of being unable to locate and implement global solutions. Therefore, they can become stuck in the local optimal zone.

Meta-heuristics integrates the heuristic approaches often employed to solve combinatorial optimization problems. Meta-heuristic algorithms use creative search tactics to unearth the global optimum and avoid being entangled in local optima by guiding solution seeking with a bias to acquire more feasible options more rapidly. Some bias mechanisms encompass objective function bias, prejudice based on past judgments, experience bias, etc. [21]. This study employs varied and increased search strategies. Using a metaheuristic technique, the main purpose of the diversification strategy is to efficiently explore all probable solution space neighborhoods. In contrast, the intensification strategy entails utilizing previously acquired search skills and investigating a more localized solution subspace. There are two types of meta-heuristic algorithms: single-point and population-based search. Nature-inspired optimization algorithms are prevalent among population-based algorithms in terms of simplicity of development and greater searchability [24]. For example, the GA (genetic algorithm; affected by evolution) [25, 26], PSO (particle swarm optimization; influenced by swarm intelligence) [27], and SA (simulated annealing; influenced by metal cooling behavior) [28] are among the most dependable and efficient algorithms available.

The coral reef optimization approach (CRO) is one of the complicated bio-inspired computer techniques utilized to address engineering and scientific issues by modeling the "formation" and "reproduction" of corals in coral reefs. In 2014, Salcedo-Sanz et al. were the first to propose the method [14]. Since then, it has been applied to a number of relevant problems, such as optimum mobile network deployment [15], improved battery scheduling of microgrids [16], and wind speed prediction systems with success in "Offshore Wind Farm Design" [17]. Diverse hybrid algorithms adapted from the original version have emerged to improve performance and reduce processing time. In 2016, for instance, a combination of CRO and variable neighborhood search approach was used to solve facility layout difficulties involving uneven area sizes [29]. Alternately, another hybrid CRO approach utilizes Spark's MapReduce programming model to lower the system's total reaction time as well as various other exciting uses [30].

3 Materials and Methods

To accurately represent the problem's reality and improve the efficiency of encoding and decoding, it is vital to pick the most appropriate approach. This decision has a significant effect on the success or failure of problem-solving.

3.1   Representation of JSSP for CRO

The operation solutions are represented as sequences of decimal numbers when the coral reef optimization (CRO) method is utilized to solve JSSP problems. Several alternative techniques, such as operation-based modeling, rule-based priority recognition, machine-based representation, etc., explain the resolution of JSSP depending on the problem's particular features [31, 32]. The two primary subdivisions of these representations are direct and indirect encoding approaches.

Implementing "random keys" is our approach to defining the solution. This method has the benefit of presenting a comprehensive description of the situation. Each number in the sequence represents the number of individual tasks, and the number of repetitions of each location in the sequence shows the number of machines the work must traverse prior to completion. In this study, a "random key" approach reveals a solution to a problem that meets the following criteria:

- Each element in a solution indicates a job to be processed.
- The number of jobs appearing corresponds to the number of machines they must pass through;
- The sequence of the elements in the solution corresponds to the machine order that the job should pass through.

Figure 1 illustrates a "random key" in the context of two computers and three jobs:

Fig. 1. A random key approach depicts an example JSSP solution.

The CRO algorithm is comprised of two distinct phases: "reef construction" and "coral re-production":

A "reef" is initially created from a M × N square grid. Individual corals are drawn from the population and then randomly distributed in any available vacant square on the reef, following the free/occupation proportion r0 (zero indicating no occupancy). Each coral represents a unique solution in the solution space and will be assigned a health function; the larger the health function, the more likely the corals will survive the algorithm's subsequent generations. The fitness function, which relies on objective functions, calculates the coral health value.

During the second stage, the CRO reproduces coral by repeating five primary mechanisms to build a new coral generation (called larvae): "Broadcast Spawning" (External sexual), "Brooding" (Internal sexual), "Larvae setting," "Budding" (Asexual), and "Depredation."

In Algorithm 1, the operation of the CRO algorithm is given:

Algorithm 1: Coral Reef Optimization (CRO).

Input: $M \times N$: reef size, ρ_0: occupation rate, F_B: fraction of broadcast spawners, F_A: fraction of asexual reproduction, F_D: fraction of the worse fitness corals, P_D: the deprecated probability of the worse fitness corals.

Output: reasonable solution with best fitness

#Initialization—Reef formation phase:
1. $M \times N \leftarrow$ reef size
2. **Generate** initial coral population
3. **Calculate** the fitness value of each coral
4. **Deploy** randomly on the reef with occupied rate ρ_0
5. *#Main loop—Coral reproduction phase:*
6. **Repeat**
7. **Reproduce** coral fraction F_B by **external sexual broadcast spawning**
8. **Reproduce** coral fraction $1 - F_B$ by **internal sexual brooding**
9. **Larvae setting**
10. **Reproduce** best corals fraction F_A by **asexual budding**
11. **Predation** of F_D worst reef corals with P_D probability
12. **Until** *stop_condition*
13. **Return** *best_resonable_solution*

3.2 Objective Function

We utilize "minimize the makespan" as the objective function for solving JSSP in this work. This is the duration between beginning the first job and finishing the last. For a fundamental JSSP with n jobs and m machines, we have: Oij is the operation of the jth job conducted on the ith computer; pij identifies the processing time of the jth job done on the ith machine based on the beginning time (rij) of operation Oij; the time required to finish operation Oij may then be computed as follows:

$$C_{ij} = r_{ij} + p_{ij} \tag{1}$$

Because machines and jobs have unique and distinct completion times, c_{in} and c_{jm} are defined as the finishing time of the last (nth) operation upon ith machine and the finishing time of the last (mth) operation upon that jth job, respectively. Calculating the starting time r_{ij} is as follows:

$$r_{ij} = max(c_{in}, c_{jm}) \tag{2}$$

Lastly, makespan can be computed as the time required to conduct the final operation on the final machine:

$$makespan = C_{max} = max(C_{im}) \tag{3}$$

The efficiency of the scheduling may be determined by comparing the machine's total idle to the whole processing time of the system:

$$C' = 1 + \frac{\sum_i l_i}{\sum_{j,k} p_{jk}} = \frac{C \cdot m}{\sum_{j,k} p_{jk}} \tag{4}$$

where li denotes the idle time of machine i; m denotes the number of machines; p_{jk} represents the processing time of job i on machine k; C means makespan;

When applied to the JSSP, the method evaluates solution quality using the Objective and Fitness functions obtained from Eqs. (5) and (6), respectively. The Fitness function drives the optimization process by expressing how the suggested solution matches the given objective inextricably. In contrast, the Objective function reveals how "great" the solution is in terms of the optimized function's performance.

$$f = \frac{1}{C_{max}} \tag{5}$$

$$F_{(i)} = \frac{f_{(i)}}{\sum_1^n f_{(i)}} \tag{6}$$

where C_{max} (or makespan) is the period of time between commencing a job and finishing the last one, n is the population size and $f_{(i)}$ is the fitness function.

3.3 Local Search: Simulated Annealing (SA)

SA is the applied local search algorithm for CRO [33]. It is a technique used to imitate the cooling behavior of metal exposed to high temperatures. The metal is quickly heated up to a high temperature and then gently cooled in accordance with a "cooling schedule" in order to create the optimal crystalline structure with the lowest possible internal energy. High temperature imparts crystal grains with a high degree of energy, allowing them to "jump" easily and swiftly to their designated positions within the crystal structure. During the cooling process, the temperature gradually declines, and crystals are expected to be at their ideal positions [28] after the temperature has been sufficiently lowered. Algorithm 2 describes the SA as follows:

Algorithm 2: Simulated Annealing

Input: t: temperature, t_{min}: min temperature, α: cooling rate, F: fitness function, S: solution, $maxIter$: maximum iteration
Output: Best_solution
#Initialization:
1. $t \leftarrow$ initial temperature
2. Best_solution $\leftarrow S$
#Main loop:
While $t > t_{min}$ **do**
3. iter $\leftarrow 0$
4. **While** iter $< maxIter$ **do**
5. **Select** a random solution S'
6. $\Delta \leftarrow F(S') - F(S)$
7. **If** $\Delta < 0$ **do**
8. $S \leftarrow S'$
9. **If** $F(S') < F($Best_solution$)$ **do**
10. Best_solution $\leftarrow S'$
11. **Else if** $rand(0,1) < e^{-\Delta/t}$ **do**
12. $S \leftarrow S'$
13. iter $\leftarrow$ iter $+ 1$
14. $t \leftarrow t * \alpha$
15. **Return**

3.4 Proposal Approaches

We propose a hybrid algorithm called CROLS based on the CRO depicted in Fig. 3's flowchart.:

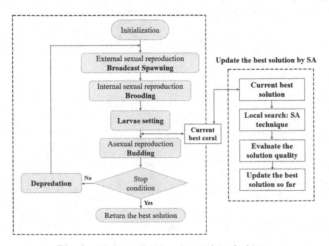

Fig. 3. CRO applied local search techniques.

Typically, algorithms that determine the best answer from a random starting solution, such as the CRO, require considerable time to provide an ideal result. On occasion, the search process becomes stuck in the local optimum and is unable to converge to the optimal solution. Combining local search methodologies is advised to shorten convergence time towards the optimal solution, prevent unnecessary local optimal, and increase search efficiency. Algorithm 3 describes the CROLS algorithm as follows:

Algorithm 3: Hybrid Coral Reef Optimization Algorithms (CROLS)

Input: $M \times N$: reef size, ρ_0: occupation rate, F_B: fraction of broadcast spawners, F_A: fraction of asexual reproduction, F_D: fraction of the worse fitness corals, P_D: the deprecated probability of the worse fitness corals.

Output: Reasonable solution with best fitness

#Initialization—Reef formation phase:

1. $M \times N \leftarrow$ reef size
2. **Generate** initial coral population
3. **Calculate** the fitness value of each coral
4. **Deploy** randomly on the reef with occupied rate ρ_0
5. *#Main loop—Coral reproduction phase:*
6. **Repeat**
7. **Reproduce** coral fraction F_B by **external sexual broadcast spawning**
8. **Reproduce** coral fraction $1 - F_B$ by **internal sexual brooding**
9. **Larvae evaluation**
10. **Larvae setting**
11. **Apply** *"Local search strategy: SA"*
12. **Reproduce** best corals fraction F_A by **asexual budding**
13. **Predation** of F_D worst reef corals with P_D probability
14. **Until** *stop_condition*
15. **Return** *best _solution*

The decision variables of the problem were handled by P_D probability in the proposed algorithm.

4   Experiment Results and Discussion

This section presents a concise and accurate summary of the experimental findings, their interpretation, and the investigation's conclusion.

4.1   Parameters Used in the Algorithm

A number of metaheuristic optimization algorithms aim their search for the best solution with parameters created at random. Therefore, creating the criteria is one of the most crucial steps. Based on the theory of basic evolutionary algorithms and JSSP tests, we determined optimal parameters for the hybrid algorithm. The following parameters are listed in Table 1:

Based on the experimental results, we think that the algorithm's parameters may vary depending on the problem's complexity and size. Even if the setup factors are equal, the outcomes in various situations are not identical. To find the optimal solution for issues of

Table 1. Parameters used in the hybrid algorithms.

Parameter	Technique	Definition	Range
$M \times N$	CRO	Reef size	$[10 \times 10, 30 \times 30]$
$Iter$	CRO	Number of iterations (generations)	$[50, 200]$
F_b	CRO	Probability of Broadcast spawning process	$[0.8, 0.9]$
F_a	CRO	Probability of Budding process	$[0.05, 0.15]$
r_0	CRO	Initial free/occupied ratio	$[0.6, 0.8]$
F_d	CRO	Probability of selecting weak individuals from the population	$[0.01, 0.1]$
P_d	CRO	Probability of removing weak individuals from the population	$[0.01, 0.1]$
k	CRO	Number of chances for a new coral to colonize a reef	$[2, 4]$
ke	CRO	Maximum number of allowed equal corals	$[0.1, 0.3]$
t_{min}	SA	Min temperature	$[0.0001, 1]$
α	SA	Cooling rate	$[0.7, 0.99]$

diverse sizes in an acceptable amount of time, it is required to experiment with different configuration choices. Using a series of tests, we employed the trial-and-error approach for adjusting parameters in order to obtain an acceptable parameter set. Table 2 provides a summary of recommended parameter settings for CROLS with distinct issue sizes.

Table 2. Suggested parameters set for different sizes of problem.

Size	$M \times N$	r_0	Fb	Fa	Fd	Pd	k	tmin	α
Small	10×10	0.6	0.9	0.05	0.01	0.1	3	0.5	0.85
Medium	20×20	0.7	0.85	0.05	0.05	0.1	3	0.5	0.85
Large	30×30	0.7	0.85	0.1	0.1	0.1	3	0.5	0.85

4.2 Experiment Results

The experimental strategy is divided into two steps: first, we will assess the influence of local search on CRO using an aggregated CRO and hybrid algorithm results in Table 3. Second, we compare the best search results of CROLS with five state-of-the-art algorithms from the literature to demonstrate that the proposed hybrid algorithms have advantageous search capabilities. The suggested method is written in Python on a computer with an Intel (R) Core i5 3.1 GHz CPU and 24 GB RAM.

4.2.1 Search Performance on CRO-Based Algorithm with Different Reef Sizes

We will assess the influence of local search on CRO using an aggregated CRO and hybrid algorithm outcome table. In this experiment, we utilize a subset of JSSP by Lawrence (1984) (LA) [34], one of the common cases for addressing JSSP, to assess the efficiency of the method with a population size of 30 × 30 and all parameters set by Table 2. The worst, mean, best and standard deviation (SD) of the makespan score determined from 30 separate executions of each method on 16 JSSP instances are shown in Table 3.

Table 3. Statistics for 16 LA cases using CRO-based methods.

Instance	Size	Method	Opt	Best	Worst	Mean	SD	Time (s)
LA01	10 × 5	CRO	666	666	674	669.55	2.7	44.27
		CROLS	666	666	671	668.09	2	20.27
LA02	10 × 5	CRO	655	655	676	665.36	6.62	44.55
		CROLS	655	655	671	663.18	6.02	18.55
LA06	15 × 5	CRO	926	926	946	935	7.82	76.36
		CROLS	926	926	940	931.18	5.04	46.55
LA07	15 × 5	CRO	890	890	922	908.18	7.38	78.09
		CROLS	890	890	916	906.91	5.29	45.91
LA11	20 × 5	CRO	1222	1222	1257	1233.45	12.58	128.82
		CROLS	1222	1222	1244	1230.73	8.52	100.18
LA12	20 × 5	CRO	1039	1039	1060	1048.27	7.96	120.09
		CROLS	1039	1039	1043	1047.45	7.27	103.45
LA16	10 × 10	CRO	945	948	1011	976.55	19.06	177.64
		CROLS	945	945	955	947.73	2.93	125.91
LA17	10 × 10	CRO	784	788	832	808.27	13.51	183.18
		CROLS	784	784	799	788.55	4.88	128.82
LA21	15 × 10	CRO	1046	1106	1250	1172.64	51.47	256.64
		CROLS	1046	1046	1066	1052.55	7.76	164.36
LA22	15 × 10	CRO	927	935	1150	1030.09	53.54	248.27
		CROLS	927	927	944	932.73	5.69	185.18
LA26	20 × 10	CRO	1218	1226	1275	1255.82	44.37	359.91
		CROLS	1218	1218	1246	1229.91	10.75	281.73
LA27	20 × 10	CRO	1235	1255	1375	1359.55	25.96	336.18
		CROLS	1235	1235	1246	1239.09	4.2	260.18
LA32	30 × 10	CRO	1850	1912	2105	1998.52	30.26	566.64
		CROLS	1850	1850	1856	1853	2.05	453.45

(continued)

Table 3. (*continued*)

Instance	Size	Method	Opt	Best	Worst	Mean	SD	Time (s)
LA33	30 × 10	CRO	1719	1805	2034	1934.91	60.59	557.82
		CROLS	1719	1719	1732	1723.45	4.97	441.73
LA39	15 × 15	CRO	1233	1332	1403	1397.21	24.37	752.09
		CROLS	1233	1233	1255	1243.09	34.44	592.64
LA40	15 × 15	CRO	1222	1342	1424	1374.33	24.88	739.82
		CROLS	1222	1228	1264	1238.25	15.89	585.45

Table 3 shows that the local search strategy has made the CRO algorithm more stable, as the amplitude of the mean between the best to the worst and the standard deviation in all cases have improved. CROLS also significantly reduces the search duration compared to the original method. Technically, CROLS has 20% more fitness function calls than the original algorithm since they employ local search techniques. Even though this increases the amount of computational work, it helps the algorithm converge quickly and experimentally shows that CROLS is still more rapid at search-than the original CRO.

To evaluate the improvement of the CROLS to CRO statistically, we performed Friedman's test on the data in Table 3. The "mean rank" and Friedman's test statistic results of three algorithms participating in the evaluation will be described in Tables 4 and 5, respectively.

Table 4. Mean rank of two CRO-based algorithms.

Algorithm	Mean Rank
CRO	2.94
CROLS	1.47

Table 5. Friedman's test statistic of two CRO-based algorithm.

	X^2	ρ
CRO-CROLS	21.556	0.000021

According to Table 4, there is little difference in the mean rank of the CRO algorithm between reef sizes. The mean rank of CROLS is significantly different from CRO, indicating that local search techniques substantially impact these two algo-rithms. Table 5 provides the test statistics for Friedman's test with a significance level $\alpha = 0.05$. All χ^2 values are larger than the critical value $\chi_0^2 = 5.991$, and all ρ values are less than 0.05, demonstrating statistically significant differences in the per-formance of two CRO-based algorithms.

Following Friedman's test made a significant result, we performed Wilcoxon's signed-rank test as a posthoc analysis to determine the difference between three CRO-based algorithms in pairwise group. The search findings of three reef sizes will be aver-aged to feed the Wilcoxon's test with a statistical significance of 0.05. Table 6 provides the statistical results of the Wilcoxon's test.

Table 6. Wilcoxon's test statistic of two CRO-based algorithms.

	CRO-CROLS
Z	−3.516
p	0.000438

Using the Z distribution table, we can find the critical value of Z is 1.96 at a statis-tical significance of 0.05. According to Table 6, the statistical findings of the pair CRO-CROLS is $Z = -3.516$ ($|Z| > 1.96$) and $p = 0.000438 < 0.05$. So, the null hy-pothesis is rejected at statistical significance of 0.05; the advantage of local search approaches on CROLS compared to the original CRO algorithm is statistically significant.

4.3 Improvement of Search Efficiency

To measure the performance increase of the two hybrid algorithms, we use the mean deviation from the optimum makespan of CROLS that outperforms the original technique CRO in terms of search performance. The following formula is used to determine the evolution of search effectiveness:

$$PI_{(CROLS/CRO)} = \frac{S_{(CRO)} - S_{(CROLS)}}{S_{(Opt)}} \times 100\% \tag{7}$$

where $PI_{(CROLS/CRO)}$ is the percentage of improvement, $S_{(CRO)}$ is the minuscule makespan by CRO, $S_{(CROLS)}$ is the minuscule makespan by CROLS, $S_{(Opt)}$ is the minuscule makespan in comparing between CRO and CROLS.

Table 7 depicts the percentage performance improvement of CROLS over CRO.

Analyzing Table 7 demonstrates that the local search techniques have improved the search performance of the original CRO algorithm. Most PI measurements are below 3% in the basic situations (LA01–LA22), indicating that the improvement is not all that evident. However, as the issue complexity rose, CROLS performed far better than the original CRO. Even in LA40, where it is difficult for the CRO to identify the best-known solution, the PI achieves a high of roughly 10%, which happens in reefs of all sizes. This highlights the effect that local search algorithms have on search performance.

226   C.-S. Shieh et al.

Table 7. Improve performance of hybrid algorithm.

Instance	Size	PI
LA01	10 × 5	0
LA02	10 × 5	0.15
LA06	15 × 5	0
LA07	15 × 5	0
LA11	20 × 5	0
LA12	20 × 5	0
LA16	10 × 10	0.32
LA17	10 × 10	0.51
LA21	15 × 10	0.96
LA22	15 × 10	0.86
LA26	20 × 10	0.66
LA27	20 × 10	1.62
LA32	30 × 10	3.35
LA33	30 × 10	5
LA39	15 × 15	8.03
LA40	15 × 15	9.33

4.3.1 Comparing the Computational Outcome of CRO-Based Algorithms to Other State-of-the-Art Algorithms

To further evaluate the efficacy of CRO and suggested hybrid algorithms, we conducted comprehensive tests on the 12 previously described LA instances, Fisher and Thompson [35]: FT06, FT10, FT20; Applegate and Cook [36]: ORB01–ORB09; and five of Adams et al. [37] marked ABZ05 to ABZ09. The results of two CRO-based algorithms were compared to those of five state-of-the-art algorithms discovered in the literature: hybrid PSO enhanced with nonlinear inertia weight, and Gaussian mutation (NGPSO) [38], multi-Crossover Local Search Genetic Algorithm (mXLSGA) [39], single seekers society (SSS) algorithm [40], genetic algorithm with a critical-path-guided Giffler and Thompson crossover operator (GA-CPG-GT). As a performance criteria, the best makespan produced by the CRO-based algorithms with reef size 30 × 30 from 30 separate runs was employed. Table 8 displays the experimental findings for the 34 cases, including the instance name, problem size (number of jobs × number of machines), best-known solution (BKS), and best solution obtained by each comparison method.

We recognize that the original CRO algorithm can only find the best value in a few simple scenarios, such as LA01; LA02; LA06; LA07; LA11; LA12 and FT06, but the rest of the CRO results are acceptable and are comparable to GA-CPG-GT. While the CROLS showed efficiency, it also produced outcomes that were superior or on par with those of five cutting-edge algorithms in 11/12 LA instances, 2/3 FT instances, 3/5 ABZ

Table 8. Experimental findings for 34 instances are compared with CRO-based algorithms and other state-of-the-art algorithms. "Not evaluated in that instance" is denoted by the symbol "-."

Instance	Size	BKS	CRO	CROLS	mXLSGA (2020)	NGPSO (2020)	SSS (2020)	GA-CPG-GT (2019)	DWPA (2019)
LA01	10 × 5	666	**666**	**666**	**666**	**666**	**666**	**666**	**666**
LA02	10 × 5	655	**655**	**655**	**655**	**655**	**655**	**655**	**655**
LA06	15 × 5	926	**926**	**926**	**926**	**926**	**926**	**926**	**926**
LA07	15 × 5	890	**890**	**890**	**890**	**890**	**890**	**890**	**890**
LA11	20 × 5	1222	**1222**	**1222**	**1222**	**1222**	**1222**	**1222**	**1222**
LA12	20 × 5	1039	**1039**	**1039**	**1039**	**1039**	-	**1039**	**1039**
LA16	10 × 10	945	955	**945**	**945**	**945**	947	946	993
LA17	10 × 10	784	788	**784**	**784**	794	-	**784**	793
LA21	15 × 10	1046	1056	**1046**	1059	1183	1076	1090	1105
LA22	15 × 10	927	935	**927**	935	**927**	-	954	989
LA26	20 × 10	1218	1226	**1218**	**1218**	**1218**	-	1237	1303
LA27	20 × 10	1235	1255	**1235**	1269	1394	-	1313	1346
LA32	30 × 10	1850	1912	**1850**	**1850**	**1850**	-	**1850**	**1850**
LA33	30 × 10	1719	1805	**1719**	**1719**	**1719**	-	**1719**	**1719**
LA39	15 × 15	1233	1332	**1233**	1258	1662	-	1290	1334
LA40	15 × 15	1222	1342	1228	1243	**1222**	1252	1252	1347
FT06	6 × 6	55	**55**	**55**	**55**	**55**	**55**	**55**	-

(continued)

Table 8. (*continued*)

Instance	Size	BKS	CRO	CROLS	mXLSGA (2020)	NGPSO (2020)	SSS (2020)	GA-CPG-GT (2019)	DWPA (2019)
FT10	10 × 10	930	934	**930**	**930**	**930**	936	935	-
FT20	20 × 5	1165	1197	1174	**1165**	1210	**1165**	1180	-
ABZ05	10 × 10	1234	1255	**1234**	**1234**	**1234**	-	1238	-
ABZ06	10 × 10	943	988	**943**	**943**	**943**	-	947	-
ABZ07	20 × 15	656	755	731	**695**	713	-	-	-
ABZ08	20 × 15	665	720	709	713	729	-	-	-
ABZ09	20 × 15	679	817	**707**	721	930	-	-	-
ORB01	10 × 10	1059	1120	1070	**1068**	1174	-	1084	-
ORB02	10 × 10	888	927	899	**889**	913	-	890	-
ORB03	10 × 10	1005	1097	**1021**	1023	1104	-	1037	-
ORB04	10 × 10	1005	1121	**1005**	**1005**	**1005**	-	1028	-
ORB05	10 × 10	887	904	890	889	**887**	-	894	-
ORB06	10 × 10	1010	1085	1020	**1019**	1124	-	1035	-
ORB07	10 × 10	397	418	**397**	**397**	**397**	-	404	-
ORB08	10 × 10	899	988	912	**907**	1020	-	937	-
ORB09	10 × 10	934	955	**938**	940	980	-	943	-
ORB10	10 × 10	944	1010	967	**944**	1027	-	967	-

cases, and 5/10 ORB occurrences. The results of CROLS surpass SSS, GA-CPG-GT, DWPA algorithms, as well as competitive comparisons with mXLSGA and NGPSO. In certain cases, such as ORB01; ORB03; ORB08; and ORB10; CROLS even outperforms NGPSO.

5 Conclusions

This study introduces the innovative hybrid algorithm CROLS, which makes use of many search techniques. In order to locate the global optimal solution and avoid the local optimal, the CROLS method uses simulated annealing (SA). This method reduces execution time while increasing the chance of getting the best result. This search strategy uses the potential of the entire reef and increases its convergence in an effort to produce new, superior individuals. The article provides insights into how the local search approach to the CRO algorithm might be improved, as shown by encouraging testing results. When the hybrid algorithm's best search results are compared to the best-known outcomes, its effectiveness is further demonstrated. For more complex problems, a variety of multi-objective optimization methods like JSSP have been proposed. In the future plan, we ought to create the fastest processing algorithm possible for multi-objectives problems. An attractive future research direction to improve the applicability of JSSP in manufacturing is the development of algorithms to handle multi-objective optimization problems.

Acknowledgment. This research was partly supported by National Science and Technology Council, Taiwan with grant numbers 111-2221-E-992-066 and 109-2221-E-992-073-MY3.

References

1. Marco Baptista: How important is production scheduling today? Opcenter (2020)
2. Ben Hmida, J., Lee, J., Wang, X., Boukadi, F.: Production scheduling for continuous manufacturing systems with quality constraints. Prod. Manuf. Res. **2**, 95–111 (2014)
3. Jiang, Z., Yuan, S., Ma, J., Wang, Q.: The evolution of production scheduling from Industry 3.0 through Industry 4.0. Int. J. Prod. Re. **60**, 3534–3554 (2022)
4. Graves, S.C.: A review of production scheduling. Oper. Res. **29**(4), 646–675 (1981)
5. Johnson, S.M.: Optimal two- and three-stage production schedules with setup times included. Naval Res. Logistics Quart. **1**, 61–68 (1954)
6. Garey, M.R., Johnson, D.S., Sethi, R.: The complexity of flowshop and jobshop scheduling. Math. Oper. Res. **1**, 117–129 (1976)
7. Zhang, J., Ding, G., Zou, Y., Qin, S., Fu, J.: Review of job shop scheduling research and its new perspectives under Industry 4.0. J. Intell. Manuf. **30**(4), 1809–1830 (2017). https://doi.org/10.1007/s10845-017-1350-2
8. Xiong, H., Shi, S., Ren, D., Hu, J.: A survey of job shop scheduling problem: the types and models. Comput. Oper. Res. **142**, 105731 (2022)
9. Xhafa, F., Abraham, A.: Metaheuristics for Scheduling in Industrial and Manufacturing Applications (2022)
10. Pinedo, M.L.: Planning and Scheduling in Manufacturing and Services (2022)
11. Türkyılmaz, A., Şenvar, Ö., Ünal, İ, Bulkan, S.: A research survey: heuristic approaches for solving multi objective flexible job shop problems. J. Intell. Manuf. **31**(8), 1949–1983 (2020). https://doi.org/10.1007/s10845-020-01547-4

12. Guzman, E., Andres, B., Poler, R.: Matheuristic algorithm for job-shop scheduling problem using a disjunctive mathematical model. Computers **11**, 1 (2022)
13. Viana, M.S., Contreras, R.C., Morandin Junior, O.: A New frequency analysis operator for population improvement in genetic algorithms to solve the job shop scheduling problem. Sensors **22**, 4561 (2022)
14. Salcedo-Sanz, S., Del Ser, J., Landa-Torres, I., Gil-López, S., Portilla-Figueras, J.A.: The coral reefs optimization algorithm: a novel metaheuristic for efficiently solving optimization problems. Sci. World J. **2014**, e739768 (2014)
15. Salcedo-Sanz, S., García-Díaz, P., Portilla-Figueras, J.A., Del Ser, J., Gil-López, S.: A coral reefs optimization algorithm for optimal mobile network deployment with electromagnetic pollution control criterion. Appl. Soft Comput. **24**, 239–248 (2014)
16. Salcedo-Sanz, S., Camacho-Gómez, C., Mallol-Poyato, R., Jiménez-Fernández, S., Del Ser, J.: A novel coral reefs optimization algorithm with substrate layers for optimal battery scheduling optimization in micro-grids. Soft. Comput. **20**(11), 4287–4300 (2016). https://doi.org/10.1007/s00500-016-2295-7
17. Salcedo-Sanz, S., et al.: Offshore wind farm design with the coral reefs optimization algorithm. Renew. Energy **63**, 109–115 (2014)
18. Bedoya-Valencia, L.: Exact and Heuristic Algorithms for the Job Shop Scheduling Problem with Earliness and Tardiness over a Common Due Date. Old Dominion University (2007)
19. Brucker, P., Jurisch, B., Sievers, B.: A branch and bound algorithm for the job-shop scheduling problem. Discret. Appl. Math. **49**, 107–127 (1994)
20. Çaliş, B., Bulkan, S.: A research survey: review of AI solution strategies of job shop scheduling problem. J. Intell. Manuf. **26**(5), 961–973 (2013). https://doi.org/10.1007/s10845-013-0837-8
21. Muthuraman, S., Venkatesan, V.P.A.: Comprehensive study on hybrid meta-heuristic approaches used for solving combinatorial optimization problems. In: 2017 World Congress on Computing and Communication Technologies (WCCCT), pp. 185–190 (2017). https://doi.org/10.1109/WCCCT.2016.53
22. Aarts, E., Lenstra, J.K. (eds.): Local Search in Combinatorial Optimization. Princeton University Press (2003)
23. Gendreau, M., Potvin, J.-Y.: Metaheuristics in combinatorial optimization. Ann Oper Res **140**, 189–213 (2005)
24. Yang, X.-S. (ed.): Nature-Inspired Optimization Algorithms. Elsevier (2014)
25. Davis, L.: Job shop scheduling with genetic algorithms. In: Proceedings of the 1st International Conference on Genetic Algorithms, pp. 136–140. L. Erlbaum Associates Inc. (1985)
26. Holland, J.H.: Adaptation in Natural and Artificial Systems: An Introductory Analysis with Applications to Biology, Control, and Artificial Intelligence. MIT Press eBooks, IEEE Xplore (2022)
27. Kennedy, J., Eberhart, R.: Particle swarm optimization. In: Proceedings of ICNN'95 – International Conference on Neural Networks, vol. 4, pp. 1942–1948 (1995)
28. Kirkpatrick, S., Gelatt, C.D., Vecchi, M.P.: Optimization by simulated annealing. Science **220**, 671–680 (1983)
29. Garcia-Hernandez, L., Salas-Morera, L., Carmona-Muñoz, C., Abraham, A., Salcedo-Sanz, S.: A hybrid coral reefs optimization—variable neighborhood search approach for the unequal area facility layout problem. IEEE Access **8**, 134042–134050 (2020)
30. Tsai, C.-W., Chang, H.-C., Hu, K.-C., Chiang, M.-C.: Parallel coral reef algorithm for solving JSP on Spark. In: 2016 IEEE International Conference on Systems, Man, and Cybernetics (SMC) (2016)
31. Cheng, R., Gen, M., Tsujimura, Y.: A tutorial survey of job-shop scheduling problems using genetic algorithms—I. representation. Comput. Indus. Eng. **30**(4), 983–997 (1996)

32. Cheng, R., Gen, M., Tsujimura, Y.: A tutorial survey of job-shop scheduling problems using genetic algorithms, part II: hybrid genetic search strategies. Comput. Ind. Eng. **36**, 343–364 (1999)
33. Lee, Y.S., Graham, E., Jackson, G., Galindo, A., Adjiman, C.S.: A comparison of the performance of multi-objective optimization methodologies for solvent design. In: Kiss, A.A., Zondervan, E., Lakerveld, R., Özkan, L. (eds.) Computer Aided Chemical Engineering, vol. 46, pp. 37–42. Elsevier (2019)
34. Lawrence, S.: Resource constrained project scheduling: an experimental investigation of heuristic scheduling techniques (Supplement). Graduate School of Industrial Administration. Pittsburgh, Pennsylvania, Carnegie-Mellon University (1984)
35. Fisher, C., Thompson, G.: Probabilistic Learning Combinations of Local Job-shop Scheduling Rules, pp. 225–251. Industrial Scheduling (1963)
36. Applegate, D., Cook, W.: A computational study of the job-shop scheduling problem. ORSA J. Comput. **3**, 149–156 (1991)
37. Adams, J., Balas, E., Zawack, D.: The shifting bottleneck procedure for job shop scheduling. Manage. Sci. **34**, 391–401 (1988)
38. Yu, H., Gao, Y., Wang, L., Meng, J.: A hybrid particle swarm optimization algorithm enhanced with nonlinear inertial weight and gaussian mutation for job shop scheduling problems. Mathematics **8**, 1355 (2020)
39. Viana, M.S., Junior, O.M., Contreras, R.C.: An improved local search genetic algorithm with multi-crossover for job shop scheduling problem. In: Rutkowski, L., Scherer, R., Korytkowski, M., Pedrycz, W., Tadeusiewicz, R., Zurada, J.M. (eds.) ICAISC 2020. LNCS (LNAI), vol. 12415, pp. 464–479. Springer, Cham (2020). https://doi.org/10.1007/978-3-030-61401-0_43
40. Hamzadayı, A., Baykasoğlu, A., Akpınar, Ş: Solving combinatorial optimization problems with single seekers society algorithm. Knowl.-Based Syst. **201–202**, 106036 (2020)

Efficient Human Activity Recognition Based on Grouped Representations of Multimodal Wearable Data

Guillaume Habault[(✉)] and Shinya Wada

KDDI Research Inc., Fujimino, Japan
{xgu-habault,sh-wada}@kddi.com

Abstract. Human Activity Recognition (HAR) is a vast and complex research domain that has multiple applications, such as healthcare, surveillance or human-computer interaction. Several sensing technologies exist to record data later used to recognize people's activity. This paper aims to linger over the specific case of HAR based on multimodal wearable sensing devices. Corresponding HAR datasets provide multiple sensors information collected from different body parts. Previous approaches consider each information separately or altogether. Vision HAR methods consider each body segment and their position in space in order to perform activity recognition. This paper proposes a similar approach for Multimodal Wearable HAR (MW-HAR). Datasets are first re-sampled at a higher sampling rate (i.e., lower frequency) in order to both decrease the overall processing time and facilitate interpretability. Then, we propose to group sensing features from all the sensors corresponding to the same body part. For each group, the proposal determines a different representation realm of the group information. This abstracted representation depicts the different states of the corresponding body part. Finally, activity recognition is performed based on these trained abstractions of each considered body part. We tested our proposal on three benchmark datasets. Our evaluations first confirmed that a re-sampled dataset offers similar or even better performance for activity recognition than usual processing. But the primary advantage is to decrease significantly the training time. Finally, results show that a grouped abstraction of the sensors features is improving the activity recognition in most cases, without increasing training time.

Keywords: Human Activity Recognition · Data Abstraction · Data Processing

1 Introduction

Human Activity Recognition (HAR) is a complex research topic [29], as it has several sensing technologies and multiple applications.

Depending on the sensing technology used, data collected for HAR can be divided in three groups: (i) Ambient-based: where sensing devices placed at

© ICST Institute for Computer Sciences, Social Informatics and Telecommunications Engineering 2023
Published by Springer Nature Switzerland AG 2023. All Rights Reserved
R. Hou et al. (Eds.): BDTA 2022, LNICST 480, pp. 232–254, 2023.
https://doi.org/10.1007/978-3-031-33614-0_16

fixed location monitor the environment variables (such as smart-homes with actuators for lights or other appliances, temperature sensors, etc.); (ii) Vision-based: where sensing devices are camera or radar either continuously monitoring an environment (such as surveillance) or set-up for specific events (such as live games); and (iii) Wearable-based: where sensing devices, embedded in our clothes or equipment we carry, purposely monitor our conditions (such as vitals, body part movements, temperature, etc.).

Some research [24] might even combine different sensing technologies together in order to cross information and gain in knowledge.

Nevertheless, HAR research proves to be useful in various domains, such as:

1. Healthcare: preventing domestic accidents or detecting anomaly with elderly people [28] as well as assisting people with disabilities or in rehabilitation after an accident [5,14];
2. Live monitoring: preventing crimes or threats [25] or it could also be used to assist live sport events;
3. Human Computer Interaction: interacting with people through games (for fitness game or for rehabilitation of people with disabilities) [10,18]. We can even imagine future applications in virtual worlds, such as in the meta-verse.

Among all these sensing technologies, wearable-based is the most challenging [29]. In fact, placement of body-worn sensors plays an important role in the efficiency of activity recognition. For instance, a smartphone may monitor different body parts at different times, as it can be alternatively positioned in our pocket, hand, against our head (e.g., during a call) or on another object (e.g., while charging). This position uncertainty makes patterns recognition more difficult without external information or ways to determine the position [19].

In Multimodal Wearable HAR (MW-HAR) scenarios [2,23], volunteers are equipped with several sensors placed on different areas of the body. These fixed positions are usually located close to the body joints (i.e., wrist, ankle, hip, etc.) as illustrated on the bottom left part of Fig. 1. This scheme allieviates the position uncertainty, but such scenarios are for now unrealistic. Indeed, these days people are carrying/wearing at most two devices (i.e., a smartphone and perhaps an activity tracker). However, with the progress of Internet-of-Things (IoT) (e.g., smart-clothing) and our life being progressively more digital, more of these monitoring devices might be available in the future. In the past years, we have already witnessed the adoption by a large part of the population of activity trackers (such as smart-watch). Therefore, it is fair to assume that in a few years from now, we might carry more of these *wearable sensors*.

According to [7], features extraction and data interpretability are some of the remaining challenges in Wearable HAR. Indeed, sensors' data are noisy [8], (i) presenting lots of fluctuations because of sensors' high precision (capturing micro movements); or (ii) having outliers because of sensors imperfections or calibrations. These variations make it difficult for us to accurately interpret the data, especially when recording long sequences. In addition, machines might interpret these fluctuations as sub-activities and, at the end, reduce their efficiency. Therefore, there is a need for a higher level of abstraction of the sensing features in order to simplify both (a) the training and learning process for the machine; and (b) the understanding and interpretation for human.

Several researches have been conducted in order to improve recognition efficiency. Most of the proposed solutions are either based on novel Deep Learning (DL) architectures [29] or data augmentation [30] (some solution even use both [17]). Nevertheless, data handling and pre-processing are often neglected in favor of more complex and more efficient architectures.

This paper aims to determine whether a different approach could improve both recognition efficiency and interpretability. For this purpose, we propose to focus on data handling of MW-HAR scenarios. We posit that proper representation of the data associated with current state-of-the-art (SOTA) architectures could further enhance activity recognition. Our approach is twofold:

1. Decrease the amount of samples used during training; and,
2. Accordingly group modalities and generate an abstracted representation.

The contributions of this paper are the following:

1. Compare the relevance in terms of recognition accuracy and training time of different pre-processing methods;
2. Initiate a unified labelling of human activities;
3. Evaluate four grouping strategies and two abstraction techniques to produce a higher level representation of a given group of body-worn features;
4. Visually analyze the impact of the proposal on the data.

The rest of this paper is organized as follows. The subsequent section presents how multimodal wearable data is handled in the literature. In Sect. 3, we describe our approach that aims at (i) re-sampling the dataset to a lower frequency; and (ii) grouping sensing features and defining another representation of such grouped data. Then, we explain our methodology and how our proposal is evaluated, as well as the metrics used. Section 4 describes in details the selected datasets and a start on proposing a unified labelling of human activities. Results of our evaluations are described in Sect. 6. In this section, we also analyze the impact and visual interpretability of our proposal. Before concluding this paper, we further discusses these results in Sect. 7 and we provide new fields of endeavor.

2 Background

To the best of our knowledge, in HAR scenarios, the recognition operations can be summarized as follows:

1. Handle missing data
2. Normalize data
3. Extract additional information (interval-based, frequency-based or using other transformations, such as shapelet)
4. Select important features (either manually or in an automated way)

5. Defining inputs (based on points or sampling, for instance with a sliding window method)
6. Train the model

Wearable HAR (W-HAR) research follows all or some of these steps in order to recognize human activity [26]. Based on the literature, missing measurements are usually ignored or interpolated [6]. Similarly to other Machine Learning (ML) researches, raw sensors' data might lead to issues such as vanishing gradient [31]. Normalization enables to limit these problems. The most commonly employed methods in W-HAR are *min-max* and *standardization*. As mentioned previously, sensors' data present lots of fluctuations. These irregular variations – occurring even within the same activity – make it more difficult for models to differentiate activities only based on raw data. Extracting information or transforming data can therefore provide additional information on a feature or a set of features. Chen et al. [7] surveyed the different methods to produce such additional information. This step commonly uses all raw features, but it can also be sensor-based or feature-based with either a dedicated or shared generation process. Statistical methods (such as determining minimum, maximum, mean and variance over a sliding window) are the basis for such a generation of additional features. However, adding multiple statistics increases the computational cost and often requires domain knowledge. To cope with this issue, Qian et al. [22] proposed a method for generating only relevant statistics. Another way to reduce the impact of these additional features is to select the most relevant ones. Several strategies defined in time-series studies (such as regularization, correlation or even more complex one [13]) exist to perform this step.

The final set of features is either used altogether or each of them separately to perform the recognition task. We believe that such an approach is the main reason for the lack of interpretability. In fact, even though the number of features is decreased, considering all of them together requires very complex architecture [20]. But with such architectures, we let *black-box* models discover any correlations – more generally, any relations – between activities and data from all these features. But the more complex the architecture is, the less it provides tools to interpret its decisions [1]. For instance, a multimodal-based architecture, which investigates both auto- and cross-modal relationships, such as [32], will see its complexity exponentially increase with the number of modalities. As a consequence, the usage of very complex architectures hinders understanding or visualizing the interpretations of these models.

All these reasons motivate us to seek for a different approach to the pre-processing phase when dealing with multiple body-worn sensing devices.

3 Proposed Approach

Based on the previously mentioned observations, we adopted a different point-of-view on human activity data when targeting recognition. Our approach takes place at the pre-processing level and can be divided into two parts.

3.1 Re-sampling Dataset

We consider to re-sample the measurements in order to decrease the number of inputs in the dataset. This preliminary step basically changes the resolution of the measurements to a coarser level (i.e., sampling frequency). The main effect of this step is to reduce the impact of micro fluctuations and any outliers by acting as a low-pass filter. In addition, it will take care of dealing with most missing data within the dataset. As a result, we hypothesize that with fewer samples to manage, the model will find relations between features and activities more easily. Consequently, it decreases the associated cost when manipulating them (processing and training). Moreover, when plotting the data, there will be fewer points to visualize, therefore simplifying both analysis and interpretation.

However, these benefits mitigate the coarser the selected re-sampling gets. Therefore, this rate needs to be selected depending on the targeted applications in order to maintain most of the measured information.

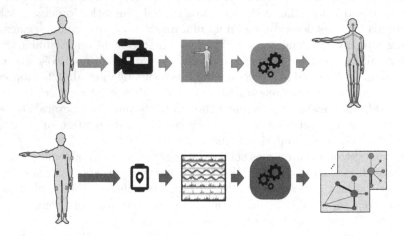

Fig. 1. Illustration for our proposal (bottom pipeline) compared to the camera-based process (top pipeline). Camera-based produces body graph from pictures. In the same way, we propose to produce abstractions of groups of sensing features (depicted here as state transition graph).

3.2 Specific Features Grouping and Data Abstraction

In other HAR studies, information directly related to some activities can be extracted. In smart-home scenarios, some ambient sensors monitor objects explicitly linked to an activity or a set of activities. For instance, when the entrance door is opened, the model can limit the potential activities to *leaving* or *entering* home [11]. Information from other sensors will then settle the decision. For vision-based studies, recognition of surrounding objects can also give hints and restrict the potential activities [15]. Such information about the environment and surrounding objects is highly beneficial for activity recognition. However, for W-HAR, these types of information are usually not available (unless combined with others [6]). Moreover, as aforementioned, wearables' position uncertainty hinders the learning process of relations between activities and sensors' data.

On the other hand, camera-based HAR has an interesting way of treating images in order to recognize activities performed. From an image, a coarse body representation is produced [3]. In this graph-like representation –referred as body-graph in the rest of the paper–, each segment represents a body part, while nodes depict the body joints. Finally, a sequence of body graphs (i.e., sequence of stances/postures) can relate to an activity. In camera-based HAR, body graph information is used for activity recognition task, but not raw image information. On the contrary, in MW-HAR studies, raw measurements of the body parts are used to perform the activity recognition task.

Therefore, the key idea of our proposal is to process raw sensors' data in order to produce a mid-level abstraction. As illustrated in the bottom part of Fig. 1, the pipeline of our idea is similar to the one used in camera-based HAR, (top part of Fig. 1). This idea is based on the observation that, at a fixed timestep, models should be efficient in recognizing the state of different body parts, but not really the activity, or at least not directly. The activity will be efficiently recognized when considering a sequence of body parts' states. For example, with a person performing a single arm lateral raise, there are two main states (i.e., *arm along the body* and *arm raised*) and multiple transition states. Therefore, instead of using raw data (acceleration, rotation, etc.), if data can represent that the wrist is moving in-between two states, while other body parts remain in the same state (standing still), it should be easier for the model to recognize the lateral raise.

To summarize, this part consists of the following steps:

1. Group sensors that monitor the same body part
2. (optional) Extract additional information on the set of features
3. Produce abstracted representations of monitored body parts

Finally, obtained abstractions become modalities of the model tackling with activity recognition.

Table 1. Mapping of activity standardized names and original ones for the targeted datasets.

Category	ID	Activity	mHealth	PAMAP2 Protocol	LDPR
1	10	Passive Standing	Standing still		
	11	Active Standing		Standing	
	12	Passive Sitting	Sitting and relaxing		Sitting
	13	Active Sitting		Sitting	
	14	Passive Lying	Lying down		Lying
	15	Active Lying		Lying	
	16	Passive Walking	Walking	Walking	Walking
	17	Active Walking			
	18	Falling			Falling
	19	On All Fours			On all fours
2	20	Standing Up			Standing up from sitting
					Standing up from sitting on the ground
					Standing up from lying
	21	Sitting Down			Sitting down
					Sitting on the ground
	22	Lying Down			Lying Down
3	30	Ironing		Ironing	
	31	Vacuuming		Vacuum cleaning	
4	40	Ascending Stairs	Climbing stairs	Ascending stairs	
	41	Descending Stairs		Descending stairs	
5	50	Nature Walk		Nordic walking	
	51	Jogging	Jogging	Running	
	52	Running	Running		
	53	Cycling	Cycling	Cycling	
6	60	Jumping	Jump front and back	Rope jumping	
	61	Waist Bend	Waist bends forward		
	62	Elevation Arm	Frontal elevation of arms		
	63	Knee Bend	Knees bending (crouching)		

4   Datasets

In order to test our proposal properly, we focus on MW-HAR datasets that (a) provide data from sensors monitoring different body parts, (b) if possible, include a diversity of sensors, and (c) target Activities of Daily Living (ADL) or at least full body activities (e.g., standing, sitting, etc.). Finally, we selected three datasets to test our proposal efficiency when performing ADL recognition.

4.1   Target Activities

Each dataset used different terminology for activities that often are similar. In order to simplify comparison in between these datasets, we propose a mapping between a unified terminology and the original ones in Table 1. In this table, empty cells suggest that the considered dataset does not target corresponding activities. Note that such a unified labelling could be extended for future usage.

Similarly to [20], in the first category, "Passive" refers to people being in a given stance doing nothing in particular (e.g., walking, standing or sitting still). While "Active" refers to people performing a specific activity while maintaining a stance (e.g., sitting and typing or standing and talking to someone). Therefore, "Passive" activity recognition targets recognition of a stance, while "Active" targets recognition of an activity performed in a given stance. Even though not present in these datasets, some activities can be carried out in different stances. The second category lists stance transition (targets spontaneous dataset, as for scripted one, transitions between activities are ignored). The third one presents household chores. The fourth category is related to stairs movements. The fifth one describes activities that may target transportation and/or exercise. The last category comprises exercise and fitness activities.

4.2   Datasets Presentation

Mobile Health (mHealth) [2] and Physical Activity Monitoring (PAMAP2) [23] are scripted datasets, meaning that volunteers perform each activity for a given duration (e.g., 1 min) or a given number of repetition (e.g., 20 times). Both datasets monitor the volunteer's heart from the chest, mHealth with a 2-lead electrocardiogram (ECG) and PAMAP2 with a heart-rate monitor. For both datasets, volunteers are wearing Inertial Measurement Units (IMUs) on the chest, one wrist and one ankle. IMUs comprise at least a 3D-Accelerometer, a 3D-Gyroscope and 3D-Magnetometer (except for the chest one in mHealth). Each IMU of PAMAP2 is also equipped with a temperature sensor and an additional 3D-Accelerometer. In contrast, Localization Data for Posture Reconstruction (LDPR) [16] is a spontaneous dataset. Volunteers perform activities in a given environment without specific order or duration for the activities. In this dataset, volunteers are wearing position tag on the chest, the belt and both ankles. Table 2 summarizes the main parameters of these datasets.

Table 2. Summary of the different datasets parameters: number of volunteers, sensors positions and types, as well as measurement rate.

Dataset	Num. subject	Sensors position	Sensors type	Record rate
mHealth	10	Chest	2-lead ECG	50 Hz (0.02 s)
			3D-Accelerometers	
		Right Wrist	3D-Acc.,3D-Gyroscope and	
		Left Ankle	3D-Magnetometer	
PAMAP2	9	Chest	Heart-rate Monitor	9 Hz
			Temperature, 2 3D-Accelerometers,	100 Hz (0.01 s)
		Dominant Wrist	3D-Gyroscope,	
		Dominant Ankle	3D-Magnetometer	
LDPR	5	Chest	Position	250 Hz (0.004 s)
		Belt		
		Left ankle		
		Right ankle		

Spontaneous datasets are more difficult to handle because of imbalance record among activities. In fact, scripted datasets ensure to have very similar amount of records, assuming that volunteer followed the script. Conversely, a spontaneous dataset is subject to the volunteer behavior. As a result, some activities might be under-represented (i.e., not enough or no repetitions at all). Without proper handling, it can lead to overfit the trained model to the most represented activities. Although some solutions exist to solve potential imbalance in the activity distribution, we do not consider them in this investigation. In fact, except for transition activities (category 2 in Table 1), LDPR has enough records per activity. In addition, for this study, we do not consider sub-activities, as all the corresponding records are labelled with their main activity. For instance, we labelled *Standing up from sitting* and *Standing up from lying* as *Standing up*. This labelling trick resolves the imbalance in this category. Moreover, it enables us to focus on our proposal and its impact on input recognition.

mHealth. consists of records from 10 volunteers. In this dataset, all actions performed between two scripted activities (labelled *Null*) are ignored in our study. This dataset is composed of one file per volunteer. Therefore, in order to create training, validation and evaluation sets, we randomly sampled unique data from each considered activity based on a 0.6/0.15/0.25 ratio.

PAMAP2. comprises records from 9 volunteers for the main protocol, among which 5 of them performed optional activities. In this study, we focus only on the main protocol. As shown in Table 5, the number of inputs of the ninth volunteer is extremely low compared to the others. In fact, this volunteer only performed *Jumping* in the main protocol. Thus, we removed this volunteer from our experiments, as it is pointless to perform activity recognition in this situation. In this dataset, break time actions –performed between two scripted activities– are also labelled as *Null*. Similarly to mHealth, and as suggested by the dataset's creator, we ignored them in our study. In addition, we use the same training/validation/evaluation split ratio.

LDPR. consists of records from 5 volunteers. Each volunteer performed 5 runs. For this dataset, we used runs 1 and 2 to train models. Run 3 is used for validation, while runs 4 and 5 are used for evaluating the trained models.

5   Evaluation Method

In this paper, we aim to investigate the efficiency of our proposal in recognizing ADL. In order to achieve this goal, we target to decrease the quantity of samples and group features by body parts. Associating the latter with an abstraction technique will produce a new representation of the data. We infer that the obtained abstraction of the data will represent the different states a body part can fall into (along with transitions between these states).

Table 3. Summary of the distinct steps performed within each pre-processing method.

	Basic (P1)	Common (P2)	Re-sampled (P3)
Re-sampling	X	X	✓
Handling missing data	Ignored	Linearly interpolated	
Normalization	Z-Score		

5.1   Evaluation of Preliminary Re-sampling

This evaluation consists of determining the number of inputs generated with different pre-processing as well as assessing the accuracy of the resulting dataset for inputs-based recognition task. These results are then compared in order to establish their advantages and disadvantages. As detailed in Table 3, we investigate three types of data pre-processing. The first one limits the processing to a minimum, i.e., ignoring missing data and normalizing the rest. This method is referred as the basic pre-processing (P1). Conversely, the pre- processing (P2) linearly interpolates missing data and normalizes the dataset. This pre-processing is frequently found in W-HAR publications and is considered as the baseline of this evaluation. Finally, the re-sampled pre-processing (P3) method begins with re-sampling the data to a coarser resolution. Then, similarly to P2, we interpolate the remaining missing data and normalize the dataset.

Re-sampling. A record rate close to the millisecond or tenth of milliseconds (as usually found in MW-HAR datasets) is too detailed for describing coarse body-parts states. Indeed, for ADL, our movements do not significantly change at such low time intervals. Therefore, in this study, we selected a re-sampling at 50 ms (i.e., every 0.05 s). This preliminary step averages the values of each feature over a non-overlapping 50 ms sliding window. As an example, with a dataset that recorded measurements every 0.01 s, 5 measurements are used to create one measurement of the re-sampled dataset. Note that for this pre-processing method, we ignore $50ms$ inputs in between two activities. It ends up only removing a few inputs, which is marginal compared to the tenth of thousands of remaining inputs. Finally, comparing different re-sampling rate in order to determine the optimal one is out-of-scope of this study, as optimal rate might vary depending on the application.

Normalization follows the z-score principle: $x_{norm} = \frac{x-\mu}{\sigma}$, where μ and σ are the training values mean and standard deviation, respectively, for each feature.

Table 4. Summary of the different parameters used for each grouped abstraction.

	G0	G1	G2	G3	G4
Grouping Strategy	None	Feature	Sensor	Body part	All
Data Abstraction	X	✓	✓	✓	✓

5.2   Evaluation of Grouped Abstraction

In this second evaluation, we compare the accuracy obtained with different combination of grouping strategy and data abstraction technique. As detailed in Table 4, we consider five grouping strategies. First, recognition is performed on all features together and without data abstraction (G0). Then, we test one abstracted representation for each feature (G1). This strategy may uncover if a specific and more efficient projection of a single feature can be found. Moreover, we consider one abstracted representation method for each sensor (G2) (e.g., an 3D-accelerometer representation is based on values of its three components). As explained in Sect. 3.2, we proposed to group sensing features corresponding to the same body part and to produce a representation of the different states of such a body part (G3). Finally, we also test one abstracted representation for all features together (G4). We consider G0 and G4 as baselines because previous works have already used these techniques. In addition, G2 and G4 enables us to further evaluate the relevance and assess if one abstracted representation method for each body part (G3) can be more efficient for recognition task.

Data Abstraction. The second part of our proposal relies on representing the data in such a way that it will better describe the state of different body parts.

This transformation could be performed manually by listing the different states of a given body part and perform a mapping between sensors' measurements and corresponding states. However, to the best of our knowledge, no HAR datasets provide such type of information. Furthermore, processing such information from current datasets requires a significant amount of knowledge and effort. As a result, in this paper, we investigated dimension reduction techniques. As the name implies, they enable to reduce the dimension or at least project the data into another space with the same dimension. In this evaluation, we considered two techniques: Principal Component Analysis (PCA) and Linear Discriminant Analysis (LDA). We focus on them here, as they do not require fine tuning and their computational cost is limited compared to other methods.

For group strategies G1 to G4, we trained a dedicated abstraction for each group. For instance, in G1 configuration, a representation is trained for each feature, while for G4, we trained one representation for all the considered features.

5.3   Classification Method and Evaluation Metrics

For this study, only one classification method is used: k Nearest Neighbors (k-NN) ($k = 11$ in our experiments). We omit DL methods because two of the selected datasets are scripted ones (cf. Sect. 4). For them, we assumed that sequenced inputs are unnecessary. However, SOTA activity recognition models are based on Convolutional Neural Network (CNN), Recurrent Neural Network (RNN) and Transformers, which require such sequenced inputs.

We evaluate the classification performance with two metrics: (1) the *score* of the model on the evaluation set (i.e., the mean accuracy as defined in *scikit-learn* library *KNeighborsClassifier*; and (2) the duration for training the model.

Table 5. Number of inputs for all datasets after applying the different pre-processing methods (P). mHealth has originally no missing values, so the number of inputs is the same for the first two pre-processing. LDPR has missing values on several time-steps as sensors records are not synchronized. Therefore, P1 ends up ignoring the majority of inputs. The re-sampling method decreases the number of inputs by 60%, 80% and 37% for mHealth, PAMAP2 and LDPR, respectively.

Dataset	P	Volunteer									
		1	2	3	4	5	6	7	8	9	10
mHealth	1	35174	35532	35380	35328	33947	32205	34253	33332	34354	33690
	2										
	3	14066	14210	14150	14130	13578	12880	13698	13328	13739	13476
PAMAP2	1	22590	23691	15841	20863	24592	22659	21055	23624	583	
	2	249957	263349	174338	231421	272442	250096	232776	262102	6391	
	3	49980	52661	34861	46275	54478	50013	46547	52414	1278	
LDPR	1	0	0	0	1	1					
	2	26285	29024	30695	30912	42665					
	3	16507	18432	19355	19472	26916					

6   Results

6.1   Re-sampling Performance

This evaluation aims to determine if the re-sampled pre-processing (P3) achieved similar performance to the common pre-processing (P2). For this evaluation, for each considered dataset, we first performed recognition per volunteer. Then, we carry out recognition when training a unique model for all volunteers (referred in the rest as the *1-for-all model*). The training set in this scenario is composed of the training data from all the volunteers. Finally, each volunteer's evaluation set is classified by this trained model. Because we intend to test the pre-processing performance, we fixed the grouping strategy to G0.

Table 6. Activity recognition accuracy with different pre-processing methods (P). Values in italic represent the percentage decrease (▼) or increase (▲) when using a 50 ms re-sampled pre-processing (P3) compared to the common one (P2).

Dataset	P	Volunteer										All
		1	2	3	4	5	6	7	8	9	10	
mHealth	1	0.9811	0.9600	0.9891	0.9889	0.9915	0.9948	0.9971	0.9960	0.9934	0.9954	0.9863
	2	0.9811	0.9600	0.9891	0.9889	0.9915	0.9948	0.9971	0.9960	0.9934	0.9954	0.9863
	3	0.9773	0.9468	0.9774	0.9816	0.9838	0.9926	0.9948	0.9928	0.9910	0.9911	0.9798
		▼0.39%	▼1.375%	▼1.18%	▼0.74%	▼0.78%	▼0.22%	▼0.23%	▼0.32%	▼0.24%	▼0.43%	▼0.66%
PAMAP2	1	0.9800	0.9490	0.9614	0.9701	0.9603	0.9645	0.9728	0.9746			0.9581
	2	0.9980	0.9952	0.9972	0.9978	0.9982	0.9968	0.9977	0.9979			0.9962
	3	0.9905	0.9789	0.9838	0.9857	0.9838	0.9830	0.9894	0.9868			0.9800
		▼0.75%	▼1.64%	▼1.34%	▼1.21%	▼1.44%	▼1.38%	▼0.83%	▼1.11%			▼1.63%
LDPR	1	–	–	–	–	–						–
	2	0.7367	0.7315	0.7550	0.5780	0.6817						0.7150
	3	0.7388	0.7462	0.7711	0.5784	0.6897						0.7253
		▲ 0.28%	▲ 2.01%	▲ 2.13%	▲ 0.07%	▲ 1.17%						▲ 1.44%

Table 7. Training time (in seconds) with different pre-processing methods (P) using different datasets (D). Values in italic represent the percentage decrease (▼) or increase (▲) when comparing a 50*ms* re-sampled pre-processing (P3) with the common one (P2).

D	P	volunteer										All
		1	2	3	4	5	6	7	8	9	10	
mHealth	2	21.37	21.92	22.25	20.28	19.97	17.91	19.32	18.80	21.79	19.91	1928.08
	3	3.92	4.02	3.92	3.86	3.64	3.25	3.72	3.64	4.08	3.72	310.92
		▼81.7%	▼81.7%	▼82.4%	▼81.0%	▼81.8%	▼81.9%	▼80.8%	▼80.6%	▼81.3%	▼81.3%	▼83.9%
PAMAP2	2	1184.67	1128.58	533.80	972.34	1419.79	1006.05	945.23	1155.67			102537.39
	3	46.07	46.24	22.00	40.32	51.46	44.16	39.75	48.78			4226.43
		▼96.1%	▼90.8%	▼91.2%	▼90.5%	▼90.9%	▼90.9%	▼90.4%	▼90.3%			▼91.9%
LDPR	2	5.42	5.52	5.58	5.78	10.02						75.89
	3	2.75	3.02	3.16	3.52	5.16						39.72
		▼49.3%	▼45.3%	▼43.4%	▼39.1%	▼48.5%						▼47.7%

Table 5 lists the total number of inputs obtained after each pre-processing. Because of the asynchronicity of the measurements in LDPR, P1 ends up ignoring most of the inputs, as shown in this table. Nonetheless, from this table, we can notice that *not ignoring missing data* (P2) significantly increases the total number of inputs for PAMAP2 – there is no impact on mHealth as it has no missing data. However, this number is greatly decreased with the preliminary re-sampling step (P3). At the end, mHealth [resp. PAMAP2, LDPR] obtained on average a drop of 60% [resp. 80%, 37%] compared with the common method.

Table 6 describes the accuracy obtained for activity recognition with the different pre-processing methods for the targeted datasets. From these results, we notice that the common pre-processing (P2) is performing better than the others for mHealth and PAMAP2. However, results obtained with the re-sampled pre-processing (P3) are fairly close, with on average a drop in accuracy of 0.59% and 1.21% for mHealth and PAMAP2 respectively. But as shown in Table 7, in returns, the training time is decreased by approximately 81.4% and 90.7% for mHealth and PAMAP2 respectively. Even though not presented in this paper, a re-sample rate of 25 ms can further improve the accuracy performance for mHealth and PAMAP2, while still substantially reducing training time. Conversely, P3 is the best for LDPR and improve accuracy on average by 1.13%. Besides, it still decreases the training time by approximately 45.1% (cf. Table 7).

As a result, the re-sampled pre-processing (P3) is worth considering for MW-HAR scenarios. Its advantages (reducing the number of inputs, while smoothing the data) will prove to be especially important for configuration tackling activity recognition task with more complex architectures and large datasets.

As a conclusion, this evaluation shows that the re-sampled pre-processing (P3) can achieve similar and even better performance than the common pre-processing (P2). However, there is a trade-off to be considered between the re-sampling rate (which affect the number of inputs and the training time) and recognition accuracy.

6.2   Grouped Abstraction Performance

In this evaluation, in order to simplify the analysis, we do not integrate P1 and concentrate on the other pre-processing methods. In addition, as shown in Table 8, we listed only the recognition accuracy of the best- and worst-performing volunteers from previous evaluations. We also included the performance of the *1-for-all model*. Based on our previous experiment, volunteer 2 [resp. 2, 4] and 7 [resp. 1, 3] are the ones with respectively the worst and best performance for mHealth [resp. PAMAP2, LDPR]. Table 8 presents the performance of different group strategies using either PCA or LDA as the abstraction technique. In this table, bold colored [resp. italic] value represents the best [resp. the second best] performance for a given scenario (i.e., combination of a pre-processing, a grouping strategy and an abstraction technique for a given volunteer).

As one could expect, we can first conclude that LDA is generally better than PCA for producing a different representation of the data. For scripted datasets

246   G. Habault and S. Wada

Table 8. Activity recognition accuracy for all datasets (D) with different (i) pre-processing (P), (ii) grouping strategies (G) and (iii) abstraction techniques (A = {PCA, LDA}). Results are presented for the best- and worst-performing volunteers on each dataset, as well as the scenario with a unique model for all volunteers (*1-for-all*). Results in bold [resp. italic] depicts the best [resp. second best] performance for the considered scenario (i.e., one pre-processing, one grouping, and one abstraction).

D	G	Worst	Best	All	Worst	Best	All	Worst	Best	All	Worst	Best	All
mHealth	0	0.9600	0.9971	0.9863	0.9600	0.9971	0.9863	0.9468	0.9948	0.9798	0.9468	0.9948	*0.9798*
	1	*0.9581*	**0.9956**	**0.9830**	0.9632	*0.9982*	0.9846	*0.9460*	**0.9918**	**0.9770**	0.9542	*0.9962*	0.9796
	2	*0.9581*	**0.9956**	**0.9830**	*0.9633*	0.9992	0.9850	*0.9460*	**0.9918**	**0.9770**	0.9564	0.9977	0.9802
	3	*0.9581*	**0.9956**	**0.9830**	0.9653	0.9992	*0.9852*	*0.9460*	**0.9918**	**0.9770**	**0.9556**	0.9977	0.9802
	4	0.9488	0.9916	0.9702	0.9541	0.9975	0.9773	0.9272	0.9892	0.9627	0.9454	0.9959	0.9714
PAMAP2	0	0.9952	0.9982	0.9974	0.9952	0.9982	0.9974	0.9789	0.9905	0.9852	0.9789	0.9905	0.9852
	1	*0.9937*	*0.9978*	*0.9954*	*0.9993*	0.9995	*0.9968*	*0.9755*	**0.9885**	**0.9810**	0.9949	*0.9971*	*0.9843*
	2	*0.9937*	*0.9978*	*0.9954*	0.9994	0.9995	*0.9968*	*0.9755*	**0.9885**	**0.9810**	0.9951	0.9968	0.9841
	3	*0.9937*	*0.9978*	*0.9954*	0.9994	0.9995	*0.9968*	*0.9755*	**0.9885**	**0.9810**	**0.9957**	0.9974	0.9839
	4	0.9796	0.9891	0.9737	0.9994	*0.9994*	0.9895	0.9566	0.9723	0.9480	0.9967	*0.9971*	0.9705
LDPR	0	*0.5780*	0.7550	0.7150	0.5780	0.7550	0.7150	*0.5784*	*0.7711*	0.7253	0.5784	0.7711	0.7253
	1	*0.5780*	0.7550	0.7150	*0.5994*	0.7917	0.7242	*0.5784*	*0.7711*	0.7253	*0.6062*	0.8032	0.7354
	2	*0.5780*	0.7550	0.7150	0.6179	*0.7795*	0.7282	*0.5784*	*0.7711*	0.7253	0.6281	*0.7818*	0.7396
	4	0.5863	*0.7541*	*0.7127*	0.5807	0.7614	*0.7258*	0.5807	0.7749	*0.7199*	0.6040	0.7676	*0.7366*
		PCA			LDA			PCA			LDA		A
			2						3				P

(mHealth and PAMAP2) with any grouping strategy, PCA always failed to provide improvement compared to the configuration where all features are considered without data abstraction (G0). For LDPR (the spontaneous dataset), considering all features (G4) with PCA data abstraction improved only the accuracy of the worst-performing volunteer when using the common pre-processing (P2). While with the re-sampled pre-processing (P3), it improved the accuracy of both volunteers. Nevertheless, PCA abstraction always failed to improve accuracy for the *1-for-all* scenario. As a consequence, the rest of our analysis focuses on LDA.

We directly noticed that, for worst-performing volunteers, LDA abstractions with higher level of grouping strategies (G3 and G4) perform better. While, for best-performing volunteers, lower-level ones are to be considered (G1 to G3).

We draw from this observation that volunteer's data that do not have obvious patterns benefit from a higher level of grouped abstraction. Nonetheless, for scripted datasets, LDA associated with any grouping strategies mostly failed to improve the accuracy of the *1-for-all* scenario. This observation implies that it is difficult to produce a generic abstraction from data collected from different volunteers – some might have particularities preventing from such a generalization.

When considering scripted datasets and common pre-processing (P2), we noticed that the accuracy obtained with grouped abstractions was almost the same despite the grouping strategy. Conversely, with re-sampled pre-processing (P3) there are more fluctuations between the performance of each grouping strategy.

Thus, for mHealth, G3 is the best grouping strategy with P2. However, with P3, G3 is slightly less efficient than G2 for the worst-performing volunteer. Otherwise, their performances are the same. Considering that G3 is computationally less expensive, G3 combined with LDA offers the best performance for this dataset for both pre-processing methods.

Focusing on PAMAP2 results, we observe that with P2, G2 and G3 have the same performances. However, G3 and G4 have better recognition accuracy with P3. Therefore, determining which one is better in this dataset depends on the computational cost requirement. For a faster training time, higher levels of grouping should be preferred, otherwise lower level ones should be selected.

When considering LDPR, readers can notice that there is no row for the grouping strategy G3. As mentioned previously, LDPR used only one type of sensor that monitors the spatial coordinate of the considered body part. Therefore, grouping by sensor or by body part is the same for this dataset. Then, only G2 appears in Table 8. For this dataset, G2 [resp. G1] is the best grouping strategy for the worst-performing [resp. best-performing] volunteer as well as the *1-for-all* scenario. This observation is valid for both pre-processing methods, but the re-sampled one (P3) is providing the best results in all scenarios (i.e., worst- and best-performing volunteers as well as *1-for-all*). Therefore, G2 combined with LDA is offering the best performance. Based on previous results, we can suppose that G3, combined with an abstraction technique, will also perform well in an MW-HAR spontaneous dataset.

As a conclusion, this evaluation shows that the re-sampled pre-processing (P3) associated with a grouped abstraction of the sensing features offers better performance compared to a scenario not using grouped abstraction (G0). Unless a unique model for all volunteers is necessary, as for such a scenario, it will depend on the type of dataset. In addition, grouping sensing features is not necessarily increasing the overall computational complexity. Indeed, the bigger the number of features in a group, the fewer the number of abstractions. Therefore, bigger groups limit the cost and impact of the abstraction technique. We assume that more complex abstraction techniques will achieve even greater activity recognition accuracy. However, there will be a trade-off to consider between the computational cost (the overall training time) and recognition accuracy.

Based on these evaluations, for all datasets and any pre-processing method, one abstracted representation method for each body part (G3) appears to be a suitable compromise for efficient computational performances (accuracy and processing time). In addition, worst- and best-performing volunteers are unknown in a real scenario, therefore G3 appears as the optimal default grouping strategy.

6.3   Visualization of Grouped Abstraction

This section aims to visualize the effect of both the re-sampled step and the grouped abstraction. Thus, we focus on scripted datasets that have more sensors. Due to space limitation, we do not show plots of all sensors and all volunteers.

Table 9 shows 3D scatter plots of training measurements from three sensors worn by the volunteer 4 of PAMAP2. We selected this volunteer as it presents average performances in the results of Sect. 6.1.

Table 9. 3D scatter plots of 3 sensors (Chest and wrist accelerometers and wrist gyroscope) for volunteer 4 from PAMAP2 after either P2 or P3 pre-processing. P2c and P3c rows represent the same plots with colors per activity showing that, even with colors, re-sample only is not sufficient to visually differentiate activities.

In order for recognition models to perform efficiently, measurements corresponding to the same activity [resp. different activities] have to be close to [resp. distant from] each other.

From these figures, we observe that it is impossible to distinctively identify activities. The re-sampled pre-processing (P3), even though removing some outliers and decreasing the total number of points, does not make this identification easier. Finally, associating a color per activity, can sometimes simplify this task, but it mostly remains difficult. Therefore, with such a raw data/representation, activity recognition is subject to errors (especially with spontaneous datasets).

Table 10 compares 3D scatter plots without (G0) and after grouped abstraction (G3 combined with LDA). In this table, we concentrate on mHealth and its worst- and best-performing volunteers according to the experiment of Sect. 6.1. From these plots, we first notice that raw measurements (G0) from the wrist gyroscope have already a good per activity separation for volunteer 2 (i.e., the worst-performing one). These separations are even more distinct for volunteer 7 (i.e., the best-performing one). Nonetheless, the proposal ends up losing this specificity. On the other hand, such demarcations are not clear from the raw measurements of the ankle accelerometer. However, the considered grouped abstraction improves the separation for the volunteer 2. The demarcations are significantly better for the volunteer 7 with a clear cloud per activity.

As a result, these plots show that our proposal is not necessarily beneficial for all features of a given group. Some features would benefit from the knowledge of the group, while other should remain in their raw format. For instance, as shown in Table 10, for the best-performing volunteer, a recognition model would benefit more from using the raw representation (G0) of the wrist gyroscope and the G3 representation of the ankle accelerometer. Another way to enhance the performance of grouped abstraction could be to use feature selection mechanisms (such as the ones presented in [4]). Such an additional step will enable the model to select the most significant abstracted features and probably to achieve a better recognition. Finally, dimension reduction could also be a solution to solve the degradation of some features resulting from our proposal. With such a reduction, data from multiple sensors belonging to the same body part could be projected in a lower dimensional space. For instance, a three-dimensional space for easy interpretation. The resulting data would represent different body part states and provide higher-level knowledge of sensors' data.

Last but not least, these visualizations of raw sensor data also help us determine that activities with the same name from different datasets could potentially be different. For instance, we assume that *Running* and *Cycling* were performed either indoor (i.e., on a machine) or on a straight and flat path for PAMAP2. While for mHealth, the same activities were probably realized outdoor, on a path that has elevation gains and curves. Indeed, in the former chest acceleration mostly follows a single axis. When in the latter, measurements present variations on all three axes. Further investigations are then required in order to clarify these disparities and update accordingly the terminology work initiated in Sect. 4.1. Such a task would improve the global recognition knowledge.

Table 10. 3D scatter plots of 2 sensors (Ankle accelerometer and wrist gyroscope) for volunteers 2 (Worst performance) and 7 (Best performance) from mHealth without (G0) and with grouped abstraction (G3 + LDA). Grouped abstraction can, depending on the measurements (sensor and user), worsen or improve the separation of activities.

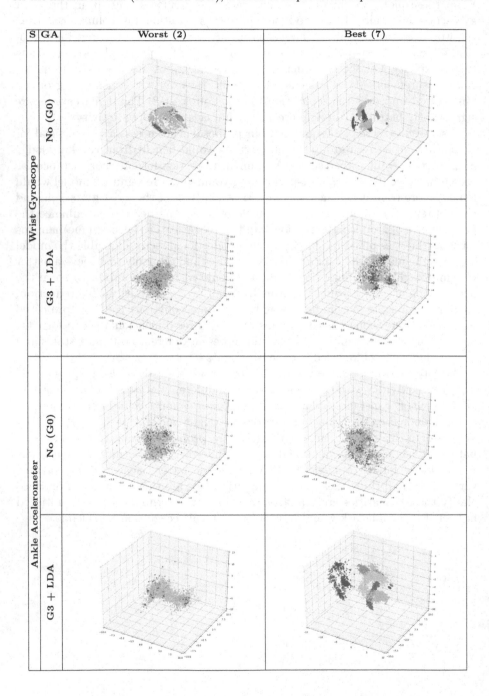

7   Discussion

These experiments show promising results, but open up to several questions and remarks.

As we demonstrated in this paper, re-sampling datasets may lessen the recognition accuracy. But on the other hand, this additional step significantly decreases the number of inputs. This curtailment will definitely be an advantage when combining such a re-sampling with SOTA recognition models. Indeed, it will greatly mitigate their training time (as there will be fewer inputs to handle). However, it is important to determine how to define the optimal re-sampling rate.

In addition, we notice that the recognition accuracy varies from one dataset to another. Besides, among dataset, there are also discrepancies in performance between volunteers. Therefore, we suppose that both the type and the calibration of used sensors play a significant part in the performance. Moreover, Fong et al. [9] showed that classification accuracy can increase significantly when a specific processing is applied on bio-signals, such as ECG. The noteworthy good performance of the per feature abstraction (G1) lets us suppose that other IMU features might also require a specific processing.

These results also pave the way for more future investigations. Indeed, as mentioned previously, there are several options to produce a different representation of a feature or set of features. For that reason, additional experiments should be conducted in order to determine the most appropriate one. For instance, such experiments could consider more sophisticated techniques, such as Neighborhood Components Analysis (NCA) [12] or t-distributed Stochastic Neighbor Embedding (tSNE) [27]. Another option would be to use the latent representation of DL models as the abstracted representation. In fact, architectures such as Variational Auto Encoder (VAE) could be trained to learn the latent representation of a group of body-worn sensors data. Once trained, the obtained latent representations will become the inputs for training the classifier.

Furthermore, in this paper, either all features have a new representation or none of them have. We did not investigate a more complex architecture, as illustrated in Fig. 2. An architecture where some features will be grouped in order to produce abstracted representations (such as features $\{f_2, f_3\}$ or $\{f_4, f_5, f_6\}$ in Fig. 2); some features will be unchanged (such as f_1); and others will be projected into another space (f_N). Indeed, as shown by the data plots in Sect. 6.3, some sensors' data are already well represented. Conversely, for others, computing a new representation significantly improves the interpretability and thus enhances the activity recognition. Therefore, there might be further research to pursue in this direction. We imagine that a multimodal architecture such as the one proposed in [21] could be particularly adapted in this situation. An architecture that could automate whether a new representation is required, based on some prior analysis of the features, their auto- and cross-dependencies.

Finally, by projecting the representation on lower dimensions, it would probably be possible to better interpret the impact of each body part state on the final decision. Coupled with some attention mechanisms, it could help us determine which features are the most important and when to use them.

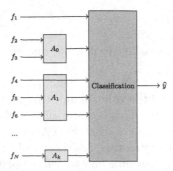

Fig. 2. Generic illustration of the grouped representation proposal. In a generic version, some features are grouped and have a high level representation, while others might only be pre-processed. $A_i, i \in \{0, ..., k\}$ is the technique used to transform a group of features into a higher level representation.

At the end, all the knowledge acquired from multimodal wearable sensing devices could benefit to other HAR research. As mentioned previously, there is uncertainty of the sensor's location at a given time in uni-modal HAR research (e.g., using a smartphone). Analysis based on MW-HAR scenarios provides knowledge of the different range of motion/values from all monitored body parts. This knowledge could help uni-modal HAR models estimate where the sensor is placed on the body. Such a transfer learning will eventually improve the understanding of what is monitored during a given period. As a result, models will better grasp associated gestures and consequently recognize more efficiently corresponding activities.

8   Conclusion

This paper describes an alternative approach to process multimodal wearable sensors' data. The presented results attempt to answer whether this proposal is the key for solving HAR task. Although it is difficult to be unequivocal on this point, this proposal depicts interesting aspects and performance over the tested datasets. These results would need to be automated and generalized to other datasets in order to settle this question. The first part of this proposal is to re-sample the data to a coarser resolution. After some pre-processing, sensing features monitoring the same body-part are grouped. For each resulting group, we train a new representation of its data. This proposal reduces the computational cost and improves the comprehension of multimodal sensors' data.

This study opens up to a multitude of possibilities. In the future, we will extensively study this proposal with more complex recognition models, different abstraction techniques, and other spontaneous Multimodal Wearable HAR datasets. We also plan to further investigate the visualization of the generated abstraction in order to better understand the advantages of this proposal.

References

1. Adadi, A., Berrada, M.: Peeking inside the black-box: a survey on explainable artificial intelligence (XAI). IEEE Access **6**, 52138–52160 (2018)
2. Banos, O., et al.: mHealthDroid: a novel framework for agile development of mobile health applications. In: Pecchia, L., Chen, L.L., Nugent, C., Bravo, J. (eds.) IWAAL 2014. LNCS, vol. 8868, pp. 91–98. Springer, Cham (2014). https://doi.org/10.1007/978-3-319-13105-4_14
3. Cao, Z., Hidalgo, G., Simon, T., Wei, S.E., Sheikh, Y.: OpenPose: realtime multi-person 2D pose estimation using part affinity fields (2019)
4. Chandrashekar, G., Sahin, F.: A survey on feature selection methods. Comput. Electr. Eng. **40**(1), 16–28 (2014)
5. Chang, Y.J., Chen, S.F., Huang, J.D.: A Kinect-based system for physical rehabilitation: a pilot study for young adults with motor disabilities. Res. Dev. Disabil. **32**(6), 2566–2570 (2011)
6. Chavarriaga, R., et al.: The opportunity challenge: a benchmark database for on-body sensor-based activity recognition. Pattern Recogn. Lett. **34**(15), 2033–2042 (2013)
7. Chen, K., Zhang, D., Yao, L., Guo, B., Yu, Z., Liu, Y.: Deep learning for sensor-based human activity recognition: overview, challenges, and opportunities. ACM Comput. Surv. **54**(4) (2021)
8. Ferrari, A., Micucci, D., Mobilio, M., Napoletano, P.: Trends in human activity recognition using smartphones. J. Reliable Intell. Environ. **7**(3), 189–213 (2021)
9. Fong, S., Lan, K., Sun, P., Mohammed, S., Fiaidhi, J.: A time-series pre-processing methodology for biosignal classification using statistical feature extraction. In: Proceedings of the IASTED International Conference on Biomedical Engineering, BioMed 2013 (2013)
10. Gerling, K., Livingston, I., Nacke, L., Mandryk, R.: Full-body motion-based game interaction for older adults. In: Proceedings of the SIGCHI Conference on Human Factors in Computing Systems, CHI 2012, pp. 1873–1882. Association for Computing Machinery, New York (2012)
11. Gochoo, M., Tan, T.H., Liu, S.H., Jean, F.R., Alnajjar, F.S., Huang, S.C.: Unobtrusive activity recognition of elderly people living alone using anonymous binary sensors and DCNN. IEEE J. Biomed. Health Inform. **23**(2), 693–702 (2019)
12. Goldberger, J., Roweis, S., Hinton, G., Salakhutdinov, R.: Neighbourhood components analysis. In: Proceedings of the 17th International Conference on Neural Information Processing Systems, NIPS 2004, pp. 513–520 (2004)
13. Gu, K., Vosoughi, S., Prioleau, T.: Feature selection for multivariate time series via network pruning. In: 2021 International Conference on Data Mining Workshops (ICDMW). IEEE (2021)
14. Hayes, A.L., Dukes, P.S., Hodges, L.F.: A virtual environment for post-stroke motor rehabilitation (2011)
15. Joshi, A., Parmar, H.R., Jain, K., Shah, C.U., Patel, V.R.: Human activity recognition based on object detection. IOSR J. Comput. Eng. **19**, 26–32 (2017)
16. Kaluža, B., Mirchevska, V., Dovgan, E., Luštrek, M., Gams, M.: An agent-based approach to care in independent living. In: de Ruyter, B., et al. (eds.) AmI 2010. LNCS, vol. 6439, pp. 177–186. Springer, Heidelberg (2010). https://doi.org/10.1007/978-3-642-16917-5_18
17. Kwon, H., Abowd, G.D., Plötz, T.: Complex deep neural networks from large scale virtual IMU data for effective human activity recognition using wearables. Sensors **21**(24), 8337 (2021)

18. Lawrence, E., Sax, C., Navarro, K.F., Qiao, M.: Interactive games to improve quality of life for the elderly: towards integration into a WSN monitoring system. In: 2010 Second International Conference on eHealth, Telemedicine, and Social Medicine, pp. 106–112 (2010)
19. Miyamoto, S., Ogawa, H.: Human activity recognition system including smartphone position. Procedia Technol. **18**, 42–46 (2014)
20. Münzner, S., Schmidt, P., Reiss, A., Hanselmann, M., Stiefelhagen, R., Dürichen, R.: CNN-based sensor fusion techniques for multimodal human activity recognition. In: Proceedings of the 2017 ACM International Symposium on Wearable Computers, ISWC 2017, pp. 158–165 (2017)
21. Perez-Rua, J.M., Vielzeuf, V., Pateux, S., Baccouche, M., Jurie, F.: MFAS: multimodal fusion architecture search. In: 2019 IEEE/CVF Conference on Computer Vision and Pattern Recognition (CVPR), pp. 6959–6968 (2019)
22. Qian, H., Pan, S.J., Da, B., Miao, C.: A novel distribution-embedded neural network for sensor-based activity recognition. In: Proceedings of the Twenty-Eighth International Joint Conference on Artificial Intelligence, IJCAI-19, pp. 5614–5620. International Joint Conferences on Artificial Intelligence Organization (2019)
23. Reiss, A., Stricker, D.: Creating and benchmarking a new dataset for physical activity monitoring. In: Proceedings of the 5th International Conference on PErvasive Technologies Related to Assistive Environments, PETRA 2012 (2012)
24. Rossi, S., Capasso, R., Acampora, G., Staffa, M.: A multimodal deep learning network for group activity recognition. In: 2018 International Joint Conference on Neural Networks (IJCNN), pp. 1–6 (2018)
25. Ryoo, M.S.: Human activity prediction: early recognition of ongoing activities from streaming videos. In: 2011 International Conference on Computer Vision, pp. 1036–1043 (2011)
26. Straczkiewicz, M., James, P., Onnela, J.P.: A systematic review of smartphone-based human activity recognition methods for health research. NPJ Digit. Med. **4**(11), 1–15 (2021)
27. Van Der Maaten, L.: Accelerating T-SNE using tree-based algorithms. J. Mach. Learn. Res. **15**(1), 3221–3245 (2014)
28. Vo, Q.V., Lee, G., Choi, D.: Fall detection based on movement and smart phone technology. In: 2012 IEEE RIVF International Conference on Computing & Communication Technologies, Research, Innovation, and Vision for the Future, pp. 1–4 (2012)
29. Wang, J., Chen, Y., Hao, S., Peng, X., Hu, L.: Deep learning for sensor-based activity recognition: a survey. Pattern Recogn. Lett. **119**, 3–11 (2019)
30. Wang, J., Chen, Y., Gu, Y., Xiao, Y., Pan, H.: SensoryGANs: an effective generative adversarial framework for sensor-based human activity recognition. In: 2018 International Joint Conference on Neural Networks (IJCNN), pp. 1–8 (2018)
31. Zeng, M., et al.: Convolutional Neural Networks for human activity recognition using mobile sensors. In: 6th International Conference on Mobile Computing, Applications and Services, pp. 197–205 (2014)
32. Zhang, L., Zhang, X., Pan, J., Huang, F.: Hierarchical cross-modality semantic correlation learning model for multimodal summarization. In: Proceedings of the AAAI Conference on Artificial Intelligence (2022)

Artificial Intelligence and Data Mining
in Education

Pose+Context: A Model for Recognizing Non-verbal Teaching Behavior of Normal College Student

Yonghe Zhang, Bing Li[✉], and Xiaoming Cao

Normal College, Shenzhen University, Shenzhen 518060, China
libingioo@szu.edu.cn

Abstract. Normal college students practice their teaching skills to prepare for their teacher career. However, due to the complexity of teaching skills and the overburdening of instructors, their needs for instructional feedback are often not met. To server automatic feedbacks to normal college students, this paper proposes a deep learning model, called Pose+Contex, to recognize three types of non-verbal teaching behaviors (*NVTB*). The model includes three parts: (1) context detection, (2) pose estimation, and (3) behavior recognition. Our model is featured by the context detection component, and experiments show that it performs better than a similar model without this component.

Keywords: deep learning · computer vision · pose estimation · classroom behavior analysis

1 Introduction

Teacher training system in China has produced a large number of teachers to K12-education, and the training of teacher's teaching skills is highly valued by the education department. Before teaching career, normal college student (also called normal students) practice their teaching skills mainly in campus. Among various training activities for teaching skills, post-class reflection is a critical part for the self-improvement of normal students, which relies on feedbacks from the instructors. Due to the complexity of teaching skills and the overburdening of instructors, the needs for instructional feedback are often not met, and instruction in non-verbal teaching behavior is particularly lacking.

Compared with verbal expressions, teachers' nonverbal behavior is a kind of "silent language", including the position in classroom, gesture, gaze and facial expressions, etc. [1]. Many researchers believe that teachers' nonverbal behaviors in the classroom have a non-negligible impact on student learning [1–6], such as the improvement of teacher-student relations, the enhancement of classroom teaching effects and student learning efficiency [1]. However, normal students' nonverbal behavior problems are often exposed during the teaching practice, due to the lack of practical experience, relevant training and self-confidence of normal students, as well as overburdening of instructors.

R. Hou et al. (Eds.): BDTA 2021/2022, LNICST 480, pp. 257–264, 2023.
https://doi.org/10.1007/978-3-031-33614-0_17

Although the related research on teacher reflection by video analysis has been studied for a few decades [7], the analysis of non-verbal behavior still needs to be further expanded in the field of classroom teaching analysis. With the new development of big data and artificial intelligence, Computer Vision (CV) has reached an unprecedented state. In the field of CV, human pose estimation is one of the major breakthroughs have been made. It is promising to develop video analysis systems based on this technology to diagnosis non-verbal behavior problems for normal students just in time. Therefore, this article explores the extension and application and of pose estimation technology in helping normal college students' training.

2   Related Work

2.1   Category of Teachers' Non-verbal Behaviors

The classification of NVTB is the prerequisite for detecting and analyzing normal college students' teaching behavior pattern. Prof. Shen classified NVTB into seven categories based on the level of teachers' support for students, including enthusiasm-support, acceptance-help, elaboration-guidance, intermediate, avoid-falter, neglect, and disagree [14]. Cui and Wang divide NVTB into two categories, including body language and scene according to the relationship between the communicator and the context [15]. Tang classified NVTB into static behaviors, such as people's spatial position and body posture, and dynamic behaviors, such as sign language and head Sentimental language, gaze and facial expressions [16]. Liu's extend Tang's theory to add interpersonal communication as a new type of NVTB, such as interpersonal distance, body orientation, etc. [17].

2.2   Human Pose Estimation and OpenPose

In computer vision research, pose estimation refers to the process of recovering human joint points from a given image or a video, which is a very challenging research problem [19]. The key points of human skeleton are of great significance for describing human posture and predicting human behavior, such as behavior recognition, task tracking, and gait recognition [18]. Human pose estimation algorithms can be divided into two methods, based on traditional methods and methods based on deep learning. The traditional pose estimation algorithm is mainly based on the image structure model [20, 21], which is not robust caused by data factors such as shape, angle, and occlusion. The pose estimation algorithm based on deep learning has been developed rapidly in recent years [21]. So far, the methods of using deep learning for multi-person pose estimation are roughly divided into two types: top-down method and bottom-up method. Top-down (top-down), that is, the human body is detected first, and then the posture of a single person is estimated [22, 25–27]. Bottom-up (Bottom-up) is to first detect the human body joint points, and then connect the human body skeleton according to the detected joint points [23, 24, 29]. Generally speaking, the top-down pose estimation method has higher accuracy, but its processing speed is lower; the bottom-up method has a slightly lower accuracy than the former, but it runs faster than the former and can achieve real-time Detection [29].

OpenPose is currently a commonly used gesture recognition model. Using a bottom-up method, it can quickly and accurately obtain the skeleton key point coordinates of the characters in the image, which is suitable for single and multi-person recognition [28]. OpenPose can realize the recognition and estimation of the key points of the skeleton of multiple people's bodies, faces and hands. It has good robustness, so it can be used for application research related to gesture recognition [28–30].

To summarize the related works of this paper, we argue that the current research on non-verbal behavior analysis and its application in normal college students' training is still in the preliminary stage. There are particularly few studies aiming at recognizing normal college students' attention-related non-verbal behavior, like focusing on the audience, podium and the classroom screen. These behaviors may have influenced their teaching performance [14], and statistics analysis of this data would be inspiring for moderating allocation during normal college students' teaching practice.

3 The Pose+Context Model

The aim of this work is to recognize normal college students' attention-related non-verbal behavior, including:

- C_a: a normal student focus on the audience in classroom.
- C_p: a normal student focus on the podium (teacher's desk).
- C_s: a normal student focus on the classroom screen.

The proposed model is called the Pose+Context model as shown in Fig. 1. It has three components: (1) Context detection: locate the area of the podium through the object detection algorithm in each image. (2) Pose estimation: extract the skeleton key points of normal college students, and drop the unreliable key points according to confidence scores. (3) Behavior recognition: Based on the results of previous steps, posture recognition is performed to recognize normal college students' attention-related non-verbal behavior.

The context detection and pose estimation components provide input vectors for the multi-class classifier which predicts the type of behavior. The context detection components can be implemented by the architecture of object detection which trained to detect podiums and applied to provide context data. we use YOLOv5 [31] to implement this component in our experiments. As for pose estimation, a pre-trained Openpose model [28] is used to extract pose data in our experiments. The results of the first two components' 2D tensors are flatten and joint into a vector as the input of behavior recognition. For behavior recognition, a multi-class classifier is typically a deep learning model. In the following experiments, we build the model with a nine-layers perceptron with 32 to 128 nodes in each hidden layer. Batch normalization and ReLU activation are also set up after each hidden layer.

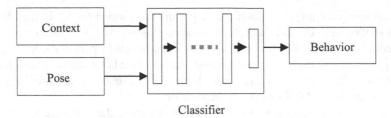

Fig. 1. The Pose+Context Model.

4   Experiment

4.1   Dataset Construction

This experiment was completed in micro-teaching classrooms in a normal college. In each micro-teaching classroom, there is a podium and a screen on wall in the frontal area, and audience desks and chairs in the rest area. Videos are captured by two cameras to produce views of teacher and the whole classroom (Table 1).

Table 1. Examples of normal college students' attention-related non-verbal behavior

C_a	1	0	0
C_p	0	1	0
C_s	0	0	1

In the experiment, videos of teaching practice were collected by a teaching-assisted system. A total of 23 normal students participated in this experiment, each of them completed 6 teaching practices. After data preprocessing, we constructed a labeled dataset of 1638 images. Labels of a sample include behavior type and a box marking the podium in it. Then we divided the dataset in cross-subject manner into training, validation and test subset by the ratio of 6:1:3 approximately.

4.2   Evaluation Metric

Our experiment compares the two cases: with context (Pose+Context) and without context (Pose only) as input for the behavior recognition model. Our hypothesis is that the Pose+Context model would enhance the recognition by the effect of context. We repeated the entire evaluation process (training, verification, and testing) for the two methods 40 times in order to avoid interference factors caused by data. For each time of the process, we set 300 epochs for training and use the same train-test division of the dataset. The evaluation metric is micro-averaged F1 score shown as Eqs. (1–3).

$$Micro\_F1 = \frac{2 \times Micro\_P \times Micro\_R}{Micro\_P + Micro\_R} \qquad (1)$$

$$Micro\_P = \frac{\sum_i TP_i}{\sum_i TP_i + \sum_i FP_i} \qquad (2)$$

$$Micro\_R = \frac{\sum_i TP_i}{\sum_i TP_i + \sum_i FN_i} \qquad (3)$$

where TP_i is the total number of true positive predictions of i-th class, FP_i is the total number of false positive predictions of i-th class, FN_i is the total number of false negative predictions of i-th class, and $i \in (C_a, C_p, C_s)$.

4.3 Experiment Results

The experimental processing was performed on a high-performance computer with 32GB memory, Intel i7 2.9GHz CPU, and NVIDIA GeForce GTX 3090 graphics. The results arc shown in the Table 2.

Table 2. Micro-averaged F-1 score of the Pose+Context model and the Pose only model.

	N	mean	std	max
Pose+Context	40	**0.84**	0.05	**0.90**
Pose only	40	0.81	0.05	0.87

We performed independent samples T-test for the two groups of results, and the outcome $p = 0.008 < 0.05$ indicates that the two sets of means have very significant differences. The Pose+Context model has a higher mean of F-1 scores than the Pose only model. One of the recognition instances of each class by the Pose+Context model is shown in Table 3.

Table 3. Metrics of the Pose+Context model

	precision	recall	f1-score	support
C_a	0.81	0.69	0.75	101
C_p	0.93	0.93	0.93	168
C_s	0.91	0.98	0.94	220

The recall value of C_a is relatively low. We look into the error samples to explore the difficulties in the recognition process of our model. Two typical false cases shown in Fig. 2 where context and pose marks are shown. From our observation, the model may have overused the distance between teacher and podium or the direction between them for inference. Hence, the context input component of the model has side effects in certain degree leading to the low recall score for C_a.

Case 1: Truth=C_a, Predition=C_p Case 2: Truth=C_a, Predition= C_s

Fig. 2. Error recognition instances of the Pose+Context model

5   Application

To demonstrate applications of the proposed model, we related the NVTB predations of the model and instructors' scores for teaching practices. Each teaching practice is marked with a score which is ranged from 1 to 5, and higher scores means better teaching performance. Ratios of predicted labels are also counted for each teaching practice. Figure 3 shows the ratio of C_a (focus of audience) increases and the one of C_p (focus of podium) decreases when scores go higher. This application shows the NVTB prediction by our model can be play as indices for normal students' teaching performance, and it is promising to server as diagnosis feedback for them to improve their teaching skill.

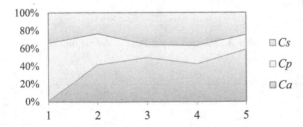

Fig. 3. An application to show NVTB labels distributions among difference scores of teaching.

6 Conclusions and Future Work

The goal of the non-verbal behavior analysis of normal college students' teaching practice is to provide feedbacks in time for teaching skill improvement. The Pose+Context model proposed in this paper has been proven to be effective to recognize three types of attention-related non-verbal behaviors with overall F1-score 0.84.

The experimental process and results of this research are constrained by a variety of factors, and further research has the following ideas: First, identify more context factors in the teaching process, and perform correlation analysis with teacher students' postures to improve the accuracy of teacher students' non-verbal behavior recognition; Second, combine speech behavior analysis methods to achieve multi-modal behavior analysis, and comprehensively describe the quantitative characteristics of the teaching process; third, improve the hardware environment, collect high-resolution eye image data, and promote eye tracking technologies to improve the outcomes.

Acknowledgements. This research was supported by the Ministry of Education in China (project: Research on the Identification Mechanism of Learning Participation Based on Multimodal Fusion in a Smart Learning Environment, 20YJA880001) and the Collaborative Innovation Research Institute of Sports Psychology Education of Shenzhen University Normal College (project: Recognition of Learning Engagement Based on Multi-view Stereo Vision).

References

1. Jinling, T.: A review of the research on teachers' classroom nonverbal behaviors. Zhejiang Educ. Sci. **1**, 10–12 (2010)
2. Cooper, P.J.: Speech communication for the classroom teacher. Gorsuch Scarisbbrick (1988)
3. Huang, L.: The impact of non-verbal behavior psychological semantics on classroom teaching. China Elect. Power Educ. **35**, 81–82 (2011)
4. Cheng, Y.: The significance and methods of using non-verbal communication strategies in college music classrooms. Northwestern Med. Educ. **18**(03), 566–569 (2010)
5. Zhou, M.: The influence of several typical nonverbal behaviors of teachers on classroom atmosphere in multimedia teaching. J. Hunan Med. Univ. (Soc. Sci. Ed.) **12**(04), 184–185 (2010)
6. Zhou, P.: A Brief Discussion on Teachers' Non-verbal Behavior Research. Nationalities Publishing House, Beijing (2006)
7. Tian, L., Zhang, Z., Chen, Y.: Research on the effect of video promoting micro-teaching reflection of normal students. Mod. Educ. Technol. **25**(10), 54–60 (2015)
8. Flanders, N.A.: Analyzing Teaching Behavior, p. 34. Addision-Wesley Publishing Company, New York (1970)
9. Yang, P., Liu, J., Luo, P.: Discussion on the teaching behavior classification system VICS. Teacher **6**, 3–4 (2009)
10. Fu, D., Zhang, H., Liu, Q.: Educational Information Processing (2nd ed). Beijing Normal University Press, Beijing, vol. 92, pp. 98–100 (2011)
11. Mu, S., Zuo, P.: Research on the analysis method of classroom teaching behavior under the information teaching environment. Audio-Vis. Educ. Res. **36**(09), 62–69 (2015)
12. Cheng, Y., Liu, Q., Wang, Y., et al.: Research on the construction and application of the cloud model of classroom teaching behavior analysis. J. Dist. Educ. **2**, 36–42 (2017)

13. Jin, J., Gu, X.: Analysis and research on classroom teaching behavior in information technology environment. China Audio-Vis. Educ. (9), 82–86 (2010)
14. Shen, L.: Non-verbal behavior in the classroom. Foreign Element. Second. Educ. **6**, 33–34 (1983)
15. Cui, Y., Wang, J.: Interpretation of non-verbal behaviors in classroom teaching from the perspective of cognitive pragmatics. Educ. Teach. Forum **42**, 98–100 (2014)
16. Tan, J.: A review of the research on nonverbal behavior of teachers in classroom. Zhejiang Educ. Sci. **1**, 10–12 (2010)
17. Liu, Y.: A Study on Nonverbal Behavior of Junior Middle School Music Novice Teachers. Master's Degree Thesis of Nanning Normal University (2019)
18. Iqbal, U., Milan, A., Gall, J.: PoseTrack: joint multi-person pose estimation and tracking. In: Computer Vision and Pattern Recognition, pp. 4654–4663, IEEE (2017)
19. Johnson, S., Everingham, M.: Learning effective human pose estimation from inaccurate annotation. CVPR, IEEE (2011)
20. Fischler, M.A., Elschlager, R.A.: The representation and matching of pictorial structures. IEEE Trans. Comput. **1**, 67–92 (1973)
21. Deng, Y., Luo, J., Jin, F.: Overview of human pose estimation methods based on deep learning. Comput. Eng. Appl. **55**(19), 22–42 (2019)
22. Huang, S., Gong, M., Tao, D.: A coarse-fine network for keypoint localization. IEEE International Conference on Computer Vision, pp3047–3056, IEEE (2017)
23. Cao, Z., Simon, T., Wei, S.E., et al.: Realtime multi-person 2D pose estimation using part affinity fields. In: 2017 IEEE Conference on Computer Vision and Pattern Recognition (CVPR). IEEE Computer Society (2017)
24. He, K., Zhang, X., Ren, S., et al.: Spatial pyramid pooling in deep convolutional networks for visual recognition. IEEE Trans. Pattern Anal. Mach. Intell. **37**(9), 1904–1916 (2015)
25. Papandreou, G., Zhu, T., Kanazawa, N., et al.: Towards accurate multi-person pose estimation in the wild. In: Proceedings of the IEEE Conference on Computer Vision and Pattern Recognition, pp. 4903–4911, IEEE (2017)
26. Chen, Y., Wang, Z., Peng, Y., et al.: Cascaded pyramid network for multi-person pose estimation. In: Proceedings of the IEEE Conference on Computer Vision and Pattern Recognition, pp. 7103–7112, IEEE (2018)
27. Fang, H.S., Xie, S., Tai, Y.W., et al.: Rmpe:Regional multi-person pose estimation. In: Proceedings of the IEEE International Conference on Computer Vision, pp. 2334–2343, IEEE (2017)
28. Yang, M., Li, J., Guo, R., Tang, X.: Realization and research of human sleeping posture recognition based on OpenPose. Phys. Exp. **39**(8), 4549 (2019)
29. Gong, W.: Design and implementation of student learning behavior recognition system based on bone key point detection. Jilin University (2019)
30. Zheng, Y.: An evaluation method of teacher's teaching behavior based on gesture recognition. Softw. Eng. **4**, 6–9 (2021)
31. YOLOv5 Homepage: https://github.com/ultralytics/yolov5. Last accessed 29 Aug. 2021

Dropout Prediction in MOOC Combining Behavioral Sequence Characteristics

Xiaoxuan Ma[1], Huan Huang[2(✉)], Shuai Yuan[3], and Rui Hou[1]

[1] School of Computer Science, South-Central University for Nationalities,
Wuhan, China
hourui@mail.scuec.edu.cn
[2] School of Education, South-Central University for Nationalities, Wuhan, China
huanghuan@mail.scuec.edu.cn
[3] School of Computer, Hubei University of Euducation, Wuhan, China

Abstract. In the past decade, online education platforms led by MOOC have developed rapidly around the world, bringing great changes to the education industry. MOOC aim to provide high-quality, free and open courses for global learners. However, different from the traditional classroom education, MOOC suffers from a significant high dropout rate due to its online mode. In previous studies, researchers mostly use some well-designed features by handcraft. Such methods can be time-consuming and complicated. In this paper, we combine the unsupervised algorithm with machine learning algorithm to solve the problem of dropout prediction in MOOC. Our model use the sub-sequences identified in the participant's behavior sequence as features, which simplifies the complexity of the features design. And a large number of experiments have been carried out on a public datasets, the experimental results show that the performance of the proposed method can be compared with the method using the high-dimensional and complex features used by other researchers.

Keywords: MOOC · Dropout Prediction · Behavioral Sequence

1 Introduction

Massive Open Online Courses (commonly known as MOOC) are open courses designed to provide world-wide educational courses to a large number of learners through an online platform [1]. Most MOOC courses are free and of high quality, which are usually recorded at great universities in various countries. Since 2010, MOOC have gradually come into the public view, and the rapid development of online learning platforms led by MOOC has become a new popular trend. Relies on the real-time and high-quality courses offered by the MOOC platform, learners can freely choose the learning content they are interested in and the learning time more suitable for them. At the same time, learners can constantly adjust their learning progress or choose different learning content in time according to their

R. Hou et al. (Eds.): BDTA 2022, LNICST 480, pp. 265–278, 2023.
https://doi.org/10.1007/978-3-031-33614-0_18

learning habits. These are advantages that MOOC online learning platform have that traditional classroom learning does not have. The most obvious feature of MOOC is that they offer a variety of courses, and is not limited by the number of learners, so the same course can accommodate more participants compared to traditional classroom learning. It is also these factors that have caused a widespread problem in MOOC platforms, that is only a small number of people finish the course. MOOC has high dropout rates [2]. And it is reported that the completion rate on Coursera is only 7–9% [3].

We know that an unavoidable problem of online education platforms is that learners have too much autonomy in learning, which leads to their failure to complete the course. This is also a common problem faced by many online education platforms. In recent years, it has attracted wide attention from scholars.

Generally, these studies about dropout prediction can be divided into two categories. In the first category, the traditional machine learning model is used for modeling to predict the dropout rates. Researchers select the datasets they are interested in, implement feature engineering to extract the effective features, and use these features for modeling to predict the dropout rates.

In traditional machine learning approach, researchers use handcrafted features. Researchers need to construct complex features to get a good prediction result, It can also be understood intuitively that more features can better represent the underlying rules of the data. However, manual feature design is a time-consuming and laborious task. And an effective feature extraction strategy is not universal for different datasets. Some researchers use the number of single behavior features in click-stream data to represent the data. In this way, the extracted features is independent and lose the temporal relation in behavior sequence to some extent. The following studies prove the validity of our point. In [12]. They use raw click-stream data without this feature engineering, claiming that it removes an important sequential pattern of the click-stream. Still, these end-to-end models may overlook important patterns in the data by taking only a single objective into account. In [13], this naturally leads researchers to consider unsupervised methods to capture meaningful patterns.

The second category is the method of neural networks, it can automatically extract features during training. Using neural networks approach is the hot spot of recent years, researchers often use multi-layer network or combination of different network model. The method of neural networks improve the performance of the prediction. However, it still has problems in this way. That is, the complex network structure and the poor interpretability of the model, what scale of deep learning network model should be used for different datasets, and also a lot of uncertainty about parameter tuning of the model.

For those two reasons, this paper try to construct a more effective dropout prediction model from the perspective of traditional feature engineering. In order to achieve this purpose, this paper only adopts the most widespread records as features in feature engineering. These features are the data that users interact with the MOOC platform. Therefore, our feature engineering can be easily implemented on similar datasets based on user behavior.

The structure of the paper is as follows. Section 2 provides a related work on what has been researched about dropout prediction in MOOC. Section 3 introduce the datasets used in this paper. Section 4 introduces the proposed method in this paper. Results and discussion are in Sect. 5. Finally, the conclusions are described in Sect. 6.

2   Related Work

In this section, we briefly review some significant results of MOOC dropout prediction research in recent years.

In [1], they present an approach that works on click-stream data. And their algorithm takes the weekly history of student data into account and thus is able to notice changes in student behavior over time. In [4], they build predictive models weekly, over multiple offerings of a course. Based on logistic regression, they propose two transfer learning algorithms to trade-off smoothness and accuracy by adding a regularization term to minimize the difference of failure probabilities between consecutive weeks. In [5], a decision tree was used to predict dropout and perform feature analysis. In [6], a survival model was developed to measure the influence of factors related to student behavior and social positioning within discussion forums using standard social network analysis techniques. In [14], they extracts features mainly from discussion forums and video lectures, and employs Hidden Markov Models(HMMs) to predict student retention.

Also, there are some researchers using ensemble methods to improve the prediction ability of the model, such as in [7], a composition and ensemble of the naive Bayes (NB), multilayered perceptron (MLP), SVM, and decision table (DT) was used to give the final dropout prediction. Some researchers have used more information about participants to help improve the model's predictive ability, such as In [8], they used students related variables (gender, age, grade in high school and so on) collected during the admission of student and pre-university information (high school marks, family income of students, parents' qualification), and they tested a variety of decision tree models, and the results show that using students' relevant information can improve the performance of the model.

Neural network has become popular in recent years, with the proposed and application of CNN and RNN network models, many researchers have built prediction models based on these neural networks, such as: In [9], by regarding dropout prediction as a sequence classification problem, they propose some temporal models for solving it. And they propose a recurrent neural network (RNN) model with long short-term memory (LSTM) to predict dropout. Through extensive experiments on a public dataset, they show that the proposed model can achieve results comparable to feature engineering based methods. In [10], their model is a deep neural network, which is a combination of Convolutional Neural Networks and Recurrent Neural Networks. In their model, features are extracted automatically from raw records by convolutional and pooling layers in the lower part of the model. Characteristics of time series data are considered by recurrent layer in the upper part of the model. Experimental results show that their model can achieve comparable results to those obtained by feature engineering based methods. In [11], they propose a deep neural network model, which is a combination of Convolutional Neural Network, Long Short-Term Memory network and Support Vector Machine in a bottom-up manner. Also their model can automatically extract features from the raw data, moreover they takes into account the impact of the sequential relationship of student behavior and class imbalance on dropout, and the model they proposed reinforce the performance of dropout prediction. In [9–11], researcher used deep learning model to extract features automatically, and their model really achieve good results compared to feature engineering based methods.

3   Dataset

This section introduces the dataset used for the experiment in this article. In order to prove the effectiveness of our proposed method, we select a public dataset as the research data: the dataset of KDD Cup 2015.

This dataset contains information about 39 courses in the online Platform Xuetangx and these courses all last one month. And it directly give the label of each participant whether the participant is dropout or not, which simplifies our discussion of how to define dropout and allows us to focus more on the problem solving itself.

This dataset contains three csv files: enrollment_train.csv,log_train.csv (see Table 1), and truth_train.csv, where, enrollment_train records the student's participation with the course, with enrollment_id as the unique identifier; Log_train records the behavior record of participants interacting with the MOOC system. Here are seven types of behavioral data (see Table 2). This table is also uniquely identified by enrollment_id; Truth_train is the real label for the dataset, also uniquely identified with enrollment_id. So enrollment_id represents the different participant, our task is to give the dropout prediction for every participant based on their behavior records.

The size of this dataset is as follows: 39 courses, 120,542 enrollment_ids, 815,7277 events. The distribution of behavior in the events is shown in Fig. 1.

Table 1. Table in log_train.csv.

Attribute	Meaning
enrollment_id	id of the participant
time	the time of the event
source	event source ("server" or "browser")
event	behavior record for participant
object	object participant access or navigate to

Table 2. Behavior data of students

Attribute	Meaning
problem	working on course assignments
video	watching course videos
access	accessing other course objects except videos and assignments
wiki	accessing the course wiki
discussion	accessing the course forum
navigate	navigating to other part of the course
page_close	closing the web page

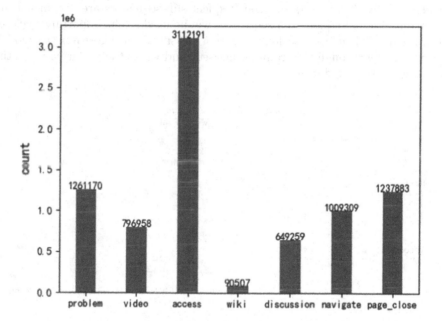

Fig. 1. Distributions of seven behavior records.

4 Proposed Method

4.1 Overview of the Method

From the previous work, we can know that the dropout prediction problem is actually a sequence prediction problem. Our task is to take a sequence of the participant, which is generated by participant's learning behaviors in time order, and then use classification model to predict whether the participant will eventually dropout. This can be summarized as a time series binary classification problem. The following is the overview of proposed method:

First of all, we divide the whole datasets into training datasets and testing datasets by 4:1. Therefore, 80% of the data is taken as training datasets and 20% of the data is taken as testing datasets. Then, we do preprocess on dataset. The preprocessing includes two parts. The first part is carried out on the whole datasets to aggregate the behavior records of participants from raw datasets into behavior sequences, and each participant corresponds to one behavior sequence. The second part is only carried out on the training datasets. Based on the time of the each behavior record, the behavior record are aggregated into different sub-sequences, each sub-sequence corresponds to one learning process, so that each participant will correspond to several sub-sequences. The whole sequence of learning behaviors obtained in this part are taken as the input of the Sequence Pattern Mining Algorithm, and the frequent sub-sequences are obtained from the output. These frequent sub-sequences will be used as the important features in our model. Then, we use four common classification algorithms to model, train the model through the training datasets, and verify the performance of the model on the testing datasets (Fig. 2).

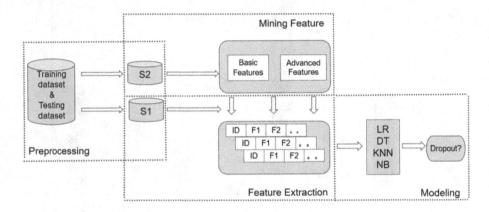

Fig. 2. Distributions of seven behavior records.

4.2   Data Preprocessing

First of all, we extract enrollment_id, time, event from log_train.csv file. Then the extracted data is cleaned to prepare for the next step of processing. Among them, "event" contains seven behavior types, and each type of behavior corresponds to one type of operation of the participant interacting with the learning system, and for the convenience of processing, we map these seven learning behaviors into 1 to 7 in the following order: problem, video, access, wiki, discussion, navigate, and page_close. The following is the main process of preprocessing, which is divided into two parts:

Part I: In this part, we directly aggregated the behavior records of each participant into an behavior sequence in chronological order, so that the learning activity of each participant was corresponding to one behavior sequence, and we could obtain the behavior sequence of all participants in this way. The experimental results generated in this part can be expressed as follows: The behavior sequence of the participant with Enrollment_id 1 is, and all behavior sequences are denote as dataset S1. For example, the behavior sequence corresponding to the participant with Enrollment ID 1 was 63331..., the length of this behavior sequence is 314.

Part II: In this part, we aggregate the participants' behavior records to varying degrees. We also draw some lessons from the previous studies, the researchers aggregate the behavior records of the participants in a day or a week's time, which make the behavior sequence more tidy on the format, but still not enough to find more underlying rule because the time granularity is not small enough. Therefore, with the time of each behavior record takes place, we aggregate the records with a time interval of no more than 30 min between adjacent behaviors in a day into one sequence. In this way, each participant's learning activity corresponds to several sequences, and each sequence represents one learning process. (The time interval used to divide is an empirical value adopted on the basis of fully studying the rules of the dataset.) The experimental results generated in this part can be expressed as follows: the behavior sequence corresponding to the participant with enrollment_id i is, where is participant's total number of learning processes. All behavior sequences are denote as dataset S2. And both the S1 and S2 datasets will be used in Sect. 4.3.

4.3 Mining Features

In this section, we describe the feature engineering in detail. The features adopted in this paper are mainly composed of two parts, one is the basic features, the other is the advanced features obtained through the Sequence Pattern Mining Algorithm. There are nine basic features, seven of them are the frequency of seven basic learning behaviors, which have been introduced in Part 3, including problem, video, access, wiki, discussion, navigate, and page_close. The other two basic features can be obtained through the processing in the second part of Sect. 4.2. One is the total number of the participant's learning process, represented by t_i, where i is the enrollment_id. The other is the total time of participants' learning activities, represented by T_i, $T_i = \sum T_{it_i}$, where T_{it_i} is the duration of the t_ith learning process for the participant whose enrollment_id is i.

Advanced features are obtained through the Sequence Pattern Mining Algorithm. Sequence pattern mining is a kind of association analysis algorithm in data mining. Different from ordinary association analysis, inputting sequence of this algorithm is ordered, and the output sub-sequences are also ordered. Sequence pattern mining refers to the knowledge discovery process, which aim to find frequent sub-sequences as patterns from the original sequence dataset, that is, inputting a sequence dataset and outputting the sub-sequences that are not less than the minimum support degree. Therefore, the sub-sequences obtained through sequence mining can represent more valuable information contained in the original sequence. In this paper, the dataset adopted for sequence pattern mining is the S2 dataset obtained in Sect. 4.2, which contains all behavior sequences of all participants in the training dataset. In this paper, we use the idea of Apriori algorithm to design a simple sequence mining algorithm. Starting with seven single learning behaviors as a candidate item set, the whole S2 dataset is searched and count the support degree for each candidate item. The items whose support degree is greater than the minimum support threshold are entered into the next iteration as candidate items. In the process of generating the candidate binomial set, we only combine the items whose support degree is greater than the minimum support threshold to generate the candidate binomial set, and then iterate the above steps. Finally, the resulting frequent sub-sequence is used as the advanced features. Where, the support degree is the proportion of sub-sequences occurring in the entire dataset. The formula is as follows:

$$\text{Support}(seq) = P(seq) = \frac{\text{number}(seq)}{\text{num}(\text{AllSamples})} \tag{1}$$

4.4   Feature Extraction and Modeling

Firstly, we introduce the details of feature mining. The basic features obtained in Sect. 4.3 include the frequency of the seven basic behaviors, as well as the number of participants' learning processes and the total time of participants' learning activities. In the training stage, the frequency of the seven basic behaviors needs to be obtained from the training dataset in S1, and the other two basic features are obtained from the training dataset in S2. The pattern sub-sequences used as the advanced features are obtained from the training dataset in S2, which are a series of frequent sub-sequences of participants' behavior sequences. We calculate the frequency of these pattern sub-sequences occurred in S1, then we get the advanced features values. The extracted basic features and advanced features are taken as the features of participants, and all of these features are used for training. In the test stage, similar to the processing in the training stage, the frequency of the seven basic behaviors needs to be obtained from the testing dataset in S1, and the other two basic features are obtained from the testing dataset in S2. The advanced features are obtained by using the sub-sequence extracted in the training stage to get their frequency from the testing dataset in S1. The basic features and advanced features obtained in this way are used as features of participants, and all of these features are used for testing.

In modeling, we adopted four common classification algorithms, including Logistic Regression, Decision Tree, K-Nearest Neighbor and Gaussian Naive Bayes. These four models are briefly introduced as follows: Logistic Regression: Logistic Regression is a commonly used classification algorithm in machine learning. Its principle is to classify different data by fitting a decision boundary, which can be expressed as: $w_1 x_1 + w_2 x_2 + \ldots + w_n x_n + b = 0$, Suppose $h_w(x) = w_1 x_1 + w_2 x_2 + \ldots + w_n x_n + b < 0$ represents that sample X belongs to category 0, and then when $h_w(x) > 0$, means that sample X belongs to category 1. Logical regression algorithm adds a layer of sigmoid function on this basis, so that $0 \leq h_w(x) \leq 1$. The final logistic regression calculation formula is:

$$y = \frac{1}{1 + e^{-(w^T x + b)}} \tag{2}$$

Decision Tree: Decision Tree is a commonly used classification algorithm. A decision tree is a tree-shaped structure in which each internal node represents a judgment on an attribute, each branch represents the output of a judgment result, and finally each leaf node represents a classification result. The decision tree classifies the samples by their different judgment results on each attribute.

K-Nearest Neighbor: K-nearest Neighbor algorithm is one of the simplest machine learning algorithms. The idea of this method is as follows: In the feature space, if most of the nearest k samples near a sample belong to a certain category, then the sample also belongs to this category.

Gaussian Naive Bayes theorem: Naive Bayes theory hypothesis that each input variable is independent of each other. And it build the model through the calculation of the probability of each category denoted as $P(Cj)$, and conditional probability of each attribute denoted as $P(Ai \mid Cj)$.

5 Experiment

The experiment of this paper mainly includes dataset preprocessing, feature mining, feature extraction, modeling, training and testing with four classification algorithms. All the codes used in the experiment were coded in Python language, and the four classification algorithms were coded with the package of Scikit-Learn Algorithm. In the training process, we use the GridSearchCV module provided in Scikit-Learn to tune the model's parameters.

Section 5.1 is divided into three parts. Section 5.1.1 introduces feature mining, experimental details in the modeling, and parameter tuning strategies in the modeling; Sect. 5.1.2 introduces the criteria for model performance evaluation adopted in the experiment. Section 5.2 is the analysis of the experimental results in this paper and the comparison with the experimental results we referenced.

5.1 Experiment Settings

Experiment Settings and Details. This section describes the setup of the experiment, including details of the feature mining and modeling. In Sect. 4.3, we have introduced the feature mining method proposed in this paper, including the mining of basic features and advanced features, in which the basic features can be obtained only by further processing on the basis of S1 and S2 datasets, and the process is not complicated. However, advanced features, that are frequent pattern sub-sequences contained in participants' learning activity sequences, need to be obtained by repeated iteration of sequence pattern mining algorithm on the basis of S2 dataset. Therefore, in feature mining experiments, we mainly introduce the details of this part of the experiment.

The key step in the sequence pattern mining algorithm is calculating the support degree of candidate sub-sequences and select the candidate for the next round according to the support degree result. Here we start from seven individual behavior as the initial candidates, according to the output of the algorithm, we make heuristic choices. And this selection method is very simple, that is to divide the candidate sequence into a group with high support and a group with low support according to the experimental result. The threshold for dividing needs to be determined according to the specific results of the experiment.

Here we directly present the experimental results obtained according to the advanced features mining method in Sect. 4.3, and the results are shown in the following three figures:

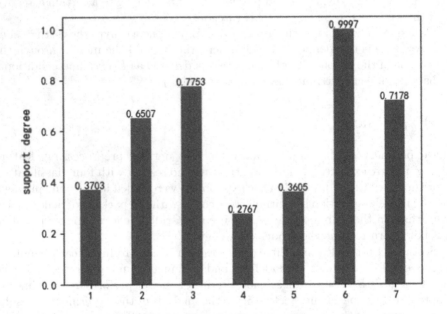

Fig. 3. Support degree of one element item set.

It can be clearly concluded from Fig. 4 that, in one element item set, we should select 2, 3, 6 and 7 to enter the next iteration of the algorithm. Then, we combine them into the binomial sequences: 23, 26, 27, 32, 33, 36, 37, 62, 63, 66, 67, 77, 72, 73, 76, 76, 77. These sequences are fed into the algorithm to calculate their support degree, and the same heuristic rules mentioned above are used to select the binomial sequences as the next round candidates. Then do the same iteration. According to the results in Fig. 3, 4 and 5, we set the minimum support threshold as 50% to obtain the pattern sub-sequence that meets our requirements. Finally, we obtained two sets of advanced features:

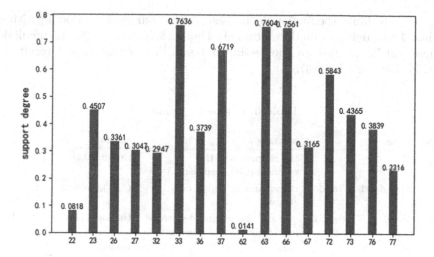

Fig. 4. Support degree of two elements item.

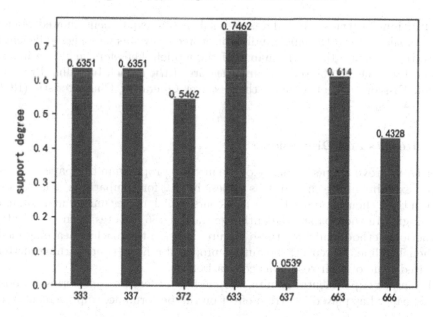

Fig. 5. Support degree of three elements item.

the two elements sub-sequences are 33, 37, 63, 66, 72; The three elements sub-sequences are 333, 337, 372, 633, 663. We refer the nine basic features mentioned above as feature set A, the five binomial sequences as feature set B, and the five trinomial sequences as feature set C.

In the experiment above, we get three groups of progressive feature sets, which are A, A+B and A+B+C respectively. The three feature sets are respectively used to build the model on the basis of the four classification algorithms, so that 12 models are finally obtained. The performance of the 12 prediction models will be verified on the testing datasets. The experimental results are given in Sect. 5.2 (Table 3).

Table 3. Parameter tuning.

Model	Parameter	Meaning	Range
LR	C	the reciprocal of the regularization coefficient λ	(0.1–0.5,0.1)
DT	Max_depth, Criterion	the maximum depth, creation strategy	(1,21),(entropy, gini)
KNN	Weights, N_neighbors	consider the weight of distance or not, number of neighbors	(uniform, distance), (1–11,1)
NB	none	none	none

Evaluation Metrics. The datasets used in our experiment showed obvious class imbalance, and the single indicator of Accuracy was no longer sufficient to accurately measure the performance of the model. Therefore, multiple indexes are used together as the prediction indicators of the model, Including Precision, Recall, F1-score and area under the Receiver Operating Characteristic (ROC) curve (AUC).

5.2   Results and Discussion

In order to prove the performance of the method proposed in this paper, we refer to the experimental results of this papers in [10] for comparison. The datasets used in these their papers is the same as ours, which makes our comparison more meaningful. In their paper, the author extracted 186 features by manual feature extraction method, and used these features to train the machine learning model as their baseline. Moreover, the author proposed a novel deep learning method. We cited some of their results as comparison.

From our experimental results, the method of feature engineering proposed in this paper has played a certain effect on the performance improvement of the

Table 4. Some experimental results in [10].

Method	Precision	Recall	F1-score	Auc
LR	89.17	96.12	92.52	87.70
DT	84.57	97.87	90.74	80.03
NB	89.89	92.52	91.18	77.40
CNN-RNN	88.62	96.55	92.41	87.42

Table 5. Experimental results in our experiment.

Method	Precision	Recall	F1-score	Auc
LR(A)	85.11	95.71	90.10	69.91
LR(A+B)	85.40	95.70	90.25	70.55
LR(A+B+C)	85.41	95.69	90.26	70.57
DT(A)	91.04	95.24	93.09	81.98
DT(A+B)	91.21	95.53	93.32	82.41
DT(A+B+C)	91.29	95.50	93.35	82.54
KNN(A)	93.07	96.40	94.70	86.22
KNN(A+B)	93.50	96.76	95.11	87.16
KNN(A+B+C)	93.60	96.89	95.21	87.38
NB(A)	85.31	94.82	89.82	70.18
NB(A+B)	86.38	93.99	90.02	72.26
NB(A+B+C)	86.77	93.64	90.07	72.99

four models. Taking the experimental results of DT model as an example, the Auc-score is 81.98% when only the basic feature set A is used. When feature sets A and B are used, the Auc-score is 82.41%. When all feature sets A, B, and C are used, the Auc-score is 82.54%. Similarly, this trend of improvement appears on the other three models, which indicates that the advanced features that we extract can improve the performance of the model (Tables 4 and 5).

By comparing the experimental results of the same model in the paper we quoted, it can be found that the performance of our proposed method on DT and KNN models is comparable to its best results, in which our Auc-score on DT and KNN model is higher, and our performance on LR model and NB model is poor. However, we should point out that the experiment in this paper adopts a simple feature extraction scheme, and the maximum number of features used in the experiment is only 19. Compared with the 186 features manually extracted in the citation paper, it is obvious that the feature engineering scheme in this paper is more efficient. At the same time, the experiments in this paper have shown good results on the KNN model, which is comparable to the performance of the depth model proposed in the citation paper.

6 Conclusion

In this paper, the Sequence Pattern Mining Algorithm is used to extract the subsequences contained in the long sequence, which can better represent the hidden rules in the sequence of learning behaviors. At the same time, the features used in this paper are all from the behavioral data and do not include other types of additional data recorded by the platform. Through extensive experiments, we can find that the method proposed in this paper has a good performance on DT and KNN based models. In future work, we hope to verify the performance of the model on more datasets. In addition, we will further study and analyze the performance of our feature mining method on different classification algorithms.

References

1. Kloft, M., Stiehler, F., Zheng, Z., Pinkwart, N.: Predicting MOOC dropout over weeks using machine learning methods. In: Proceedings of the EMNLP 2014 Workshop on Analysis of Large Scale Social Interaction in MOOCs (2014)
2. Khalil, H., Ebner, M.: MOOCs completion rates and possible methods to improve retention - a literature review. In: World Conference on Educational Multimedia, Hypermedia and Telecommunications 2014 (ED-Media) (2014)
3. Peng, D., Aggarwal, G.: Modeling MOOC dropouts. Entropy 10(114), 1–5 (2015)
4. Bailey, J., Zhang, R., Rubinstein, B., He, J.: Identifying at-risk students in massive open online courses. In: AAAI (2015)
5. Sharkey, M., Sanders, R.: A process for predicting MOOC attrition, pp. 50–54 (2014). https://doi.org/10.3115/v1/W14-4109
6. Yang, D., Sinha, T., Adamson, D., Rose, C.P.: "Turn on, tune in, drop out": anticipating student dropouts in massive open online courses. In: NIPS Workshop on Data Driven Education (2013)
7. Manhães, L., Cruz, S., Zimbrão, G.: Evaluating performance and dropouts of undergraduates using educational data mining (2014)
8. Pal, S.: Mining educational data to reduce dropout rates of engineering students. Int. J. Inf. Eng. Electron. Bus. 4(2), 1–7 (2012)
9. Fei, M., Yeung, D.Y.: Temporal models for predicting student dropout in massive open online courses. In: IEEE International Conference on Data Mining Workshop (2015)
10. Wei, W., Han, Y., Miao, C.: Deep model for dropout prediction in MOOCs. In: The 2nd International Conference (2017)
11. Wu, N., Zhang, L., Gao, Y., Zhang, M., Sun, X., Feng, J.: CLMS-Net: dropout prediction in MOOCs with deep learning, pp. 1–6 (2019). https://doi.org/10.1145/3321408.3322848
12. Whitehill, J., Mohan, K., Seaton, D., Rosen, Y., Tingley, D.: Delving deeper into MOOC student dropout prediction (2017)
13. Sinha, T., Li, N., Jermann, P., Dillenbourg, P.: Capturing "attrition intensifying" structural traits from didactic interaction sequences of MOOC learners. In: EMNLP Workshop on Modelling Large Scale Social Interaction in Massive Open Online Courses [SHARED TASK WINNER] (2014)
14. Balakrishnan, Eecs, G.: Predicting student retention in massive open online courses using hidden Markov models (2013)

CVO: Curriculum Vitae Optimization by Recommending Keywords to Undergraduate Students

Cibele Santos[1]([✉]) [ID], Fabrício Góes[2] [ID], Carlos Martins[3] [ID],
and Felipe da Cunha[4] [ID]

[1] Post-Graduation Program in Electrical Engineering, Pontifícia Universidade
Católica de Minas Gerais, Belo Horizonte, MG 30535-901, Brazil
`cibelesimoesoliveira@gmail.com`
[2] Informatics Department, University of Leicester, Leicester, UK
`fabricio.goes@leicester.ac.uk`
[3] Post-Graduation Program in Informatics, Pontifícia Universidade Católica de
Minas Gerais, Belo Horizonte, MG 30535-901, Brazil
`capsm@pucminas.br`
[4] Department of Computer Science, Pontifícia Universidade Católica de Minas
Gerais, Belo Horizonte, MG 30535-901, Brazil
`felipe@pucminas.br`

Abstract. Candidate selection platforms have been widely used in companies that seek agility in the process of hiring. Candidates who do not meet the requirements of a job vacancy are disqualified in the first step, called screening. This stage has been automated due to the large volume of curriculum vitae (CV) of candidates per vacancy, particularly for internship vacancies. As a consequence, candidates receive little to none feedback and do not know how to improve/optimize their CVs for new applications. The goal of this paper is to realize the curriculum vitae optimization (CVO) process for internship vacancies by implementing a recommendation system that given an undergraduate student CV, it suggests the addition of relevant keywords, taking into account the student's undergraduate course. This system is implemented based on the clustering of CVs keywords, from an internship recruitment private company database, into profile groups which are linked to internship vacancies. The experimental results showed that recommendations improved students CVs similarity (competitiveness within a specific field) from 18.83%, with 3 keywords recommendation, up to 50.67%, with 10 words.

Keywords: Clustering · Curriculum Vitae Optimization · Keywords Recommendation

1 Introduction

The undergraduate student career starts with an internship, where they can practice the skills learned at the university. However, there is an increasing competition for internship vacancies, in which students are first evaluated by their

R. Hou et al. (Eds.): BDTA 2022, LNICST 480, pp. 279–293, 2023.
https://doi.org/10.1007/978-3-031-33614-0_19

curriculum vitae (CV) [14]. However, crafting a CV is not an easy task, particularly in online recruitment. Each CV can be seen as a webpage and requires the careful use of relevant keywords to be better ranked in recruitment search engines such as Linkedin. This process is similar to SEO (search engine optimization) techniques for improving website ranking on search engines. We thus call the process of improving CVs in this context CVO (curriculum vitae optimization) [15]. Most online services for internship applications are focused on making it easier and efficient for companies recruiters to identify potential candidates instead of helping undergraduate students improve their CVs, increasing their odds of being invited for an internship interview.

This problem has been identified in previous work such as [6], the majority of recommendation systems focus on job search services and simple recommendations, ignoring the specific needs of undergraduates seeking a first job opportunity. Those students usually do not have any professional experience and the required skills for a full job position. One way used by authors was to propose a system that uses the student grade in university combined with machine learning algorithms to find the best match between students and internships. On the other hand, to find similarity between profiles, [16] focuses his research on calculating the similarity between two profiles where values of shared characteristics are extracted and clustered for a specific job position. Both approaches are aimed at classifying skills according to the job position rather than providing feedback for candidates on how to improve their CVs.

This paper aims to realize the curriculum vitae optimization (CVO) process for internship vacancies by implementing a recommendation system that gives an undergraduate student CV; it suggests the addition of relevant keywords, taking into account the student's undergraduate course. This system is implemented based on the clustering of CVs keywords, from an internship recruitment private company database, into profile groups that are linked to internship vacancies. It enables undergraduate students to improve their CVs using skill recommendations and feedback to achieve effectiveness in an internship job. The profile groups were able to cluster students into 9 groups, covering the most popular undergraduate courses. The recommendations improved students' CVs similarity (competitiveness within a specific field) from 18.83% with three keywords recommendation. The main contributions are listed below:

1. We developed a methodology using machine learning-based clustering and classification techniques with similarity functions are used to enable the undergraduates to understand their CVs.
2. The use of NLP techniques focused on undergraduate students, not on the recruitment process.
3. The recommending CVs keywords made it possible to know the level of an internship candidate's resume about its competitors and enable undergraduate students to improve their CVs.

   The rest of this paper is organized as follows. In Sect. 2, the Related Work is presented. In Sect. 3, there is the Methodology. Next, Sect. 4 presents and analyzes the Experimental Results. This paper is concluded in Sect. 5.

2   Related Work

This section presents the related work regarding candidates skills selection, clustering techniques and recommendation systems for job positions.

2.1   Candidate Skills Selection

According to [9], The skills selection of a candidate for a vacancy is determined by two aspects: the technical aspect, known as hard skills, and by the personal aspect, known as soft skills. This second determines the motivational aspects of an individual, generally ignored in selection systems, since such systems correlate job requirements with candidates' hard skills. However, looking for these characteristics, recruiters use recommendation platforms to group characteristics in job positions. Also, the authors have innovated using the concepts of gamification and crowdsourcing to rank candidates according to job requirements but selecting deterministic characteristics, such as Sex and Age, that reduced the diversity of the database.

The work of [16] emphasizes the importance of pre-processing the characteristics before associating the candidate with others. The authors highlighted three steps for the correct selection of profiles. The first step is screening, removing insignificant records, in some cases with too many missing values or with a slight variation to be helpful. The second is the classification of attributes, allocating the established importance of each attribute. The third step is the selection that identifies the cluster of resources to apply subsequent models. This pre-processing allows to focus on the relevant parts of the data and improve the algorithm's capacity. The paper focused mainly on job positions and not candidates.

In [8], the authors used the NLP (Natural Language Processing) to extract the words of a resume. It was possible to load single or multiple resumes into the program and convert them into a standard text format which is later analyzed for the necessary information. The Extracted data is organized in a defined standard format to be later downloaded in CSV format. As a result, the authors classified the primary data of the candidates into their standard text format with processed and clean text. In [19], IBM created a platform for internal transfer of professionals in positions at IBM, statistically measuring employees who could or could not be transferred based on the keywords of their CVs. This search was done by using the experience taxonomy of the positions with the requirements of the jobs. Although they used keywords of skills like "Cisco certification" to correspond the employee with the job positions, these authors did not use any techniques to calculate the correspondence between profiles. A taxonomy was also used by [5] that created a recommendation system of job positions using profile data from Facebook and LinkedIn. The researchers used the statistical technique of frequency inversion TF-IDF combined with the SVM algorithm to search jobs for people with similar interests.

In the selection of characteristics, the difference of this research among the others is the focus of intern profiles that, in the majority, do not have pre-defined experiences. The database diversity is also considered to avoid bias, so characteristics such as sex and age are not established in the private database used. The unprecedented steps in [16] and [8] are relevant in this research, with the difference of the focus being not vacancies but intern profiles. Finally, statistical measures are also used as applied on [19] and [5].

2.2   Clustering of CVs

The second step after selecting characteristics is to find similarities between profiles that share common characteristics. This similarity can be achieved through the technique known as clustering [16], specifically Text clustering, which is an unsupervised machine learning technique [11].

In [18], clustering algorithms such as K-Means, fuzzy C-Means, and classification were used to understand which attributes are most determinant in the selection of recently graduated candidates. The results showed that classification algorithms like Decision Tree had better accuracy than the other algorithms when evaluated separately. However, the combination of clustering algorithms with classification algorithms was not evaluated for profiles. In this same context, [7] combined the use of classification and clustering algorithms to predict the academic performance of students. The authors highlighted the importance of these techniques for the decision-making process and used the Confusion Matrix and ROC curve to verify which students would possibly have better academic performance in the exams.

The research of [6] used the student historical academic data to find intern positions according to the grades of students at university. The system reads the academic data of the university candidate for the position, evaluates the profile, and presents positions opened by companies in this same system. The proposed algorithm involving probabilistic neighborhood selection and clustering of priority k-Medoids (a K-Means partition) are used to help improve the accuracy and diversity of recommendation results.

To segment, a large amount of big data job recruitment information, the work of [4] combined with stuttering word segmentation and regular uses K-means text clustering to divide big data jobs into ten different categories (using the sum of squares method) and explore the needs of big data jobs. As a result, the actual perspective of the big data industry was presented, especially about the experience level of job positions.

In clustering of CVs, the contribution of this research compared to other works is the identification of the profiles clusters based on the classification of the characteristics that generate the clustering of the approved candidates and the similarity of the skill set of the candidate's profile. Therefore, a cluster that generates a significant distance from the profile to the internship position through the keyword trend should be shared with the candidate for possible change or adaptation of this tendency CV.

2.3   Recommendation Systems

Recommendation Systems were developed through a set of tools and techniques that give suggestions to a user about specific items that can be of their interest [10]. According to [21] in their research, the concepts among recommendation systems involve the Target User, the Desired Profile, and the similarity between these entities. Once these entities are identified, the research highlighted three different types of recommendation systems such as *Collaborative Filtering Recommenders (CFRs)*, *Content-Based Recommenders (CBRs)* and *Knowledge-Based Recommenders (KBRs)*, which is the concept of development of a recommendation system.

Using Content-Based recommendation systems, in [1], the objective of the research was the recommendation of candidates for job positions by quantifying the suitability of a candidate for a job through intervals. They used structured and unstructured data in which each candidate received a value for each of the required qualifications. Finally, according to the qualification, the candidates were indicated or not to the job position using the distance of Minkowski. In work proposed by [3], the authors focused on necessary and desirable skills (also referred to as preferred skills) that are not identified by recommendation systems, such as different grades. Their research showed how plain keyword-based vacancy-to-jobseeker matching might result in improper matching, which means that it is essential to recommend skills that make sense with the candidate's CV.

In order to find better accuracy in skill recommendation, some systems use the combination of more than one machine learning model creating Hybrid Recommendation Systems (*Hybrid Recommenders (HR)*). In [12], were identified necessary skills for allocating people in jobs using the combination of the algorithms BayesMatch and NpBayesMatch models as recommendation algorithms and associating with other members. Combining Machine Learning Classification SVM algorithm and Content-Based Recommendation, [17] used Cosine Similarity Index in their recommendation model to take the job description and CVs as input and provide the list of CVs which are closest to a provided job description. The proposed approach effectively captures the resume insights, their semantics and yielded an accuracy of 78.53% with a linear SVM classifier.

In recommendation, the works focused on the indication of vacancies, not worrying about the recommend of the profile of a candidate that did not pass in a processor was no indication for a vacancy, for example. As [17], we used Cosine Similarity Index but focused on the undergraduate students and groups. In this work, we intend to characterize the groups in order to evolve them where, in addition to the recommendation of skills to intern positions, we also provide feedback, based on the keywords of the curriculum related to the *hard skills* of the candidates.

3   Methodology

This methodology section presents the techniques, database, and tools used to cluster the profile groups by keywords and build the recommendation system. Figure 1 shows the methodology. The remaining subsections follow this flowchart.

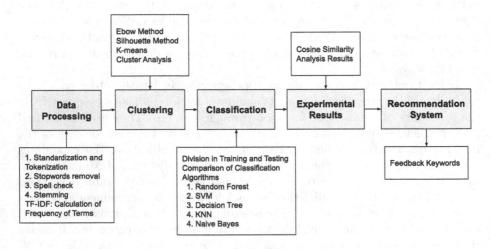

Fig. 1. Methodology steps from NLP to Experimental Results

3.1   Dataframe

The analysis of this research is focused on the keywords of undergraduate students CVs focused on internship vacancies. The private dataset consists of a database with user identifiers, courses, cities and keywords previously 163885 undergraduate students CVs from Brazilian universities (the database is in Portuguese) available in JSON format by an internship recruitment company.

3.2   Data Processing

In the NLP stage, the preprocessing of the data was made. During this preprocessing, the words were unified by a user, creating a single record for each user. After this unification, the normalization step started.

In the normalization step, in addition to removing columns that contained duplicate information, the vectorization process allowed the cleaning of words, removing special characters and null records. In this stage, words like "turno" (shift) and "habilidades comportamentais" (behavioral skills) were also removed since the focus is on hard skills. The words related to the courses have been removed since the objective is to seek as many skills as possible. This step was reduced to 7202 candidates/CVs (rows) and three columns: User ID, Course, and Standardized Keywords.

The second stage of data processing was the removal of stopwords, which are words that are considered irrelevant in a search. For example: "do", "da", "os"; generally used in names of courses and technologies such as "computer science", in this case "da", is a *stopword*. In this step, the Python NLKT library was used, and then all the stopwords from the Portuguese dictionary were imported. The functions below were used to remove *stopwords* for each record of each user: *remove_stop_words()*, *remove_pt_br_char_by_text()* and *replace_ptbr_char_by_word()*

In the third step, stemming was performed, that is, given the set of words from the *corpus*, the lexicographic parts of the terms are obtained. In short, this generalizes the words, transforming each user's words to a set of words in common with other users. For example, the words "engenheiro", "engenharia"(engineer), "engenheira" have the same radical "engenh", so the algorithm transforms these words into this single radical.

TF-IDF. After normalizing the data, the Term Frequency-Inverse Document Frequency (TF-IDF) method was used, which calculates the frequency of a document in the set of documents (corpus). Equation 1 shows its formula.

$$tf\_idf_{t,d} = tf_{t,d} \cdot log \frac{N}{df_t} \tag{1}$$

$tf\_idf_{t,d}$ = Inverse frequency of the term in the document.
$tf_{t,d}$ = Occurency of the frequency of the term t in the document d.
N = Total number of documents.
df_t = Number of documents with the term t.

The calculation was done by importing the TfIdfVectorizer method, found in the sklearn module (library also in Python). The result of this method was a numerical set of the frequency of terms in each document. An essential point of this stage was the use of bigrams; that is, a bigram is an n-gram for n = 2, this means the composition of terms with two words like "banco dados" (database).

3.3 Clustering

In order to find the optimal number of clusters, two techniques were used: the Elbow Technique (Elbow Method) [20] and the Silhouette [20]. Both were applied in the range of 2 to 30 K values. Moreover, they demonstrated that after 9, there were not many variations in the distance of the terms in the set. After obtaining this optimum number, the K-means algorithm was used in the cluster, wherein Fig. 2 the result of the clustering is presented.

Then, we analyzed the terms closest to the centroid, and we created a dictionary of clusters with names that made more sense to the words found in each cluster. The suggested names based on course names were: *Generic Administration; Accounting Sciences; Psychology; Civil Law; Web Development; Human Resources; Generic Customer Service; Advertising and Journalism* and *Civil*

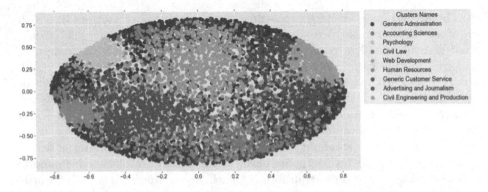

Fig. 2. Clustering result of profiles by each cluster (Color figure online)

Engineering and Production. Among the analyzed clusters, one in particular, consisting of sets of words present in most of the others, however, without much intensity. This cluster was called "Generic Administration" and can be seen in dark blue in Fig. 2.

In Fig. 3, as the words get closer to the cluster center, the more related among the profiles of that cluster they are and the larger the word size also in the presentation. For example, in the "Civil Law" cluster, the radicals "tributari", "civil" and "trabalh" are closer to the radical "direit". This means that resumes of candidates for "Law" job positions have mostly these words highlighted.

Fig. 3. Top 50 words by each cluster

3.4   Classification

After the grouped dataset and the respective clusters, the data was divided into 80% training and 20% testing using the module *train_test_split* from the sklearn library of the python library to then classify the data. Five classification algorithms were chosen for comparison: *Random Forest* [2], *SVM* [17], *Decision Tree* [18], *KNN* [13] and *Naive Bayes* [7].

After the execution of the algorithms, two metrics were obtained, the *Score* where the algorithm with the best classification performance was the *SVM* with 0.9269 according to Table 1 and the metric *Accuracy*, where the algorithm with the best performance was also *SVM* with 94.71%. The accuracy metric was obtained through the *Cross Validation* validation method, which consists of assessing the generalization of the model. This metric was also used by [17] to evaluate the performance of the models. All executions were performed on the same training and test set in each algorithm.

Table 1. Classification Score and Accuracy of Execution Results.

Method	Score	Accuracy (%)
SVM	0.92694	94.71
Random Forest	0.90472	92.29
Decision Tree	0.81725	85.84
KNN	0.75963	77.24
Naive Bayes	0.65741	76.87

Once the classifier was chosen, in this case, using the SVM algorithm, the profiles were classified. The generic cluster("Generic Administration") is the largest one with 2591 CVs. This large size is due to the low variability of words in the profile or words not very relevant to the cluster in question. These 9 clusters cover the majority of the profiles in the private base.

4   Experimental Results

After the model is trained and the CVs are classified, it is time to calculate the distance of each CV to the clusters. Also, it is essential to understand the cluster itself, which means the cluster's relevance is due to vacancies.

4.1   Cosine Similarity

The 50 terms (remembering that the bigrams are involved) closest to the cluster's centroid were obtained to calculate the cosine similarity. This calculation is done by comparing two vectors that evaluate the cosine value of the angle between them. In this case, one of the vectors is the TF-IDF matrix of the 50 words closest to the cluster, and the other is the result of this matrix in vocabulary resulting from the words of the CV itself in each record of the data set.

It was observed in Fig. 4 that the cluster with the largest interval is the "Web Development" cluster. This means that this cluster has more adherent profiles and more common words among them. In other words, their cosine similarity has the highest levels. In contrast, the "Generic Administration" cluster has lower levels of cosine similarity.

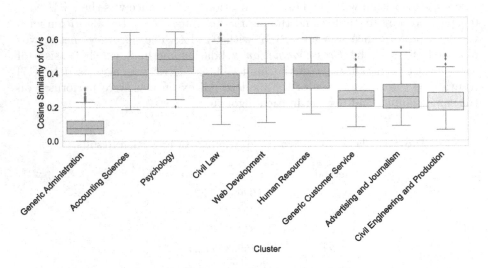

Fig. 4. Box-plot distribution of the cosine similarity among the clusters.

Once the profiles had the cosine similarity calculated, the cluster similarity was calculated with the words of internship vacancies found on job vacancy sites on the web. These words passed through an intersection, considering only the ones in the defined vocabulary. Using these vacancy words was created a classification profile quality, and the result can be seen in Fig. 5.

Labels were assigned to facilitate the understanding of the similarity calculation. Bellow the following classifications were considered:

1. If the CVs have more than 50% similarity with the cluster, it is considered "skilled."
2. If the CVs are between 25% and 50% similar to the cluster, it is considered "medium."
3. If the CVs have less than 25% similarity, it is considered "inexperienced."

For example, a profile with the words "sql sql sql banco dados banco dados redes comp...", with a similarity of 0.276385, has a profile considered "medium" because it does not yet have the most important words for a specific area. This is delivered as feedback to the student.

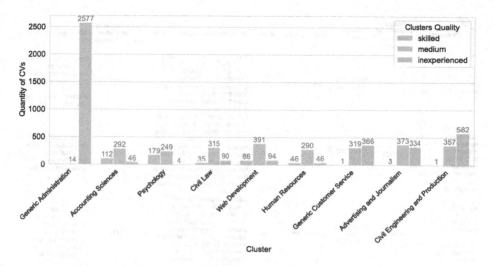

Fig. 5. Distribution of profiles quality among the clusters

4.2 Recommendation System

Once a candidate has already been classified into a cluster, and the similarity of cosine with the cluster was obtained, the result is the recommendation of keywords. The recommendation is based on the most relevant words in the cluster, that is, terms not present in the profile of the current candidate but are present in the profiles of the best candidates. In addition, the recommendation also presents feedback.

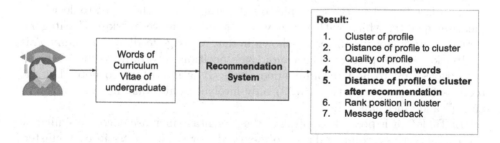

Fig. 6. Flow of undergraduate result feedback.

Figure 6 shows all the feedback that the model recommends, and Fig. 7 provides the complete feedback information for three different CVs. In these three records, it is possible to observe the keywords extracted from the CV in the column "CV words", the similarity of the cosine calculated with the words about the cluster, and the quality of the profile.

CV words	Cosine similarity of profile to cluster	Cluster name	Profile quality	Rank	CV words with recommendation	Cosine similarity of profile after recommendation	Message feedback
accounting accounting nursing nursing accounting accounting nursing nursing	0.2498	Accounting Sciences	inexperienced	1st	accounting accounting nursing nursing accounting accounting nursing nursing fiscal fiscal marketing point windows commercial law receptionist excel accounting department department personnel linkedin invoice fiscal accounting	0.4322	You are among the top 10 of the inexperienced profile on your cluster. Check our skills recommendations and improve your profile.
accounting secretary receptionist management people human resources accounting accounting secretary receptionist management people human resources accounting	0.2324	Accounting Sciences	inexperienced	17th	accounting secretary receptionist management people human resources accounting accounting secretary receptionist management people human resources accounting fiscal fiscal marketing point windows commercial law excel accounting department department personnel linkedin launch fiscal accounting point point	0.4321	Your profile is inexperienced. Check our skills recommendations and improve your profile.
adobe illustrator photoshop illustrator photoshop design marketing linkedin adobe illustrator photoshop illustrator photoshop design marketing linkedin	0.4652	Advertising and Journalism	medium	9th	adobe illustrator photoshop illustrator photoshop design marketing linkedin adobe illustrator photoshop illustrator photoshop design marketing linkedin graph linkedin behance social media digital content marketing excel premiere attendance networks english campaign media	0.5717	You are among the top 10 of the medium profile on your cluster. Check our skills recommendations to improve and have a skilled profile.

Fig. 7. Complete feedback results.

The first record shows a profile with an "inexperienced" category, which although it has this qualification, this profile is the best within the "Accounting Sciences" cluster with this qualification. Using a recommendation of 10 terms in the first record, as shown in the column "CV words with recommendation", it is possible to notice that if this profile is improved. It can reach a medium-quality profile, increasing the similarity from 0.2498 to 0.4322, according to the column "Cosine similarity of profile after recommendation" as well as the other profiles in the example had increased according to the word recommendation.

The last record in the example, on the other hand, shows a profile with a medium quality, which with the new terms, can achieve a "skilled" category, that is, suitable for vacancies, as shown in the "Message feedback" column. This feedback message presents the candidate's position according to his level and encourages him to add recommended words. It is important to note that the records for recommendation (6739) only involve profiles qualified as "inexperienced" and "medium".

In Table 2, it is possible to observe the percentage increase in cosine similarity according to the recommendation of keywords for student CVs in each cluster. The calculation of the percentage of increase was obtained from the average similarity before and after the recommendation of keywords, according to the columns. On average, all clusters had a significant increase when applying 3, 5, and 10 keywords recommendations. It is important to note that the comparison of these words from the CV and the recommended keywords were compared and calculated with the 50 keywords closest to the centroid of each cluster, that is, the most important keywords. Thus, the mean of the previous and following clusters of the recommendation was obtained.

Table 2. Result of recommendation with 3, 5 and 10 words in each cluster.

Cluster name	Similarity increase by suggesting 3 words (%)	Similarity increase by suggesting 5 words (%)	Similarity increase by suggesting 10 words (%)
Generic Administration	62.41	99.99	146.24
Accounting Sciences	12.01	17.32	38.26
Psychology	15.78	24.93	33.86
Civil Law	27.37	49.62	77.22
Web Development	15.24	22.39	36.58
Human Resources	9.73	20.07	33.70
Generic Customer Service	18.14	28.95	48.63
Advertising and Journalism	13.77	21.55	42.36
Civil Engineering and Prod.	32.62	57.83	86.32

Table 3. Result of general recommendation in clusters.

Recommendation	Mean cosine before recommend	Mean cosine after recommend	Similarity increase after keywords recommendation (%)
Recommendation of 3 words	0.289304	0.343768	18.83
Recommendation of 5 words	0.289304	0.379977	31.34
Recommendation of 10 words	0.289304	0.435906	50.67

Finally, Table 3 shows the Mean Cosine before and after a recommendation and the similarity in percentage with 3, 5, and 10 keywords. The results were positive with a minimum increase of 18.83% using only 3 terms, optimizing the student's CV.

5 Conclusion

The grouping of curriculum keywords brought up groups of profiles relevant to the context of the undergraduate students. In addition, it was possible to evaluate the classification of CVs in the groups generated by comparing different types of algorithms, where the algorithm with greater precision was the *SVM* method. It was possible to understand the distance of the profiles of undergraduate students in each cluster and the distance of this cluster with the vacancies. The use of clustering techniques allowed a reduction and optimization of comparisons of a candidate's profile with a vacancy.

The feedback for the inexperienced students, in terms of distance from a profile considered "skilled", made students aware of their CV competitiveness for internships in their respective fields. Once the candidate is in a cluster that does not match his course, he is also informed of this profile trend. Another essential piece of information is the student rank in a cluster. The experimental results showed that recommendations improved students' CVs similarity (competitiveness within a specific field) from 18.83%, with 3 keywords recommendation, up to 50.67%, with 10 words. It was also possible to provide a feedback message to the candidate and qualification of his profile and ranking against other candidates.

As future work, it is intended to expand the dataset to find new profiles of undergraduate CVs. Also, Deep Learning techniques can be implemented to find more keywords and skills relevant to the profiles of students who are starting their professional careers.

References

1. Almalis, N.D., Tsihrintzis, G.A., Karagiannis, N., Strati, A.D.: FoDRA - A new content-based job recommendation algorithm for job seeking and recruiting. In: IISA 2015–6th International Conference on Information, Intelligence, Systems and Applications. Institute of Electrical and Electronics Engineers Inc. (2016). https://doi.org/10.1109/IISA.2015.7388018
2. Bicego, M.: K-Random forests: a K-means style algorithm for random forest clustering. In: Proceedings of the International Joint Conference on Neural Networks. vol. 2019-July. Institute of Electrical and Electronics Engineers Inc. (2019). https://doi.org/10.1109/IJCNN.2019.8851820
3. Chala, S., Harrison, S., Fathi, M.: Knowledge extraction from online vacancies for effective job matching. In: Canadian Conference on Electrical and Computer Engineering. Institute of Electrical and Electronics Engineers Inc. (2017). https://doi.org/10.1109/CCECE.2017.7946793
4. Debao, D., Yinxia, M., Min, Z.: Analysis of big data job requirements based on k-means text clustering in china. PLoS ONE 16(8), 1–14 (2021). https://doi.org/10.1371/journal.pone.0255419
5. Diaby, M., Viennet, E.: Taxonomy-based job recommender systems on Facebook and LinkedIn profiles. In: Proceedings - International Conference on Research Challenges in Information Science. IEEE Computer Society (2014). https://doi.org/10.1109/RCIS.2014.6861048
6. Ding, Y., Zhang, Y., Li, L., Xu, W., Wang, H.: A reciprocal recommender system for graduates' recruitment. In: Proceedings - 2016 8th International Conference on Information Technology in Medicine and Education, ITME 2016, pp. 394–398. Institute of Electrical and Electronics Engineers Inc. (2017). https://doi.org/10.1109/ITME.2016.0094
7. Durairaj, M., Vijitha, C.: Educational data mining for prediction of student performance using clustering algorithms. Technical report Bharathidasan University, Tiruchirappalli, India (2014). 10.1.1.567.8824. https://www.ijcsit.com
8. Goyal, U., Negi, A., Adhikari, A., Gupta, S.C., Choudhury, T.: Resume data extraction using NLP. In: Singh, J., Kumar, S., Choudhury, U. (eds.) Innovations in Cyber Physical Systems. LNEE, vol. 788, pp. 465–474. Springer, Singapore (2021). https://doi.org/10.1007/978-981-16-4149-7_41
9. Harris, C.G.: Finding the best job applicants for a job posting: a comparison of human resources search strategies. In: IEEE International Conference on Data Mining Workshops, ICDMW. vol. 2017-November, pp. 189–194. IEEE Computer Society (2017). https://doi.org/10.1109/ICDMW.2017.31

10. Kanwal, S., Nawaz, S., Malik, M.K., Nawaz, Z.: A review of text-based recommendation systems. vol. 9, pp. 31638–31661. Institute of Electrical and Electronics Engineers Inc. (2021). https://doi.org/10.1109/ACCESS.2021.3059312
11. Liu, W., Lin, F., Hu, Z., Zhang, J.: Optimized clustering based on semantic similarity of components for short text. In: 2019 IEEE International Conference on Signal, Information and Data Processing (ICSIDP), pp. 1–6. Institute of Electrical and Electronics Engineers (IEEE) (2020). https://doi.org/10.1109/icsidp47821.2019.9173343
12. Maurya, A., Telang, R.: Bayesian multi-view models for member-job matching and personalized skill recommendations. In: Proceedings - 2017 IEEE International Conference on Big Data, Big Data 2017, vol. 2018-January, pp. 1193–1202. Institute of Electrical and Electronics Engineers Inc. (2018). https://doi.org/10.1109/BigData.2017.8258045
13. Narayanan, B.N., Djaneye-Boundjou, O., Kebede, T.M.: Performance analysis of machine learning and pattern recognition algorithms for Malware classification. In: Proceedings of the IEEE National Aerospace Electronics Conference, NAECON, pp. 338–342. Institute of Electrical and Electronics Engineers Inc. (2016). https://doi.org/10.1109/NAECON.2016.7856826
14. Pierre, J., Marie Jeanne, J.: Exploring the relationship between internship and employability. Tech. rep. (2020). https://researchspace.ukzn.ac.za/handle/10413/19258
15. Ramanath, R., et al.: Towards deep and representation learning for talent search at LinkedIn. In: International Conference on Information and Knowledge Management, Proceedings. vol. 9, pp. 2253–2262. Association for Computing Machinery, New York, NY, USA (2018). https://doi.org/10.1145/3269206.3272030
16. Rodriguez, L.G., Chavez, E.P.: Feature selection for job matching application using profile matching model. In: IEEE 4th International Conference on Computer and Communication Systems (ICCCS), pp. 263–266. Institute of Electrical and Electronics Engineers (IEEE) (2019). https://doi.org/10.1109/ccoms.2019.8821682
17. Roy, P.K., Chowdhary, S.S., Bhatia, R.: A machine learning approach for automation of resume recommendation system. Procedia Comput. Sci. **167**, 2318–2327 (2020). https://doi.org/10.1016/j.procs.2020.03.284, https://www.sciencedirect.com/science/article/pii/S187705092030750X. International Conference on Computational Intelligence and Data Science
18. Sivaram, N., Ramar, K.: Applicability of clustering and classification algorithms for recruitment data mining. Tech. Rep. 5, National Engineering College, Kovilpatti, India (2010). https://doi.org/10.5120/823-1165
19. Wei, D., Varshney, K.R., Wagman, M.: Optigrow: people analytics for job transfers. In: Proceedings - 2015 IEEE International Congress on Big Data, BigData Congress 2015, pp. 535–542. Institute of Electrical and Electronics Engineers Inc. (2015). https://doi.org/10.1109/BigDataCongress.2015.84
20. Yuan, C., Yang, H.: Research on k-value selection method of k-means clustering algorithm. Mult. Sci. J. **2**(2), 226–235 (2019). https://doi.org/10.3390/j2020016, https://www.mdpi.com/2571-8800/2/2/16
21. Zheng, S., Hong, W., Zhang, N., Yang, F.: Job recommender systems: a survey. In: ICCSE 2012 - Proceedings of 2012 7th International Conference on Computer Science and Education, pp. 920–924 (2012). https://doi.org/10.1109/ICCSE.2012.6295216

Hardware and Software Solutions
for Big Data Storing and Management

Big Data in Healthcare Institutions: An Architecture Proposal

José Lopes[1]⊙, Regina Sousa[2](✉)⊙, António Abelha[2]⊙, and José Machado[2]⊙

[1] University of Minho, Gualtar Campus, 4710-057 Braga, Portugal
a82207@alunos.uminho.pt
[2] ALGORITMI Research Center, School of Engineering, University of Minho,
Gualtar Campus, 4710-057 Braga, Portugal
regina.sousa@algoritmi.uminho.pt, {abelha,jmac}@di.uminho.pt

Abstract. Healthcare institutions are complex organizations dedicated to providing care to the population. Continuous improvement has made the care provided a factor of excellence in the population, improving people's daily lives and increasing average life expectancy. Even so, the resulting aging has caused patterns to increase day by day and the paradigm of medicine to shift from reaction to prevention. Often, the principle of evidence-based medicine is compromised by lack of evidence on pathogenic mechanisms, risk prediction, lack of resources, and effective therapeutic strategies. This is even more evident in pandemic situations. The current data management tools (centered in a single machine) do not have an ideal behavior for the processing of large amounts of information. This fact combined with the lack of sensitivity for the health area makes it imminent the need to create and implement an architecture that performs this management and processing effectively. In this sense, this paper aims to study the problem of knowledge construction from Big Data in health institutions. The main goal is to present an architecture that deals with the adversities of the big data universe when applied to health.

Keywords: Big Data · Healthcare Information Systems · Real-Time Information System · System Architecture

1 Introduction

Since 1985, with the invention of X-rays, medicine has been intrinsically linked to technology in such a way that it is considered dependent on it [1].

The innovations that have since been sprung up have guaranteed improvements in the quality of life of the community as well as cost reductions in the services provided to it. If, at first sight, everything is beneficial, and social and economic developments increase average life expectancy, the need for investment in health increases accordingly. In view of all this, the philosophy of the institutions has moved from medicine based on the interpretation of symptoms to solving a problem to a medicine that is not only preventive but also predictive [2,3].

© ICST Institute for Computer Sciences, Social Informatics and Telecommunications Engineering 2023
Published by Springer Nature Switzerland AG 2023. All Rights Reserved
R. Hou et al. (Eds.): BDTA 2022, LNICST 480, pp. 297–311, 2023.
https://doi.org/10.1007/978-3-031-33614-0_20

In healthcare institutions, all data are relevant. From the results of laboratory analyses, imaging methods (radiography, magnetic resonance imaging, etc.), to the collection of vital signs through sensors (blood pressure, heart rate, respiratory rate), everything is information with potential knowledge. In short, all data are important and necessary and as a consequence it is increasingly necessary and frequent to collect and store information with interest for the construction of knowledge and consequent evolution. With the evolution of the activity, the data associated with health are generated and aggregated continuously, resulting in large amounts of information in its raw state. This is how the concept of Big Data associated to health emerges [4,5].

The current management tools do not have an ideal behavior for the processing of large amounts of data [6]. Often, the principle of evidence-based medicine is compromised by lack of evidence on pathogenic mechanisms, risk prediction, lack of resources and effective therapeutic strategies. This is even more evident in pandemic situations [7].

Big Data as a research topic has as many opportunities as adversities. Issues such as ambiguity, resistance to change, privacy and information security, reliability and so many others, appear as soon as the subject is discussed. In this way, a robust architecture is essential, so that large-scale organizations, such as health institutions, can demonstrate rigorous evidence based on current techniques and technologies. Only then the progress be believed in a real context of data-driven business.

2   Main Concepts

2.1   Big Data in Healthcare Institutions

Today, Big Data is rooted in various business sectors, yet the health sector is one of those that contains this term, but only flying over all other information systems issues. Health institutions produce large amounts of data, although not everything is in digital format. This makes the processing of this data even more difficult. Besides the diversity of new forms of data (biometric sensors, three-dimensional images, among others), the need arises to digitize data previously recorded on paper [8].

Potential and Challenges of Big Data in Healthcare. With the emergence of several companies interested in the research and use of Large Data in health institutions, several gaps have been defined as priority research needs.

Therefore, the most pointed branches have been:

- The support of research, in a genetic context;
- Transformation of data into information;
- Support for self-care.

However, research on these issues is not always an easy process, much due to the resistance to change present in the nature of health professionals who have become accustomed to making decisions without the help of any other technology [9]. Moreover, whatever information technology is associated with health, it requires considerable investment with no certainty of return, which makes investment initiatives in this field more scarce than desired [10].

In recent years, the issue of privacy, data security and data ownership has been added to these two challenges, requiring great care with regard to access and processing of third party data [11,12]. Even so, over the years, some goals have been set with regard to the development of information systems. Goals such as increasing the efficiency of healthcare providers, reducing costs and errors, patient-centered and prevention-oriented medicine and personalized medicine have received much attention and investment.

Large data tools have a clear advantage over older technologies and approaches, allowing data analysis, management and processing regardless of format. Therefore, the same tool or processing technology can be used for structured, unstructured or semi-structured data, leading to the construction of relevant knowledge for healthcare institutions and professionals.

Data Sources in Healthcare Institutions. The data sources, in hospital environment, are embedded in the process of electronic health record, medical images, clinical notes or even genetic data [13,14]. Various information can be extracted from the electronic record, such as laboratory results, prescription records, billing data and examination details. In this way, it is necessary to understand the nature, format and use of each type of information:

1. Billing data: Billing data use various codes to document patient symptoms, clinical records and laboratory results;
2. Laboratory data: Laboratory data and vital signs are mostly in structured format. Currently, many dictionaries and various algorithms are developed to reduce complexity of laboratory data;
3. Drug records: Medication records are used to identify the precise characterization of the phenotype. In addition, drug registries are also used to improve disease diagnosis and drug recommendation in the healthcare industry;
4. Clinical notes: Clinical documentation often appears in an unstructured form. Clinical notes are also considered large data and scalable algorithms are used to process such large data;
5. Medical Images: Medical imaging is most often used for diagnosis, planning and therapeutic evaluation. Such data require huge storage space and fast algorithms to process and diagnose diseases. The main challenge with imaging data is that they are not only large in size, but also complex and multidimensional;
6. Documentation of Reports and Tests: Currently, the cost of human genome sequencing is decreasing rapidly with the refinement of high-performance sequencing tools and methods;
7. Sensor devices: Today, more viable medical devices are developed for the continuous monitoring of patient health. These devices generate an enormous amount of health data on an ongoing basis [15].

Data Types in Healthcare Institutions. The data, mainly in health institutions, comes from several sources with quite distinct natures. Thus, they can be classified as Structured, semi-structured or even Unstructured. Excel files, log files, imaging exams (X-rays) are examples of the three types of data, respectively. The following table presents the main differentiating characteristics of the three types of data (Table 1):

Table 1. Differences between structured, semi-structured, and unstructured data. Adapted from [16].

STRUCTURED DATA	SEMI-STRUCTURED DATA	UNSTRUCTURED DATA
Well defined schema	There is not always a scheme	There is no scheme
Regular Structure	Irregular Structure	Irregular Structure
Data independent structure	Embedded Data Structure	Data source-dependent structure
Reduced Structure	Extensive Structure	Extensive Structure
Not evolutive, rigid structure	Very evolutive structure	Very evolutive structure
Closed schemes, integrity restrictions	No associated data scheme	No associated data scheme
Clear distinction in data structure	Distinction in data structure	No distinguish between data structures

2.2 Big Data Engine - Hadoop

Definition. The term Hadoop is one of the most common in today's research technology vocabulary. With a distributed, open source processing structure it manages the processing and storage of data in scalable computer server clusters. To increase the processing capacity of the Hadoop cluster, it is possible to add more servers without having to have expensive memory and CPU resources.

Due to its extreme flexibility it allows organizations to frame and modify the system according to their needs. This technology is the center of an ecosystem of big data technologies that, dealing with various forms of data (structured, unstructured, semi-structured), collect, analyze and manage databases.

Although Hadoop is not considered a data warehouse, it acts as a software structure. Its operation is very briefly based on the distribution of large amounts of data to different nodes, combining the various results later. Therefore, Hadoop provides a high level of durability and availability, which makes it the ideal choice for large loads such as Big Data.

Advantages:

- Scalability: The system can grow easily, just add nodes so you can handle even more data;
- Flexibility: The pre-processing task is no longer necessary. The data can then be stored in its pure state;
- Low cost: The open source framework is free-of-charge and runs on low-cost standard hardware;
- Fault Tolerance: Jobs are always secured since the nodes automatically redirect the work in case of failure;

- Computing Power: Its distributed computing model quickly processes large data, without the components having to have high memory resources, CPU, among others.

Disadvantages:

- Security: Given the various levels of storage and Hadoop network that are unencrypted;
- Vulnerable: The framework is written almost in java, that is heavily exploited by cybercriminals;
- Does not fit for small amounts of data;
- Potential Stability Issues: Since it is an Open source project, there are several programmers working constantly on the project.

Hadoop in Healthcare Institutions. In healthcare institutions in particular, real-time patient monitoring is proportionate to much more detailed supervision of the situation the patient is in and how it has developed since the beginning of the process. Real-time data processing makes it possible to alert the healthcare professional at the immediate moment when the patient's condition changes. Thus, and given that 75/100 of patients' data, present in healthcare institutions, is not structured in nature, a careful analysis of this data in real time can not only eliminate and/or incorrectly classify exams and wrong diagnoses, but also decrease the costs of the healthcare institution.

The term real time is often associated as something instantaneous, but there are deadlines for data entry and exit that are variable from institution to institution. Ideally, the system should have the ability to receive data in a continuous flow, producing and sending results in a matter of milliseconds. However, in some cases (e.g., a wind turbine), if the response is produced in a period of one minute or even two, this processing is also considered real time, since there is a whole mechanical process from the sensor in the turbine to the system that is receiving the data.

Most healthcare institutions are still investigating the best tools for Big Data treatment in order to improve patient care. Hadoop is in fact a very viable solution that tries to address some challenges in the hospital environment such as electronic health records (EHR) as these have too many free text fields for clinical notes.

There are several advantages of using Hadoop in healthcare institutions. As has been mentioned, currently much of the information is in the form of unstructured data. This category includes medical notes, laboratory reports, imaging examinations, physiological signs, among others. In addition, the average data storage capacity in healthcare facilities is three days of data per patient, which seriously limits the opportunity for data analysis. Therefore, Hadoop allows the storage and availability of data without the cost of these tasks being astronomical. In addition, this tool can also serve as a data organizer and analyst.

3   Proposed Architecture

This proposal seeks to create an open-source architecture that is suited for the capture and real-time processing of large volumes of information within the healthcare area, which when later analyzed are valuable for the acquisition of useful outcomes that provide solutions to support health professionals in the decision-making process.

Moreover, through various big data sources, the aim is to develop a clinical decision support system based on real-time knowledge discovery, while maintaining reliability and availability, as well as allowing easy adaptation in terms of scalability.

The proposed architecture is illustrated in Fig. 1 and can be divided into five layers: data layer, data aggregation layer, data analytics layer, data security and information exploration.

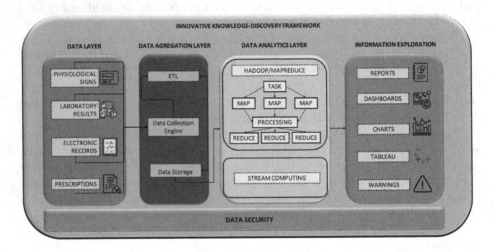

Fig. 1. Proposed Architecture.

3.1   Structure

The next step is to understand each layer of this framework, along with its associated components.

Data Layer. The proposed architecture takes advantage of high volumes of data from numerous healthcare sources, mainly physiological signs, laboratory results, electronic records, and prescriptions. The data's composition may differ due to their structured/unstructured nature, so this architecture must have the ability to collect data in all its formats.

Data Aggregation Layer. This layer concerns the collection, incorporation, transformation, and storage of data. This is an important step since the accuracy of results from data analysis depends heavily on the amount and quality of the exploited data. Therefore, it is important to gather high-quality, accurate data in a large enough amount to create relevant results.

Data Collection
The data collection engine decides how the data is collected from several data sources in order to build the data pipeline. Thus, data collection is where the extraction portion of the ETL process is performed.

At the initial collection stage, initial metadata can be generated, which facilitates subsequent aggregation or look-up methods.

ETL Process
An Extract-Transform-Load (ETL) process is an ordered sequence of operations that seeks to systematically process data so as to make it available in a more accessible format.

The implementation of an ETL process focuses on the following tasks:

1. Extract: Data extraction from different sources;
2. Transform: The extracted data is converted into the user's required format. For processing and validating the data, it is required some sort of data transformations, such as data cleansing, filtering, standardization, flow validation, joining, splitting, sorting, among others;
3. Load: In the final stage of the ETL process, the processed data is loaded into the destination, usually a database or a distributed file system [17].

Data Storage
Storage of Big Data is an important issue for its management. Management is only possible when the storage of data is done properly and efficiently such that the retrieval of data from huge datasets is simpler and user-friendly.

Data for batch processing is normally stored in a distributed file store that can maintain high volumes of large files in various formats.

Data Analytics Layer. Here the aim is to process and examine all the collected data in order to uncover meaningful patterns, relations and other insights.

With the currently available technology, it is possible to analyse data in real-time, through stream computing.

Information Exploration. In the final layer, the focus is on gathering data value and extract business intelligence, providing an ergonomic and user-friendly representation of the data-driven outcomes, in terms of graphs, tables and/or images.

Components

Apache Kafka

Apache Kafka is a distributed high-throughput platform for a real-time environment using a publish-subscribe messaging system, used for high-performance data pipelines, stream processing, log aggregation, and data integration [18].

Advantages:

- Low Latency: Handles messages with a low latency value (on the millisecond's scale), even when handling a large number of messages;
- High-Throughput: Due to low latency, Kafka can manage high-velocity and high-volume data;
- Fault-Tolerance: Provides resistance to node/machine failure within a cluster;
- Distributed: Contains a distributed architecture which makes it scalable. Uses capabilities such as partitioning and replication;
- Scalability: Handles a large number of messages simultaneously. Kafka can be scaled-out by adding additional nodes without incurring any downtime;
- Durability: Presents a replication feature, which makes data/messages persist on the cluster;
- High Concurrency: Kafka can deal with thousands of messages per second in low latency conditions with high throughput, allowing the reading and writing of messages into it at high concurrency;
- Easily accessible: Since all data gets stored in Kafka, it becomes easily accessible;
- Consumer Friendly: Allows producers and consumers to operate independently and at separate times. Moreover, Kafka can integrate well with a variety of consumers written in a variety of languages;
- Real-Time Handling: Able to handle real-time data pipelines;
- All the data that a producer writes go through Kafka. Therefore, a single integration is sufficient to automatically integrate with each producing and consuming system;
- Kafka allows data/messages to integrate directly into applications using APIs, providing additional features and functionalities.

Disadvantages:

- Kafka does not contain a complete set of management and monitoring tools;
- Kafka's high performance depends on whether the message requires additional processing. It can perform well if the message is unchanged because it uses the capabilities of the system, but its performance is significantly reduced if additional processing is required;
- Kafka only matches with the exact topic's name, not supporting wildcard topic selection. This is related to the fact that selecting wildcard topics makes it incapable to address certain use cases;
- As the messages' size increase, brokers and consumers start compressing them, increasing memory usage. After decompressing the data flow, the node memory gets slowly used. This compressing and decompressing of messages affects its performance and throughput;

- When the number of queues in a cluster increases, Kafka's performance decreases [19].

Talend

Talend Open Studio is an open-source project that supports ETL-oriented implementations and is provided for on-premises deployment as well as in a Software-as-a-Service (SaaS) delivery model [17]. Talend Open Studio for Big Data helps to develop faster with a drag-and-drop User Interface (UI) and pre-built connectors and components [20].

Advantages:

- It is a very flexible, scalable and performance-driven solution for executing data manipulation and extraction on Big Data;
- Since it is open-source, it enables users to access, transform, move and synchronize data through big data components such as Hadoop, Hive, Kafka, Spark and NoSQL databases (e.g. HBase), making them easier to use;
- Customizes and creates components and code to extend a project. It can generate both MapReduce and Java code;
- The user usually just needs to drag and drop the components and configure a few parameters;
- Connects with several big data distributions like Apache, MapR, Cloudera, HortonWorks, and other cloud solution providers [20,21].

HDFS

In the Hadoop ecosystem, the Hadoop Distributed File System (HDFS), as its designation suggests, is a distributed and scalable file system and the primary data storage system used by Hadoop applications [22].

Advantages:

- Large data storage: stores a variety of data of any size and format;
- Provides scalable and fast data access;
- Can store files across multiple machines;
- Cost effectiveness: relies on much less expensive commodity storage disks and can be implemented on low cost and easily replaceable hardware;
- Fast recovery from hardware failure: HDFS is highly fault-tolerant and can automatically recover on its own;
- Streaming data access: HDFS is built for high data throughput, which is best for access to streaming data.
- Shares its hardware with MapReduce. Thus, HDFS is optimized for MapReduce workloads and provides high performance for sequential reads and writes [23].

MapReduce

MapReduce allows the scalability of countless servers (nodes) in a Hadoop cluster. Its purpose is to divide the collected data in order to be analysed into smaller and independent parts, and to be processed in parallel, reducing the processing time [22].

Advantages:

- Scalability: MapReduce can scale across thousands of nodes;
- Flexibility to process different types of data from various sources;
- Memory requirements: MapReduce does not require large memory, meaning that it can work with a minimal amount of memory and still quickly produce results;
- Fast: MapReduce is located in the same servers as HDFS, which allows for faster data processing;
- Parallel processing: Tasks are divided in a way that allows their execution in parallel. Parallel processing allows multiple processors to take on these divided tasks, which helps them run programs in less time;
- Availability: MapReduce processes data by sending it to an individual node, as well as forwarding the same set of data to other nodes in the network. Therefore, in case of failure in a particular node, other copies are available and can be accessed whenever the need arises;
- Fault Tolerance: MapReduce has the ability to quickly recognize faults and then apply a quick and automatic recovery solution;
- Cost-effective: Due to its high scalability, MapReduce reduces the cost of storage and processing in order to meet the growing data requirements;
- Security and Authentication: MapReduce works with HDFS security that allows only approved users to operate on data stored in the system [24].

Tableau
The Tableau platform is a usual choice for modern business intelligence and is known for rapidly turning data into useful insights, helpful in the decision-making process.

Advantages:

- Ease of use;
- High performance;
- Multiple data source connections;
- Remarkable visualization capabilities.

Disadvantages:

- High cost and inflexible pricing;
- Limited data preprocessing;
- Time- and resource-intensive staff training [25, 26].

Monitoring and Alerting. Modern-day's information systems require real-time performance controls for a better understanding and interpretation of data.

The monitoring process helps to supervise the data flow in a system. It allows users to find complications before they develop into problems and helps to maintain high availability and quality of service. Therefore, monitoring aims to identify faults and assist in their elimination, providing helpful assistance in the decision-making process.

Alerting is somewhat allied to the monitoring process. It involves the capability of a monitoring system to detect and notify users about abrupt changes in the system's state. Thus, alerting is essentially an automated way to send notifications to users when there is an immediate problem in the system [27].

In the proposed architecture, the monitoring process is done through the conception of reports, where we organize the retrieved data into visual indicators such as dashboards, charts, tables, and time-series, in order to keep track of its performance. Since we are dealing with data originated from healthcare institutions, it is important to be aware of what is happening with the extracted information in real-time. Thus, reporting helps to alert, in the form of warnings or notifications, when the data falls outside of expected ranges (or some other pre-defined criteria), inducing us to react and take appropriate action, as necessary. For example, if a patient's blood pressure increases alarmingly, the system will send a warning in real-time to the designated doctor who will then take measures to lower the patient's blood pressure.

Data Security. Tied to the vital activities to manage the access to the system's data and services, Security involves:

1. Authentication: Verify and validate the identity of a user or service, so that only legitimate users have access to the data and services.
   - In Hadoop, it is common to authenticate with Kerberos and use LDAP as a backend. Depending on the Hadoop component, other authentication possibilities are available, such as SAML, OAuth and classic HTTP authentication;
   - Apache Kafka's authentication is done with SSL or SASL.
2. Authorization: Ensures that the user or process has the rights to access resources or services. In other words, it provides permission to the user (or process) whether he can access the data or not.
   - In Hadoop, access to HDFS is managed through UNIX access rights where users are assigned to user groups;
   - On other Hadoop components, such as Apache Kafka, authorization is controlled by role-based Access Control Lists (ACLs), which include features such as regular expressions for pattern matching.
3. Data Protection: Involves the use of techniques such as encryption and data masking, vital in preventing sensitive data access by unauthorized users and applications.
   - Hadoop provides encryption for HDFS. Thus, since several Hadoop components write their temporary files to HDFS, those files will automatically be secured. This HDFS-level encryption allows applications to run transparently on the encrypted data, while also preventing filesystem or OS-level attacks;

- In Apache Kafka, data is encrypted using SSL/TLS, which keeps data encrypted between the producers and Kafka, as well as the consumers and Kafka;
- In some cases, if data encryption is not required by law or business reasons, partial encryption of data can be done, mainly beneficial for performance purposes. For example, MapReduce uses format-preserving encryption and masking techniques, facilitating faster analytical processing between applications.

4. Auditing: Keeping track of events that happen within the system to support forensic analysis in the event of a breach or corruption of data. Auditing also monitors the activity of an authenticated and authorized user or process, including what data was accessed, added, and modified.
   - Each of the Hadoop components offers audit capabilities to ensure that the users and administrator's activities can be logged;
   - Every component of a big data platform allows logging, either to the local file system or into HDFS [28,29].

3.2 Hands-On: Proposed Process

After an extensive description of each specific layer and its associated tools, this section will focus on the clarification of the exact data flow process throughout the entire architecture. This proposal involves a hybrid architecture that seeks to build an ecosystem capable of supporting both batch and stream processing, combining similar or related components and APIs, and visualization of information in real-time.

Firstly, we start by presenting the different data sources available. In this case, the ones accessible in healthcare institutions. Thereby, the beginning of this process is characterized by the capture of data derived from these healthcare data sources.

To deliver real-time ingestion, Apache Kafka is connected to these data. This connection to Kafka can be accomplished by different approaches: the usual recommendation, which is to use the APIs developed by the Apache Software Foundation, or to use additional technology to facilitate its handling.

Furthermore, Kafka will be used for both data ingestion and stream processing. Since we want a real-time (or near real-time) architecture, the low latency provided by Kafka, meaning that it is optimized to deal with a very high volume of data messages with minimal delay, allows real-time ingestion and real-time processing with time frames shorter than milliseconds. Also, its easy configuration, fault tolerance, high scalability, and the fact that a single tool will be used to collect and process data, makes a Kafka ingestion - Kafka streaming connection an ideal choice for this proposal.

However, we cannot perform ETL transformations in Kafka. Thus, for an ETL-oriented implementation, Kafka's data can then be integrated into Talend Open Studio through its standard connectors and components. Talend's graphical design environment enables the exporting and execution of standalone jobs in runtime environments. Following Talend's connection to an existing Kafka topic, we can persist data in the data object and perform end-to-end ETL transformations. Afterwards, Talend can create a job that writes these data in an HDFS (it can also access data that is stored in an HDFS if necessary).

Alternatively to Kafka's stream processing, we use Hadoop to perform batch processing. After the transformed data's storage in an HDFS, we use it in the analysis layer for batch processing. In batch processing, batches undergo processing through MapReduce, which can later be, once more, stored in an HDFS.

Lastly, following the data's processing and analysis, it is possible to consume and explore the acquired information, where it can be displayed in a more understandable and intuitive form. To do so, we will use Tableau. Tableau connects to Apache Kafka and, through this connection, it is possible to obtain near real-time results, which will be continuously updated in dashboards as new data is ingested and processed. Despite this, and due to Tableau's higher cost, it is advantageous to make use of another tool. So, while Tableau constructs evaluation parameters, we will additionally make our own evaluation, where we will view these parameters and manipulate them, creating, for example, warnings based on the acquired information from Tableau.

4   Discussion and Conclusions

The proposed architecture is capable of supporting healthcare analytics by providing batch and real-time results, combined with an extensible storage technology solution, which will benefit healthcare institutions to a great extent. In fact, its main advantage is the ability to combine historical data with real-time data and produce results in real-time.

Moreover, the insertion of a stream processing tool is beneficial for handling healthcare data that require an almost immediate response. In doing so, the data processing framework achieves low latency, while also presenting in-memory computing, indicating that nearly all processing is performed in the cluster's memory and only the final output is stored on a storage disk.

Throughout the paper, several tools were introduced and briefly clarified, followed by their specific insertion in each layer of the architecture. Hadoop's MapReduce was employed for batch streaming, performed on data stored in HDFS, while Apache Kafka was implemented for stream processing.

However, since historical data is extensive and new information is constantly produced, it can be difficult to maintain the production of real-time results. Thus, this architecture carries a substantial implementational complexity. Also, since batch and stream processing use different technologies, they need to be developed separately, requiring higher efforts in the architecture's implementation.

It is also important to denote that other open-source tools are available. Regarding data collection tools, Apache Flume and Apache NiFi are some usual choices. As for stream processing systems, Apache Spark, Apache Flink, and Apache Storm are often employed.

Since this paper mainly focuses on the theoretical side of the architecture, offering a possible architecture for dealing with Big Data in healthcare institutions, future work primarily concerns its practical implementation, so as to evaluate its performance and establish how its execution is beneficial when dealing with huge amounts of healthcare data.

Acknowledgments. This work is funded by "FCT-Fundação para a Ciência e Tecnologia" within the R&D Units Project Scope: UIDB/00319/2020.

References

1. Editors, H.: Scientist discovers X-rays (2019)
2. Barnes, T.J.: Big data, little history. Dialogues Hum. Geogr. **3**(3), 297–302 (2013)
3. Sivarajah, U., Kamal, M.M., Irani, Z., Weer-akkody, V.: Critical analysis of big data challenges and analytical methods. J. Bus. Res. **70**, 263–286 (2017)
4. Ramage-Morin, P.L.: Successful aging in health care institutions. Statistics Canada (2005)
5. Neves, J., et al.: A deep-big data approach to health care in the AI age. Mob. Netw. Appl. **23**(4), 1123–1128 (2018)
6. Neto, C., Brito, M., Lopes, V., Peixoto, H., Abelha, A., Machado, J.: Application of data mining for the prediction of mortality and occurrence of complications for gastric cancer patients. Entropy **21**(12), 1163 (2019)
7. Wang, Y., Kung, L., Byrd, T.A.: Big data analytics: understanding its capabilities and potential benefits for healthcare organizations. Technol. Forecast. Soc. Chang. **126**, 3–13 (2018)
8. Feldman, B., Martin, E.M., Skotnes, T.: Big data in healthcare hype and hope. Dr. Bonnie **360**, 122–125 (2012)
9. Pereira, A., et al.: Improving quality of medical service with mobile health software. Procedia Comput. Sci. **63**, 292–299 (2015)
10. Bates, D.W., Saria, S., Ohno-Machado, L., Shah, A., Escobar, G.: Big data in health care: using analytics to identify and manage high-risk and high-cost patients. Health Aff. **33**(7), 1123–1131 (2014)
11. Raghupathi, W., Raghupathi, V.: Big data analytics in healthcare: promise and potential. Health Inf. Sci. Syst. **2**(1), 3 (2014)
12. Kruse, C.S., Goswamy, R., Raval, Y.J., Marawi, S.: Challenges and opportunities of big data in health care: a systematic review. JMIR Med. Inform. **4**(4), e38 (2016)
13. Neto, C., et al.: Different scenarios for the prediction of hospital readmission of diabetic patients. J. Med. Syst. **45**(1), 1–9 (2021). https://doi.org/10.1007/s10916-020-01686-4
14. Martins, B., Ferreira, D., Neto, C., Abelha, A., Machado, J.: Data mining for cardiovascular disease prediction. J. Med. Syst. **45**(1), 1–8 (2021). https://doi.org/10.1007/s10916-020-01682-8
15. Manogaran, G., Thota, C., Lopez, D., Vijayakumar, V., Abbas, K.M., Sundarsekar, R.: Big data knowledge system in healthcare. In: Bhatt, C., Dey, N., Ashour, A.S. (eds.) Internet of Things and Big Data Technologies for Next Generation Healthcare. SBD, vol. 23, pp. 133–157. Springer, Cham (2017). https://doi.org/10.1007/978-3-319-49736-5_7
16. Li, G., Ooi, B. C., Feng, J., Wang, J., Zhou, L.: Ease: an effective 3-in-1 keyword search method for unstructured, semi-structured and structured data. In: Proceedings of the 2008 ACM SIGMOD International Conference on Management of Data, pp. 903–914 (2008)

17. Sreemathy, J., Nisha, S., Prabha, C., RM, G.P.: Data integration in ETL using Talend. In: 2020 6th International Conference on Advanced Computing and Communication Systems (ICACCS), pp. 1444–1448. IEEE (2020)
18. The Apache Software Foundation. Apache Kafka Documentation. https://kafka.apache.org/intro. Accessed 11 Mar 2021
19. DataFlair: Advantages and Disadvantages of Kafka (2019). https://data-flair.training/blogs/advantages-and-disadvantages-of-kafka/. Accessed 12 Mar 2021
20. Talend. Talend Open Studio for Big Data. https://www.talend.com/products/big-data/big-data-open-studio/. Accessed 28 Mar 2021
21. Katragadda, R., Tirumala, S.S., Nandigam, D.: ETL tools for data warehousing: an empirical study of open source Talend Studio versus Microsoft SSIS (2015)
22. White, T.: Hadoop: The Definitive Guide. O'Reilly Media Inc (2012)
23. TutorialsCampus. HDFS Overview. https://www.tutorialscampus.com/hadoop/hdfs-overview.htm. Accessed 29 Mar 2021
24. Tutorialspoint: Advantages of Hadoop MapReduce Programming. https://www.tutorialspoint.com/advantages-of-hadoop-mapreduce-programming. Accessed 29 Mar 2021
25. Tableau. Business Intelligence and Analytics Software. https://www.tableau.com/why-tableau. Accessed 14 Mar 2021
26. SaM Solutions: Pros and Cons of Tableau Software for Data Visualization (2017). https://www.sam-solutions.com/blog/tableau-software-review-pros-and-cons-of-a-bi-solution-for-data-visualization/. Accessed 14 Mar 2021
27. Ligus, S.: Effective Monitoring and Alerting. O'Reilly Media Inc. (2012)
28. Chang, W.L., Boyd, D., Levin, O.: NIST big data interoperability framework: volume 6, reference architecture. National Institute of Standards and Technology (2019)
29. Deloitte Consulting GmbH: Five key principles to secure the enterprise Big Data platform (2017)

New Domains and Novel Applications Related to Big Data Technologies

Analysis of Knowledge Map on Rural Culture Tourism in China

Guoxin Tan[1], Qimin He[1(✉)], and Huan Huang[2]

[1] Central China Normal University, Wuhan, China
qmhe@mails.ccnu.edu.cn
[2] South-Central University for Nationalities, Wuhan, China

Abstract. Based on the literature on rural cultural tourism in China National Knowledge Infrastructure (CNKI) from 1992 to 2019, this paper uses bibliometric analysis method and citation analysis software CiteSpace to draw the knowledge map of rural cultural tourism in China, and describes and analyzes the research status and hotspots. The results show that the overall research results of rural cultural tourism show a steady growth; Research institutions are mostly distributed in tourism colleges and universities, and there is a cooperative relationship between more institutions; the core keywords of rural cultural tourism research at this stage are rural tourism, rural culture and tourism development. In terms of research content, it involves macro-analysis of rural cultural tourism policy and micro-study of specific regional rural cultural tourism. The research methods include qualitative and quantitative research and multidisciplinary cross-study, which enriches the research compatibility of rural culture and cultural tourism. In the future, we should strengthen the integration and development of rural cultural tourism research, broaden the research content of rural cultural tourism, and pay attention to the innovation of research methods of rural cultural tourism, so as to promote the development of rural cultural tourism.

Keywords: Rural cultural tourism · CiteSpace · Knowledge map · Hot topics

1 Introduction

Rural cultural tourism is a new form and development of rural tourism, so in the study of rural cultural tourism, most scholars at home and abroad extend from rural tourism to the excavation of rural culture. At present, the existing foreign research is more mature, such as Frochot refines rural tourists into four types: entertainment, active, sightseeing and rural. Empirical research shows that the majority of tourists want to understand rural culture and the target of rural tourism market should be targeted at rural culture [1]. Swarbrooke in the study of rural tourists' motivation analysis, experience of rural culture and rural life is the main reason for rural tourists travel [2]; Lane puts forward the protection of rural characteristic culture in the analysis of rural tourism development, emphasizing the sustainable development of culture for rural tourism [3]. Through investigation and study, Royo-Vela M puts forward that the key of rural cultural

© ICST Institute for Computer Sciences, Social Informatics and Telecommunications Engineering 2023
Published by Springer Nature Switzerland AG 2023. All Rights Reserved
R. Hou et al. (Eds.): BDTA 2021/2022, LNICST 480, pp. 315–329, 2023.
https://doi.org/10.1007/978-3-031-33614-0_21

tourism marketing lies in the construction of rural cultural image [4]. Anderson W takes rural areas in Kilimanjaro as an example to analyze the positive effect of rural cultural tourism on poverty alleviation policies in the region [5].

The attention and academic research on rural cultural tourism in China are increasing day by day. In the national policy level, the No. 1 document of the State Council in 2016 emphasized that leisure agriculture and rural tourism should be vigorously developed, and rural tourism should become a new pillar industry in rural areas relying on local cultural resources [6]. In 2017, the report of the 19th National Congress of the Communist Party of China proposed the policy of rural revitalization, which included vigorously developing rural tourism to build a new engine for rural revitalization [7]. After the relevant policies are put forward, rural cultural tourism has attracted increasing attention from tourists and relevant researchers. On the level of tourists' feelings, rural culture is the inherent attribute of rural tourism, which can effectively meet the cultural experience and spiritual needs of tourists [8]. At the level of industrial planning, the development of rural tourism can promote the industrial combination of rural tourism resources and cultural resources. Moreover, rural culture is the highlight of the development of rural tourism. The integration of rural culture and rural tourism is the inevitable choice to achieve sustainable development, and is the inevitable choice for the development of tourism industry and the excavation of cultural connotation [9]. At the level of social research, researchers have studied rural tourism, cultural tourism and current rural cultural tourism from different perspectives. It is not difficult to see that the research of rural cultural tourism at home and abroad is starting from rural tourism, analyzing the role and significance of culture in it, and promoting the deeper development of rural tourism through culture.

Therefore, a comprehensive review of domestic research literature on rural cultural tourism and the excavation of research hotspots at the emerging stage will not only help improve the development path of government and other decision-making institutions for rural cultural tourism, but also improve people's satisfaction with rural cultural tourism in decision-making optimization. However, in the face of a large number of documents, the research status of rural cultural tourism summarized by manual reading will be missed reading and one-sided understanding. In order to avoid this kind of situation, this paper attempts to analyze and think about rural cultural tourism research by mining and visualizing the existing research literature on rural cultural tourism in China, so as to provide reference for relevant researchers.

2   Data Sources and Research Methods

2.1   Data Source

This study selected CNKI journal full-text database as the data source. When conducting data retrieval in this database, considering that rural cultural tourism is the background of the combination of rural tourism and cultural tourism, the retrieval conditions are 'rural tourism', 'cultural tourism' and 'rural cultural tourism'. The relationship between the three is 'or contains'. Taking 'theme' as the retrieval requirement, the literature sources are 'core journals' and 'CSSCI', the retrieval time is 1992–2019, and the retrieval condition is 'accurate'. A total of 10723 records are retrieved. In order to improve the quality and correlation of data sources, 9837 valid literature samples were obtained by manually screening and eliminating literatures with inconsistent topics or conditions, such as news, catalogues, scholars' essays and conference notices. The literature is exported in Refwork format and transcoded to form a sample database of rural cultural tourism research.

2.2 Research Methods

Knowledge graph is a graph that shows the relationship between the development process of literature knowledge and the structure of literature. It describes literature knowledge resources through visualization technology, and excavates, constructs, draws and displays the relationship between literature knowledge resources [10]. CiteSpace is one of the most widely used tools in knowledge mapping software, which is sufficient to draw co-word clustering map and time zone map. The advantage of CiteSpace is that it can record the literature based on co-citation analysis theory and path-finding network algorithm to explore the evolution and content of research hotspots [11]. The analysis process mainly includes data collection, data processing, parameter and node setting, knowledge map visualization, map optimization setting and interpretation map. This study uses CiteSpace 5.6 R2 version to visualize the dimensions of rural cultural tourism related literature publishers, authors, keyword co-occurrence analysis, keyword time zone analysis, mutation detection and keyword clustering analysis [12], which is of great significance to fully understand the overall situation of rural cultural tourism research results and obtain research hotspots in this field.

3 Analysis of the Trend in Rural Cultural Tourism Research in China

3.1 Distribution of Years

In this study, the annual publication statistics of 9837 core journals and CSSCI source journals related to rural cultural tourism since 1992 are carried out and plotted as a broken line, as shown in Fig. 1. In the past 20 years from 1992 to 2011, the relevant research literature has been showing a steady upward trend, in which the annual growth rate was high from 2006 to 2011. After the peak of relevant research, the research bottleneck period from 2011 to 2012 showed a downward trend. At the same time, this development trend is also in line with the Price literature index. After the decline in the number of publications in the bottleneck period, the literature growth rate slowed down from 2012 to 2016, showing a low-speed fluctuation trend; However, due to the promotion of rural tourism industry driven by the national major planning of rural revitalization strategy, the research literature has been on the rise since 2017, and the annual number of core journals has remained at about 200, entering a new stage of stable development.

3.2 Institutional Distribution Characteristics

From the perspective of publishing institutions, the domestic research forces are concentrated in colleges and universities, and the colleges of tourism in colleges and universities are mainly such as the College of Tourism of Sun Yat-sen University, the College

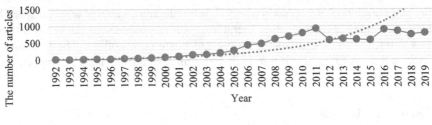

—●— Annual Publication Trend

Fig. 1. The distribution of domestic rural cultural tourism research literature by age

of Tourism and Environment of Shaanxi Normal University, and the College of Tourism of Beijing Union University, as shown in Table 1, indicating that colleges and universities and their teams in this field are the main forces of related research, and they also undertake a number of scientific research projects related to rural cultural tourism. However, at present, the number of relevant papers published by domestic scientific research institutions is relatively low, and the publishing institutions are concentrated in tourism colleges. The research on rural cultural tourism involves tourism, culture, economics and other disciplines, and only focuses on tourism colleges, lacking the deep participation of cultural, economic and their units.

The cooperation network of publishing institutions shows that the Institute of Geography and Resources, Chinese Academy of Sciences, Chinese Academy of Tourism, School of Tourism, Hunan Normal University, graduate students of Chinese Academy of Sciences, and School of Tourism and Environment, Shaanxi Normal University have deep cooperation relationships, as shown in Fig. 2. Most other research institutions are scattered, and a few institutions have cooperative relations, such as Nanjing Normal University and Beijing Union University, Sichuan University and Southwest University for Nationalities, but the intensity of cooperation is insufficient.

3.3 Analysis of Authors

The core author is the academic leader in the research field, which has a significant impact on the development of this field. The most intuitive manifestation is that the quality and quantity of academic papers published by him are significantly higher than those of scholars in the same field [13]. According to the largest number of papers published by Professor Sun Jiuxia, School of Tourism, Sun Yat-sen University, a total of 28 papers, it is concluded that the number of core authors is $0.749 \times 28 \approx 4$, that is, the number of authors with ≥4 papers is the core author, and there are 172 qualified authors in the sample database.

Table 1. The distribution of the top 10 institutions in China's rural cultural tourism

NO.	Institution	Article	Region	Proportion/%
1	Institute of Geographic Sciences and Natural Resources Research	172	North China	1.75
2	School of Tourism Management, Sun Yat-Sen University	80	South China	0.81
3	College of Geography, Nanjing Normal University	71	East China	0.72
4	College of Tourism and Environment, Shaanxi Normal University	63	Northwestern China	0.64
5	School of Tourism, Beijing Union University	54	North China	0.55
6	College of Land Resources and Tourism, Anhui Normal University	53	North China	0.54
7	College of Tourism, Guilin University of Technology	48	South China	0.49
8	Center for Tourism Development and Planning, Sun Yat-sen University	46	South China	0.47
9	School of Tourism, Sichuan University	44	Southwestern China	0.45
10	China Tourism Academy	42	North China	0.43

Fig. 2. The maps of domestic rural cultural tourism research institutions

4 Analysis on the Research Hotspots of Rural Cultural Tourism in China

4.1 Keywords Co-word Analysis

Keywords, as an important indicator in scientific research, are binding on research topics and important evaluation indexes in bibliometric analysis [14]. Set the node parameter category to Keyword, and get the keyword statistics table of domestic rural cultural tourism research, as shown in Table 2.

Table 2. Keywords Statistics of Domestic Rural Cultural Tourism Research

	Keywords	Frequency	No.	Keywords	Frequency
1	Rural tourism	1910	11	Development	223
2	Tourism	555	12	Tea culture	223
3	Tourism development	401	13	Intangible cultural heritage	213
4	Cultural tourism	322	14	Ecotourism	163
5	Tourism resources	280	15	Cultural industry	147
6	Tourism industry	261	16	New Rural Construction	142
7	Rural revitalization	261	17	Influencing factors	125
8	Sustainable development	252	18	Tourism products	122
9	Tourism	235	19	Leisure agriculture	112
10	Countermeasures	227	20	Industrial integration	112

Keywords basically reflect the core theme of rural cultural tourism research, but high-frequency keywords are mainly tourism-related vocabulary, indicating that the existing research results are mostly analyzed from the perspective of tourism, while ignoring the soft power of rural culture. At the same time, simple word frequency statistics cannot show the relationship between keywords, so the co-occurrence analysis of keywords is carried out, as shown in Fig. 3.

In the keyword co-occurrence map, nodes with high co-occurrence frequency will gather together, indicating the close degree of links between keywords, such as rural tourism, tourism industry, rural revitalization and other keywords, reflecting the role of policies in rural cultural tourism. Key words such as culture, tea culture, development, tourists and countermeasures are gathered together, reflecting the integrated development of specific rural culture and tourism.

4.2 Keyword Mutation Detection

Mutation detection technology and algorithm detect words with high frequency change rate from a large number of keywords through the time distribution of keywords frequency [15]. Therefore, mutation detection of keywords, specifically lists the top 10

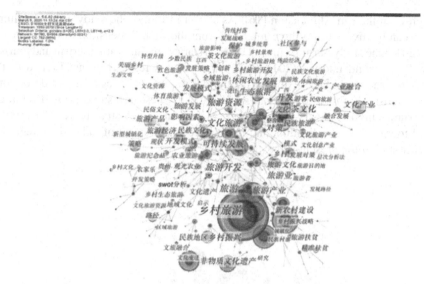

Fig. 3. Keywords Co-occurrence Map of Domestic Rural Cultural Tourism Research

keywords of mutation intensity, the higher the mutation intensity indicates that the topic is a hot topic in the mutation period, as shown in Table 3.

Table 3. Keywords Mutation Strength of Domestic Rural Cultural Tourism Research

	Keywords	Mutation strength	Mutation period/Year
1	Tea culture	88.0526	2016–2017
2	Rural revitalization	86.9254	2018–2019
3	Rural tourism	42.0563	2003–2007
4	Targeted poverty alleviation	26.8158	2017–2019
5	all-for-one tourism	24.5965	2016–2019
6	Tourism agriculture	19.4071	1992–2006
7	Traditional villages	13.8966	2017–2019
8	Beautiful countryside	13.3659	2016–2019
9	Cultural industry	12.5205	2012–2015
10	Rural Tourism Development	11.9663	1992–2007

4.3 Time Zone Analysis of Keywords

The time zone diagram of keywords can show the distribution and changes of keywords in a certain research at different time periods, and grasp the hot topics and trends of research from the time dimension [16]. As shown in Fig. 4, the study of rural cultural tourism can be divided into three intervals from the time dimension: the first interval (1992–2011),the study of rural cultural tourism started, mainly rural tourism and tourism policy; The second interval (2012–2016), the relevant research is not limited to the analysis of macro policies, extended to the development strategy and mode of rural cultural tourism; In the third interval (since 2017), the research subjects are diversified, such as rural tourism industry, cultural tourism integration industry, showing the trend of cultural tourism industrialization, and in line with the concept of industrial integration and cultural IP at the present stage.

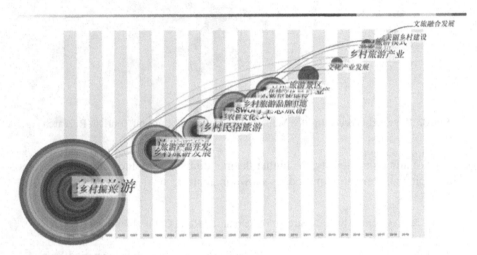

Fig. 4. Hot keywords time zone map of domestic rural cultural tourism research literature

4.4 Analysis of Keywords Clustering Map

Cluster analysis combines research objects according to similar categories, and high frequency keywords of the same category are aggregated into a cluster [17]. The keywords of domestic rural cultural tourism research literature are clustered and the themes in this category are identified, and 23 categories of research are obtained, as shown in Fig. 5.

Topics and keywords were identified by statistics. Clusters with too few words or repetitive meanings were screened out combined with keyword co-occurrence analysis. Research hotspots of rural cultural tourism were summarized from two dimensions of research methods and research contents, as shown in Table 4.

Focus on Content Research at the Macro Level

The keywords of 'rural revitalization', 'tourism development', 'sustainable development', 'tourism' and 'eco-tourism' reflect the content research of rural cultural tourism tending to the macro level. The research time span of this category is roughly from 1992 to 2011, and its content covers a wide range, mainly in the context of rural tourism to

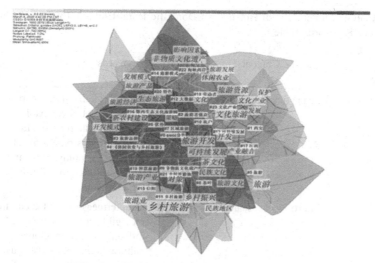

Fig. 5. Keywords Clustering Map of Domestic Rural Cultural Tourism Research Literature

analyze the effect of rural culture, the development of rural culture, the integration of tourism resources and the inheritance of rural culture.

Zhang Shanfeng et al. studied the status of rural culture in rural tourism planning. Starting from the cultural nature of rural tourism, they formulated corresponding rural cultural expressions based on rural material culture, institutional culture and spiritual culture, emphasizing the significance of rural cultural heritage [18]. Zhang Yan defines rural tourism and rural culture. Based on the dynamic model of rural tourism, this paper analyzes that rural culture is the motivation of rural tourism from the perspective of tourists, and puts forward three rural cultural development models, such as cultural sightseeing model, cultural experience model and cultural comprehensive model [19]. Based on the analysis of the current situation and problems of the development of cultural tourism resources in China [19]. Zhenhua Han et al. proposed seven aspects of in-depth development, such as the promotion of celebrity resources, the use of folk resources and the use of modern science and technology, finally, they proposed the integration idea of rural cultural tourism resources from the four dimensions of concept, interest, image and transportation [20]. From the perspective of cultural inheritance, Zhang Yujun et al. combed the positive and negative impacts of rural tourism on rural culture at home and abroad, and proposed that the research focus should be on how to maximize the positive impact of rural tourism and reduce its negative impact on rural culture. How to form a benign and smooth cultural inheritance mechanism is a new idea for the development of rural tourism and the protection of rural culture [21].

The content research at the macro level focuses on the comprehensive review or suggestion of rural cultural tourism research, which provides a general direction for

Table 4. Analysis Dimensions of Hotspots in Domestic Rural Cultural Tourism Research and Corresponding Keywords Table

Analysis Dimension	Specific Content	Keywords
Research contents	Macro-level research	Rural Revitalization, Tourism Development, Sustainable Development, Tourism, Ecotourism, Cultural Industry, Tourism Products, Tourism Economy, Tourism Culture, Cultural Protection, Tourism Development, etc
	Micro-level research	Countermeasures of tea culture, intangible cultural heritage, influencing factors, global tourism, cultural heritage, tourist souvenirs, cultural creativity, etc
Research methods	Qualitative and quantitative study	Countermeasures, influencing factors, path, development mode, strategy, SWOT analysis, present situation analysis, analytic hierarchy process, grounded theory, comprehensive evaluation, etc
	Multi-disciplinary investigation	Spatial structure of rural culture, spatial and temporal distribution of cultural heritage, GIS, etc

related research. However, since the research is in the early stage of development, there is no specific analysis combined with cases, and there is no case support.

Focus on Content Research at the Micro Level

The keywords of 'tea culture countermeasures', 'intangible cultural heritage', 'global tourism', 'cultural heritage' and 'cultural creativity' reflect the micro-level content research of rural cultural tourism. Relevant research combined with the case analysis of specific rural areas to verify the implementation effect of macro strategy to a certain extent. Lin Jinping and others took the Sanyuan Village of Lijiang Guifeng, the world cultural heritage, as the research object of rural tourism, focused on the national culture and customs of Naxi and Dongba, and analyzed the feasibility principles of transforming Dongba culture into tourism resources [22]. Chen Qiuhua et al. took Qipanzhai Mulberry Picking Garden in Fuzhou City, Fujian Province as the research object to develop cultural and creative tourism products from the perspective of five senses, namely vision, hearing, smell, taste and touch, so as to enrich the multidimensional experience of tourists and meet the needs of tourists' experience [23]. Zhang Zhong took Xinyang Maojian Tea as the research object, analyzed the development value of Xinyang tea culture tourism from the natural environment, tea industry base, tea culture accumulation, and tea culture ecological tourism market, integrated the cultural connection between Xinyang Maojian Tea and other tourism resources, and built Xinyang tea capital characteristic tourism brand [24].

The content research at the micro level focuses on the case analysis of the development of specific rural cultural tourism. In the macro context, due to the differences in various attractions, the strategy analysis of rural cultural tourism is carried out according to local conditions. At the same time, by reading the relevant papers one by one, it is found that the research theme of the paper is related to the area where the author ' s work unit is located, indicating that the relevant research of rural cultural tourism in local colleges and universities can form different academic circles.

Focus on Qualitative and Quantitative Methodological Research

The keywords of 'SWOT analysis', 'current situation analysis', 'analytic hierarchy process', 'grounded theory' and 'comprehensive evaluation' reflect various research methods of rural cultural tourism. There are both qualitative analysis methods such as SWOT analysis and grounded theory, and quantitative analysis methods such as analytic hierarchy process and factor analysis. For a certain research topic, the use of different research methods to show the research conclusion is different, which is of great significance to the development of the research topic.

In the study of rural cultural tourism, the attraction of rural cultural tourism is a hot topic for tourists. From the perspective of qualitative analysis, Li Hui believes that folk customs have a positive effect on the development of rural cultural tourism. Through literature analysis, this paper summarizes the factors restricting the integration of folk customs into rural cultural tourism, such as the enthusiasm of rural residents to participate in the development of rural tourism is not high. Finally, according to the reasons for restricting the development, aiming at the purpose of attracting tourists, this paper puts forward improvement strategies such as providing food, accommodation, transportation and purchase of ' integrated' services [25]. From the perspective of quantitative analysis, Zhou Jing and others take Hetuala Village in Liaoning Province as the research object, to understand the attractiveness of local rural cultural tourism as the research purpose, from the perspective of tourists' demand to design the evaluation index system, using Delphi method and empirical research to construct multi-level tourism attraction evaluation, using quantitative method to intuitively draw the attraction of rural cultural tourism, and adjust the development strategy through the attraction comparison [26].

According to the keyword co-occurrence map, the relationship between the new rural construction of rural cultural tourism and the new urbanization is studied. By examining and reflecting on the current situation of rural cultural tourism development in the context of new urbanization, Huang Zhenfang and Lu Lin believed that rural culture is the source and an important part of Chinese culture. However, under the impact of urbanization, the traditional rural culture is facing the dilemma of destruction or even disappearance. Therefore, it is necessary to take rural tourism as the carrier, strengthen the regional types and cultural values of rural tourism culture, and put forward to promote the deep integration of culture and rural tourism, such as the intelligent reproduction supported by science and technology according to local conditions, the clustering construction of theme culture, the commodity development of cultural extension and the industrialization expansion of cultural tourism integration [27]. Taking rural cultural tourism in Jiangxi Province as the research object, Lu et al. constructed the coupling evaluation model between the two to explore the coupling and coordination relationship between them and the construction of new urbanization. Through empirical research on 11 prefecture-level cities in Jiangxi Province, the coupling coordination degree and evaluation of specific cities are obtained. Combined with empirical conclusions, counter-measures and suggestions are put forward, such as differentiated development of cities in Jiangxi Province, highlighting local cultural characteristics, such as Ji'an red culture and Jingdezhen ancient porcelain culture [28].

Qualitative research is mostly based on literature review, while quantitative research is mostly based on empirical data. Its purpose is to promote the development of rural cultural tourism in a certain perspective. The combination of qualitative and quantitative research on rural cultural tourism is also a research method that scholars pay attention.

Focus on Multidisciplinary Methodological Research
According to the statistics of high-frequency publishing institutions, in addition to domestic tourism colleges, there are also colleges of geography science and colleges of land and resources. At the same time, the papers combing the database show that relevant publishing institutions also involve information management colleges. Huang et al. sorted out and summarized the literature on the cultural impact of rural tourism destinations in China and abroad, and applied the theory of stress ecology, namely, adverse or negative impact, which covered many fields such as ecology, environmental science, urban research and management. The study constructs a research framework of tourism development on rural culture stress including social, temporal and spatial dimensions, forms a stress model of tourism development on rural culture, and provides strategic analysis for rural culture protection under rapid urbanization and tourism development [29]. Based on the perspective and method of human geography theory, Zheng Zili analyzed the problems existing in the development of rural cultural tourism in China, such as improper political representation, excessive cultural integration, and slug-gish transformation of kinetic energy, and put forward countermeasures to standardize the power relationship and political representation in the development of rural cultural tourism, and promote the differentiated integration and protective development of cul-tural resources in the development of rural cultural tourism [30]. From the perspective of public cultural services and rural cultural tourism public services, Li Guoxin proposed that public cultural services should be embedded in tourist attractions such as public reading places, cultural and historical exhibition halls and rural creative workshops, so that rural tourism public service centers have dual functions of tourism and culture [31] The multidisciplinary approach enriches the related research of rural cultural tourism, but the research subject of rural cultural tourism includes tourism and culture. At present, some research results have been formed in the cultural dilemma, cultural protection and cultural tourism development of rural areas [32], lacking the participation of cultural scholars, deep mining of rural cultural resources and close integration with tourism.

5 Conclusion and Discussion

With the continuous promotion of rural revitalization policy and the development of tourism and the vigorous construction of beautiful villages, rural cultural tourism is facing opportunities and challenges, which are reflected in research institutions, research authors, research subjects, research contents and research methods. Combined with the current research content and the overall understanding of the sample literature, it can be found that there are two main elements in the research field, one is rural tourism, and the other is rural culture. Rural tourism focuses on the form and development mode of tourism in rural specific environment, and cultural tourism considers the integration of rural cultural resources development and rural tourism. Previous research topics and content are mostly based on these two main elements, such as intangible cultural heritage, tea culture, tourism resources and other keywords reflect the rural culture, tourism industry, ecological tourism, leisure agriculture and other keywords reflect the rural tourism. At present, the research is not limited to simply analyzing and summarizing these two main elements, and the research content and methods have also begun to expand and deepen, such as the combination of cultural industry analysis, the use of geographic information system and remote sensing technology, but technology is only an auxiliary means. In the study of rural cultural tourism, many literatures do not highlight the cultural subject, and most of the research focuses on tourism, while ignoring the status of 'culture'. Therefore, the study of rural cultural tourism in the future should strengthen the following three aspects:

Firstly, to strengthen the development of rural cultural tourism research strength, from the current research institutions and research authors point of view, most of the research is carried out in the college of tourism as the center, the intensity of cooperation between research authors is not high, which will lead to scattered conclusions.

Secondly, it is necessary to broaden the research content of rural cultural tourism. At present, the research content is mostly based on the analysis of the significance of policy and the development strategy of a single region, which cannot include the research content of the whole rural cultural tourism. In the study of tourism, one of the most important elements is tourists, which can carry out tourist satisfaction assessment or feedback on tourists to develop rural cultural tourism development programs.

Thirdly, strengthen the innovation of rural cultural tourism research methods, the current research methods are mostly qualitative analysis and quantitative analysis, qualitative analysis mainly for literature reading, field investigation, etc., quantitative analysis mainly for mathematical model, combined with geographic information technology and other methods. What will be broken through in the future is the deep integration of qualitative analysis and quantitative analysis, so that the application of new technologies can break through the bottleneck of the original research and establish a research system with both scientific and cultural characteristics. For example, combined with the current technologies such as big data and artificial intelligence, the spatio-temporal big database of rural cultural tourism is constructed. Through knowledge mining technology, the comprehensive evaluation of rural cultural tourism in different regions of China is carried out, and more reasonable and scientific strategies and suggestions are provided for relevant national institutions.

Acknowledgements. This research was supported by the Technological Innovation Special Major Project of Hubei Province "Key technology research and development application of big animation information platform" (No.2018AAA069) and the Science and Technology Innovation Project of National Cultural and Tourism "Innovative application on digital communication of intangible cultural heritage in Hubei Province".

References

1. Frochot I. A benefit segmentation of tourists in rural areas: a Scottish persperctive. Tour. Manag. **26**, 335–346 (2005)
2. Swarbrooke, J.: Culture, tourism, and sustainability of rural areas in Europe. Robinson, M., Evans, N., Callaghan, P.: Managing Cultural Resources for the Tourist: Tourism and Culture—Towards the 21st Century(Conference Proceedings) (2000)
3. Lane, B.: Rural tourism and sustainable rural development. Channel View Publications, UK (1994)
4. Royo-Vela, M.: Rural-cultural excursion conceptualization: a local tourism marketing management model based on tourist destination image measurement. Tour. Manage. **30**(3), 419–428 (2009)
5. Anderson, W.: Cultural tourism and poverty alleviation in rural Kilimanjaro, Tanzania. J. Tour. Cult. Chang. **3**, 1–17 (2014)
6. The Central Government and the State Council: The Central Document No.1 Document of 2016 [EB/OL]. http://www.moa.gov.cn/ztzl/2016zyyhwj/
7. Xi, J.: Report to the General Assembly on behalf of the eighteenth Central Committee [EB/OL]. http://www.12371.cn/special/19da/bg/
8. Cai, X., Deng, X.: The impact of rural culture on rural tourism demand. J. Southwest Univ. National. (Human. Soc. Sci. Ed.) **32**(11), 144–147 (2011)
9. Liu, Y., Gao, R.: Research on the core competitiveness of rural tourism from the perspective of cultural and tourism integration. Theoretical Monthly (1), 92–100 (2020)
10. Qin, C.R., Hou, H.: Knowledge Map – new areas of information management and knowledge management. Univ. Libr. Sci. **27**(1), 30–37+96 (2009)
11. Chen, Y., Chen, C., Liu, Z., Hu, Z., Wang, X.: Methodology function of CiteSpace knowledge map. Sci. Res. **33**(2), 242–253 (2015)
12. Chen, C.M.: CiteSpace II: detecting and visualizing emerging trends and transient patterns in scientific literature. J. Am. Soc. Inform. Sci. Technol. **57**(3), 359–377 (2006)
13. Liu, K., Li, C., Bai, F.: Bibliometric study on name specification in the field of library and information in China. Libr. Work Res. **12**, 66–71 (2017)
14. Cheng, F.-F., Huang, Y.-W., Hsin-Chun, Y., ChinShan, W.: (2018) Mapping knowledge structure by keyword co-occurrence and social network analysis: evidence from Library Hi Tech between 2006 and 2017. Libr. HiTech. **36**(4), 636–650 (2018)
15. Chen, Y., Zhou, T.: Visualization analysis of domestic network public opinion governance research—method based on scientific knowledge map (CNKI). Inf. Sci. **34**(11), 101–106 (2016)
16. Feng, Y., Hu, C., Li, S.: Knowledge map and hot topics of domestic academic resources research. Inf. Sci. **37**(10), 3–7+19 (2019)
17. Zhao, B., Dong, Y., Yang, X.: Knowledge map and hot topics of domestic information ecology research—based on co-word analysis of bibliometrics. Inf. Sci. **35**(9), 61–66+164 (2017)
18. Zhang, S.: The expression of rural culture in rural tourism planning. Shanghai J. Agri. (2), 127–130 (2008)

19. Zhang, Y., Zhang, Y.: Rural culture and rural tourism development. Econ. Geogr. **3**, 509–512 (2007)
20. Han, Z., Wang, S.: Research on the development and integration of rural cultural tourism resources. Reform Strat. **25**(9), 91–93 (2009)
21. Zhu, D., Zhang, Y.: Research on the impact of tourism on rural cultural heritage. J. Beijing Forestry Univ. (Social Sci. Ed.) (2), 58–62 (2008)
22. Lin, J., Zhou, H., He, Y.: Research on the inheritance of national cultural tradition and the development of rural tourism in Naxi Dongba—Taking the development of rural tourism in Sanyuan Village of Lijiang, Yunnan as an example. Hum. Geogr. (5), 84–86 (2005)
23. Xie, C., Chen, Q., Su, Y., Xiao, T.: Research on the development of rural creative tourism products from the perspective of five senses – Taking Qipanzhai mulberry garden as an example. Forestry Econ. Prob. **35**(1), 63–67+74 (2015)
24. Zhang, Z.: Exploration of Xinyang rural ecotourism development strategy from the perspective of tea tourism industry integration. Fujian Tea **39**(1), 125–126 (2017)
25. Li, H.: Folk customs add luster to rural cultural tourism. People's Tribune **25**, 92–93 (2017)
26. Shan, F., Zhou, J., Li, X.: Multi-level evaluation of rural cultural tourism attraction – taking the village of Hetuala in Liaoning as an example. J. Arid Land Resour. Environ. **31**(12), 196–202 (2017)
27. Huang, Z., et al.: Rural tourism development under the background of new urbanization-theoretical reflection and dilemma breakthrough. Geog. Res. **34**(8), 1409–1421 (2015)
28. Lu, J., Yan, L.: Construction of coupling evaluation model for rural cultural tourism complex and new urbanization—Taking Jiangxi Province as an example. Enterprise Econ. **36**(07), 118 124 (2017)
29. Xu, D., Huang, Z., Li, D., Hong, X., Yu, F.: The Research progress and framework construction of cultural impact of rural tourism destinations from the perspective of stress. Hum. Geog. **34**(6), 17–25 (2019)
30. Zheng, Z.: Problems and countermeasures of rural cultural tourism development from the perspective of human geography. Mod. Econ. Discussion (6), 128–132 (2019)
31. Li, G., Li, Y.: Thoughts on the Integrated development of cultural and tourism public services. Libr. J. **38**(10), 29–33 (2019)
32. Huang, Z., Huang, R.: Rural culture research under the background of urbanization and tourism development : academic debate and research direction. Geog. Res. **37**(2), 233–249 (2018)

A Visual Analysis of E-Government Research in China Based on Co-word Clustering

Chuan-ming Sun[1], Yan Zhou[1(✉)], and Shuai Yuan[2]

[1] Central China Normal University, Wuhan, China
675261872@qq.com
[2] School of Computer, Hubei University of Education, Wuhan, China

Abstract. The application of emerging technologies has promoted the rapid development and popularity of e-government. This paper takes 372 CSSCI papers in the field of e-government in China as the research object, and uses bibexcel, UNICET and SPSS software to perform co-word clustering analysis and visualize the clustering relationships. The research hotspots of e-government in China were found to include research on the development trend of e-government, research on the integration of e-government and new media, research on e-governance in the information society, and research on government information management and data governance. The analysis of the research hotspots provides references for the further development of e-government in China.

Keywords: e-government · big data · informatization · visualization and analysis

1 Introduction

China's e-government started in the 1980s with the construction of office automation systems. With the continuous development of digital technology, e-government has moved from the Internet era into the era of the Internet of Wisdom, and its construction has continued to develop in the direction of greater efficiency and quality. Therefore, to promote the development of e-government has become a worldwide trend and trend. From the launch of the "Government Internet Project" in 1999, to the implementation of the "Regulations of the People's Republic of China on Government Information Disclosure" in 2008, to the "Guidance on Accelerating the Work of "Internet + Government Services" in 2016, China's e-government is in the midst of the development of the Internet. China's e-government is in the process of continuous development and progress. At present, e-government research has become a hot area of common concern in information science, management and other disciplines [1].

Based on keyword clustering analysis, visual co-word network graph analysis and multi-dimensional scale analysis, this paper summarizes China's e-government research, reveals the research hotspots and main areas in e-government in China, and further clarifies the research trends in e-government.

R. Hou et al. (Eds.): BDTA 2021/2022, LNICST 480, pp. 330–342, 2023.
https://doi.org/10.1007/978-3-031-33614-0_22

2 Data Sources and Research Methodology

2.1 Data Sources and Preparation

In this paper, the CSSCI journals included in China Knowledge Network (CNKI) are used as data sources, mainly including "E-Government", "Modern Intelligence" and "Journal of Intelligence", and "e-government" is used as a keyword for the preliminary search. 2014 is the year when the Central Leading Group for Network Security and Informatization was formally established, which is an important step in the national informatization strategy. It is also a key point in the history of e-government development, so the search period was set from 2014 to 2020. After counting, 458 relevant papers were retrieved in this study. After excluding irrelevant papers such as conference announcements, volume headings, comparative studies on e-government at home and abroad and duplicate papers, the final number of sample papers was 372.

2.2 Method

In this paper, the methods of co-word analysis and cluster analysis are mainly used in analysing hotspots of e-government research. Co-word analysis refers to the number of times two or two keywords appear in the same document, and thus determine the affinity between keywords [3]. On the basis of co-word analysis, cluster analysis is used to divide keywords that are close together into one category, each category representing a specific focus of the literature [5]. Currently, co-word cluster analysis appears in the fields of economics, tourism, policy, intelligence studies, and education. For example, based on this approach, Huang Zui et al. conducted a quantitative analysis of science innovation policy changes in China, and found that China's science and innovation policies have changed significantly in four areas: "international cooperation", "human resources", "institutional reform" and "research and development priorities" [4]. Ding Xueyang et al. used the method to analyse the stages of research on educational equity and the areas and themes covered by the research focus [5].

Using the co-word analysis method, with the help of software bibexcel, frequency statistics as well as co-occurrence matrix were generated for high-frequency keywords. Using the social network analysis software UCINET to draw visual knowledge maps, and similarity matrices were obtained through Excel and entered into SPSS software for clustering analysis. Accordingly, the hotspots and trends of e-government research in China are analysed in depth.

3 Analysis and Discussion

3.1 High Frequency Keyword Word Frequency Statistics and Analysis

Keywords are the result of a high degree of condensation of the content and methods of research in the literature, and word frequency statistics and analysis of keywords can transform keyword information into quantifiable data. The 372 documents were imported into NoteExpress and keyword statistics were performed. Finally, 697 keywords were obtained, and the top 31 keywords were selected as high-frequency keywords in this paper, as shown in Table 1.

Table 1. High frequency keyword word frequency table

Key words	Word frequency	Key words	Word frequency	Key words	Word frequency
E-government	351	Data sharing	19	Mobile government	12
Public services	50	Service-oriented government	17	Performance evaluation	11
Big data	39	Information resources	17	Public participation	9
E-governance	29	Digital government	15	Online government	8
Government websites	26	Cloud computing	14	Internet public opinion	7
Internet+	26	Government governance	14	Information security	7
Government microblogs	25	Government-people interaction	14	Open government	7
Informed society	23	New media	14	Social media	7
Public management	22	Data governance	13	Top-level design	7
Government services	21	Information disclosure	13		
Smart city	20	Government WeChat	12		

3.2   High Frequency Keyword Co-word Analysis

As can be seen from Table 1, these keywords appear more frequently in China's e-government research papers, except for the keyword "e-government" which is exactly the same as the subject term, and to a certain extent, these keywords indicate the research hotspots of Chinese scholars. Next, the co-occurrence matrix was used to generate a keyword co-occurrence network, and the relationship between these high-frequency keywords was explored based on this network diagram. Therefore, the co-occurrence frequencies in 372 papers were counted using bibexcel software, forming a 31 × 31 co-occurrence matrix, as shown in Table 2.

According to the co-occurrence matrix, with the help of UCINET, the co-occurrence network diagram of high-frequency keywords of e-government research from 2014 to 2020 was obtained, as shown in Fig. 1, 31 high-frequency keywords formed a very close interlocking network with each other, each node represented a keyword. The size of the interconnected nodes represents the centrality of the keywords, and the thickness of the connecting line between the nodes represents the frequency of occurrence of the two sets of keywords between the nodes. From Fig. 1, we can see that: (i)the concepts in

Table 2. High frequency keyword co-occurrence matrix (part)

	Big data	E-government	E-governance	Top-level design	Service-oriented government	Public services	Public management	Public participation	Internet +
Big data	39	36	1	2	0	5	0	1	3
E-government	36	351	27	7	15	50	22	9	24
E-governance	1	27	29	0	1	6	8	1	1
Top-level design	2	7	0	7	0	0	0	0	0
Service-oriented government	0	15	1	0	17	5	3	0	1
Public services	5	50	6	0	5	50	6	1	6
Public management	0	22	8	0	3	6	22	0	0
Public participation	1	9	1	0	0	1	0	9	0
Internet+	3	24	1	0	1	6	0	0	26

the core area are "e-government", "public services" and "big data", which are the three largest nodes, representing their highest frequency and influence in the field. These three nodes are the largest, which means that they are the most frequent and have the greatest influence in the field. (ii) "Online government", "government-public interaction", "information-based society", "public management" and "government governance" are in the transitional area. These keywords are the bridge between the central keywords and the peripheral keywords, and are also the focus of current research. (iii)Keywords in the marginal zone such as "data governance", "public participation" and "new media" are more specific concepts and the actual focus of researchers. Although they account for a relatively small proportion of the current research, they are also indicative of research trends in e-government.

At the same time, the social network-based analysis method specifies the position and importance of an individual in the network by calculating the centrality of the nodes. The degree centrality of a point indicates the direct connection between a point at the 'core' of a series of relationships and other points; the betweenness centrality of a point measures the degree of control an actor has over other resources in the network; and the closeness centrality of a point indicates how much it is not controlled by others, the smaller the proximity centrality value of the point is, the more critical the point is to the network [5]. Therefore, after excluding the keyword "e-government", the UCINET software was used to calculate the degree centrality, betweenness centrality and closeness centrality of high-frequency keywords to explain the power index of high-frequency keywords in the co-occurrence network knowledge graph (as shown in Table 3). Among the three indicators, "public services", "big data", "e-governance", "information society", "public management", "government websites", "government governance", "government-public interaction" and "data sharing" all ranked in the top 10, indicating that these keywords are at the core of the network and are hot spots in the field of e-government research. The fact that "cloud computing" and "information disclosure" ranked in the top 10 of more than one kind of indicators also indicates that they have important research value in the field of e-government, and the analysis results are basically consistent with the results of the co-occurrence network diagram of high-frequency keywords.

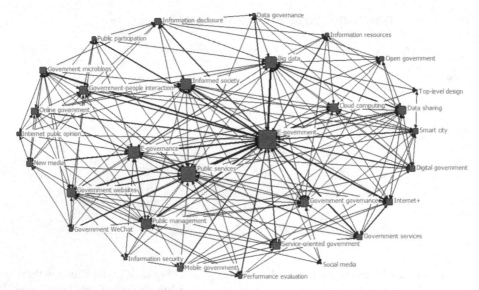

Fig. 1. High frequency keyword co-occurrence network diagram

Table 3. High-frequency keyword network centrality (part)

Num	Degree centrality		Closeness centrality		Betweenness centrality	
1	Public services	82.759	Public services	85.294	Public services	13.879
2	Big data	65.517	Big data	74.359	Big data	8.619
3	E-governance	65.517	E-governance	74.359	E-governance	7.422
4	Informed society	58.621	Informed society	70.732	Public management	4.925
5	Public management	55.172	Public management	67.442	Government websites	4.663
6	Government websites	51.724	Government websites	67.442	Informed society	3.943
7	Data sharing	48.276	Data sharing	65.909	Government governance	3.719
8	Government governance	48.276	Government governance	65.909	Government-people interaction	3.264
9	Government-people interaction	48.276	Government-people interaction	65.909	Data sharing	2.693
10	Cloud computing	44.828	Cloud computing	64.444	Information disclosure	2.4

3.3 High Frequency Keyword Clustering Analysis

The essence of cluster analysis is to divide the entire data into a number of finite categories, such that the differences in attributes within the same category are infinitely small and those between different categories are infinitely large [7]. Cluster analysis diagrams can visually reveal the research hotspots and research classifications in the field of e-government [8].

Firstly, Excel was used to convert the co-word matrix into a similarity matrix, part of which is shown in Table 4. In the similarity matrix, the closer the value is to 1, the closer the relationship between the two keywords is. It can be seen from Table 4 that "big data" is more closely related to other keywords and is one of the research centres.

Table 4. High frequency keyword similarity matrix (part)

	Big data	E-government	E-governance	Top-level design	Service-oriented government	Public services	Public management	Public participation	Internet +
Big data	1.000	0.738	0.476	0.614	0.445	0.580	0.458	0.531	0.550
E-government	0.738	1.000	0.731	0.679	0.699	0.806	0.740	0.714	0.715
E-governance	0.476	0.731	1.000	0.422	0.510	0.640	0.770	0.522	0.487
Top-level design	0.614	0.679	0.422	1.000	0.433	0.465	0.430	0.462	0.445
Service-oriented government	0.445	0.699	0.510	0.433	1.000	0.662	0.616	0.462	0.511
Public services	0.580	0.806	0.640	0.465	0.662	1.000	0.674	0.558	0.626
Public management	0.458	0.740	0.770	0.430	0.616	0.674	1.000	0.489	0.463
Public participation	0.531	0.714	0.522	0.462	0.462	0.558	0.489	1.000	0.457
Internet+	0.550	0.715	0.487	0.445	0.511	0.626	0.463	0.457	1.000

Next, the similarity matrix was imported into SPSS statistical software for cluster analysis, and the obtained cluster analysis is shown in Fig. 2. Finally, SPSS was used to conduct a multi-dimensional scale analysis of high-frequency keywords in e-government, resulting in a visual mapping, as shown in Fig. 3. Stress $= 0.1921 \leq 0.2$, RSQ $= 0.8269 \geq 0.6$, representing a good fit for this time. The multidimensional scaling method is a statistical research method that classifies and then analyses similar relationships between samples or variables in complex dimensions as distances in a two-dimensional plane.[3] Multidimensional scaling diagram more visually show the position of individual keywords in the research field and the distance of their relationship to each other.

As can be seen from Figs. 2 and 3, the above keywords can be divided into four clustering groups, as shown in Table 5. Cluster 1 focuses on the development trend of e-government, which is an Internet-based platform for government services that makes mobile government a reality and is gradually becoming a new means of government governance. Cluster 2 focuses on the specific application of e-government in the new media, effectively play the role of new media, correctly guide online public opinion, and enhance social governance capacity. Cluster 3 focuses primarily on e-governance in the information society, government websites and other platforms are important platforms for the

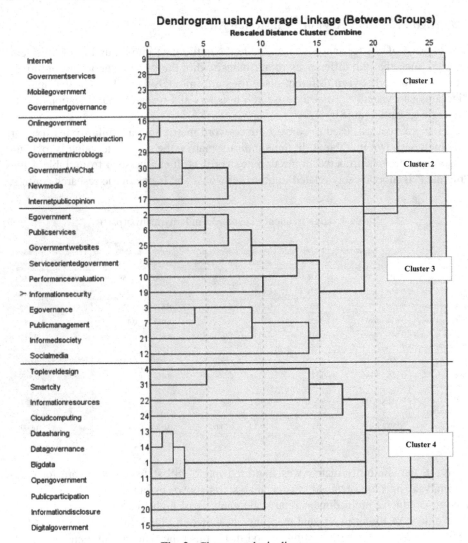

Fig. 2. Cluster analysis diagram

government to release information and interact with the public, create a service-oriented government while ensuring information security. Cluster 4 focuses on government information management and data governance, making full use of information resources and maximising their usefulness, improving the availability and authenticity of information resources; data governance and sharing can effectively solve the problem of data ownership, avoid the fragmented development of data and provide support for building a digital government.

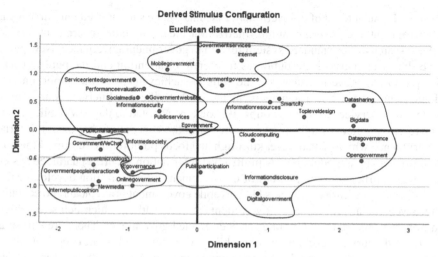

Fig. 3. Multidimensional scaling diagram

Table 5. Clustering results

Clusters	Clustering results
Cluster 1	Internet+, Government services, Mobile government, Government governance
Cluster 2	Internet governance, Government-people interaction, Government WeChat, Government Microblog, New media, Online public opinion
Cluster 3	E-government, Public services, Government websites, Service-oriented government, Performance evaluation, Information security, E-governance, Public management, Information society, Social media
Cluster 4	Top-level design, Smart city, Information resources, Cloud computing, Data sharing, Data governance, Big data, Open government, Public participation, Information disclosure, Digital government

4 Findings

Based on the results of the above co-word analysis, cluster analysis and multi-dimensional scale analysis, and combined with relevant literature, the research hotspots in the field of e-government in China in recent years can be further analysed and studied, this section analyses and discusses the research hotspots in the field from the following four perspectives.

4.1 Researches on the Development Trend of E-Government

New public service theory, service-oriented government theory, information security theory, holistic governance theory and open government theory are the theoretical foundations for the development of e-government. Based on the above theories, the research on the development trend of e-government in China can be summarised into three areas: the development of e-government informatization, the research on government services and the research on the standard system related to government governance. New public service theory emphasises the public as the centre of attention and the public service as the purpose of government work and thus the achievement of the public interest. [9] E-government itself is a management model that relies on Internet technology to provide public services to social groups. It should be adapted to the new public service theory to create a new form of public service with the concept of "big data + Internet + government", which is also a breakthrough and focus point for the reform of the government governance model [10]. A multi-level information security guarantee system should be constructed in the process of e-government informatization development to solve information security problems [11]. Mobile government is a typical representative of the development process of e-government informatization, which helps to achieve open government affairs and build a service-oriented government. There are still some problems in the current development of mobile government, such as the overall quality of service, unclear planning and design, the phenomenon of fragmentation of services and uneven levels of public use [12]. In order to improve the quality of government services, it is necessary to consider the impact of policy requirements, technological application capabilities, political drive, and institutional environment on the city government's Internet service capabilities [13]. Holistic governance emphasizes the use of integration, coordination and networking to solve problems in government governance and reform. In order to cope with the problems such as information silos in the development of e-government, research on standard systems mainly including four areas: construction of e-government informatization standards, construction of a standard system for government services, standardization of open government services at the grassroots level and exploration of a standard system for e-government interoperability. However, in the current research process, the theoretical and practical combination is not close enough. It is necessary to start from the construction of the current situation, analyze the root of the problem, test the research results in practice, and promote the high-quality development of e-government as well as the reform of government governance model.

4.2   Research on the Integration of E-Government and New Media

In the context of big data, government microblogs, government weibo and government APPs have emerged one after another in response, enriching the channels of online information services. In 2018, the State Office issued the Opinions on Promoting the Healthy and Orderly Development of New Media for Government Affairs, elevating new media for government affairs as "an important channel for the Party and government to contact the masses, serve the masses and bring them together" [14]. The scope of research by Chinese scholars has focused on the communication effects of new government media, the optimization path and the governance of online public opinion. The new government media has the function of releasing government information, guiding social opinion and improving the government's social governance capacity. With the help of big data technology, the appropriate "soft text" communication strategy can be used to enhance the communication effect of the new media of government [15]. With the increasing number of new government media, the problems in practice have been exposed, such as the lack of influence of new media for government affairs on the image of the government and the public, the lack of initiative in platform construction and the lack of interaction between new media platforms, as well as the lack of full use of government data resources, all of which have affected the communication effect [16]. The government should attach importance to the construction of new media for government affairs, rely on the advantages of big data, adhere to the people-centered approach, and make use of the development mechanism combining multiplemodes to optimize the its development and improve its social influence [17]. As one of the mainstream media in China, the new media for government affairs should actively participate in the governance of online public opinion. Online public opinion governance includes early warning of online public opinion, the need for guidance and the formulation of guidance strategies. When participating in online public opinion management, new media for government affairs should establish a positive concept of public opinion, harness the power of multiple guidance and flexibly use public opinion response methods, so that the public opinion guidance mechanism and the new government media matrix can play a linkage role [18]. Therefore, its necessary to focus on the synergistic development of e-government and new media, the construction of a new media matrix, the diversity of communication strategies and the improvement of the ability to integrate and utilise big data resources, in order to achieve the social communication effect of "1 + 1 > 2".

4.3 Research on E-Governance in the Information Society

E-governance is an important part of the national governance system, including public management and services, e-government information construction and other aspects. Domestic scholars' research on e-governance in the information society mainly covers three aspects: public services, continuous use of government websites and government performance evaluation. As early as 2011, Ning Jiajun pointed out that building a service-oriented e-government centered on the public will improve the government's basic public service capabilities [19]. Government websites are an important part of the construction of service-oriented e-government, and the study of users' continuous use behaviour on government websites is conducive to improving the construction of government websites and, in turn, the information construction of e-government. Research on the sustained use of government websites has gone through four stages: the technology acceptance model, the information system success model, the expectation confirmation theory and the expectation confirmation model of sustained use of information systems [20]. The public intention to continue using government websites influences the construction of government websites to a certain extent, while the quality of information, system quality and service quality of public service centres significantly affects the public's intention to use government websites as well as government performance [21]. In addition, e-government performance evaluation is a new model of government management services and governance, and the current research areas are mainly in government information disclosure, government website construction and application, and electronic government public service system construction and application. In order to improve user experience and build a service-oriented government, the performance evaluation system should be based on three aspects: the level of content construction, the degree of functional perfection and the effectiveness of user experience [22]. According to the current situation in specific provinces and cities, an overall performance management model for e-government can be established that is integrated, linked and coordinated with "government openness, 'Internet+ government services' and government website intensification" [23]. Currently, the national integrated online government services platform has been put online for trial run in 2019, which to a certain extent reflects the service capability of "one network for all". But in the process of service government transformation, the integration of online and offline services has not been fully achieved. In the future, important issues such as system building for e-governance, public participation and interaction, information security in information technology construction and evaluation of the effectiveness of policy implementation will require continuous attention.

4.4 Research on Government Information Management and Data Governance

At the national level, a number of documents on information management and data governance have been promulgated since 2015, including the Action Plan for Promoting the Development of Big Data, the Interim Measures for the Management of Government Information Resources Sharing, the Guidelines for the Construction of the "Internet+ Government Services" Technical System and so on, the documents provide a plan for effectively promoting data sharing in e-government [24]. In academic research, three aspects of information management and data governance are mainly studied: the current situation, framework system design and relevant policy standards. Local governments in China have insufficient capacity to apply data analysis techniques, inadequate internal management and external collaboration mechanisms, and inadequate security to prevent risks in the process of data governance [25]. One of the main reasons for these problems is that the framework system for government information management and data governance in China is not perfect, and a data governance framework can be constructed in accordance with relevant theories, focusing on government information management aspects and realizing embedded government data governance [26]. Policy support is essential for the governance of the current situation and the design of the framework system. Therefore, it is necessary to study and interpret the relevant policies. The relevant policy research mainly focuses on government data openness policy, data security policy, privacy protection policy, open licensing policy, infrastructure policy and government data governance policy, etc., and suggestions can be made accordingly. For example, the open government data subject system can be improved in four aspects: the legal subject system, the subject integration system, the coordination system of responsibilities and powers, and the subject exemption system [27]. And in the process of data opening, the principles of openness, quality, timeliness, equality, balance of interests and security should be followed [28]. Our government, as one of the subjects of e-government information management and data governance, should not only establish a reasonable concept of data governance, and build a dynamic balance mechanism for information security and privacy protection, but also grasp the extent of data utilization wisely to avoid leading to an over-reliance on data [29]. Therefore, it is necessary to consider the characteristics of information sharing and existing problems in the era of big data and the current situation of data governance in China, and further deepen the research on the optimization of data emergency management system and information sharing security, so as to guarantee the effectiveness of information management and data governance in China.

5 Summary

The continuous development of the Internet has brought development opportunities and challenges for e-government. Through a visual analysis of the CSSCI-included literature in the field of e-government in China from 2014 to 2020, this paper finds that the research hotspots of e-government in China broadly involve four fields. Although the research results of e-government have gradually increased in recent years, there are still problems such as a single research perspective, insufficient integration of theory and practice, and lack of dynamic analysis of research. Therefore, a systematic, relevant, dynamic and universal paradigm of e-government research should be established to promote the in-depth development of e-government theoretical research. There are also some shortcomings in this study: (i) the sample data is limited, and there may be bias in grasping the research hotspots. (ii) the research data is time-sensitive, which may make the analysis of research hotspots and research status have stage characteristics; (iii) the bibliometric analysis can reflect the hot spots and research trends in this field, but the interpretation of the visual charts is somewhat subjective and generalised.

At present, the accelerating process of internationalisation and modernisation and the rapid spread of new technologies will certainly bring new impetus to the field of e-government in China. Therefore, the future development of e-government in China still needs to be studied in depth and on an ongoing basis.

References

1. Li, Y., Yan, H., Zhao, Y.: Knowledge graph analysis of domestic e-government research based on CSSCI. E-Government (04), 112-121 (2016)
2. Yang, D.: The current situation of e-government development in China and the outlook of the 13th five-year plan. E-Government (03), 53-60 (2017)
3. Callon, M., Law, J., Rip, A.: Mapping the Dynamics of Science and Technology: Sociology of Science in the Real World. Macmillan (1986)
4. Huang, C., Zhao, P., Li, J.: A quantitative analysis of China's science and technology innovation policy changes based on co-word analysis. Chin. Public Adm. (09), 115-122 (2015)
5. Ding, X., Cheng, T.: Hotspots and future trends of China's educational equity research since the 21st century--a knowledge map analysis based on co-word matrix. Distance Educ. China (01), 9–17+46+92 (2019)
6. Liu, J.: Lecture Notes on Holistic Network Analysis - A Practical Guide to UCINET Software, pp. 97–107. Gezhi Press, Shanghai (2009)
7. Zhang, W.: Advanced Tutorial on SPSS Statistical Analysis, pp. 238–246. Higher Education Press, Beijing (2004)
8. Guo, W.: Knowledge graph: a new technique for content visualization research of educational literature. J. East China Normal Univ. (Educ. Sci.) **34**(01), 45–50+114 (2016)
9. Gu, L.: New public service theory and its implications for China's public service reform. Nanjing J. Soc. Sci. (01), 38–45 (2005)

10. Zhai, Y.: Research on the change of government governance model from the perspective of overall government: the example of "Internet+government services" in Zhejiang, Guangdong, Suzhou and Shanghai. E-Government (10), 34–45 (2019)
11. Li, F., Wu, C., Wang, M.: Information Security Theory and Technology. Xi'an University of Electronic Science and Technology Press (2018)
12. Zheng, Y., Wang, H.: The current situation, problems and countermeasures of mobile government. Public Adm. Policy Rev. **8**(02), 74–84 (2019)
13. Li, H., Gu, L.: Technical rationality, political rationality and online government service capacity building: an empirical study based on the Internet service capacity building of Chinese prefecture-level municipal governments. E-Government (06), 86–97 (2020)
14. Huang, H.: The policy evolution of "digital government" in China: the relationship between "digital government" and "e-government." Adm. Tribune **27**(03), 47–55 (2020)
15. Zhang, F., Yang, Y, Wu, L.: An experimental study on the effect of "soft text" communication in government weibo. Journalism Mass Commun. Monthly (01), 59-73 (2020)
16. Zhang, D.: How to break the "information silo" in the new media of government affairs. People's Tribune (09), 52-53 (2020)
17. Zhang, L., Mei, G.: Research on the optimization path of governmental jitterbug based on SWOT analysis. E-Government (09), 113–124 (2019)
18. Ye, Y.: A study on the strategy of government weibo for responding to emergencies. J. Editing (03), 107–111 (2017)
19. Ning, J.: Integrated planning, innovative services, and solid promotion of e-government construction in the new era. E-Government (10), 49–58 (2011)
20. Wu, S.: Research on the Model of Public's Intention of Continuous use of Government Websites. University of Electronic Science and Technology of China (2017)
21. Ming, C., Xu, X., Chen, T.: Service quality and citizen satisfaction in public service centres: the moderating role of citizen participation. Nanjing J. Soc. Sci. (12), 71–77 (2016)
22. Wang, J., Yang, D.: Performance evaluation of government websites based on user experience: exploration and practice. E-Government (05), 35–41 (2014)
23. Shou, Z., Huang, X., Guo, Y., Chen, Z., Xu, J., Wang, X.: Study on the transformation of overall performance assessment of e-government services--a review and reconstruction of the problems of Anhui model. E-Government (10), 108–116 (2019)
24. Zhang, H., Hu, S.: Research on the promotion strategy of cross-sector data sharing for "Internet + government services." J. Intell. **37**(12), 168–174 (2018)
25. Zheng, Y., Gan, Q., Zhang, C., Zhang, X.: The current situation and problems of local government data governance-an empirical study based on 43 government hotline departments. E-Government (07), 66–79 (2020)
26. Huang, J., Zhou, R.: Research on the construction of government data governance framework based on information lifecycle management theory. E-Government (09), 85–95 (2019)
27. Chen, C., Deng, Z.: Research on the path to improve the system of open government data subjects. Inf. Sci. **37**(01), 3–8+21 (2019)
28. Jiao, H.: Exploration of the principles that should be followed for the opening of government data in China. Libr. Inf. Serv. **61**(15), 81–88 (2017)
29. Tan, B., Liu, R.: The UK government data governance system and its inspiration for China: towards "good governance." J. Inf. Resour. Manage. **10**(05), 55–65 (2020)

Research on Virtual Simulation Teaching Platform Based on Convergent Media

Qing Fan[1,2(✉)], Liang Xia[1], and Chuanming Sun[1]

[1] National Research Center of Cultural Industies, Central China Normal University,
Wuhan 430079, China
43132944@qq.com
[2] Jingchu University of Technology, Jingmen 448200, China

Abstract. Analyze and summarize the existing metadata at home and abroad. Based on DC metadata, combined with the characteristics and forms of intangible cultural heritage, it further explores the metadata-based intangible cultural heritage knowledge organization based on relevant resource description standards. National intangible cultural heritage-Wuhan woodcarving ship model as an example, to control the application of metadata in intangible cultural heritage knowledge organizations, and to provide new ideas for the protection of national intangible cultural heritage and digital communication.

Keywords: intangible cultural heritage · metadata · knowledge organization

1 Preface

Today, with the rapid development of new media, the college new media specialty is precisely the current strong demand of the industry and society. Colleges and universities should integrate the media experimental teaching platform as the college new media. The core of convergence media is media convergence, that is, with the development of media technology and the breaking of some barriers, the continuous advancement of television, network, and mobile technologies, all kinds of news media will be integrated [1]. However, the integrated media experiment platform is an important training platform for college journalism majors. It is an important part of news collection, digital reporting, data analysis and public opinion monitoring. It not only provides important information for media digital research, digital communication and scientific research results conversion. The foundation, but also to improve students' practical ability of digital news production and innovation ability cannot be underestimated.

However, how to build a media convergence platform that integrates the capabilities of news gathering, editing, and writing is an important issue for the cultivation of journalism professionals in contemporary universities. Through our teaching research, it is found that the talents currently cultivated in colleges and universities are out of touch with the needs of society. Social media needs complex, high-quality talents, but our schools cultivate a single, theoretical, but little practice. Talent training programs

R. Hou et al. (Eds.): BDTA 2021/2022, LNICST 480, pp. 343–355, 2023.
https://doi.org/10.1007/978-3-031-33614-0_23

are backward is out of touch with the times. To this end, on the one hand, we should continue to improve our talent training program according to social needs, plus theoretical knowledge to keep pace with the development of the times, on the other hand, we recommend a media experiment platform for journalism professionals to allow students to do from theory to practice Gapless docking.

1 Development status of converged media

With the rapid development of the global Internet, the emergence of smart phones, mobile networks, various cloud platforms, and various online video tools has exploded since media users have exploded, and online micro-videos have become popular. With the help of digital cloud platforms, virtual reality, augmented reality and other technologies, traditional news media have entered the stage of real-time news production and reporting. On March 7, 2017, CNN announced the formal establishment of a virtual reality (VR) news department called "CNNVR", focusing on immersive VR news and live broadcasting, and launched a 360-degree panorama every week Video [2]. At the same time, foreign media such as Face book, Twitter, etc. are attracting more attention to the investment of big convergent media, in order to attract more users of social platforms, and enhance their online voice.

In 2015, the country proposed the "Internet+" plan, which is the external power and necessary way to promote a new round of conmunication of traditional media. Traditional media can use the Internet to complete its own innovation and reform through intelligent upgrades, operational upgrades, and service upgrades [3]. At the same time, the network livestreaming platforms and the continuous development of digital media technology have become the new driving force for the conmunication and development of domestic news media. At the same time, mobility, real-time, interactivity, integration and virtuality have become the highlights of the development of convergence media. All traditional media are changing to new media and converged media. The construction of converged media represented by People's Daily's "Central Kitchen" has promoted the conmunication and development of traditional media of all sizes across the country. Build a converged media platform and do a good job of "two micro-ends". According to survey statistics, the top three with the highest total readings of public accounts in 2018 are "People's Daily", "Xinhua News" and "CCTV News". "People's Daily" published 8,156 articles in 2018, with a total reading of 810 million and likes of 94.43 million [4]. In addition, the construction of a cloud platform for media integration has also been the focus of recent development. For example, Hubei Radio and Television Group contacted the Yangtze River Cloud established by TV stations in various cities in the province to create a news production and a real-time resource sharing. These are the differences between traditional media and integrated media Trial and innovation.

The applicable and practical characteristics of journalism majors in colleges and universities require schools to build integrated teaching platforms that meet the daily teaching of students, including news gathering, editing, writing, sending and live broadcasting. Similarly, this kind of integration platform is different from the integration media of social media companies. It should also have the characteristics of integration of teaching and experiment, multi-platform action, and cross media. It is required that the school's journalism major teaching tasks can complete training on this converged experimental platform, and it must also achieve resource sharing and seamless integration with various processes. On the integrated media platform, students can completely simulate the process from content production to news broadcast according to the social media model. Can intuitively and quickly train students' actual combat ability.

2   Achieve Functions of Convergence Media Experiment Platform

The Convergence Media Lab is an important experimental training base for journalism majors in colleges and universities, and an important place for students to carry out practical teaching and connect with society. The construction of the laboratory should be able to meet the needs of on-campus training, including the environment of the venue and the number of equipment [5]. It should be technically practical, efficient and advanced, based on the current needs of teaching research and social services, and give due consideration to the advanced nature of technology [6]. At the same time, from the perspective of construction funds, efficiency, safety and scalability, we should maximize the effectiveness of the integrated media experimental teaching platform.

The construction of converged media solutions is based on the integration of content aggregation, production, and publishing. It integrates all aspects of media acquisition, editing, storage, and management. At the technical design level, it must provide a long-term uninterrupted operation, high reliability and high processing capacity, multi-service support platform with strong scalability. Therefore, the technology design and implementation of the integrated media teaching platform should be comprehensively considered from the aspects of advancement, stability, security, openness and scalability.

From a news perspective, the production of the content of each news requires unified command and collaborative production and collection are highly compatible, and the content is released at the same time when it is released on the "two micro ends". In the actual experimental teaching, considering the actual situation of the university, we adopt the "platform + tools + service" technology model to carry out the integrated production of news to cover the overall collection, editing, preservation and management of news. In terms of the overall rest of the network, we divide it into three parts: the school intranet, the teaching network, and the Internet. Each network has independent devices and service platforms. To achieve the integration of the overall system to respond to business, the process is effectively interoperable, and the technology is seamlessly connected. The function of the integrated media experiment teaching platform is shown in Fig. 1.

According to the function, we divide it into four parts: business collection, collection of news materials, management, production and preservation. The external collection includes literature, sound and pictures.

In the aggregation function, the platform supports materials such as hardware devices (cameras, computers, mobile phones, etc.), cloud clues, user news breaking news, news collection and other materials to enter the converged media experiment platform online. In the cloud clue, through the big data analysis and mining system, real-time monitoring of hot events of the media in the entire network, real-time tracking of special events and local news, so as to realistically achieve mainstream domestic media, including newspapers and websites under the media, Weibo, WeChat, news mobile client manuscript

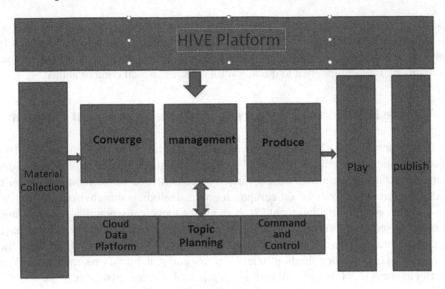

Fig. 1. Converged Media Functions

monitoring and hot spot mining. To achieve unified and integrated material management. For the collection of multiple materials, various types of non-edited materials are supported, including text, pictures, sound, and video.

In the aggregation function, the platform externally supports the materials of hardware devices (camera, computer, mobile phone management functions are the core of this experimental teaching platform, responsible for the management of content library materials, unified transcoding of video formats, and the topic selection of news Planning and management to manage the flow of content production. Traditional media content is produced in a standardized form, and then delivered and sent to everyone through specific channels and media, and converged media is more in the state of simultaneous operation of multiple media. Use the integrated media model to classify and integrate a large amount of information, so that traditional and new media forms such as paper media, mobile media, television media and online emerging media can be merged into a huge gathering place for media resources. Information can be edited and published simultaneously in the group Integrated operation of all internal media. The management of the integrated media experimental teaching platform can realize the unified management and personalized display of the content resources of the content library, including the specific elements: index, metadata management, life cycle management, permissions Etc. Use the index to analyze the content Labeled, sorted, organized, fast retrieval and presentation, while using the metadata management to complete meta data entry and inheritance media files, media files to achieve unity.

In addition, in the platform's resource library management, from multiple levels and angles, multiple links provide information retrieval functions for platform management, including personal information space and information management of the platform's public resource library, including storage of data, Add, delete, archive and other processing. In the business process, the key chain technology is used to manage the news content in a pipelined manner to ensure that different people will not process the news information repeatedly. In the management module, another important function is to perform permission management for different personnel. News planning, production, production, and broadcasting all have a strict data grouping and encryption mechanism to allow personnel with different permissions to access different data to ensure Data security.

The production function includes the design and support of various production tools including the content published on the Internet and traditional news production tools. For example: multimedia video editing tools, BS short video editing tools, multimedia manuscript editing tools, etc. It can arrange the content of WeChat, Weibo, APP, website and other Internet publishing channels, and provide a large number of template styles for editing. It can implement comparative editing, achieve multi-level auditing, and realize unified platform and interface management for multiple channels and multiple accounts. In the production tool software, it has the support to support the mobile phone to the school's business, such as mobile phone material back transmission, mobile topic planning, mobile manuscript writing, mobile review, and prompting business process news at any time.

In the news topic selection planning, it has unified planning and management of the integration business to meet the needs of the integrated media for the overall teaching business. From the perspective of command reporting and topic selection planning, it is Internet-based, paperless, and process-oriented. Realize the management and tracing of topic selection, and the top-level design management of different businesses. The specific functions include: new topic selection, topic selection management, topic selection assignment, task management, and support for planning single management topic selection. Select, enter, manage, and assign topics through the mobile phone and the PC, which is convenient for teachers in the school to operate the topics and improve work efficiency.

In the command report module, it includes the overall display of business data and business processes, the status of student positioning and material collection, and the function of on-site connection to communicate and command students and equipment. Realize the need for intuitive monitoring of daily business and command planning of sudden major accidents. Through the statistics and analysis of productivity business data, business processes, and published data, it helps to measure and analyze the performance of business processes, and find the key problems of business processes through visualized processes and data, which is conducive to improving the speed and quality of business processes and production processes. And efficiency.

After the news production is completed, after the review is correct, the program will be broadcast or published on the Internet. The release on the network platform includes the release of news content on WeChat public account, Sina Weibo, APP, and website. These releases only need to be edited, managed and arranged by the integrated media teaching platform.

3 Construction of a Converged Media Experiment Platform

3.1 General Frame Design

The convergence media experiment teaching is a comprehensive news media processing platform. The data processed is huge, including videos, pictures, texts, sounds, etc., the distributed technology is used to manage the media, and the micro-service design is used to realize the system Decoupling and reconstruction, etc. In the design of the experimental platform, we are next divided into three levels, namely the tool layer, the platform layer and the basic resource layer, as shown in picture 2

At the tool layer, the boundaries of traditional systems are broken, the tools in each system are classified and aggregated, and the relevant tool units are designed according to the aggregation, management, production, and release links to support the development of multiple businesses. In the tool layer, there are news business, variety show production, studio broadcasting, mobile media business and "two micro-ends" business. In the application of tools, it breaks the boundaries of traditional systems, classifies and aggregates the tools in each system, and focuses on the design of related tool units in accordance with aggregation, management, production, and release to support the development of multiple businesses.

At the media platform layer, the basic resource layer is a virtual management platform to manage private basic service resources, and through virtual division and integration, four virtual services supporting computing, network, database and storage are constructed. At the platform level, there are four basic service modules: data services, media processing services, management services, and other services. The servers corresponding to all modules are designed with a distributed service framework to meet the principles of load balancing and high availability. And in response to the actual service support needs of colleges and universities, multiple units are integrated, and the content service center and process-driven service center will be the core services that support the operation of the cloud platform in the future. The public service components in the platform service layer implement distributed deployment, load balancing, and high availability. The services are loosely coupled and use a unified calling method.

Both the tool layer and the platform layer adhere to the open design to meet the excellent user experience and platform service capabilities. The construction method of separating the background service from the terminal application tools is adopted to expand the choice of terminal application tools. Through the unified platform access specification, you can access the production tools of mainstream manufacturers, and use unified resource management to facilitate the access of multi-vendor editing tools. As the hardware support of the entire converged media platform, the basic resource layer has certain requirements on the hardware configuration and performance. The bottom layer of the entire basic resource is also the core layer. The entire hardware design uses HP workstations, including Graphics Processors Unit, Central Unit Storage Arrays, Non-linear Editing Workstations, Video and Audio Encoder, Network Management Module, I/O Load Balancing Module, etc., as shown in Fig. 2.

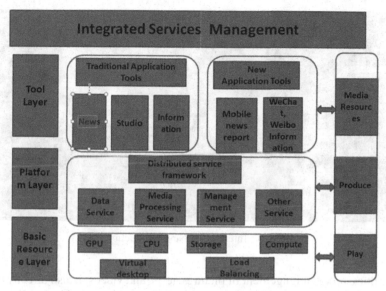

Fig. 2. Converged media technology architecture diagram

3.2 News Production Design

The teaching platform construction is to integrate video, multimedia manuscripts, audio processing, mobile information processing and news information release, and also requires teachers to be able to conduct real-time monitoring and guidance. This requires that the media information needs to be processed by different terminals, and has a flexible website processing style and unified material management.

1. The media video editing tool is an online video editing tool based on HTML5 that adopts the B/S architecture. It only needs a browser to work, and it achieves true Internet editing, which can realize fast video cutting, subtitles, and special effects. Such as a variety of efficient and fast video processing. After simple editing is completed, the background is automatically packaged for subsequent sharing and distribution services. The storyboard generated by editing can be directly entered into the production platform, and can be directly opened by non-editing software for subsequent processing. Provide B/S web version editing software based on the video content library. Users can log in to the media platform through the browser anytime and anywhere using a computer, open the tool, and directly edit the material directly, including video editing, stripping, common effects, and subtitles And other functions, the edited content is automatically packaged in the background for subsequent use, as shown in Fig. 3.

2. The multimedia editing tool not only undertakes the content distribution function of WeChat and Weibo and other mainstream platforms; it also includes the management and editing of published content, provides a rich material library and template library, provides topic selection management, and is more convenient for the management of news articles, Editing and task tracing; at the same time, it has powerful editing

Fig. 3. Interface of News production

capabilities, mixed arrangement of pictures, texts, and videos; it also directly embeds pictures and video edits on the picture and text editing pages to achieve unified editing in a true sense. Use the editor in the multimedia work to carry out picture editing and intelligent matching of short videos and GIFs; at the same time, use intelligent technology to intelligently identify subtitles in video clips, which can synthesize subtitle overlays with one click, which can greatly improve Editing efficiency.

3. Precise video editing tools. The main function of tools in the system is to complete the editing and production of the program. The professional terminal NOVA provided by the system platform edits the high bit rate material through NOVA. Professional video processing terminals use high-performance workstations and professional video and audio I/O cards in terms of hardware to ensure that they meet the requirements of the integrated media system in terms of real-time editing. The precise editing workstation realizes the rapid production of video programs, and provides users with different types of video editing tools, including complete editing and initial editing, supports commonly used high-definition video files, standard-definition video editing, and various high-definition format mixed editing. The editor provides a variety of special effects and provides subtitle processing and other functions. In the video precision editing tool, it supports offline mode editing, and the project file supports backup and recovery. In terms of function, you can directly replace text, pictures, videos, model elements in the edit bar, and make video news quickly and conveniently in a templated way. Provides rich 3D synthesis effects, can perform 3D model transitions, manually draw animations and other functions, and provides various types of template components including subtitle templates, non-editing effect templates, sound effect libraries, and 3D packaging templates.

4. Dubbing tools. In this project, the professional dubbing software is separated from Non-line Editing as an independent workstation, which is mainly used for the later dubbing of the program. The software follows the main style of Nova, and on the basis of it, it has been redesigned specifically for dubbing, and a powerful teleprompter function has been added to make it more suitable for dubbing business environments.

The dubbing workstation can dub the high and low bit rate programs according to the different types of programs, and is equipped with a professional sound card to achieve a professional-level dubbing effect. Targeted dubbing design, extract the content of the program manuscript while dubbing, so that users can see the content of the manuscript directly on the display screen, instead of the previous way of holding the manuscript in the hand to dub, which simplifies the voice The cumbersome preparation of the manuscript before the dubbing allows the voice actor to see the manuscript and the video screen, grasp the speed, and control the sound. The secondary adjustment in the dubbing tool is also very convenient, and various sound effect processing makes the dubbing effect more abundant. The platform dubbing supports two processes of dubbing, namely, dubbing by picture and dubbing by voice, so that users can either dub first and then edit the program after completion; or they can dub the dubbing workstation and complete the dubbing after that, it can be sent to the synthesis server for synthesis.

5. Information release system. With the rapid development of information technology and the continuous accumulation of multimedia technology, the traditional Internet-based multimedia technology and its single distribution channel can no longer meet the requirements of the current media audience. New media such as mobile phones, Internet TV, and WeChat are constantly emerging, which broadens the channels for digital media release, and also requires a platform to comprehensively manage the digital resources of various media. The project solution for the construction of the experimental teaching platform of media fusion in universities has made a very open and convenient design for Internet publishing. The system can realize the direct release of WeChat public account, Sina Weibo, APP and website. In order to effectively manage existing teaching resources and digital resources, provide content support for the operation of new media businesses, and lay a resource foundation for future business development, we have designed a new content publishing system, namely SCMS, SCMS Based on LAMP technology architecture and MVC + OOP mode development, it adopts modular development method to facilitate secondary development and expansion. SCMS takes "practical + easy to use" as the basic concept and provides an integrated solution from information publishing, organization, communication, interaction, data mining to profitability. It is the preferred CMS product for educational new media websites.

SCMS is located at the top of PC website, APP terminal, and WeChat public account, and publishes information content to each terminal in a unified manner. Content creators, editors, and publishers use SCMS to submit, modify, approve, and publish content, including graphics, atlases, videos, live broadcasts, special topics, and other information you want to publish to the terminal. At the same time provide additional functions such as content collection, access statistics, advertising, editing and assessment. Users can get rid of the shackles of technology and programming language, break through technical bottlenecks and reduce labor costs.

3.3 Media Aggregation Module

We can use the media aggregation module for Non-line editing, PPT, network big data, national regional news, video real-time collection and local material upload.

In network data aggregation, data mining technology are used to monitor the latest and hottest news hotspots in the entire network in real time. In order to realize the monitoring of domestic mainstream media, including newspapers, websites, Weibo, WeChat, and news mobile client manuscripts under the media, and hot spot mining. In order to ensure the timeliness of hot news, for every hot news found in the hot news of the media, the system will update the heat every 5 min. The heat value is affected by factors such as the number of media reprinted, media weight, and time. When the reprint rate per unit time is higher than the parameter of decreasing the heat value by the passage of time, the heat value of the news continues to rise. When the reprint rate per unit time is lower than the parameter that the time elapses and the heat value decreases, the heat value of the news will continue to decline. The system does not simply reflect the heat of a certain point, but monitors the entire life cycle process of each hot news, and reflects the news heat value from the process; adding the consideration of time factor increases the scientificity of the heat value calculation and also allows the calculation The heat value can be truly reflected in the actual application scenario. Media hotspot monitoring supports two dimensions, time sorting and popularity sorting, and supports retrieval functions. In addition, the module also uses the article's semantic intelligent learning system to classify each hot news into 15 major categories (social, education, current affairs, economy, military, technology, sports, art, transportation, entertainment, cars, real estate, weather, Travel, food), to facilitate editing of different columns, and quickly extract the required news from different news categories.

PCG backhaul, PGC backhaul module mainly implements mobile phones, tablet computers and other mobile terminals to send back breaking news through the mobile network. As an important auxiliary means for emergency reporting, it can return files taken by mobile terminals to the cloud aggregation platform, Rapid production release through cloud editing, can also be directly downloaded to the school for rapid production.

3.4 Design of Media Resource Management System

The design of MAS for Internet thinking, MSA (Micro Service Architecture) aims to achieve centralized management of solutions by decomposing functions into discrete services. MSA goes from the system to the components inside the system. MSA is divided into business and packaged with smaller granularity, which provides conditions for the system to achieve more elaborate elastic scaling and decentralization, which is conducive to independent deployment and operation, independent operation, and Support different advanced technology implementation methods.

According to the characteristics of media applications, service management is subdivided from three dimensions. One is to subdivide on the horizontal expansion capability, the second is to subdivide on the level of refinement of business services, and the third is to subdivide on data attributes. This design allows the system to easily expand the system horizontally, following the principle of service-oriented, to achieve a real building or split system like building blocks, and at the same time the system can break the system barriers to achieve flexible data interaction and achieve data And system disaster recovery. Use a variety of Internet technologies to achieve the development and design of this system architecture, such as the use of Docker/Swarm technology for service containerized management; the platform uses HTTP/Restful interface technology to achieve standard open and lightweight and efficient service invocation; using Zookeeper to achieve services Cluster management; high availability and load balancing of services are achieved through HAProxy + Keepalive; data is segmented according to Scale Cube theory, and comprehensive database technologies such as Mongodb, MySQL, Codis, ElasticSearch, etc. are used to achieve distributed storage of converged content, Efficient access and performance scaling; Logstash and ElasticSearch achieve unified management of logs, as shown in Fig. 4.

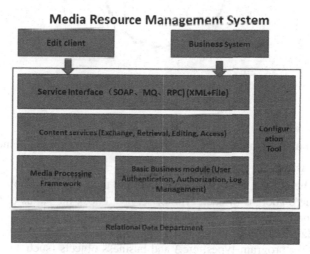

Fig. 4. Media Resource Management System

SaaS service design (Platform-as-a-Service) uses distributed computing technology. Distributed computing technology divides the project to be processed into several data blocks, and distributes these data blocks to multiple computing nodes for calculation, and monitors each computing node at the same time. Therefore, distributed computing can not only ensure the security of the calculation, but also improve the calculation efficiency of the system, and also can automatically load balance. In the era of all media, the production, dissemination and interactive Internetization of programs is an inevitable trend. The distributed application system can provide users with dynamically scalable virtualized resources.

The SaaS service integrates multiple replicas to form a cluster, and provides multiple tools with the cooperation of corresponding switches. In fact, in the background architecture, nodes can scale horizontally according to user needs to enhance computing power. The PaaS service layer provides a series of clear and clear SaaS interface definitions aimed at providing SaaS software services with a more standardized access to the cloud platform, enabling unified management of various business applications and unified exchange of business data. Therefore, the design of SaaS software services should follow the standardized interface design, as shown in Fig. 5.

For many PaaS services and interface definitions, the platform service management also provides visual service, configuration management, and interface definition queries.

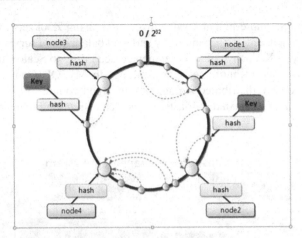

Fig. 5. SaaS Distributed Computing

You can see the management overview of the entire cluster on the homepage, mainly including:

1. Determine whether the network is accessible and detect the status of cluster nodes.
2. Determine the c address of each type of service, check the status of the service on each node, and view the log records.
3. Visual metadata modeling of PaaS layer data objects (such as cataloging layer, recording tasks, EDL, program types, etc.) and business objects (such as video services, audio services, picture services, document services).
4. Configure the functional permissions, roles, content permissions, and functional permissions of PaaS services and tools. At the same time, it provides an API interface to facilitate the third-party business system to quickly access the platform.

4   Conclusion

In the process of constructing the integrated media experimental teaching platform, it is necessary to meet the teaching needs of university teachers and students, and adhere to the principles of practicability and applicability. At the technical level, there can be a real-time, non-stop, high-reliability, high-processing capability, and scalability multi-service support platform, and the relevant hardware and software configuration should meet the requirements of media information processing. Through the integration of different modular functions, the integration of news content collection, production and release is completed, and all aspects of media collection, editing, storage and management in the new media era are brought together. The construction of the integrated media experimental teaching platform can better provide a good platform for college students, stimulate students' learning initiative, and better match school teaching with social news production.

References:

1. Gao, G., Chen, X.: Some thoughts on media convergence. Chinese J. Journalism Commun. (09) (2006)
2. Yang, Y.G.: Reform strategy of sports journalism education in the new media era. Media (20) (2017)
3. Ke, N.: Establishing a demand-oriented network public opinion response mechanism. Chin. High. Educ. (11) (2015)
4. Can global media actively distribute bets on VR products, can VR find treasure? People's Daily, http://media.People.Com.cn/n1/2017/0315/c40606-29147167 html 03 (2017)
5. Hudson, L.: Stay woke bot helps activists explain racism to Twitter randos. [OL]. Boingboing, 21 July 2015
6. Liu, X., Li, X.: In-depth, intelligent and interactive: integrated development in the context of intelligent media. China Broadcasts (2) (2019)
7. Wang, W.T., Wang, Y.G.: On the discourse space of mainstream culture in the age of self-media. Future Dev. (02) (2018)
8. Peng, L.: Mobility, socialization, and intelligence: the three major paths of traditional media transformation. Journalism Mass Commun. Monthly (01) (2018)
9. Huang, C.X., Peng, Y.J.: China Media Integration Development Report. Mod. Commun. (4) (2018)
10. Zhang, J.: Public Account 2018. new list, January 4, 2019, https://mp.weixin.qq.com/s/riw 2rye54Iopzi BDe4y POQ
11. Wu, H., Chi, X.W., Li, X.F., et al.: Reform of the experimental teaching system of outstanding engineers in safety science. Res. Explor. Lab. 33(8) (2014)
12. Liang, K.W., Cai, Z.Y., Jia, S.L., et al.: Highlight the teaching function to build a safety engineering laboratory. Res. Explor. Lab. (30) (2011)

Author Index

© ICST Institute for Computer Sciences, Social Informatics and Telecommunications Engineering 2023
Published by Springer Nature Switzerland AG 2023. All Rights Reserved
R. Hou et al. (Eds.): BDTA 2022, LNICST 480, pp. 357–358, 2023.
https://doi.org/10.1007/978-3-031-33614-0

Printed in the United States
by Baker & Taylor Publisher Services